P9-DYZ-670

Praise for *Presumed Guilty*

"An incredible read. *Presumed Guilty* and *Helter Skelter*
are the two best true crime books of all time."
—GERALDO RIVERA, *Fox News*

"This is a very smart lawyer."
—BARBARA WALTERS

"Jose Baez is the most sought-after
criminal defense attorney in the country."
—*Los Angeles Times*

"Baez's courtroom strategy is stunning!"
—*ABC News*

"Jose Baez is really the new Johnnie Cochran…If you're in trouble,
you want the best go-to person in the criminal-justice system.
Right now, that person is Jose Baez."
—SUNNY HOSTIN, *In Session*

"The jury was faced with a very difficult task
but probably made the right decision."
—JOHN GRISHAM, *bestselling author*

"Baez is one of the best lawyers in America."
—*Fox News Latino*

PRESUMED
GUILTY

PRESUMED GUILTY

CASEY ANTHONY:
The Inside Story

JOSE BAEZ
AND
PETER GOLENBOCK

BENBELLA BOOKS, INC.
DALLAS, TEXAS

Presumed Guilty copyright © 2012 by Jose Baez
"Afterword" Copyright © 2013 by Jose Baez
First trade paperback edition 2013

All rights reserved. No part of this book may be used or reproduced in any manner whatsoever without written permission of the publisher, except in the case of brief quotations embodied in critical articles or reviews.

The facts presented in this narrative have been pieced together from testimony in the trial, public record, and interviews and research done by the authors.

BenBella Books, Inc.
10440 N. Central Expressway, Suite 800
Dallas, TX 75231
www.benbellabooks.com
Send feedback to feedback@benbellabooks.com
BenBella is a federally registered trademark.

Printed in the United States of America
10 9 8 7 6 5 4 3 2

Library of Congress Cataloging-in-Publication Data
Baez, Jose, 1968–
  Presumed guilty : Casey Anthony: the inside story / Jose Baez, Peter Golenbock.
     pages cm
  Includes bibliographical references and index.
    ISBN 978-1-937856-77-9 (pbk.)—ISBN 978-1-937856-38-0 (trade cloth)—
ISBN 978-1-939529-21-3 (electronic) 1. Anthony, Casey, 1986—Trials, litigation, etc. 2. Trials (Murder)—Florida—Orlando. 3. Anthony, Caylee, 2005-2008. 4. Baez, Jose, 1968- I. Golenbock, Peter, 1946- II. Title.
    KF225.A58B34 2012
    345.759'025230975924—dc23   2013023262

Cover design by Kit Sweeney
"About the Author" photo by Dr. Enrique Monasterio
Text design and composition by John Reinhardt Book Design

Behind a good man stands an even better woman... This book is dedicated to the wonderful women in my life who have made me a better man: my mother, Carmen, who sacrificed so much and only asked for love in return; my wife, Lorena, who endured far more than she deserved; my daughter, Christina, who was my inspiration; my three sisters, Ruthy, Mildred, and Lucy, who made me as tough as nails; and my very special law partner, Michelle Medina, who is as loyal and dedicated as the day is long. I love you all.

To the seventeen men and women who served on our jury. I am ashamed at how our system has treated you. May this book shed light on why your decision was not only the lawful but true verdict.

J.B.

To Wendy Sears Grassi, who helps me enjoy every day. My love.

P.G.

CONTENTS

ACKNOWLEDGMENTS

I WANT TO THANK all of the people who supported me on this journey beginning with our defense team, both past and present: Dorothy Clay Sims, Cheney Mason, Michelle Medina, William Slabaugh, Lisabeth Fryer, Ann Finnell, Linda Kenney Baden, Andrea Lyon, Todd Macaluso, Pat McKenna, Jack Weiss, Jeanene Barrette, Katie Delanie, Mort Smith, Michael D. Walsh, Jonathan Kasen, Diana Marku, Coreen Yawn, Audrey Paul, Jim Lucas, and Tyler Benson; Legal GraphicWorks; and all of our wonderful and talented interns from Florida A&M University College of Law, George Paul Lemieux and Robert Haney; all of our wonderful and talented expert witnesses, Werner Spitz, Jane Bock, Ken Furton, Barry Logan, Kathy Reichs, William Rodriguez, Larry Daniels, Josh Restrivo, Larry Kobilinsky, Nick Petreco, Richard and Selma Eikelenboom, Timothy Huntington, Henry Lee, Richard Gabriel, and Sally Karioth; my law partners, Ronald J. Manto and Juan M. Gonzalez, for supporting me and believing in the cause to serve our clients in the search for justice.

Also a very special thanks to Howard Messing. If it weren't for his unbelievable acts of kindness, I wouldn't be a lawyer today. And to Professor Tim Chinaris, who always made sure that everything we did was done ethically and professionally.

Also to Glenn Yeffeth, for believing in me; Michael Wright, for his expertise and his friendship, and his partner, Leslie Garson; Frank Weimann for arranging the deal; and a special thanks to Peter Golenbock for being my partner in this endeavor.

And finally, to Casey Anthony for giving me the permission to tell my story. May you find the strength and peace in God to mourn and move forward in your life.

—JOSE BAEZ

I WISH TO THANK Frank Weimann, for insisting that I get involved with this project; Jose Baez, an inspiration and a man I am proud to call my friend; and to all my friends in St. Pete who have supported me over the years.

—PETER GOLENBOCK

When I see hatred that faces the accused in high-profile cases I am reminded of a passage in *A Man for All Seasons* that reads in part:

WILLIAM ROPER: So, now you give the Devil the benefit of law!

SIR THOMAS MORE: Yes! What would you do? Cut a great road through the law to get after the Devil?

WILLIAM ROPER: Yes, I'd cut down every law in England to do that!

SIR THOMAS MORE: Oh? And when the last law was down, and the Devil turned 'round on you, where would you hide, Roper, the laws all being flat? This country is planted thick with laws, from coast to coast, Man's laws, not God's! And if you cut them down, and you're just the man to do it, do you really think you could stand upright in the winds that would blow then? Yes, I'd give the Devil benefit of law, for my own safety's sake!

That is what justice requires...

CHAPTER 1

LIAR, LIAR, PANTS ON FIRE

THE POSTMAN ambled up the cement walkway toward the front door of the peach ranch-style home at 4937 Hopespring Drive in Orlando, Florida, and rang the doorbell. When no one answered, he duly filled out a form, dated it July 7, 2008, and stuck it to the door. The orange notice requested that the homeowners, George and Cynthia Anthony, go to their neighborhood post office and pick up a certified letter. Even though the notice went unanswered for more than a week, the postman failed to leave a second and final notice, per post office policy, according to George Anthony.

It was July 15, 2008, one week after the arrival of that notice, when George, a well-built man in his early fifties with a full shock of neatly kept white hair, drove to the post office to pick up the letter. In the letter, Johnson's Wrecker Service informed him that it had possession of his 1998 Pontiac Sunfire. The letter gave the address where he could come and claim the vehicle.

The title of the Pontiac was in George and Cynthia's names, but was being driven by their twenty-two-year-old daughter, Casey. George drove a black 2007 Chrysler PT Cruiser, while Cindy drove a dark green 2005 Toyota 4Runner.

George called Cindy at work and said, "You're not going to believe this, but I got a notice from a towing company that they have Casey's car."

1

This caused immediate concern for Cindy, because Casey had supposedly driven that car to Jacksonville. She demanded loudly that George go and pick up the car immediately. But they agreed to go together to pick up the vehicle. They drove together to Johnson's Wrecker Service. Before leaving, George went to a shed in the backyard, grabbed a cylindrical gas can filled with gasoline and threw it in the trunk of his PT Cruiser.

When they arrived at the tow yard, Cindy, a middle-aged, tanned blonde, spoke to an employee through bulletproof glass. She demanded to know why it had taken so long for the company to notify her about the car.

"We have policies that we have to follow," replied the employee behind the glass. "We have to send out a certified letter on the third business day to the registered owner."

Cindy, an intelligent and strong-willed woman, wasn't satisfied. The employee politely explained that the problem could have occurred because the letter was sent during the Fourth of July holiday. Cindy stated she and her husband had been out of town for a few days. (Her telephone records and later testimony would show otherwise.)

George and Cindy went to a nearby ATM and withdrew $500. After paying the bill, George walked with the manager of the tow company, Simon Burch, to the gated lot that held George's Pontiac Sunfire.

They discussed how long the tow yard had held the car.

"Three weeks," Burch said.

George replied, "The car had been at the Amscot for three days before you towed it." Burch fleetingly thought to himself, *We had no idea how long the car had been there before we towed it. How did he know?* He also wondered how George knew it had been picked up at the Amscot Financial store parking lot.

As they walked toward the car, George apologized for Cindy's rude behavior.

"I'm sorry," he said. "We're having a rough time. Our daughter had the car. And our granddaughter is missing. And she told us lies. We'll probably get divorced over this."

Burch felt sorry for the man but felt awkward about a stranger divulging such private family details. He didn't engage him further but instead offered his condolences, saying, "Okay, I'm sorry. No big deal."

The car was locked, and there was no key in the ignition. George reached into his pocket, brought out a set of keys, opened the driver's side door, and got in. As soon as George opened the door, Burch was struck by a terrible, overpowering odor coming from the inside of the car.

"Whoa, that stinks," said Burch.

"Yeah, that's pretty rough," said George.

George put the key in the ignition but thought better about starting the car. He asked Burch, "Can you open the trunk with me?"

George would later tell the cops that as he was opening the trunk under his breath he said, "Oh God, please don't let this be Casey or Caylee."

At the same time, Burch was thinking to himself, *I know what that smell is, and I don't want to think about it.* The yard had once held a car that had a corpse in it, and it seemed like a very similar smell was coming from the Pontiac.

When George opened the trunk, Burch looked inside, half expecting to see a body. Instead there was a large white kitchen garbage bag, pulled tight at the top. Burch told George that it was obvious that the garbage, left in the summer heat to cook for three weeks, was the source of the smell. George reached into the trunk, opened up the garbage bag, and looked inside. Inside were some three-week-old pizza remnants, a crumpled pizza box, and other garbage.

"You want me to get rid of this?" asked Burch. George did. The bag wasn't very heavy, and Burch tossed it over the chain-link fence near a Dumpster and slammed shut the trunk.

George sat in the driver's seat of the Pontiac, opened the driver-side window, and turned the key. The engine turned over, but it wouldn't start. Burch, who had a world of experience with cars that had run out of gas, leaned over and noticed that the gas gauge was on "E."

"It's probably out of gas," Burch said.

"Yes, it's out of gas," stated George.

Burch, having been told of the stress George was under, felt bad for the man. He was fighting with his wife, his granddaughter was missing, he had paid a small fortune to get his impounded car back, and now the car wouldn't start. Burch was about to offer one of his gas cans so George could walk to the nearest gas station and get some gas, but George surprised him by saying, "I've got gas with me."

Under the procedures of the impound lot, Burch had to accompany George back to his PT Cruiser. George opened the trunk, pulled out the metal gas can, and took it back to the Pontiac. He poured the gas from the can into the car.

George got back in the Pontiac, and the car roared to life after three or four cranks of the engine. Burch walked to the gate and pushed a button to open the gate. When George reached the exit, he thanked Burch for his help.

"Sorry about the wife," Burch said.

"No big deal," said George, driving off.

AFTER GEORGE AND CINDY arrived home, Cindy opened the trunk of Casey's Pontiac and sprayed an entire bottle of Febreze air freshener into the trunk in an attempt to kill the foul odor. Both then headed to their respective places of employment. When Cindy arrived at her job at Gentiva Health Services, Inc., where she was a clinical supervisor, her coworkers were waiting for her with a barrage of questions.

Cindy is a talker, and the entire office was a hothouse of gossip, so her coworkers all knew that Cindy hadn't seen her granddaughter Caylee for a month. During that period, Casey would call and tell her mother where she was. For a time, Casey said she was in Jacksonville visiting a boyfriend by the name of Jeff Hopkins. Another time she said she was in Tampa. On the days Casey didn't call, Cindy would call her. Each time, Cindy would ask about Caylee's whereabouts, and every time Casey would come up with a different excuse why she couldn't put Caylee on the phone. Casey would say Caylee was with Zenaida Fernandez-Gonzalez, the nanny, at the beach, or sleeping, or at Walt Disney World. Casey would tell her mother that she felt Caylee and her mother were too close and that she wanted to keep her out of the picture while she bonded with her daughter. Day after day Cindy called Casey trying to talk to Caylee, and every day for a month she was rebuffed. Cindy would wring her hands and tell her coworkers that Casey was lying.

Miserable because her daughter wasn't allowing her to see or talk to her granddaughter, Cindy had gone on Myspace and vented, railing about the way Casey was treating her. The subject of the post was "My Caylee Is Missing," and it was posted on July 3:

> Now she is gone, and I don't know why. All I am guilty of is loving her and providing her a safe home. Jealousy has taken her away. Jealousy from one person that should be thankful for all of the love and support given her. A mother's love is deep, however there are limits when one is betrayed by the one she loved and trusted the most. A daughter comes to her mother for support when she is pregnant, the mother says without hesitation it will be ok. And it was. But then the lies and the betrayal began. First it seemed harmless, as, love is blind. A mother will look for the good in her child and give them a chance to change. This mother gave chance after chance for her daughter to change, but instead more lies, more betrayal. What does the mother get for giving her daughter all of these chances? A broken heart. The daughter who stole money, lots of money, leaves without warning and does not let her mother now speak to the baby that her mother raised, fed, clothed, sheltered, paid her medical bills, etc. Instead tells her friends that her mother is controlling her life and she needs her space. No money, no future. Where did it go? Who is now watching out for the little angel?

With the discovery of Casey's car, Cindy couldn't face the possibility that Casey or Caylee or both of them might be dead. After Cindy returned to work, her coworkers wanted to know what was going on.

"We found Casey's car," said Cindy. "We took it home, and the baby's car seat was in the back, and a backpack and her favorite doll."

"Where's the baby?" asked Debbie Polisano, her boss.

"I don't know," said Cindy, who was becoming agitated.

"I want you to go home," said Polisano.

Cindy then said, "There was a very terrible odor in the car."

"Did you open the trunk?" asked Polisano.

Cindy didn't answer. She paused.

"It's a very, very bad odor," said Cindy. "George said it smelled like a dead body had been in the car. I'm a nurse and I know that smell."

"Call the police," said the coworkers.

"I want to give Casey a chance to explain," said Cindy.

Polisano went to her supervisor and said, "You need to tell Cindy to go home and take care of her personal business, because something bad is going on, and she needs to be home."

"Cindy, I'm ordering you to go home," said Nilsa Ramos, the woman in charge.

"Okay," Cindy said and, in tears, she packed up and left.

Sent home from work, Cindy now had to confront the reality of her situation. She searched Casey's Pontiac. She found Casey's purse inside and a slip of paper with the phone number of Amy Huizenga, one of Casey's girlfriends. She called her.

"Amy, this is Cindy," she said, "and I'm very worried. Have you seen Casey?"

"Yes," Amy said. "She just picked me up at the airport. She's at her boyfriend's house."

"I don't know where that is," said Cindy. "Can you take me there?"

Amy, hearing the agitation in Cindy's voice, agreed.

Cindy drove to The Florida Mall, picked up Amy, and together they drove to the apartment of Tony Lazzaro in East Orlando.

Amy knocked on the door, while Cindy hid around the corner. When Casey came to the door, Cindy rushed up to confront her.

"Where's Caylee?" Cindy asked.

"She's at the nanny's house," said Casey.

"You're taking me to her right now."

"No, I'm not," said Casey. "She's sleeping. I'm not going to do that."

"You're going to take me right now," said Cindy. "You're coming with me right now."

"No, I'm not."

"Yes, you are. You're coming with me right now or I'm calling the cops."

Inside the apartment, Tony sat in the living room with several college friends watching the All-Star baseball game on television. Tony was a college kid studying musical production at Full Sail University. He worked part-time as a club promoter for an Orlando nightclub called Fusion Ultra Lounge.

Casey finally agreed to go with Cindy. Before she left, Cindy stuck her head in the door and screamed to Tony, "I hope you're rich, because she's going to rob you blind."

No one said very much during the car ride to take Amy back home. All Cindy wanted to know from Casey was, "Where's Caylee?" She demanded, "Take me to her."

"I'm not doing that."

"All right, I'm going to call the cops."

Cindy drove to a police substation on Pershing Street, only to find it closed. She parked the car, pulled out her cell phone, and dialed 9-1-1. Her first question was, "Where can I find out where to take someone to the police department?"

"What are you trying to accomplish by bringing them to the station?" was the reply.

"I have a twenty-two-year-old person that has, um, grand theft, sitting in my auto with me."

"So the twenty-two-year-old person stole something?" the dispatcher asked her.

"Yes."

The dispatcher asked if the person was a relative.

"Yes," Cindy said.

"Where did they steal it from?"

"Um, my car, and also money."

"Okay, is this your son?"

"My daughter."

Cindy then related the saga of the impounded car.

"My car was stolen. We've retrieved it today. We found out where it was at and retrieved it. I want to bring her in. I want to press charges."

"Where did all of this happen?" asked the dispatcher.

"Oh, it's been happening," said Cindy.

"I know," said the dispatcher, "but I need to establish a jurisdiction."

"I live in Orlando," Cindy said, and she gave her address, 4937 Hopespring Drive.

The dispatcher told her that was the jurisdiction of the sheriff's department, not the Orlando Police Department.

"All righty," said Cindy.

While the dispatcher was transferring the call to the sheriff's office, Cindy threatened to get a court order to force Casey to give Caylee to her.

"That's not the way I want to do it," said Casey. "Give me one more day."

"No, I'm not going to give you another day," said Cindy. "I've given you a month."

Cindy, frustrated, hung up, and she and Casey drove to the Anthony home. Prior to arriving, she called George's cell phone, but there was no answer. George, after seeing the missed call, dialed his son, Lee, age 26, and told him, "I need you to go to the house immediately and check on your mother. Something is terribly wrong." Lee did so immediately. When Cindy and Casey arrived, Lee was already waiting in the garage by the Pontiac Sunfire, which had the trunk open to air out the smell that Lee would later describe as something that "hit you like a wave as soon as you walked in the garage." Casey got out of Cindy's 4Runner and briskly walked past him, saying nothing as Cindy explained to Lee what was going on. Cindy then asked him to go and try to talk some sense into his sister.

Lee walked into Casey's room and began to ask her where Caylee was, but Casey wasn't talking. Since Lee was not getting anywhere with Casey, Cindy made another call to 9-1-1, and when she was connected to someone in the sheriff's office, she informed them, "I have someone here that needs to be arrested in my home, and a possible missing child. I have a three-year-old that's been missing for a month."

"A three-year-old?"

"Yes," said Cindy.

"Have you reported that?"

"I'm trying to do that now, ma'am."

"What did the person do that you need arrested?"

"My daughter."

"For what?"

"For stealing an auto and stealing money."

"So she stole your vehicle?"

"Yeah."

"When did she do that?"

"On the 30th [of June]. I just got it back from the impound. I'd like to speak to an officer. Can you have someone come out to my house?"

"What's her name?"

"My name?"

"Her name."

"Casey Anthony."

"And your name?"

"Cynthia Anthony."

"Casey's there right now?"

"Yes, I got her. I finally found her after a month. She's been missing for a month. I found her, but we can't find my granddaughter."

"Does she have any weapons on her?"

"No."

"Is Casey not telling you where her daughter is?"

"Correct."

The dispatcher promised to send out a deputy as soon as one was available.

Lee continued to try to persuade Casey to tell him where Caylee was. She was hemming and hawing, and finally Lee said to her, "This is futile. Mom has called the cops. And when the cops get here the first thing they are going to do is say, 'Miss Anthony, can you please take us to where your daughter is?' Then you're going to have to take them. Why are you taking things this far? Why would you let the police get involved? You should just tell me so I can tell her, and we can go get Caylee."

"All right," said Casey. "You want me to tell you the truth?"

"Yes."

"The truth is I haven't seen Caylee in thirty-one days."

And just as Casey was telling Lee this, Cindy walked within earshot.

"Oh my God," said Cindy. "What have you done? Why didn't you tell me? We could have done something before."

Flipping out, Cindy made a third 9-1-1 call to the police, this time in tears.

"I called a little bit ago," she said. "I found out my granddaughter has been taken. She's been missing for a month. Her mother finally admitted that she's been missing—admitted that the babysitter stole her. I need to find her."

"The baby is where?" asked the dispatcher.

"The babysitter took her a month ago. My daughter's been looking for her. I told you my daughter was missing for a month. I just found her today, but I can't find my granddaughter. And she just admitted to me that she's been trying to find her herself. There's something wrong. I found my daughter's car today and it smells like there's been a dead body in the damn car."

"Okay, what is the three-year-old's name?"

"Caylee—C-A-Y-L-E-E—Anthony."

"Is she white, black, or Hispanic?"

"She's white."

"How long has she been missing for?"

"I have not seen her since the 7th of June."

When the dispatcher asked Cindy the date of Caylee's birth, she became distraught and began to cry hysterically. Right at this moment, George entered the scene.

"George, Caylee's missing," cried Cindy.

"What?" George responded softly.

"Casey has admitted Zanny took her a month ago. She's been missing for a month."

George, composed and stoic, said nothing.

Cindy was crying so hard that the dispatcher asked her to give the phone to Casey, who told her, "My daughter's been missing for the last thirty-one days. I know who has her. I've tried to contact her. I actually received a phone call today now from a number that is no longer in service. I did get to speak to my daughter for a moment, about a minute."

The dispatcher then asked about the stolen vehicle.

"No, this is my vehicle," said Casey. "It's a '98 Pontiac Sunfire."

The dispatcher, who could not have possibly figured out what in the world was going on, told her a deputy was en route to her home.

The dispatcher asked Casey more questions, and Casey told her that the name of the babysitter who took her baby was Zenaida Fernandez-Gonzalez.

"She's been my nanny for about a year and a half, almost two years," said Casey.

"Why are you calling now?" asked the dispatcher. "Why didn't you call thirty-one days ago?"

"I've been looking for her and have gone through other resources to try to find her, which was stupid, but…"

Casey was still on the phone when the officers arrived.

The first officer to arrive at the scene, Corporal Rendon Fletcher, thought the call was about a stolen car, which was what the dispatcher's printout said. When Fletcher arrived at the home, he noticed that Cindy was yelling at Casey, "ranting and raving," as he put it. Cindy was pacing back and forth between the kitchen and the living room.

When Fletcher asked Casey what was going on, she paused and then said, "My daughter is missing."

Once he realized there was a missing child involved, he called his supervisor, Sergeant Reginald Hosey. Shortly thereafter, several more officers, including Deputies Adriana Acevedo and Ryan Eberlin, arrived at the Anthony home. All the officers would later testify that Cindy and Lee were visibly upset while George and Casey were remarkably calm.

It was around nine in the evening. At first the police weren't sure it was a case about a missing child. They figured this was a domestic issue, and that, for some reason, Casey didn't want to bring her child home. After talking with Casey, the thinking was that there was a rift between Casey and her mother, and that Casey was using the baby as a pawn in a power struggle with Cindy. Cindy was also telling the officers that Casey had stolen some credit cards and money from her and that she wanted to press charges since Casey would not tell her where Caylee was. Hosey instructed Eberlin to handcuff Casey and place her in the back of his squad car.

When a suspect has her freedom curtailed by law enforcement—meaning a reasonable person feels no longer free to leave—the legal process begins, and if the police choose to question that suspect, they must read that person her Miranda rights. But they didn't.

Hosey then spoke on the phone with Detective Yuri Melich, the detective on call. Cindy asked Hosey, "What's going on?"

"We're taking the handcuffs off her because a detective is coming to talk to her," said Hosey. They opened the squad car door, let her out, and took off the handcuffs. In effect, they were "unarresting" her. (There's no such thing as "unarresting" someone though.)

From the moment of Casey's arrest, the police demonstrated an unbelievable degree of carelessness. As you will see, Casey's arrest and unarrest was only the beginning.

Casey then told the police that she had dropped Caylee off at the Sawgrass Apartments in Orlando. The police asked Casey to take them there. Casey said the apartment was on the second floor.

"You go straight over one speed bump, and it's the first building on the right-hand side. There's a welcome sign. There's a little shed close to the building, maybe ten yards away."

Casey rode in the back of Acevedo's squad car. Fletcher followed in a second squad car.

Acevedo lowered Casey's backseat window, and Casey pointed out the apartment. Fletcher knocked on the door, but no one answered. He then went to the management office of the apartment complex, where he learned Casey wasn't telling him the truth. No one had lived in the apartment for almost six months.

Detective Melich arrived at the Anthony home around 1:00 A.M. After being briefed by Hosey, Melich was pulled aside by George, who informed him that he was a former law enforcement officer in Warren, Ohio. George told Melich that Casey was not being truthful and that her car smelled of human decomposition. Melich, ignoring George, concentrated on reading Casey's statement about Zenaida taking her baby rather than going to inspect the car.

"This sounds very suspect," Melich said to Casey. "Are you sure, before we go any further, that you don't want to change anything in here?"

Casey didn't.

"Okay," said Melich, "Let's take your sworn statement." So Casey regurgitated the same story about Zenaida, her nanny of two years, taking her baby, Caylee. She described the directions to Zanny's apartment in great detail. She said she met Zanny through a mutual friend, Jeffrey Hopkins.

"She was his son's nanny at the time," she said. She described how Hopkins had moved to North Carolina and then back to Jacksonville. When asked for his telephone number, Casey said she didn't have it on hand. She said Hopkins had a four-year-old son named Zack. She said that her nanny before Zenaida was a woman by the name of Lauren Gibbs.

In an effort to make headway, Melich asked Casey if she knew where Zenaida's mother lived.

"She lived off of Michigan," Casey said. "It's not a very well-marked neighborhood. It crosses over Conway. It's one of the big stretches of neighborhoods."

When asked if she could find the house, she said she thought so.

Melich asked Casey what she remembered about June 9, the day she dropped her child off with the nanny, and the last day she said she saw Caylee.

"I got off work," Casey said, "left Universal, driving back to pick up Caylee like a normal day. And I show up at the apartment, knock on the door. Nobody answers. So I called Zenaida's cell phone and it's out of service. So I sit down on the steps and wait for a little bit to see if maybe it was just a fluke or if something happened. And time passed. I didn't hear from anyone. No one showed up to the house, so I went over to Jay Blanchard Park and checked a couple other places where maybe possibly they would have gone. A couple stores, just regular places that I know Zenaida shops at and she's taken Caylee before. And after about 7:00 P.M., when I still hadn't heard anything, I was getting pretty upset, pretty frantic. And I went to a neutral place. I didn't really want to come home. I wasn't sure what I'd say about not knowing where Caylee was. Still hoping that I would get a call or, you know, find out Caylee was coming back so I could go get her... and I ended up going to my boyfriend Anthony's house, who lives in Sutton Place."

When Melich asked Casey whether she told any of this to her parents, she said she didn't. Did she tell anyone? She said she had told Jeffrey Hopkins and Juliette Lewis, another coworker at Universal Studios, and said she attempted to call Zenaida's mother, Gloria.

"Do you know Gloria's telephone number?"

She didn't.

When he was done, Melich said to her, "I asked you this at the onset, and before we went on tape, and I'll ask you again just to make sure we're clear. Is there anything about this story that you're telling me that's untrue?"

"No."

"Is there anything that you want to change or divert from what you've already told me?"

"No, sir."

"Did you hurt Caylee or leave her somewhere and you're..."

"No."

"...worried that if we find that out that people are gonna look at you the wrong way?"

"No, sir."

He then asked whether she had any problems with drugs, narcotics, cocaine, ecstasy, meth, anything like that.

"Nothing like that."

"Have you ever been to Lakeside?" he asked, referring to a local mental health facility.

"No."

Melich said, "You said Zenaida had family in New England or New York or something."

"Yes, she has family down south. Her mother, her sister, and her brother are in New York. She's originally from New York."

"And where down south?"

"Miami area."

"Where's she originally from?"

"New York."

"She was born and raised in New York?" asked Melich.

"As far as I know, she pretty much grew up there, moved down here, went to the University of Florida."

"She Puerto Rican, Dominican, or white?"

"She's mixed. She's black and Puerto Rican."

Melich asked Casey, "Does Juliette Lewis still work at Universal?"

"Yes, she does," said Casey.

"And what does she do there?"

"She's an event coordinator."

"Can I have her phone number?"

"Oh," said Casey, suddenly changing direction, "she moved up to New York two months ago."

"So she doesn't work at Universal anymore?" asked Melich.

"No, she does not."

Melich asked if he had forgotten to ask her anything.

Casey told him that Caylee had very distinctive features and that even if someone had cut her hair, people would recognize her dark hazel eyes. "They're brown and green. She has a birthmark on her left shoulder."

"What kind of birthmark?"

"It's just like a small line. It almost looks like a small little beauty mark."

"Anything else?"

"I just want my daughter back."

Melich then had her raise her right hand and swear that everything she had told him was the truth.

After taking down her statement, Melich said, "Okay, take me to where you showed the police officers." They went back to the same apartment complex. Then he asked, "Do you know any other places where Zenaida lived before she lived here?"

"I know where her mother Gloria used to live," she said, and she took Melich to another apartment complex, which turned out to be a home for the elderly.

Melich checked. The people at the home had never heard of Gloria Gonzalez. Later police would discover that the complex was across the street from one of Casey's former boyfriends, Ricardo Morales. And the Sawgrass Apartments, where Zenaida supposedly lived, was the home of Dante, the boyfriend of her best friend, Annie Downing.

After driving Casey around until three in the morning, Melich drove her back to her home.

"Okay," he said, "we'll talk tomorrow. We're going to keep investigating."

Before Melich left, George pulled him aside.

"My daughter has been lying to you," he said. "Something's very suspicious. I don't think she's being truthful. You need to look into this a little bit more."

"Don't worry," said Melich. "We will."

George then told him about finding the car at the impound lot and again mentioned the smell in Casey's car.

The car was in the garage of the Anthony home with the trunk open. As the police were coming in and out of the house that night, they entered through the garage. Any of them could have smelled that car, and not one said a word about it. Even though George had told him, "The car smells of death," the detective was either grossly incompetent or believed the smell from the car came from the trash that had been in the car, as apparently did all the police on the scene. In Melich's five-page, detail-rich initial report, not a word was said about any smell in the car. If the car smelled uniquely of human decomposition, none of the officers noticed it. As I will show later, decomposition is decomposition and no one can uniquely detect human decomposition.

Melich drove back to his precinct and met with Sergeant John Allen around seven in the morning. During breakfast Melich briefed Allen about the case.

As they discussed it, the new strategy was to see how far Casey would go with her lies.

Casey had told the police she didn't have Zenaida's cell phone number because she had left the cell phone in her office at Universal Studios.

"The number of everyone who knows about Caylee being missing is on that SIM card on the cell phone in the office," said Casey.

"Let's go to Universal and get it," said Melich. "We'll get your cell phone out of your office, and you can get the numbers."

She quickly changed her story.

"My phone was stolen," she said. "I reported it to loss prevention, and they're looking for it."

Melich, sensing another lie, decided to drive over to Universal Studios and see what Casey's coworkers could tell him about this strange tale-spinning woman whose child was missing.

It was July 16, 2008, and in speaking with Universal's head of security, Leonard Tutura, Melich learned that Casey was fired from her job at Universal Studios on April 24, 2006, after not showing up for work one day. Melich asked about Casey's coworkers, including Hopkins and Lewis. When Melich checked, he found that Hopkins had once worked at Universal but was fired in 2002, so he couldn't have known about Caylee's disappearance during the thirty days when she was missing. And Lewis wasn't found in the company's database.

Melich called Casey from Universal and asked for the name of her supervisor.

"Tom Frank," she told him.

He also asked for Casey's number at work and her extension.

Melich checked the database. No supervisor by the name of Tom Frank existed, and though she knew the main number for the Universal Studios switchboard, extension 104 didn't exist. Melich asked for the building number. Casey said she couldn't remember it.

Melich told her, "I'll have an officer pick you up, and you can meet me here at Universal. We'll go find your office and we'll talk to some people here to see if we can find Jeff Hopkins or Juliette Lewis."

She cheerfully agreed.

Around noon Allen drove over and picked her up with Officer Appling "Appie" Wells. Casey had not slept all night. During the early morning, Casey and Cindy had been building Facebook and Myspace pages in their attempt to spread the word about Caylee's disappearance. They were texting hundreds of people trying to organize a search for Caylee.

Casey and the two cops arrived at Universal. When they arrived at the gate, the security officer asked for her ID.

"I lost it," Casey said.

The police asked if he would please let them in so she could show them the location of her office.

He agreed.

Casey led them into an office building in the back area of Universal Studios. She made a left turn, kept on walking, began to walk down a hallway, and then stopped.

"Okay," Casey said, "I don't work here."

The detectives, growing more incredulous by the moment, took her into a conference room and began to question her. They hit her with her lies.

Talk about going around in circles. It was such a red flag. I don't know how Melich didn't realize right then and there that he was dealing with someone with serious mental health issues. Why didn't he see this was a clear sign that something just wasn't right? She gave such vivid details from her imagination. This was a bit more than just lies.

Though confronted with the fact she had been lying, Casey stubbornly stuck to her story: the scenario, in effect, that her nanny had taken Caylee and she didn't know where she was.

The police pounded away at her. As the interrogation was coming to a close, Melich received a phone call from Cindy.

What Cindy wanted Melich to know was that on the day Caylee disappeared, the ladder on the outdoor above-ground swimming pool was up, meaning Caylee would have had access to the pool.

"We're religious about taking that ladder down," Cindy said, "and it was odd that it was still up. Something is not right, and we are very concerned. We just don't understand what's going on."

What Cindy was telling Melich was that her suspicion was that Caylee had drowned in the swimming pool that day. Armed with this new information, Melich returned to question Casey. Did he ask her about the ladder? Did he ask her anything about the swimming pool? Not a word. Focusing in on the missing nanny, he asked more questions about her and asked Casey to look at some photographs to see if perhaps the faces in the photos were Zenaida.

It was clear to me that Melich didn't ask Casey about the ladder and the pool because he had already made up his mind that she was a prime suspect in a possible murder case. He knew there was a missing child, who was presumed to be dead, and he knew Casey was lying, and probably figured that after a night in jail she would come forward and confess. *Don't give her an out,* was probably his thinking. *Confessions are the quickest way to close a case. Let's get an incriminating statement and we can pack up and go home.*

After showing Casey the pictures of women at the police station, none of which she identified as Zenaida, they told her, "We're arresting you. Unless you come clean and tell us the truth, we're arresting you now."

"I am telling the truth," she said defiantly.

"Okay, then, you're under arrest."

She was arrested around three in the afternoon. Two hours later, the police alerted the media. In Orlando, the police like to do perp walks, where they take the accused out of the police station and march them in front of the television cameras. The TV and newspaper reporters then ask the suspect questions. The strategy is to try to get recorded statements that can be used in court. Or, at the very least, the police department gets more publicity for a big arrest.

So the cops handcuffed her and walked her out. In front of the one camera crew that appeared, Casey didn't answer a single question. Casey wore a light blue hoodie with the number 82 in bright yellow. The news crew had no idea that the B-roll it had just shot would be replayed and broadcast across the country for the next three-and-a-half years.

You might wonder why the cops arrested her so quickly. According to Melich, the reason they did so was what occurred in the Melinda Duckett case. Duckett was a young woman from Lake County, Florida, who had a missing child. After going on the *Nancy Grace* show, where Nancy Grace attacked her repeatedly, Duckett came home and took her own life. She shot herself in her grandparents' home on September 8, 2006. Melich said they didn't want a repeat of what happened to Duckett. But this case was different. Casey had shown no signs of depression. What was their hurry?

I have always believed that at this crucial moment in the investigation, the police made a horrible decision. They should have stopped and realized, *Wait a minute, we're not dealing with someone who's playing with a full deck here.* How much more evidence did the police need to see that this girl was taking them on a wild goose chase? Rather than thinking, *This is a guilty person who's a horrible liar,* why didn't they consider, *This is a person who has built some kind of fantasy world, someone who lives within a mythical reality?*

I just can't fathom that after going down to Universal and watching her make up names of coworkers and a fictitious office, saying she worked there when she didn't, why the cops wouldn't say, *Wait a minute. Maybe we should have a psychologist come in and talk to her and see what we're dealing with here.*

That moment at Universal Studios was the time and place to confront this girl in a different manner. It was the time to bring in a mental health professional and say, *We're dealing with something beyond our comprehension.* Instead, they went old school with a good cop/bad cop routine and mounted an accusatory interrogation.

They slapped the cuffs on her. They thought they were going to pull the truth out of her and that after a night in jail she'd break down and tell them everything. If they had just let her remain free, they could have bugged her phones, watched her movements, followed her, and perhaps would have gotten a better idea of the extent of her involvement in Caylee's disappearance. But within twenty-four hours they arrested her and made her a suspect. She immediately got herself a lawyer (yours truly), which meant they had no more access to her. I'd have to say that was a really stupid move on their part.

The police took Casey to the Orange County jail, and the next morning she had what is called a first appearance. The judge read the police report. He told her, "You're not cooperating. We need to know where Caylee is."

Casey said nothing, and despite being held for child neglect and lying—minor crimes—the judge held her without bond, which was odd. Casey had a public defender at this point (she hadn't yet hired me), so I can't answer why this wasn't fought more vociferously.

Several hours later I came to see her, and my life would never be the same.

CHAPTER 2

THE PHONE RINGS

I N THE SUMMER OF 2008, our little firm was growing. We were really rocking and rolling. I had moved my practice from Orlando to Kissimmee, Florida, which is a suburb of Orlando. It had almost tripled in revenue because I had built a strong practice specifically catering to the Hispanic market.

There are three units in the building where my office is: two small units on the side and a larger unit in the middle. At the time I met Casey we had just finished moving from one of the smaller units to the big one. An appraisal firm, our neighbor, moved into my smaller office, and I moved into its bigger one.

I had put in close to $30,000 in renovations. We hired an interior designer and installed hardwood floors because we really wanted to show that we were a boutique law firm on the rise. One hundred percent of my business was based on referrals. We did not advertise. The only way to build a strong referral-based practice is by delivering results. And that is how the phone rings.

Later, when the media described my office as being in a "strip mall," it upset me, because we had put so much work into our office, and the entire firm was so proud of it. It was one of the first attempts to paint me as a small-time lawyer with no prospects, even though my cases were taking on greater importance.

The last case I tried before Casey's, the Nilton Diaz trial, had been an ordeal. Diaz was accused of murdering his girlfriend's two-year-old daughter.

I strongly believed that Diaz was innocent. It was a pediatric head-injury case in which our defense contended that the mother was the one who struck the child, and after she hit her, the child went through a lucid interval, a common occurrence in such head-injury cases. While the mother ran out to the store, leaving the child in Diaz's care, the child had a seizure. Diaz immediately took the child to get help, but she died anyway. The police arrested him and charged him with child abuse and first-degree felony murder.

Our defense was excellent. We answered every question we thought the jury would have and raised a significant amount of doubt. But what I didn't understand yet was that in child death cases, juries want someone to pay. I really believe the jury thought Diaz was innocent, but it felt someone had to be held responsible so it came back with a compromise verdict. The jury found him guilty of child abuse and manslaughter and sentenced him to fifteen years.

I was devastated. It had been a long trial, and I had dedicated a significant amount of my personal time to it. I needed to do something where I could relax a little bit and find an activity I could do outside my office. I was living in Florida and figured that boating would be relaxing, so I joined a boat club. Members got to rent boats at reasonable rates. I was sure this would be a wonderful activity for my wife, Lorena, and me to do together.

As part of the process of becoming a member, I went out with one of the owners to learn the workings of the boats. He and I were talking, and I told him I was a criminal defense lawyer, and after a day of training he said, "Jose, we're trying to get the word out about the club. We're having a local newspaper do an article on it. Do you mind if they call you and you can talk about the club? We'd like other professionals like you to join."

"Sure," I said, "no problem." And I forgot about our conversation.

About a week later, on July 17, 2008, I was driving in downtown Orlando when I called my office to check my messages. My secretary told me to go see a prospective client. She said a relative of an inmate called and wanted me to go to the Orange County jail to see an inmate by the name of Casey Anthony.

It's just another case, I thought. I didn't think anything of it. I was going to the jail anyway.

"I'll go see her," I said.

After a twenty-minute drive, I was at the Booking and Release Center, what we call the BRC, which is where they house the newly arrested inmates who are going to bond out shortly. While I was waiting in the building, I noticed a whiteboard on the wall, and I saw the name *Casey Anthony* written on it. *That's odd,* I thought. *Of all the inmates, why is her name up there?* I wondered if maybe she had beaten the crap out of a correctional officer and she was a high risk.

Maybe she's a live one, was my thinking. They usually only put the names of the troublemakers up on the wall.

I told the guards, "I'm here to see Casey Anthony," and I was struck by their reaction. They looked at each other as if to say, "He's here to see *her.*" A public defender, who was also waiting to see Casey, asked me, "Who are you?" I explained I had gotten a call to come see her.

"This case has been in the news," he said, "and I just came down to tell her not to talk to anyone because detectives might be coming by."

Casey walked in and sat down. The public defender told her, "A private lawyer is here to see you."

"Yes, I know," she said. "I asked someone to do that for me."

He said, "We just wanted to let you know you shouldn't talk to anyone without a lawyer being present." And then he left.

I sat down and said, "Hello. How are you?"

I saw this tiny, attractive, hip-looking girl with short dark hair and greenish-gray eyes in her early twenties. She was no more than five feet tall, weighed 105 pounds soaking wet, and looked totally out of place in the jail. She wasn't your typical inmate. She was dressed in jail blues but very well kept. Most of my clients, both male and female, are a little rougher around the edges, more street-wise. That was not Casey. In this business you mostly run across people who have been through the system. They're much more hardened. I could see Casey was a first-timer.

After I introduced myself, I could tell she was grateful that I had come to see her.

I asked her, "Do you have your paperwork with you?" meaning her police reports. We were talking through a glass partition, so she slid them underneath the glass.

"Give me a second to read your report," I said.

I saw that the specific charges were child neglect and lying to law enforcement. I thought, *Okay, she's going to be out of here pretty soon.* Then I saw, "No bond," and that was a head-scratcher. I couldn't understand how, with those relatively minor charges, she didn't have a bond.

I thought, *There's no reason she should be held without bond.*

As I was reading the arrest report line by line, I could see that this was not your typical child-neglect case. I thought, *This is a missing person's case.* I kept reading, and the report said that she hadn't seen her child in thirty days and that she had led police to an apartment that had been vacant for 142 days.

Strange, I was thinking. *They certainly have cause for suspicion.* I read further, and the report talked of statements she had made. She said that she dropped off Caylee at the babysitter's home thirty days before, and it gave a location, and that when she came back to pick up the baby from the nanny, no one was there. When the police went to verify her story, they knocked on the door and found it to be a vacant apartment. They then called the manager of the apartment complex, and he said the apartment had been vacant. So the conclusion of the police was that she was lying.

I saw she didn't have a phone number for this woman, whom she identified as Zenaida Fernandez-Gonzalez. She didn't have any information that could lead them to this woman. As I was reading this, I was thinking that this set of facts was "crazy." *Her child is missing and she takes the cops to a vacant apartment?*

I read the part of the report where she took the cops to her job at Universal Studios. She said she worked there, but with one phone call they found out she hadn't worked there for two years. They wanted to see how far she'd go with her lies, so they took her to Universal Studios, and after leading them on a wild goose chase, she said, "Okay, I don't work here."

That did not look very good for her, but I couldn't help thinking, *What are the secrets she is hiding?*

I kept reading. The report said she was arrested for not reporting her child missing and lying to law enforcement about the nanny, about working at Universal, and about where she dropped off the child.

I'm thinking to myself, *This is more than it seems. I need to be very diligent with how I deal with the situation.*

I badly wanted to hear what she had to say, certainly as much as the cops did, but I didn't want to push her too hard because if the police report was accurate, either the child was deceased and she knew something about it, or there was an actual kidnapping. I thought, *Maybe she's afraid to talk to the police and if she's afraid to talk to the police, she's got to be afraid to talk to me, a stranger she doesn't know.*

I spoke with Casey, and as we talked, I could tell she was a very bright girl.

Okay, there are probable trust issues here, I thought, so I explained to her, "Listen, Casey, everything you tell me is confidential."

When I asked her, "What happened?" she stuck to her story that she gave the cops, saying that her babysitter, Zenaida, took Caylee.

I asked her to describe Zenaida.

"She's a perfect ten," she said.

"People notice perfect tens," I replied. "A woman that attractive gets noticed."

She didn't respond.

It didn't make sense, but I took her at her word. The thing with clients in my line of work is they aren't always up front with you at the very beginning. They don't know you; it takes time to build trust. I would never say, "You have to tell me everything right here and now." Especially to someone young like her. I needed her to trust me, and to do that I needed to demonstrate that I was on her side, that I was going to do whatever I could under the law to help her through this process.

I did say to her early on, "Don't send me on fool's errands, because that's not going help you in any way." But I always had that nagging certainty, *This is a person with some serious trust issues.*

And again, here's the thing that people don't really understand: 90 percent of cases like these are marathons, not sprints, and the bond with the client is the most crucial part of the attorney-client relationship.

When I first met Casey, I had no idea that something was horribly wrong. I was sure there were trust issues, that she didn't trust people for a reason. What reason it was, I didn't know. I figured I would eventually find out when the time was right.

After spending a little bit of time with her, I was shocked that the judge hadn't granted her a bond. Based on the charges of child neglect and lying to a police officer—a third-degree felony and misdemeanors—$200 should have gotten her out of jail.

I said to her, "I've got to get you out of here, and that way you and I can talk freely." She nodded. I said, "The first thing I want to do is get the names and phone numbers of people you want me to call for two things: one, to help you put up a bond, and two, for them to come and possibly testify for you at a bond hearing." She gave me the names of her parents and stressed that I should talk to her mother, not her father. In hindsight, that should have been my first indication that there were secrets and trust issues between her and her father.

After that, we talked about her boyfriends. She gave me their phone numbers, including the number of a boyfriend she had in Jacksonville. After I wrote all those things down, we talked about my fee. I told her I would charge $5,000 to represent her. She informed me that she had $1,300 in the bank as a down payment and would work out a payment schedule. I agreed, figuring her parents might be able to contribute toward her defense. She signed a retainer agreement then and there.

Since I had a hearing scheduled later that day in another county, I said I'd come back to talk to her a bit later after I had a little bit more information. As I was leaving the jail, I was thinking to myself, *This is a possible child-neglect case that could end up a homicide for all I know.* But when I left, I really didn't give the case any higher priority than what it was—a possible child-neglect case.

I went to court in Osceola County that afternoon, came back to my office around three, and handed the retainer agreement to Myrna Kercado, my secretary.

"Go ahead and open a file," I said. "First things first. We want a motion to set bond and file notice of appearance."

About thirty minutes later she walked into my office and said, "Jose, this is a big case. You know that, right?"

"What do you mean?"

"This is all over the news right now."

"Really?"

"Yeah."

I went online and I could see this case blowing up.

Holy cow! This *was* pretty big. I figured it might get a little coverage, but I didn't realize that *everyone* around Orlando, it seemed, was curious about it.

The very first person Casey wanted me to call was her mother. I picked up the phone and introduced myself to her.

"I'm Jose Baez, Casey's lawyer," I said. "Don't worry. I want you to know that the very first thing I'm going to do is file a motion for bond just so we can get her out."

"Oh God, no," she said, "Whatever you do, please don't do that. We know where Casey's at, and she's safe, and maybe that'll get her to start talking. We don't know where Caylee is, and we need her to stay in jail."

I was taken aback. Her attitude was another head-scratcher.

"What?" I said. "I'm sorry, but that's not my job. I represent your daughter, and your daughter's interests, and she's instructed me to file a motion for a bond, which is what I have to do. I don't represent you, and you have to understand there might be times where her interests conflict with yours, and I have to go with hers. But I always think it's important to have family involvement in my client's cases. I'd be more than happy to work with you. Would you like to come to my office, and we could talk about the case? You can let me know what you want me to know."

"I'd like to meet with you," Cindy said, "but we're trying to get the word out about Caylee. Is there any way you can come here?"

"Not a problem," I said. I was thinking that this might be an opportunity to get my name in the public eye. I thought, *She's looking to get some publicity, and with any luck I'll be on the eleven o'clock news.* It's always good marketing for a criminal lawyer to have a case in the news and get a little exposure for the brand. I figured I'd get one shot and that would be the extent of it.

At the same time, this case really intrigued me. My associate Gabriel Adam and I drove to the Anthony home on Hopespring Drive, where a number of television trucks were parked up and down the block. I had never seen anything like this before. I have to be honest—the first thing I thought about was the publicity I was going to get from this case. Advertising is expensive. I had been on the Spanish TV station numerous times but only once or twice on the English-speaking news, and never as a feature story. It was always a quick blurb, nothing big. I thought I would call my wife, Lorena, and get her to record this, until I realized Lorena was out of town, so I called Myrna and asked her to tape the six o'clock news and put it on our website.

Gabe and I walked up to the home, the cameras filming us all the way. George answered the door and let us in. He was polite and cordial. Cindy greeted me as we stepped inside. Their son, Lee, who is four years older than Casey, was also in the house. I was surprised to see another lawyer, Paul Kelly. It seemed odd they were lawyering up so quickly, given they weren't suspects. But Kelly wasn't a criminal defense lawyer. He was a family lawyer who had done some work for them.

My first impression of this typical middle-class home was that it was impeccably kept. Nothing was out of place, and it was spotlessly clean.

When I sat down, it still hadn't sunk in that we were dealing with a missing child. For some reason, I was sure this was a domestic dispute. I suspected that Casey was having problems with her family and didn't want the baby around them, and that's why she was keeping them apart. That was floating around in the back of my head when I walked in, but I kept an open mind.

After I sat down, Cindy did all the talking. Even their lawyer took a backseat. Cindy took control of the room and the conversation. She recounted to me in great detail everything that had happened over the last thirty days.

"After June 9, there was a story every day," she said. "Casey would say, 'I have to crash at work, and I'm going to leave Caylee with Zanny.' Casey never came home."

She said that during the third week of June Casey called and told her she had to go to Jacksonville to go with Zanny to pick up a brand-new car. Zanny had been in an accident and her car was totaled.

Another time, she said, Casey called to say she and a coworker at Universal, Juliette Lewis, were going to stay at the Hard Rock Cafe in Tampa, Florida, because they were working at a convention. They stayed through June 20, she said. Zanny was watching Caylee and Annabelle, Lewis's daughter. Cindy said that Casey told her they were staying at the Marriott outside Busch Gardens. She said that Universal was paying for Zanny's room as well and that Caylee and Annabelle were rooming with Zanny.

Casey called on June 21, a Saturday morning, to say she would be home by noon, but then, Cindy said, she waited all day for Casey to come home. At 5:30 p.m. Casey called to say that they had one last meeting so they were leaving Sunday—the next day—instead. But on Sunday she called to say that Zanny's roommate, a woman by the name of Raquel Farrell, was with them, and they were all going to go to see the animals at Busch Gardens.

As a result, said Cindy, they stayed one more night. They were expected to return home on Monday, June 23, but then Casey said a terrible thing happened. Zanny got in a car accident. Zanny had a concussion, and Farrell had a broken arm. Casey was going to stay at the Tampa General Hospital with Zanny.

"Who's watching Caylee?" Cindy asked Casey.

"Oh, Juliette will watch her and Annabelle," Casey told Cindy.

She was supposed to come home the next day but Casey told Cindy that Zanny started vomiting and passing out—she had a laceration behind her ear that no one had noticed and needed stitches. Zanny, said Casey, was having difficulty breathing, so Casey was going to have to stay with her a couple more days. Meanwhile, said Casey, Zanny's sister and mother, who had been in the hospital herself off and on, were traveling from Orlando to see Zanny.

She talked on and on about the stories Casey was telling her, and no one else got a word in edgewise. Gabe, meanwhile, was furiously trying to write down everything she was saying on his yellow legal notepad. I wanted to bond with the family of my new client, so I relied on him to take notes.

Cindy went on. Casey then called Cindy to inform her that Zanny's sister and mother had come to the hospital to take Zanny home, but the hospital refused to release her, so the sister had to drive the mother back home because Zanny's mother had forgotten to bring her medication. Casey said she had returned to Orlando to get Zanny's insurance information.

"Couldn't they get that over the phone or fax?" Cindy asked Casey.

"The sister didn't know where to look in the apartment," said Casey. As a result, Casey drove to get them. Zanny had given her keys to the apartment and instructions on where to find them.

Cindy was talking so fast that I was having a great deal of difficulty following what she was saying. And I remember thinking to myself, *I hope Gabe is getting all of this, because I certainly am not.*

As Cindy was explaining this, she held my hand, which I found odd. We were seated on the couch. Her lawyer and his wife were sitting on chairs, as was Gabe, and George was hopping around, helping everyone and serving drinks.

Cindy continued, "On June 27, Casey said she was going straight to work with her coworker Juliette Lewis. They checked in with their boss, Tom Frank, and she was going to come home when she learned that Jeff

Hopkins was in Jacksonville. She hadn't seen him in a while and so she drove to Jacksonville to be with him from June 28 until June 30."

"I talked to her every day," said Cindy. "Every day." At first, Casey had convinced her that Caylee had been staying with Zanny, but now she wasn't so sure. She hadn't seen or heard from Caylee for days and she was frightened for her granddaughter.

The only time she stopped talking was to admit a news crew into the home. She and the crew would go into the dining room, and she'd do an interview, asking anyone who knew of Caylee's whereabouts to come forward.

On camera she'd say, "We have a missing child. We don't know where she is." And she would be very distraught and cry.

The crew would leave, and she would return to the living room, take my hand, and continue her monologue. After another twenty minutes, another news crew would come in. I have to tell you, it was such a sad situation to see them talking about Caylee and how she was missing. Cindy was so passionate and sincere she almost brought tears to my eyes.

Cindy sat there talking for at least two hours. She gave me the whole story about how she went to Universal Studios to find Casey, and how Casey wasn't there. She detailed the last fifteen days, when Casey was supposed to be in Jacksonville, Florida, while Caylee was with her nanny. She talked about the car and the tow yard, and how she and George went and brought the car back.

She was interrupted by the arrival of a detective from the Orange County Sheriff's Office. Officer Appie Wells was a large, jolly officer whose specialty was child abuse. He was about six foot two, 290 pounds, and very professional. He said to the Anthonys, "We'd like to take a look at your backyard. Do you mind if we go back there? You don't have to." He saw that lawyers were in the room and was very clear that the Anthonys weren't obligated to cooperate.

George jumped up and said, "Yes. I'll show you."

"You don't have to," said Wells respectfully. "It's entirely up to you."

"No, no, no, we'll cooperate," said George. "We want to do whatever we can."

George then took Wells to the shed. Later on, that trip to the backyard would prove significant in the case, but what I remember most vividly was George jumping up at the chance to get out of the room, something he did often. He would sit down initially, but he would jump up and want to offer you water, or get you a Coke or another drink, a snack, nuts, chips, anything so he didn't have to be engaged in the conversation. He was Mr. Nice Guy. I didn't think anything about that other than, *He's going through hell and he's trying to keep himself busy.* Every single time we went to the Anthony house, I would keep noticing that.

When I finally got a chance to talk, I explained to the Anthonys about the attorney-client relationship. I said, "You realize I represent your daughter and her interests. I don't represent you or Caylee. Finding Caylee would be phenomenal for our case—that's where our interests are aligned—but that's where it ends. I represent your daughter and her interests, even if they conflict with yours. You must understand that."

Cindy said she clearly understood. The Anthonys' lawyer told her that I was just doing my job and that it was important that we have open communications.

I stood to leave. I told them I was going to come back and that I was going to see Casey again. I said I thought we could get a bond hearing right away. We parted in a very positive way, but I couldn't help thinking, *Casey has been lying to them, and this is going to get worse before it gets any better.*

We shook hands. When Gabe and I walked out the front door, we were accosted by television news teams. This was my very first experience with the media in this case. As soon as I walked out of the Anthony home, they all came running, like fish swimming to the surface when you toss some bread in the water. They stopped just short of where I was standing, and I granted them an interview.

"My name is Jose Baez," I said. "I represent Casey Anthony. I'm just here to speak with the family."

They asked me, "What did your client say to you?" and I answered, "I can't tell you." Then Michelle Meredith from WESH Channel 2 said to me, "We just saw a crime scene investigator leaving with a long paper bag. Could that have been a shotgun?"

Gee, what a ridiculous and inflammatory question, I recall thinking. *Are they looking for some type of story that Casey had murdered the baby with a shotgun?* (What the police actually took away was a shovel, which also had nothing to do with the case.)

I immediately discounted that. I looked at Meredith and said, "There's no evidence of any kind that a shotgun was involved in this case. They are just doing their job." I thought to myself, *Yeah, Casey must have done a tremendous cleanup job after shooting Caylee with a shotgun, because there's no blood anywhere.*

"That's ridiculous," I added. "Any reports of that would be completely untrue."

And that was my first taste with how inflammatory the media could and would be. It was all about the drama. It was all about how wild and crazy things could be. It wasn't about truth or what was really going on as much as what they could make up to make it seem like it was going on. To them the case was a reality show, except that in this case there could be serious ramifications to my client because of their inflammatory nonsense. The critical thing I didn't understand at the time was how much the media and the cops were playing the same game.

Gabe and I returned to the Orange County jail that night to visit Casey, as much to get to know her as anything else. When we went in there that first night, they wanted to put us back in a room with the glass divider between us. So I said to the supervisor, "You know which case this is."

"Yeah," she said.

"I really need to talk and have unfettered access to my client because we're talking about very sensitive issues. I'm trying to find out what's going on here."

"I understand," she said. "I'll put you in the classroom."

And from that night on, I would always visit Casey in what we called the classroom, a huge room with six rows of desks and a whiteboard to the right. This was where the inmates held Bible study. The entire back wall is made of glass so the officers can look in and see everything that's going on. Sitting there, you felt like you were in a fishbowl.

From the beginning, the only thing I was certain about was that I wasn't going to let the police talk to Casey. I explained to her the importance of not talking to anyone about her case and I kept stressing that and working on that with her. Until I could get a good grasp as to what was going on, my primary function was to protect Casey from making any incriminating statements. To accomplish this, I kept her from making *any* statements at all—frustrating the hell out of the police.

That first night, Casey, Gabe, and I sat down at a table and as soon as we started talking, we heard a clicking sound coming from the intercom.

"Gabe, did you hear that?" I asked.

"Yep," he said. Casey heard it, too, proof that though we were promised privacy, the police were listening in on our conversations. I immediately complained to the corporal who was on duty that night.

I said to her, "Listen, I'm hearing clicking sounds."

She acted all upset. "That shouldn't be," she said. "You should be able to talk to her without having anyone listen in, and I'm going to talk to the powers that be. I'll take care of it."

But we didn't really trust her. I was very cautious about what we talked about in that jail, especially in the very beginning.

I never pressed Casey about Caylee's whereabouts or anything else. I had realized from the start that this girl had trust issues and I didn't want to push her. This was her child who was missing. I decided that the prudent way of dealing with the situation was to let her know what my role was and to educate her as to what I was there to do. She was bright enough to let me know if there was something she needed to tell me. When I saw she wasn't telling me certain things, I didn't take that as a sign of dishonesty as much as I took it as a sign that we needed to get out of the jail so we could talk in private.

"I met with your family," I told Casey. "They're actively looking for Caylee."

"Oh, that's great," she said.

"I will do whatever you want me to do, but what's important is for us to maintain a good relationship with them, because it will benefit you in the future," I said.

"I agree," she said. "I understand."

I told her, "Being close to your family will give us information, and there is going to be a time when your interests are aligned, so they could help us."

I left the jail around ten that night and as I was walking out the door, I was ambushed by a local Orlando television reporter from WKMG by the name of Tony Pipitone. He started to question me on camera.

"I can't tell you anything we discussed," I told him.

He said to me, "What's your reaction to the fact that cadaver dogs have just hit on something in the Anthonys' backyard?"

"I don't have any reaction," I said. "I just left the jail. I don't know anything about it."

I was shocked by how much he knew. Why would the police be call-ing him, or any other member of the media for that matter, to say they were digging up a body in the backyard? It was really beginning to piss me off how much these cops talked to the media.

When Pipitone turned off the camera, he said to me, "Sorry we had to sandbag you like that, but they just hit. The cops are digging up the body right now. I guess it's time for you to start working on your insanity defense."

You motherfucker, I thought to myself. *Who does he think he is?* It was such a condescending thing to say—besides the fact that your ordinary insanity defense is always a loser.

Gabe and I turned right around and went back into the jail to see Casey. I told her what Pipitone had told me.

"They're digging in the backyard," I said. "You have to tell me if she's back there."

Casey looked at me and said, "I don't know where she is," and it was one of the few times early on that I believed her. It was a unique moment between the two of us. I had a gut feeling she was telling me the truth.

We walked out, and I said to Gabe, "I guess we'll have to see what happens next."

And that's what a lot of legal work in criminal cases is: reacting to things police do. I returned to my office, and the news of the cadaver dogs was all over the news. Again, I was shocked at how much the cops were talking publicly about the case.

I mean, the cops weren't talking to me. They were talking to the me-dia. In fact, later on reporters would tell me this was an easy case for them to work because they didn't have to go out looking for sources. All they had to do was sit around and wait for the police to call.

I immediately began to work closely with the Anthony family because the strategy early on was simple: if we found Caylee, then Casey could get out of jail. I spent a majority of my time during the first couple of weeks sitting with the Anthonys. There were nights during that first week when I was in their home talking to them until one in the morn-ing. Their object and strategy of inviting the media in was to get the word out that Caylee was missing.

In their quest to find Caylee, George, Cindy, and Lee decided to make up flyers with Caylee's picture on it and work with existing charity orga-nizations for support. George announced he would set up a command center in front of a local Publix supermarket and, from his post at the command center, he would pass out flyers and T-shirts. Little did I know that a year later, a huge piece of evidence would come from that command center that would blow the case wide open.

The news media descended on me almost overnight and came at me like an avalanche. Two days after I took the case, my secretary, Myrna, told me that a reporter from *People* was waiting in the lobby to talk to me.

I walked into Gabe's office and said, "*People* magazine is here."

"Yeah," he said," "they want to take you out to lunch."

"Look at these messages," I said. "One is from *20/20*, another from *Dateline*, and here's one from the *CBS Morning Show*."

"Unbelievable," he said.

Myrna walked in.

"The *Osceola News-Gazette* [is] on line three," she said.

I said jokingly, "I have *People* magazine in the lobby. I have *20/20* and *Nightline* to call back. Baby, the *Osceola News-Gazette* is going to have to get in the back of the line."

"It's about the boat club," she said dryly.

Gabe and I had a good chuckle over that. And I did talk to them.

I went to lunch with the reporter from *People*. The reporter asked if I would introduce her to Casey's parents, and I agreed.

One of the reporters who showed up at my office was former Los Angeles Police Department Detective Mark Fuhrman, the star witness against O. J. Simpson in his murder trial. Fuhrman was the one who found the bloody glove and was accused of being a racist. When tapes appeared on which he uttered the N-word, he was indicted for perjury. He accepted a plea deal and was forced to leave the police force. Fuhrman was now a Fox News contributor—talk about landing on your feet. A Fox producer had called me and asked if I would go to lunch with him. When I was in law school, I had watched that trial every day, so yes, I wanted to meet Fuhrman.

I still remember the moment Fuhrman walked through my door. He was tall and handsome, and I thought to myself, *Last week I was arguing motions in a simple marijuana possession case, and today Mark Fuhrman is taking me to lunch.*

The Fox producer, Fuhrman, and I went to lunch in Kissimmee. During the meal, the producer got up and went to the bathroom. I'm sure this was planned, because as soon as he left, Fuhrman said to me, "Listen, I have a lot of connections with law enforcement and I can really help you with this case, especially in maybe negotiating with the cops. If you tell me where Caylee is, we can solve this case and you'll look like a big hero."

He said this as though I knew where she was and that, of all people, I would tell him.

When Fuhrman said that, I looked to my left and to my right to make sure no one was listening and leaned forward, saying to him, "I'll tell you where Caylee is if you tell me if you planted that glove." A bloody glove was one of the key pieces of evidence against Simpson.

He stared at me for a moment and then exploded in laughter. I could appreciate him trying to get the information out of me, even though it would have cost me my license. But I didn't appreciate the fact that he thought I was stupid enough to tell him.

I asked him for a favor. I said, "Mark, I teach at a local law school. Would you consider coming by my class tonight to speak to the students?"

"Sure. No problem."

What I failed to tell Fuhrman was that semester I was teaching at Florida A&M University College of Law, a historically black university. The second he walked in and began to speak, the students gave him a good grilling. I could have saved him, but it was just too much fun to watch.

All the national TV shows came calling, including *Nancy Grace* on HLN and *Geraldo at Large* and *On the Record with Greta van Susteren* on Fox News. They all wanted to talk to the Anthonys. Cindy agreed, but for some reason George refused to go on. I kept telling him he should do it, but he said he didn't want to make statements on television.

"That's Cindy's job," he said. "I don't feel right doing that." I found that odd.

They asked me if I would go on with Cindy. I figured I would be able to deflect any questions about Casey, so I agreed. When I asked Casey about it, she was all for it, because being on TV was part of our overall quest to find Caylee.

And so a couple days after I entered the case, I appeared with Cindy on a string of national TV shows, trying to focus attention on the search for this missing child.

The first time I did *Nancy Grace*, Grace wasn't hosting that night. Jane Velez-Mitchell was sitting in for her. It was a weird, fast-paced show, and I didn't think it was very productive.

The next day, Cindy and I were on *Today*. Matt Lauer was the host, and we told the audience about our quest to find Caylee.

The second time I appeared on *Nancy Grace*, Grace herself was there. I had never watched *Nancy Grace* before this case, so I didn't know what it was about, and I didn't know what I was walking into, though I learned quickly.

Grace, a former prosecutor from Fulton County, Georgia, grilled me about my conversations with Casey, and I told her I couldn't discuss any of that. Immediately she accused me of hiding behind the attorney-client privilege.

"I'm not hiding behind anything," I said. "I'm keeping my license, and I'm shocked you even asked a question like that."

She replied haughtily, "I don't represent criminals. I represent the victims."

I was thinking, *Who is this quack?*

I quickly discovered that Grace's show was a lot like professional wrestling, where the action and drama are more important than truth or facts. She would attack me, and we'd go to a commercial, and she'd say, "Hey, you're doing great. This is just the schtick of the show."

"I understand," I said.

"You're doing wonderfully," she said. "Keep up the good work."

As I SAID, very early on I spent a lot of time with Cindy and George. No one got much sleep the first couple of days. I chalked up their manic behavior to the situation as I knew it. Their granddaughter had been kidnapped and was missing, and they were terrified that something had happened to her.

I thought, *These people are going through a horrible, horrible experience, and this would make anybody crazy. It would make anybody act differently.* It took me a while before I realized that not only was there something off about Casey but something was off about her parents as well. At first glance the Anthonys seemed like the all-American family.

They worked very hard to maintain an amazing façade of normalcy, one that I bought into hook, line, and sinker. It took a significant amount of time before I realized, *There's something off here.* Exactly how "off" I would discover much later.

Everything suggested that when it came to Caylee that this was a loving family. Cindy was the protector. She swore up and down that Casey would never harm Caylee, and everyone else said the same thing. Her brother Lee said it. Even George said it. They all talked about what an incredible mother Casey was. After discovery was made public, not one incident of child abuse or child neglect on Casey's part ever came to light. There was nothing that would lead anyone to believe this child was anything less than doted on and loved and cared for by her mother and grandparents.

And you could see it throughout the house. You could see it everywhere—this child was *loved.* From a defense attorney's perspective, I was being more reactive than proactive, because I was trying to get a grasp of the situation. Early on, as I was starting to acknowledge to myself that there was a possibility that Caylee was dead and trying to determine whether Casey—or anyone else—was involved, I thought, *This has got to be an accident. These people truly loved this child and took good care of her.* That was something that you could see. A person just doesn't all of a sudden wake up one day and think, *I'm going to kill my child, whom I've loved and doted upon for the last three years.* People just don't do that. Where there's abuse, there's always a progression of violence. There's a black eye or a broken arm, or an emergency trip to the hospital for a more serious injury. Other people notice these things. There was *nothing* like that in this case. Even up until today, not a single person has ever testified that this child was anything but loved.

Casey officially hired me on July 17, 2008, and I filed a motion for a bond hearing, which was heard on July 22. Meanwhile, I went to see Casey and the Anthonys every day. I don't know what it was—I was drawn into this case immediately. It was as if everything else had to be put on hold, because I was sure that at any minute this child would either be found, or something was going to break. That's what this case did to me from the very beginning: it sucked me in, taking me away from everything else I was doing.

CHAPTER 3

THE BOND HEARING

O N JULY 22, the morning of the bond hearing for Casey, the Anthonys—George, Cindy, and Lee—came to my office. They came late, and I had to rush through our meeting with them so we could get to the courthouse on time for the 1:00 P.M. hearing. We went over the questions I was going to ask them, and I told them what to expect.

I explained to them what I was trying to accomplish at the hearing, that my goal was to establish Casey's ties to the community, to show she had no prior record, to show she had a safe place to go—the Anthony home—and to tell the judge that the Anthonys would be responsible for her and would ensure that she would show up in court.

The purpose of bail, you have to understand, is not to punish the defendant. Rather, it's to ensure the safety of the community and to make certain that the defendant shows up in court for the trial.

Those are the two goals of bail, and those were the two criteria I was trying to establish for Casey. Under Florida statutes, a defendant accused of a third-degree felony, as Casey was, normally would have bonded out for $1,000. She was also charged with two misdemeanors, for which the standard bond amount totaled $500. I figured that under the local guidelines, once she posted $150 dollars, she would be out of jail.

Months later I would find out that Lee had called Detective Yuri Melich and not only told him that the Anthonys had met with me but also told him what we talked about, including my strategy. My guess is that Lee was trying to stay on the good side of law enforcement by letting them know that just because he was testifying on Casey's behalf, it didn't mean that he wouldn't assist them. Never before or since have I ever experienced someone calling law enforcement before going to testify for a family member.

Later on I would discover that George would say some pretty negative things about me to law enforcement, and it would take quite a while longer before I found out why. But to my face both he and Lee were perfect gentlemen, as kind as they could be. They always seemed to be very encouraging when trying to help out Casey.

Because I was meeting with the Anthonys at the last minute, we were running behind. As we walked into the courtroom, Judge Stan Strickland was already seated on the bench. Not a good start for me.

I got ready and made my presentation. I called George, Cindy, and Lee to the stand. George did a wonderful job. He testified that Casey had no criminal history, that Casey had lived at the same address for twenty years, that she had significant ties to the community, that even when the police started to question her, she never ran, even though she could have.

I also went over the family's finances so the judge would have an idea of how much bond money the family could afford to post. I explained that George was a security officer making ten to fourteen dollars an hour and that Cindy was a nurse. She wasn't a practicing nurse but worked as a clinical supervisor making between $50,000 and $60,000 a year. I talked about the family assets and said they owned a home worth $250,000.

They were middle class, I said, maybe even lower than that, and they all said they would assist with the posting of bond.

After we were done, I felt I had established Casey's significant ties to the community and showed that she had no prior record, was no danger to the community, and was no flight risk.

When Cindy took the stand, the lead prosecutor, Linda Drane Burdick, asked her about financial problems, questions I felt were totally irrelevant to the issues relating to whether Casey should be freed on bond. Her questions appeared to be focused mainly on airing dirty laundry as opposed to accomplishing anything. Cindy had to admit that she had several judgments against her and that her wages had been garnished. I don't know how that established anything for the state other than showing that Cindy had financial problems.

I didn't call Casey to the stand. A lot of lawyers call their clients to the stand, but I never do that because anything and everything they say can be held against them. A smart prosecutor might push the envelope and go beyond the scope of direct examination, and a biased judge could overrule any objections that I might make. It is always a foolish move, though I see lawyers do it all the time.

That should have been the end of it. It was an open-and-shut case. Casey Anthony should have been freed on bond.

But nothing about this case ever turned out to be as simple and straightforward as it should have been. In certain cases, the judge will allow the prosecutors to call law enforcement officers to testify so they can give the judge an idea of what the case is about. However, on most occasions prosecutors just rely on the arrest report to fill the judge in on the facts alleged. In this case, Strickland allowed the prosecution to put on what amounted to a minitrial taking more than two hours. The prosecution put on a dog-and-pony show for the press, the sole purpose of which was to bash Casey.

First up was Melich, who took the stand and testified as to Casey's actions on the day she was arrested. He listed many of the false statements she made and showed how he had disproved them. He talked about going to Universal Studios with Casey, replaying her lies. He talked about smelling the car when it was at the forensics bay. Melich said that before going into missing persons he had been in homicide, and that, based on his experience, he smelled the "smell of decomposition."

Every cop who testifies always has the same line that "once you smell the smell of human decomposition, you never forget it." It's like Supreme Court Justice Potter Stewart, in his concurring opinion on *Jacobellis v. Ohio*, writing he couldn't define pornography, "but I know it when I see it."

And yet, in his five-page detailed initial report, Melich had said *nothing* about the smell of the car. He also testified about a stain in the trunk of the car that the crime scene investigators thought was "questionable." I would later find out that the test was negative—not at all "questionable," as testified to by Melich. CSI had used a product called Bluestar Forensic, a spray similar to luminol that, after applying, can reveal human bloodstains even after someone has cleaned them up. There was a small reaction in the trunk but the confirmatory test turned up negative. This is not uncommon and as an experienced detective, Melich surely should have known that.

Melich also gave testimony to finding hairs similar in color and length to that of Caylee in the trunk of the car. This is also not uncommon because the human head sheds between one hundred and two hundred hairs a day. If Casey had taken Caylee's sweater and put it in the trunk, her hair easily would have transferred to the trunk. Or Casey could have Caylee's hair on her clothing from dressing her and then gone into the trunk to retrieve something, transferring the hair in the process. Put simply, every trunk has hair in it. Melich failed to mention that Casey's hair, and even animal hair, was found in the trunk as well, but no one was accusing Casey of throwing her cats in the trunk.

I took notes feverishly and listened carefully to each witness because as a defense lawyer, even if I don't win the battle of the bail hearing, the testimony can help me win the war. Not only was I getting to hear from crucial prosecution witnesses but their testimony was on the record and locked in so they couldn't ever change it. Having them on the record so early gave us an advantage.

When the prosecution talked about cadaver dogs and the smell coming from Casey's Pontiac, I didn't know how to read them. The bond hearing was the first time that anyone had made a big deal about the smell of the car. Cindy hadn't made an issue of the smell of the car to me, so I hadn't paid too much attention to the fact that the car allegedly had some foul odor. I thought there was still a possibility that there was some crazy woman out there who had taken Casey's baby.

Next up was the dog part of the state's dog-and-pony presentation. Deputy Jason Forgey, the handler of a cadaver dog named Gerus, took the stand. He struck me as someone who was slick. And I say that because ever since the *Miranda* ruling, defendants had to be read their rights before they could be questioned, and the police know just how far they can go to get around that law. The cops know the rules. And they know the exceptions. And, in my experience, this has developed a police culture called *testilying*, police slang for when they decide to embellish or omit critical testimony regarding a criminal defendant.

Why do they do it? Because they know they can get away with it. And I strongly sensed Forgey was testilying.

He got up there and recounted how he and his dog Gerus came to inspect Casey's Pontiac. He said he deployed Gerus, who alerted Forgey to the trunk area of the car. Forgey then testified that he took Gerus into the backyard of the home, and that the dog alerted there as well. He said he then called in another dog from another county, who alerted to the same area as well.

When Forgey finished testifying, I stood up to cross-examine him. I had never had any experience dealing with a cadaver-dog handler before. On top of that, this was the first time I was hearing about this evidence, so I really had to think fast on my feet.

"Your dog alerted in the backyard?" I asked.

"Yes," he said.

"And obviously CSI dug in the backyard and found nothing."

"Correct."

"And then your dog alerted in the trunk of the car?"

"Yes."

"And obviously you didn't find a body in the trunk."

"No."

"And so," I said, "at the very best your dog was one for two, or at worst, oh for two."

And what Forgey did—and I didn't quite catch it at the time—was save himself by saying, "I'm sorry. I don't understand you."

I went over it again. I even repeated myself, but Forgey avoided answering my question by playing stupid and pretending not to understand the point I was making.

And then Strickland stepped in to save him.

"I understand your point," said the judge. "Move on."

So I did. But what I didn't know—and what Deputy Forgey knew—and what the prosecution likely knew—was that the dog who came back the next day *did not* alert in the backyard and that they brought in the other dog, and that dog *did not* alert in the back yard, either. I had a hard time believing the prosecution did not deliberately hide that information from me and from the judge at that hearing.

Forgey did say, "We went back the next day." But the prosecution didn't question him any further. A case of "what they don't know won't hurt them"?

I voiced my objections throughout. As far as I was concerned, everything the cadaver-dog handler said was hearsay. I objected to the information about what the dog found. Strickland overruled me every time.

I objected to Melich's testimony. What did his testimony have to do with whether Casey would show up in court or not?

The judge asked for arguments, and I said, "The law is the law, and we're here to enforce the law, to follow the law. And under the law, she's entitled to bond."

I said, "Sure, there's possible evidence of a possible homicide here, but they aren't charging my client with that. If they want bond commensurate with a homicide case, they need to charge her with a murder. So long as the charges are what they are, you have to give her a bond. Treat her like anyone else. She has no prior criminal record, she has significant ties to the community, and she's not a danger to anyone."

I requested the standard bond amount, $1,500.

I argued, "If she's free, she can also help search for her daughter. And it will also give me an opportunity to go over things with her," which more than anything was really what I wanted. I wanted Casey to have unfettered access to her attorney so she and I could communicate better. We couldn't talk in the jail. I didn't trust the police to give us the privacy I needed when I spoke with her.

The case wouldn't have dragged on as long as it did if I had been able to meet with her more and build trust so she could feel more comfortable talking to me. But we were in the Wild, Wild West of Central Florida. Nothing doing.

Burdick, the prosecutor, rose and said, "Now that she's a person of interest, she may run. I request a bond of $500,000."

I almost laughed. Then I became angry.

"If that's the case," I said, "why are we standing here going through the motions? If you're going to enter a $500,000 bond, that amounts to no bond at all. Why not make it a kajillion dollars? Why don't we just pack up and go home?"

The judge ruled in favor of the prosecution, setting Casey's bond at $500,000. Then Strickland did something very odd. He gave extra commentary. In open court he said, "Casey has not helped in any way to find her daughter." When he said that, I thought to myself, *She's not obligated to. She may be morally obligated to, but that's not how the law works.*

Then the judge said, "Not a bit of useful information has been provided by Ms. Anthony as to the whereabouts of her daughter. And I would add that the truth and Ms. Anthony are strangers."

The next day the headline "The Truth and Casey Anthony Are Strangers" was on the front page of the *Orlando Sentinel*.

Doesn't Judge Strickland care about the Fifth Amendment? I asked myself. It was such an interesting statement considering the Fifth Amendment of the United States Constitution ensures a defendant's right against self-incrimination. To make a statement like that to someone who's about to stand trial in his courtroom was absurd and disturbing. Considering that Casey had never taken the stand or testified, he had *zero* ability to judge her statements or her ability to tell the truth.

A judge is not supposed to show any type of prejudice against a defendant, and to say in front of a national audience that Casey was a liar didn't exactly strike me as maintaining a neutral position.

Strickland didn't instill a lot of confidence in me that Casey was going to get a fair trial. I didn't object, but for the first time, I thought about recusing him.

When George, Cindy, Lee, and I left the courtroom, the crush of press was absolute madness. It was then that Cindy, defending her daughter, threw out the theory of the moldy pizza smelling up the car. As bodies and cameras and tape recorders surrounded us, she said, "There was a pizza in the back of the car for three weeks. You know how hot it's been, and that's where the maggots came from and that's where the smell came from."

Riveted by her every word, the flock of reporters pressed closer until we were being held hostage. I finally had no choice but to make a deal with them.

"I'll talk to you if you let the Anthonys go," I said.

They agreed, and after the Anthonys made their escape, I couldn't express enough anger toward the injustice of the $500,000 bond for a third-degree felony.

I knew at that moment we were going to appeal it. To this day I cannot understand how any court could have justified a $500,000 bond for a third-degree felony.

I went back to the Orange County jail to speak to Casey about what the $500,000 bond meant for her. I explained to her that I was going to appeal the decision, that we were going to do everything in our power to raise the money to get her out, and that her parents had agreed to help in any way they could.

During the bond hearing I began to wonder whether Casey had been telling me the truth after I heard some of the things that came out. As I was telling her about the unfairly large bond, Casey whispered to me conspiratorially, "I have something I have to tell you."

"What, Casey?"

Because I had been concentrating on the witnesses at the bond hearing and not on her, she knew that I would be asking her about the cadaver dogs and about her lies, information that must have been terribly unsettling for her. She knew this conversation was coming, and so to head it off she said to me, "I have some things to tell you."

"What is it?"

"After I came back from the hearing," she said, "I was up in my cell, and one of the inmates came by, and she flashed the number 55 through the window where I could see her. She was looking at me, and I could read her lips. She was saying, "Timer 55.""

"What does that mean?" I asked her.

She said, "Caylee had had a play date with Annabelle, and they went to Jay Blanchard Park with Zenaida [Fernandez-Gonzalez] and her sister Samantha, and at one point Zenaida grabbed Annabelle and Caylee and started walking toward the car." Casey told me that she watched as the children got into the car, and when she asked Zenaida, "What are you doing?" she said that Zenaida grabbed her by her shoulders and said, "Listen, I'm taking Caylee, because you don't know what you have. You don't know how lucky you are, and I'm going to teach you a lesson."

Casey told me that she and Zenaida struggled and that Zenaida got in her car with the children, and as she was driving away, she said, "I will contact you with further instructions."

Casey said that Zenaida contacted her and told her to change all her passwords to "timer55." (When we looked at her computer records, the passwords to her Myspace and Facebook accounts were in fact "timer55.")

"Why?" I asked.

"What 'timer55' means," said Casey, "was that Zenaida was going to return Caylee in fifty-five days." (If you count from June 16, the day Caylee disappeared, to August 9, Caylee's birthday, it's exactly fifty-five days.)

She said that Zenaida would give her instructions to go to places around Orlando, and the way she would do it was through posting on Myspace or Facebook.

"Zenaida could do this," Casey said, "because she had the password, but Zenaida would post it and then delete it right away so there would be no trace of it."

She looked at me with great seriousness. What I wanted to say to her was, *You are nuts. That's hands-down the most ridiculous story I have ever heard. Listen, Casey, it's hard to believe that Zenaida was able to find someone in the jail to get to you and flash "timer55" so you won't tell the cops what's really going on. That's a very powerful conspiracy theory.*

But I didn't say any of that because I wanted her to trust me. I wanted to be her helper and I wanted to find a way to get her to tell me the truth and to stop living in this intricate fantasy world of hers.

I was really struggling to respond to her, so I finally said, "This is going to be really difficult to prove."

"I know," Casey said quietly. "I know."

I said, "You're going to have to think long and hard to help me find things to help prove some of the things you're saying, because they caught you in other lies, and if I come forward with this, it's going to be very difficult to prove just based on your word."

"I understand," Casey said, "but I don't know what to do."

I thought to myself, *Either she's a really bad liar or this poor girl desperately needs some professional help.*

I very much wanted to bring in a psychiatrist to talk to her. The problem was, I couldn't. Every time I went to see Casey at the jail, the press would report, "Jose Baez went to visit Casey Anthony today for an hour and fifteen minutes." Any visitor would become part of the public record and the subject of discussion in the media. I tried to picture the reaction if I were to bring in a psychiatrist to see Casey. The press would have had a field day. This was a clear example of how the public records law can hurt a case. I still wonder if my calling in a mental-health expert early on the case might have affected the outcome of the case.

At the bond hearing, Strickland had ordered two psychiatrists to see Casey in order to decide whether she was competent to stand trial. I was going to object, because that shouldn't have been something for the state to determine. Rather, if anyone was going to make that move, it should have been mine to make. I didn't object because I thought this might be a good time to get professionals to see her who might shed light on what her psychological problems might be.

If I had initiated it, then the media would be commenting that I was intending an insanity defense, which to a layman means, *I'm not guilty because I'm crazy.* Which was something I didn't want because, more than anything, that would have hurt Casey. Plus she was sharp enough that she might have said to me, "I'm not crazy. You're fired," which was something else I didn't want.

A couple days after Strickland handed down his ruling for a $500,000 bond, I filed an appeal with the Fifth District Court of Florida to have it overturned. To the best of my knowledge, this had been the very first time in the state of Florida that a defendant had received a $500,000 bond for a third-degree felony and two misdemeanors.

Clearly it was excessive. The appellate court denied our motion without a written opinion. We asked the appellate court to issue an opinion so we could take it to a higher court, but it refused. There's a saying that "bad cases make bad law," and I wondered whether this was an example of that.

I was in a real quandary. I was unable to communicate with Casey because the clicking of the intercom led me to believe that the police were listening to our conversations, so I needed to find a way to get her out. That's par for the course in any case. Your clients want to get out of jail. They don't want to sit there. Only I had the distinct feeling that unlike the rest of my clients, Casey *enjoyed* being in jail. When I came to see her, she was always upbeat, never depressed. She would come in feeling chipper, as though she was at a picnic rather than in jail. This, as much as anything else, really struck me as being odd. Only later would it turn out to make perfect sense.

I NEEDED TO SPEND TIME alone with my client, but after the judge hit us with a $500,000 punishment, I was at a loss for what to do. And then out of the blue I got a call from Polakoff Bail Bonds, the largest of Orlando's bail bondsmen. A man named Kalik came to my office to meet with me.

"I can post the $500,000 bond," he said. "In fact, here's the paperwork. I'm one of the few bondsmen in town who has this type of authority."

Most bondsmen require a 10 percent payment in cash and then collateral that equals the rest. In the case of the Anthonys, they would have to pay him $50,000 and own a house worth $450,000. Their house wasn't worth close to that, but Polakoff was willing to give them a break. He said that if the Anthonys made payments on the $50,000 and put their home up for collateral, he would post Casey's bail. It was exactly what the Anthonys were looking for.

I suspect the reason he was willing to do that was that it would bring a significant amount of publicity to his bail-bonds firm. I didn't care. I was thrilled to have an opportunity to get Casey out of jail.

Cindy and Lee had been going through the motions of trying to find a bondsman to bail her out, so I called Cindy to tell her the good news.

After meeting with the bondsman and spending a lot of time arranging to get Casey out, I was shocked when, at the last minute, Cindy said "no."

"George doesn't want to post the bond," she said. My jaw hit the ground, because they were sure Casey knew where Caylee was, and I couldn't understand why they weren't doing everything they could to find Caylee.

I told her that I had gone to a lot of trouble to arrange this and that I was furious she was saying no.

"He's my husband," said Cindy. "He's half owner of the house. I have to respect his wishes."

Angry as I could be, I went to see Casey. I told her that George was preventing her from getting out of jail.

"I really want to talk to him," she said.

From the start, I had instructed Casey not to accept visits from her parents or from Lee. I requested this for two reasons. First, because law enforcement was telling the Anthonys, *We can't talk to her, but you can, wink, wink,* in essence making them agents of the state in their attempt to get her to talk to them. Second and most importantly, these meetings were recorded by the police, which was bad enough, but they were also broadcast across the country through the media every time they met. Despite my counsel, she continued to accept the visits—a major source of frustration for me. I kept telling her that every word she was saying to them would be recorded and used against her in court, where it could be microanalyzed and misinterpreted by those judging her fate. But her family ties were strong, and she kept agreeing to see them. Though George refused to bond her out, Casey said she was sure that if she could just talk to him, he would relent and put up the money.

Unfortunately, I was right about the state using her conversations with her family members against her. The state would later make a majority of its case around the conversations during those visitations. The evidence would turn out to be devastating, painting her in a negative light. On certain occasions, what she said to them undermined our defense.

One of the worst examples occurred during a phone call she made to her parents on the night she was arrested. She called home, and the conversation was taped and later played in court for all to hear. During the call she started to fight with her mom, who wanted to know what she knew about Caylee's disappearance. Curtly, Casey asked for her boyfriend's phone number. Her mother said she didn't have it. Casey asked her to put Lee on the phone. Then she spoke to a girlfriend, who wailed, "If anything happens to Caylee, I'll die."

Casey can be heard saying on the tape, "Oh, my God. Calling you guys was a huge waste of time. All I wanted was my boyfriend's number."

From a defendant's standpoint, it was terrible. She sounded so cold. She came across very badly, like she was completely heartless. All these people were trying to do was find out what happened to Caylee, and she was being bitchy with them. The prosecution used the tape to bash her at trial.

Though her motivation to see her parents was to try to get them to bond her out, I repeatedly told her she was jeopardizing her case every time she talked with them. Finally I tried a different approach. I bought a book about the landmark case of *Miranda v. Arizona*, the Supreme Court case that gives each person the right to remain silent. I wanted her to read it so she could educate herself as to her constitutional rights, where they come from, and why they're important.

Basically, I gave her a homework assignment. I gave her the book and asked her to write an outline of it. When I came to visit her two days later, not only had she read the book but her report was so intelligently written, I doubt a seasoned lawyer could have written it better.

I remember thinking to myself, *Wow, this girl could have been anything she wanted to be in life. Instead, she's here in jail and in the running for Most Hated Person in America.*

But I had finally gotten through to her. She then agreed to start rejecting the entreaties of her family members to come see her.

Coincidentally, a day after she began rejecting her parents' visits, I had a meeting in my office with prosecutor Burdick, Sergeant John

Allen, and Commander Matt Irwin, supervisors from the missing persons unit. They said they wanted to set up a "private" meeting with Casey and her family in hopes Casey would tell them where Caylee was.

When Burdick suggested Casey meet with one of her relatives, I thought to myself, *Maybe this would be beneficial. Maybe she can talk them into posting bond.*

"We can set it up at your office," Burdick said. "We can bring Casey here. She can meet with whatever family members she wants."

I agreed and then went to the jail and talked to Casey about it.

"This might be something you might want to do," I said to her. "Maybe you can talk your family into bonding you out. Who would you like to meet with?"

"I only want to meet with my father," she said. "Only my father."

At that time it really didn't mean that much to me. The realization of its importance only came much later. I told the cops, "She wants to meet with her father."

The next day I received a call from Allen, who informed me that, "Unfortunately my boss won't okay bringing Casey over to your office because she's a security risk."

"A security risk?" I said with disdain. "You guys are cops."

"The media is there across the street," Allen said. "Anyone could go there. It's too high profile a place." He recommended we do it at the courthouse. I was thinking, *They didn't want to do it in my office because they couldn't get in to bug my office last night.* But I played along and said, "Okay, but this has to happen tomorrow because the next day I'm flying to New York and won't be there, and we'll have to put it off until next week." My intention to leave Florida was a piece of information I never should have given them.

They came back with the same excuse the next day.

"For security reasons we can't do it," said Allen.

"In that case," I said, "we'll see if we can do it next week."

I was flying to New York to meet with forensic experts on August 14, 2008. One of the networks wanted to fly me up to do an interview and meet its executives. I was using the trip to build a defense team on the media's dime. While the entire world thought I was doing these interviews just to get on TV, I realized that this case was going to be expensive to defend and I had to be creative and use the media to my advantage. And that's exactly what I did. Each and every time I did an

interview in New York or someplace else, I used the trip to see and work
with my experts and build a defense.

Before I left my office to go to the airport, I saw on television the
headline, "Casey Anthony Accepts Visit from Parents." I couldn't believe
it. This was despite my numerous pleadings to her not to do so.

I was very upset with her and called my associate Gabe Adam immediately. I told him, "Go over there and read Casey the riot act. Explain to
her that she can't be doing this. Tell her I'm working on getting her the
private visit."

In fairness to Casey, she wanted badly to talk to her parents about
bonding her out. They had the ability to spring her and they weren't
doing it. She was antsy and wanted them to act. I got on the plane and
flew to New York.

At the jail George reportedly told Casey, "All you need to do to make
the private meeting happen is to write a letter to the sheriff saying you
want a private meeting with me, and it will happen immediately."

Casey later said she was sure I would be notified of the meeting, but
George later said that the police told him, "If she writes the letter to the
sheriff, we don't need the lawyer." So Casey wrote the letter, gave it to a
guard, and the cops sprang into action, knowing full well I would be in
New York.

The police picked up George, took him in a squad car to the jail, and
unbeknownst to George, taped him during the entire trip. Halfway to
the jail, the police were shocked when they got a phone call from the jail
saying Casey's lawyer was at the jail with her.

"I don't understand," said one of the policemen on the recording, "I
thought he was supposed to be in New York."

But it wasn't me; it was Gabe who was reading Casey the riot act.
Later Gabe told me that when he arrived, he saw a lot of strange move-
ment. The police made him wait a long time in the waiting room. Finally, having run out of patience, Gabe said to the police, "Hey, what's
going on with my client. Why can't I see my client?"

"Don't worry," said the cops. "We're making the visit happen."

Suspicious, Gabe asked them, "What visit?"

"The one with her father."

Gabe said, "No. I want to see my client this second." And they delivered Casey to him before her father arrived at the jail.

"Jose has no knowledge of this," Gabe told Casey. "You can't do this." And at that point she rejected the visit, spoiling the police and prosecution's best-laid plans. Had Gabe not been there, they would have brought George in to see her and would have taped the two of them talking. Who knows what would have been said that they would have tried to use against her?

When I learned of the tricky business the cops were up to, I was livid. *Again*. This was a clear violation of Casey's right to counsel. It was an end-run by the police who were trying to get to her without having to deal with me. It was unprofessional, *dirty* police work. I do understand why they do it—the police sometimes think the ends justify the means—but we have a Constitution, and there's never an excuse for police officers to violate someone's constitutional rights. We have brave men and women dying every day to preserve those rights. I am a firm believer that these rights mean something and no one, especially a police officer who is sworn to uphold the law, has the right to violate them.

A huge debate arose as to whether I was cooperating with law enforcement. I had written a letter to the police saying I would be more than happy to assist them in the search efforts to find Caylee, but that under no circumstances would I allow them to interrogate Casey. I said if they wanted to run leads by Casey, I'd talk to her about it, but that Casey had no idea where Caylee was.

The police never once called me to get Casey's help, despite my offer. They had no intention of doing so. All they wanted was to go in and take a few more shots at her.

My insistence that Casey remain silent became a huge public debate.

"Is Jose Baez cooperating with law enforcement?" ran the headlines. The cops kept saying, "He hasn't contacted us once, and Casey isn't cooperating," trying to put pressure on us.

My answer: "I'm sorry. You can complain to every newspaper and TV station in the world, but I'm not letting you get close to my client. End of story."

And because I did what any competent lawyer in my position would do, I quickly gained very powerful, vindictive enemies.

Here's another underhanded thing the police did: before I stopped them, whenever George, Cindy, or Lee visited Casey, they always released the videotapes of their visits to the media. Wouldn't you know it: the only tape they never made public was their dirty business of August 14, 2008, when George told her to write a letter to the sheriff in an attempt to get around the attorney-client privilege.

When I filed a motion forcing them to turn it over, I'll never forget prosecutor Frank George saying in court, "It must have been misplaced."

I couldn't hold back the laughter on that one. Here's the biggest case in the state of Florida, maybe the country, when every statement made by Casey was being broadcast everywhere by the media through the police, and they're going to tell me they lost one of the tapes? In my mind it was no coincidence the conversation that was "missing" was the one in which George told her, "Write a letter to the sheriff, and we can make the meeting happen."

Every day, it seemed, there was a leak coming from law enforcement. They had a well-orchestrated plan to convict Casey in the court of public opinion and to taint the jury pool, as the police began to serve the media a steady diet of leaks and false information. They leaked that there was the "smell of death" coming from the trunk of Casey's car. They leaked that cadaver dogs had sniffed the trunk of Casey's car and alerted to decomposition. They leaked that a single strand of Caylee's hair found in the trunk had the "death-banding" associated with finding a dead body. They leaked that they had found a stain in the trunk and, after testing it, had found DNA. And finally, they leaked that chloroform had been found after testing the air in the trunk and that experts had discovered that Casey had looked up chloroform on her computer.

As you will see, none of this "evidence" turned out to be based on fact. But that didn't matter at all. Like in politics, this was about winning. How they won didn't matter. The prosecution and the police from the start were convinced that Casey had killed Caylee, put her body in her trunk, and disposed of her somewhere, and they were going to make sure she was convicted, no matter what facts or evidence got in the way of their version of reality.

As a public relations and prosecution strategy, it was brilliant. They may not have had the evidence but they figured if they could inflame the public and the possible jury pool, it would give them a clear advantage when selecting a jury. And if they could intimidate Casey or her so-called "rookie lawyer," maybe she would fold, accept a plea, and tell the police where Caylee's body was so everyone could go home.

I knew this was their game, but I also knew that it was all a fishing expedition. I thought to myself, *If they really had all of this evidence of her guilt, why do they need to talk to Casey so badly? Why are they resorting to cheap tricks to get her to talk?*

Her "rookie" lawyer decided we weren't going to fold just yet.

For the entire first year, whenever there was new discovery, the first place I heard it from was the television set. It was never given to me in advance.

The public records law in Florida is counterintuitive to a defendant's right to a fair trial, and early on, I filed a motion with the court asking it to delay disseminating the information about the case to the media and the public so I could have an opportunity to review it first to see if there were any objectionable reasons to making it public.

Strickland denied my motion without even a hearing.

ONE DAY I GOT A CALL from one of my paralegals.

"There's a guy who says he wants to bond Casey out," he said.

"Really?"

"He says he's a bounty hunter. He says he has a show on the National Geographic Channel, and he's willing to post Casey's bond."

The man's name was Leonard Padilla, and when I checked him out, I found out he did have a reality show on the National Geographic Channel. When he arrived in Orlando, he was met at the airport by dozens of cameras. He stood and talked with a toothpick in his mouth, telling the reporters how he was going to get Casey out, and how he believed that Caylee was still alive, and that as soon as Casey got out, he was going to give her a beer and get her to relax and tell him where Caylee was.

I didn't get to meet Padilla until the next day, when he came into my office. He had his entourage with him, including a guy who followed him around with a camcorder. As soon as he walked in the door, I told him, "He's going to have to turn the camera off, because I'm not getting involved in what you're doing." He obliged.

Leonard came into my office, and I found him to be a funny, entertaining guy. He was like a character in professional wrestling. He was a cowboy—wore a cowboy hat—and with a Mexican accent, he would say, "I'm in 'Or-lon-do,'" yet would pronounce his name "Pa-dill-ah" without the Mexican accent, where it should have been "Pa-dee-yah."

So here was this Mexican guy from Sacramento, California, with a Southern accent and a cowboy hat, but he had $50,000 in hand—apparently his nephew was a bail bondsman—and he's a bounty hunter with a reality show. He told me he wanted to be the next Duane "Dog" Chapman, the bounty hunter who had a popular show on A&E, and that he was trying to renew his show.

I could see that the reason he was agreeing to post the bond was mostly for the publicity. My first impulse was to tell him to get lost, but I had a client in jail who needed $50,000 to bond out, as well as $450,000 in collateral, and she had no way to post it. I would have been shirking my duty if I had sent him on his way. Even though I felt this wasn't the ideal situation, I took advantage of it.

I realized I would have to deal with this guy. I said to myself, *So long as he gets her out of jail and I can protect her from him, this shouldn't be a problem. He'll get his publicity, and Casey'll get out.*

We both discussed that. I told him, "I'm not going to put my client's safety or her future in your hands."

"Why don't you sign me up as an investigator?" he asked.

I didn't trust him enough to do that.

"No, no, none of that," I said. "I don't want to be affiliated with you in any shape or form."

I had him sign a confidentiality agreement.

Padilla said the only condition he would put on the deal would be to have a woman on his own security team in the Anthony house in case Casey tried to run.

"No problem," I said.

I made him sign a written agreement to these rules, some which he would later ignore. I told him, "You can't talk to her and you can't question her." He agreed. Padilla put up the money and the collateral, and Casey got her release.

CHAPTER 4

ROOKIE LAWYER

PUTTING UP WITH THE CRAZINESS of the media was almost as difficult as trying to keep up with the shenanigans of the prosecution and the police. It wasn't long before the media trucks were lined up in such numbers outside my office on Simpson Road in Kissimmee that they were taking up every space in my ten-car parking lot. My other clients were reluctant to come to my office because the media outlets were filming everyone walking in my door and putting them on the news.

Finally I put my foot down. Enough was enough. I gave them all trespass warnings and told them if they didn't park across the street in the school lot, I was going to call the police. They were incensed about that, but they complied.

By law they could park across the street, and while that was still too close, there wasn't anything I could do about it. I'd pull up in my car to go to my office, and they'd film that. And at night, when I left, they filmed that too. They would shout, "Here he comes!" and the cameras would start to roll.

There must have been ten different news outlets, and each of them would call my office incessantly. Finally I said, "I'll work with you, but stop calling. I'll make a brief statement, give you what you need, and you can go away or at least stop bothering me."

I'd walk across the street, and they'd film me crossing the street. I would be standing there, waiting for cars to pass, looking both ways, and then I'd jog across the street, and they'd film it and put it on TV.

Why couldn't they just wait for me to get there? I could only conclude that they wanted me to look bad.

I told myself, *You have to stop this too.* It was all a learning experience for me. I'd get in my car, and they'd film me backing out with my license plate number in sight, and I'd have to stop and say, "Listen, I will talk to you, but please don't film me driving away in my car. I'd like a little privacy."

They'd say, "No problem," but the next time I was backing out, again they'd start filming. I soon realized that the word of the media people meant absolutely nothing.

I would give them a statement, and they would take what I said and spin it around and make it into whatever it was they wanted to say. The perfect example of this came much later in the case when the state decided to make this a death penalty case. When I was asked whether Casey was informed, I told them, "Casey knows the forces that she's up against." The lead story that night began, "Jose Baez says there are forces against Casey," implying supernatural forces. I would just shake my head. It was the theater of the absurd. It took me awhile to understand that I wasn't just a lawyer. I was an important cast member of their reality show. And then they started digging into my background. And that *really* started to bother me.

I hadn't said a word about my past, but they soon found that I had graduated from St. Thomas University School of Law in Miami in 1997 but wasn't admitted to the bar until 2005. They insinuated that, because I had failed the bar for eight years, I must be stupid because it took me so long to pass it. Their story became, *Here is this stupid Hispanic kid who's only been a lawyer for three years and couldn't pass the bar for eight years. And his office is in a strip mall.*

The other sobriquet they would throw at me was "Kissimmee lawyer." As in *Jose Baez, Kissimmee lawyer*, an insult they'd toss off in a condescending way to show that because my office wasn't in sophisticated Orlando but rather in hayseed Kissimmee I was some kind of country, hillbilly lawyer.

Another way the media described me was to call me a "rookie lawyer" as in *Casey Anthony's rookie lawyer*. Because I had only been a member of the bar for three years, many of the so-called "legal experts" were saying, "He's over his head. He doesn't have the experience. He doesn't know what he's doing." Before long *everything* I did was second-guessed.

"That was a stupid motion."

"He doesn't know what he's doing."

Early on, one of my tactics with the state and law enforcement was to demand information. I'd file ten motions at a time rather than make one motion to ask for ten different things. I did this on purpose in an attempt to get them riled up. They would drag their feet, and I wanted the judge to make them send things to me more quickly.

When I started doing that, I heard the public criticism immediately, that I either didn't know what I was doing or that I had somehow botched a motion. One time the media accused me of forgetting the court's jurisdiction. I thought, *Whaaaaat? What are they talking about?* They would accuse me of not knowing what I was talking about.

The public may have been convinced that I was an idiot, but I let it all roll off my back. When I had worked in the public defender's office in Miami, my boss was Rick DeMaria.

"Experience is always good, but it is secondary to being skilled and prepared," he would say. "One can be a bad lawyer for a long, long time."

I won a lot of cases working in the public defender's office because I had good trial skills, and no one outworked me. If you're prepared by working hard, it trumps experience every time.

One time when I was leaving the jail, I gave Casey a hug. A female guard came over and barked at me, "Get away from her. You can't touch an inmate."

"What?"

It was the most ridiculous thing I'd ever heard. I've hugged innumerable male inmates, and no one said a word. This had nothing to do with jail policy, I knew. Rather it was their simmering prejudice against Casey.

It really angered me when she said that.

"What are you implying here?" I asked.

"We're not implying anything," she said. "You just can't have physical contact with an inmate."

I said, "You know, she's a human being, and if I want to shake her hand, or hug her, I will."

"Then we'll put her behind the glass partition, and that way you won't have any physical contact with her."

"I'll file a motion in court," I said, "and we'll see about that." Then I thought to myself, *Let it go. Assholes will be assholes. It's not that important.*

But someone from corrections leaked the incident to the media, and the story was exaggerated to say that Casey and I were hugging and that we had to be separated from our embrace. Later a jail spokesperson came out and said the report wasn't true, but that was never picked up by the media. Making things worse, other media outlets picked up the original report and made up their own version of "the day Jose Baez hugged Casey Anthony."

I should have known what was coming next. Geraldo Rivera had warned me, but I didn't believe him.

I found Geraldo to be a really down-to-earth person. While I recognized he had a job to do, he also recognized the same about me, and we never tried to overstep our boundaries with each other professionally. It was the beginning of a true friendship.

Geraldo had covered the O. J. Simpson case and had done battle with defense attorney Johnnie Cochran, who has always been one of my heroes. Geraldo would tell me some of the mistakes that Cochran made, warning me not to make the same mistakes.

"Be careful what you do personally," he said. There was an instance when Cochran confided in a former girlfriend, telling her that he was sure to win the case if he could get one black person on the jury. When the former girlfriend told the media, it became headlines. There were also reports of him having had a mistress.

"Be careful who you trust," he warned me. "Watch yourself. Don't fall into the same traps."

Geraldo was part of the media that made Cochran's life difficult, and I asked him why, because the issues he had revealed had nothing to do with the case.

"When you're in these high-profile cases," he said, "it's a blood sport. And no one will have mercy on you." I always remembered Geraldo's words when dealing with the media, even though in the end I was plenty bloodied.

About a month before the headlines aired about my hugging Casey, I was in New York hiring a DNA expert when Geraldo invited Lorena and me to go sailing on his boat. We were sitting together on the boat, and Geraldo said to me, "You know, you have a really beautiful wife."

"Yeah, I think so too," I said.

"What you should do is take her around town in Orlando and be seen with her publicly," he said.

"No," I said, "I really want to keep my family out of this." I had seen how vicious the media could be, and the last thing I wanted to do was expose my family to it.

"No. Listen, and listen carefully," Geraldo said. "If you don't do that, before you know it, they're going to accuse you of having an affair with Casey."

"What?" I said. "An affair with Casey? You're nuts." And I laughed him off.

And sure enough, about a month later, the media aired the "news" about my hugging Casey in jail, and rumors started flying that I was having an affair with her.

Geraldo, who's been in the business for forty years, saw it coming from a mile away.

When the "news" hit the airwaves, I felt helpless. First of all, I'm a legal professional, and I would never allow myself to be put in a position where I had a relationship like that with a client. Not only that, but I am married to a Hispanic woman, and if the accusation had been true, Lorena Baez would have turned into Lorena Bobbitt. It was a ridiculous charge, but there wasn't anything I could do. I told my wife about the story, and she became a little angry, but it was short-lived. In the end she knew better.

But it wasn't fun having to tell her about the charges. Trying to prove that something isn't true is not a fun situation at all. And then professors at the college Lorena was attending started asking her about it. In the middle of one class, a professor called her out and said, "Oh, I hear your husband's having an affair with Casey Anthony." It really bothered her and hurt her tremendously.

People today still bring it up. I was never concerned, because I knew it wasn't true. But having to deal with the bullshit of it all really infuriated me.

It didn't take me long to figure out that in this case I had to battle not only the media but also the prosecution, the cops, and the judge. There were times, as you will see, that the crush of the opposition almost became too much to bear.

Fortunately, I wasn't the rookie lawyer everyone said I was. My background, as unconventional as it was, had given me the tools to defend Casey in this case.

Growing up in New York City and Miami, I was raised by my mother, who moved around quite a bit to find work. I have three much older sisters on my mother's side from another marriage. I have four brothers on my father's side from another marriage. I was the only child of my parents, who split when I was four years old.

My sisters raised me while my mother worked two or three jobs. My mother worked in a nursery and in factories. She cleaned houses, taking whatever jobs she could get. Eventually my sisters went off on their own, and it was just my mother and me. I had no strong male figure in my life and, at age fifteen, I started to become rebellious. A couple times I moved out and went to live with one of my sisters. At the age of sixteen I dropped out of high school in the ninth grade. At age seventeen I met a girl and got her pregnant. She was sixteen.

I was on the road to nowhere, but then I heard the heartbeat of my daughter Christina. She would save me and put me on the path that led me to where I am today. I know I would not be a lawyer today if it were not for the motivation of becoming a father. My sole mission in life was to one day have my daughter say to me, "Dad, I am proud of you." That day came while I was representing Casey. Christina was getting her degree in public relations from the University of Florida when I asked her to come down and help me with all of the media requests that were coming in. It was the summer and she needed experience and what better experience could she have than a national high-profile case? One day she came over to me and said, "Dad, I am proud of you. You are standing by this girl when no one else will. I truly admire that." That was it. I felt my life's goal had been accomplished right then and there, and it made all that I was about to suffer worth it. It would also give me the strength to forge ahead.

I didn't want my child to be raised in a single-parent home, so I married her mother. I then joined the U.S. Navy at seventeen. My wife and daughter came with me, first to boot camp in San Diego, then to Meridian, Mississippi, for school, and then to Norfolk, Virginia, where I was stationed. While I was in the navy I got my GED and started college at Tidewater Community College. After I got out of the navy, I was able to take advantage of the GI Bill to go to Miami Dade Community College.

We got divorced after six years of marriage, but I continued to stay in my Christina's life. I transferred to Florida State University in Tallahassee and, after two years, I graduated and moved to Miami to go to law school.

Originally I had wanted to enter federal law enforcement. My dream job was to serve in the United States Secret Service. I had studied criminology at Florida State and while I was there, I filled out my application and went through the hiring process. But at this point I was engaged to a woman who was going to law school, so I decided to see if I, too, could get in. I figured I could make a bigger difference as a lawyer than as a law enforcement officer.

I was accepted into St. Thomas University School of Law. It was very difficult because I had to work full time in order to pay my child support. Mostly I worked as a security guard or in loss prevention in stores—and it was tough because, under American Bar Association guidelines, I wasn't supposed to work more than twenty hours a week. I can admit it now—sometimes I went over because I needed so badly to make money.

I lived in a boarding house in Miami. We had some very colorful characters renting rooms, including a single mother who worked as a prostitute, two mechanics who worked on their cars in the front yard, and another guy who I'm not quite sure what he did.

I drove a jalopy. When I parked in the law school parking lot, smoke would come out the exhaust; I would be parked next to a Mercedes or a BMW.

The first year of law school is difficult enough for a student with no other responsibilities, but I managed to make it through. That first summer I was going to do my internship at the state attorney's office in Miami. I was excited, but that first day on the job I felt that something wasn't quite right. I didn't enjoy it. It was a dry, angry environment.

The next day I walked across the street to the Miami-Dade Public Defender's Office and I never left. I loved it. I got to work with clients and got to be around people. The public defender's office was about helping people, working with real people and real problems, being the light of hope for people who had no hope. I fell in love with it.

I was around great lawyers and great people while I was there. I learned so much that I didn't want to go to law school anymore. I just wanted to be there. The second and third years of law school aren't nearly as hard as the first, and I was able to graduate, despite spending most of my time at the public defender's office. I was a C student, but it didn't matter to me because all I wanted was to be in the courtroom. That was my passion. It's what thrilled me and kept me in law school. The other classes, like contracts and torts, didn't do anything for me, but the advocacy of a jury trial really hooked me. The O. J. Simpson case aired during the middle of my second year; I watched it every day and was fascinated by the case. Johnnie Cochran, Barry Scheck, F. Lee Bailey, Dr. Henry Lee—these guys were like rock stars to me.

The law school library had videodiscs, like records, from the Harvard Law School trial advocacy center. The discs contained video of students conducting trials. It was from those tapes that I learned about evidence objections. I was always impressed by Harvard, and I am proud to say that this past year I was invited to be a faculty member of the same program.

By the time I graduated from law school, I had ten jury trials under my belt. I could practice under a certified legal internship as long as I had a licensed attorney by my side. I was able to pick a jury, make opening statements, cross-examine witnesses, and go through the entire trial. I learned so much and have to give credit to these fine lawyers who helped develop me as a criminal defense lawyer.

I was so excited when the public defender's office hired me. The office allowed me to start right away. Fresh out of law school, I was given one hundred and fifty cases, and that first year I tried twenty-four of them. I was in court every week. Most of the cases were minor issues like battery, domestic violence, resisting arrest, or cases where the defendants didn't plead out.

Out of the thirty-four cases I tried (including ten while in law school), I lost three, and two of those were reversed on appeal. I had a very high success rate. The Miami-Dade Public Defender's Office has a stellar reputation for developing great lawyers, among them Roy Black, Michael Haggard, and Jack Denaro. All I ever wanted was to be the next great lawyer to come from that office.

One of the most important traits I learned, one that I carry with me to this day, is the mentality of a fearless warrior. We were taught to fear no one—not the cops, not the judge, and certainly not the prosecutor. A couple of months after I graduated from law school, I had a heated cross-examination that involved Leonel Tapanes, a Miami police officer.

The next day Tapanes confronted me in the courtroom, and we nearly came to blows. He thought—as most police officers do—that I would bow to his authority, and when I didn't, he held it against me. There we stood, nose to nose, about to get into a fistfight in the courtroom.

We both restrained ourselves, but the line had been drawn and I made it clear to him that he better not cross it. Out on the street I told him, "You may be the law, but in the courtroom your ass is mine."

He later went to the upper brass at the public defender's office to tell them about the incident and to complain about me. The next day I was called in to see my boss, Rory Stein, the man who hired me. I was sure I was in big trouble. He called me into his office and showed me the complaint. As I began to shrink in my chair, Rory smiled at me and said, "Now that's the way we teach our lawyers to fight for our clients!" That was the mentality in the public defender's office. We fought for those who couldn't fight for themselves.

I know this may sound extreme, but this is the state of mind required for one to do defense work effectively. Imagine yourself in trouble, fighting for your life in a system that cares more about those who are rich and guilty than those who are poor and innocent. Who do you want representing you, a fighter or someone who'll fold at the first hint of pressure?

About a year before Casey's case went to trial, I went to trial in Miami on another murder case. I was helping Michael Walsh, a good friend of mine, by assisting him with the forensics and ran into that same cop who was now a high-ranking homicide detective. Though it was thirteen years after our confrontation, Tapanes and I recognized each other instantly. We shook hands and even hugged. That afternoon we had lunch together and laughed about our fight. Being more mature, we both could see that each of us was just doing his job, and doing it well.

Many people think that defense lawyers and police officers are natural enemies, but nothing could be further from the truth. In fact, a good defense lawyer always makes a police officer better.

I can't tell you how many times I have finished a cross-examination of a police officer and left the courtroom with a good friendship. I've built really good relationships with many police officers through my years of working in the law. I have the utmost respect for what they do. They put their lives on the line for all of us and they get paid very little to do so.

It's those police officers who violate the law and who trample over individual rights who really get to me. Those are the officers I go after as hard as I can, and unfortunately in the Anthony case, because of the high-profile nature of the case, the police always had their guard up. And I have to say that too often the officers in this case crossed the line—or at least danced on it.

I can never fully express how valuable my time at the public defender's office was. My training attorney was Rick DeMaria, and not a day went by that he did not teach me something. Rick sat and watched each and every one of my trials, and every time I would win a case, he would bring me back to earth with a long list of the things that I had done wrong.

He told me, "Be careful. Don't get too high and don't get too low. You will learn far more from your failures than your successes." He was right. Rick was *always* right. I would remember his words of wisdom for my battles to come.

After I had passed the bar, and toward the end of my first year after graduating from law school, I went through the character and fitness part of the Florida Bar, a long, drawn-out process where they go into your background and turn over every stone.

One of the people they contacted was my ex-wife.

Unbeknownst to me, she wrote a letter and accused me of being in arrears in my child support. She wrote, "He only pays me two hundred dollars a month. He needs to be paying me more now that he's a lawyer." She also noted that I was driving "a fancy car."

I went for my informal hearing, sure this was going to be no big deal. I figured the topic would be my credit, because they were asking me about my finances. I didn't hire a lawyer to come with me—I didn't think I needed one. Later I found out that everyone went with a lawyer—except me.

The hearing was like the Spanish Inquisition. That's when I found out what my ex-wife had said. They wanted me to admit I hadn't paid her, but it wasn't true, so I didn't.

It would have been very easy for me to have said, "I was poor. I didn't have money. I wasn't paying her, but I'm paying her now, and we're working it out." And I would have gotten my license immediately. But stupid or not, I felt the truth was more important so I said, "It's not true. I did pay her, but I paid her in cash mostly and occasionally with money orders. We had always had a great relationship, but it wasn't until I became a lawyer that she started wanting more money. I told her, 'I'm not a rich lawyer. I just graduated. Give me a little time. I'm a public defender.' And I told her, 'I have over $100,000 in student loans. Give me a little time.'"

That's when we started having problems. The people in charge of the hearing started thinking, *Is he lying? Because if he's lying, he doesn't have the character to be a lawyer.*

There was more: I had defaulted on a membership to a Bally's Total Fitness and had a car note of $300 a month for my Mazda Miata. If I had been driving a cheaper car, I could have paid off Bally's. And while I was in law school, I had gone on a study abroad program in Europe instead of working over the summer to pay Bally's and some other bills. And I had bounced a couple of checks, including one at a local Publix supermarket.

That was the "informal" hearing. When the formal hearing came around, this time I brought a lawyer with me. I had three judges testify on my behalf. They said, "Jose's in my courtroom every day. He's always honest. He practices as well as any lawyer I've seen and he has the character and fitness to be a member of the Florida Bar."

After each judge testified, the three judges on the panel would say, "Thank you. No questions." But when it came to the witnesses who were testifying against me, I got a grilling.

Two days later, the panel denied me admission. I had to wait two years before I could reapply.

I was devastated. Denied admission to the bar, I lost my certification, so I could no longer try cases in the public defender's office. They liked me, so they kept me on as an investigator, but I was crushed—I felt like a major league ballplayer who was no longer allowed to play the game he loves. I had the door slammed in my face and there was nothing I could do about it.

All I wanted to do was try cases. That was my purpose in life. I felt a deep sadness every day for what turned out to be the eight years I wasn't allowed in court. Every day I thought about how unfair this was. Every day I pined for my job. Because of my love for the law, I never gave up in my quest to get my license.

My whole world was the law. Everybody I associated with was a lawyer. I had built all these friendships in the legal community and I was winning case after case in court. I was really building a name for myself. And then I got my block knocked off. There were times when I refused to see my friends because they would ask me, "What's happening with the bar? When are you getting in?"

It was tough for me not to be able to practice. I was devastated the whole time. Those eight years were really tough on me psychologically and financially. I lived from paycheck to paycheck, didn't make much money, and was miserable much of the time. I saw my classmates who graduated with me go on and become successful. I was happy for them, but it was tough for me to have to sit back and not be able to practice.

I guess I could have taken my degrees and done something else, but that wasn't what I wanted. What I wanted was to defend the accused in court.

I felt that what happened to me was completely unjust. Ultimately, I was able to overcome it. As a result, I have known what it was like to experience injustice—not to the extent of some of my clients, but enough to make me a better lawyer for it. But until I was able to get admitted to the bar and resume my career as a defense lawyer, those eight years were by far the worst years of my life. The words don't come close to explaining the black hole that the rejection by the panel put me in. In a way I was a dead man walking. In order to reapply, I had to show the panel that I was rehabilitated, that I was no longer financially irresponsible, and that I respected the rights of others. To do that, I had to do community service, and working in the public defender's office wasn't sufficient to satisfy the judges.

I began by helping to raise money for homeless kids. I worked with domestic violence organizations in Miami, including one organization that was building a domestic-violence hotline.

You never know how one event in your life can impact another, but a friend of mine told me about a little girl in Colombia who was born with a major birth defect. She lacked bones from her knees down to her ankles so she had to walk on her knees. She lived in a dirt shack, and I thought to myself, *This is so sad. I should get involved and raise money for her to have an operation.* At the same time, I would use this work as my community service for the bar.

I flew to Barranquilla, Colombia, and met the girl. I wanted to videotape her so I could come back to the United States and start my fund-raising campaign so I contacted one of the local news stations, which agreed to do the filming for me. For the station it was a personal-interest story because an American was going to Colombia to try to raise money for prosthetic legs to help this little girl who couldn't walk.

The head of the TV station and I went out to dinner. While there we ran into one of his former anchors, Lorena Velasquez. We met, and she was stunningly beautiful, smart, sassy, and interesting. I was smitten. Within five minutes I turned to a friend who had accompanied me on the trip and laughingly said, "Whatever you do, don't let me marry this woman."

For a while, Lorena and I maintained a long-distance relationship, but at my suggestion she eventually moved to Miami, and after several months, we got married. Shortly thereafter, I felt stagnant working as an investigator for the public defender's office. When I finally quit, I went to work for LexisNexis, training lawyers how to do legal research online. My job was to go to law firms and courthouses in a support role. The company had an opening in Orlando, and I felt it was time to get out of Miami. Nothing was happening in my life there, and a change of scenery would be good for me.

Meanwhile, I reapplied for the bar, and the process wasn't any easier the second time around. This time the panel wanted to know why I had to use my overdraft protection so often. I explained to them that my job at LexisNexis required me to travel, and that I didn't get my money back from the company until my return, so my only choice was to spend the money knowing I had to use my overdraft protection to pay for it. My boss even wrote a letter explaining it to them.

They said they didn't believe me, so I had to go to the effort of showing them maps of where I traveled. I was then asked for a photo of my car's odometer. They wanted me to prove I wasn't lying to them. My car's odometer showed them what they needed to know. They put me through a ringer, and after I testified, shortly after my move to Orlando, they agreed to accept me into the Florida Bar.

Then I was told, "By the way, two weeks ago, your bar exam results expired. You're going to have to take the bar over again."

I was so upset. I thought, *Couldn't they have made their decision two weeks earlier?* But meetings are scheduled once a month, and this was just dumb (bad) luck. So after being out of law school for seven years,

I had to study for the bar again. I passed it and was accepted by the Florida Bar. (How many lawyers can say they passed the bar twice?)

I immediately opened an office in downtown Orlando. I had another small office in Miami and started representing Hispanic clients. Within three months, I had a very busy law practice. Being bilingual in Orlando proved to be very helpful to my career because there aren't as many bilingual lawyers in Orlando as there are in Miami.

I then took a risk and moved my practice from Orlando to Kissimmee, a small town where I could be a bigger fish in a smaller pond. I found my office next to the Osceola County Jail, and I hired two lawyers to work for me. I began trying cases again, doing the thing I really was meant to do. I caught quite a few big cases. I represented a woman accused of kidnapping an infant and got it thrown out. I represented a cop who was charged with aggravated assault with a deadly weapon and got that thrown out. I was the lawyer for a kid in a vehicular manslaughter case and got him six months. Word started getting around the Hispanic community that I was an effective lawyer. So, as things turned out, the result of the worst thing that ever happened to me—not being accepted into the bar—ended up as the best thing that ever happened to me. If they had admitted me to the bar, I would not have met my wife, I would not have my son, and I would have never have moved to Orlando and started a thriving practice. Lorena and I vacationed in Europe. I had a nice cash flow and a wonderful wife. We were doing great, but then the phone rang—changing everything that was before and everything thereafter.

CHAPTER 5

CASEY COMES HOME—
AGAIN AND AGAIN

W HILE WAITING FOR LEONARD PADILLA to get Casey out of jail, I was constantly going to the Anthony home, getting tips about where Caylee might be, when one day Cindy called me at my office.

"I need to talk to you," she said. "It's a huge emergency."

"Okay, not a problem," I said.

"I need you to get a message to Casey for me," she said. "Nothing could be more important than this."

I was thinking, *Okay, now we're on to something. Finally something has broken, and Cindy is going to tell me, and I'll be able to talk to Casey, and we're going to get down to some serious business.*

Cindy had been on TV almost every day and had become a celebrity of sorts. We needed to meet where no one would see us.

"Why don't you meet me outside the jail?" I said. "There's a church on the corner across the street."

We drove around the back of the church and met in the parking lot.

Cindy said to me conspiratorially, "I got a call from this man. He's from Maryland. It's extremely important that you ask Casey the following." (She had written it down and was reading from the piece of paper.) She said, "Tell her I want to plant a rose bush for Caylee's birthday. I want to plant an ecstasy blue rose bush. I want her to tell me where to put the bush in the backyard so I can plant it in the exact spot for Caylee."

As she was reading this, I was thinking, *Oh my God. The apple doesn't fall very far from the tree.* This wasn't long after Casey told me about "timer55." I was thinking to myself, *That poor girl. This is whom she has for a mother.*

Cindy made me swear up and down that I would read this to Casey, and I agreed. When I read it to her, she had this look on her face like, *What the fuck?* Casey said to me, "Stick the bush in the middle of the grass. I don't know what she's talking about."

When I told Cindy later that the words meant nothing to Casey, she looked so dejected.

The night before we were to go get Casey out of jail, I was at the Anthony home. It was around midnight, and I was sitting in the living room with George, Cindy, and Lee, and we were talking about what was going on with Casey.

"Why would she be hiding Caylee?" Cindy wondered.

Cindy never believed for a second that Caylee was dead. George kept quiet, and Lee went along with whatever Cindy was saying.

Cindy said to me, "Sometimes Casey and I would argue. She could be hardheaded. And maybe she just resents me."

"What do you mean, Cindy?" I asked.

"After Caylee was born," she said, "they had to stitch up Casey, and the nurses gave the baby to me first, and she never forgave me for that. She was always angry and she would throw that in my face."

That can be upsetting, but that's no reason for her to be this extreme, I thought to myself.

I said to her, "I hate to say this, Cindy, but it would have to be something much deeper, a scar much deeper than that. I'm not saying this happened, George, but take for example if you were sexually abusing her. That would be something where she would be afraid and not want to have you around the child. If that happened, I could see a mother going to these extremes."

I wasn't accusing him. I was just throwing it out as a hypothetical about why a mother might act the way Casey was acting.

As soon as I said that, there was a deafening silence in the room. No one moved. Everyone stayed very quiet. It was so impactful that I immediately noticed it. I thought, *Waaaaiiit a minute here.* I parked that in the back of my mind, and I would return to it later, but I will never forget the day I said that and the reaction I got. They all sat there *very* quietly. It was just *very* weird.

The next day we got Casey out of jail.

Prior to Casey's bond being posted, I met with jail officials and asked them, "Can you help me with some security?"

"No," they said, "no one gets special treatment. We had Governor [Jeb] Bush's daughter once, and she didn't get any special treatment. So you're not getting any special treatment either."

I had no idea what I was getting myself into.

Padilla brought with him his security detail to help keep the press away from her. I had represented a heroin dealer who didn't have the money to pay me but who gave me his old Dodge Durango SUV instead. It was black and had tinted windows. While the air-conditioner was broken, it looked like the president's security vehicle.

We pulled in. It was a rainy day, and in front of me was a scene like you wouldn't believe. Helicopters were flying overhead, and reporters and cameramen were everywhere. I couldn't believe the crowd that had assembled. We pulled in. A few of Padilla's associates were driving cars both in front of and behind my SUV. They had walkie-talkies; it looked like we had done this a million times before. We looked like the presidential motorcade, but I quickly found out I hadn't done enough.

My plan was to get Casey, put her under my umbrella, walk straight to the Durango, and go.

I went to the jail and got Casey, who was dressed in jeans and the blue hoodie she was wearing when she was arrested. She carried her paperwork and things people had sent to her while she was in jail. She had her hair up in a little ponytail. It had grown while she was in jail. When she was arrested, she had a short bob.

"Are you ready?" I said to her.

"I'm as ready as I'm going to be," she said.

"I have this umbrella," I said. "I'm going to open it up inside here. Mike [Walsh, from my office] will open the door, and we'll walk out. We'll be really close, and then we'll get in the car and go. Let's walk briskly and get out of here."

I opened the umbrella, which I had gotten when I was working for LexisNexis. You can see the logo if you watch the video on YouTube. I tilted it forward, and reporters mobbed us as we started walking out the door. Casey was under the umbrella, shielded from view, but the reporters just started attacking her.

"Casey, where's Caylee? Did you kill Caylee?"

Casey leaned over and whispered to me, "I'm innocent, and I want to walk out of here with my head high." She was asking me to fold up the umbrella so people could see her walk out with dignity, and I was just about to close up the umbrella when a local Fox reporter pushed himself under the umbrella and got right in my face.

I don't know what came over me, but it really pissed me off. If I hadn't had one arm around Casey while holding the umbrella with my other hand, I would have slugged him. I literally wanted to clock him. It was such an invasion of privacy, an outrageous move on his part. I felt like we were being assaulted physically and that I had the right to respond with physical force. If I had to do it over again, I probably would have socked him one.

But all I could do was shove the guy as hard as I could. I pushed him really hard. I started yelling, "Get away. Get away." I was ready to fight. And then Mike from my office got under the umbrella to talk to me. I was about to shove him when he said, "No, Jose, it's me." Mike and I grabbed Casey from behind and rushed her inside the Durango and drove off.

The motorcade to the Anthony home was carried live on local television. It wasn't as dramatic as O. J. Simpson's ride home in his white Ford Bronco, but it was close. People in the public were able to anticipate and follow our path, and along the route we saw signs. One said, "Burn in hell, bitch." Another read, "You killed Caylee." Others said, "I hope you die." *So much for innocent until proven guilty*, I thought.

We pulled into the garage, and George was the first one to greet us. Casey got out, and George went up and hugged her. He whispered something in her ear, and then they went inside. She wanted to do the first thing every freed inmate wants to do—take a shower in the comfort of her own bathroom. She went to the bathroom, and then we threw Padilla and his crew out of the home.

I was so upset with the way the media were acting that I went outside the house and ripped them. I told them all off, told them I had never seen anything so unprofessional in my life. It was absurd. But this being the era of reality TV, the case of the *State of Florida v. Casey Anthony* was feeding the monster.

I left because I had to go to court to make a motion for a new trial in the Nilton Diaz case. I had assigned another lawyer, Jonathan Kasen, to cover the calendar, and he was fully prepared to do so, but I had enough time to make the hearing, so I called him and told him I was on my way. He had seen what was happening on live TV and answered the phone laughing.

"Ha, ha, ha," Jonathan said, "Jose Baez, lawyer linebacker."

I went home after the hearing and told the Anthonys I was going to bring Lorena to meet them and Casey, and we did that. Cindy had asked Casey, "What do you want me to cook you your first night home," and she said, "Salmon patties." Of course, for us to get back in the house, we had to walk past ten media trucks and ten film crews.

The Anthonys were not experienced people when it came to the criminal justice system. I brought with me a tape of *48 Hours* about the Eisenbergs, a family that lost an infant daughter when someone came into the home and snatched her in the middle of the night. Police suspected the parents and bugged their home. The federal government later brought charges against the parents, claiming they had made incriminating statements in their home—they had installed a listening device in the home—despite the fact that they did not. I showed the film to the Anthonys because I wanted them to understand that there was a strong possibility that law enforcement would bug their home as well.

I played the episode, and everyone was somber and down because they were going through the same emotions as the Eisenbergs.

Under my contract with Padilla, I had agreed to let Tracy McLaughlin stay in the home to keep an eye on Casey, but I told the Anthonys, "She is not allowed to be left alone in a room with her." I explained, "Whatever Casey says to Tracy, Tracy can be called to the stand to testify against her." Everyone swore they understood. I don't know if that was followed to the letter, but Tracy never was able to provide any incriminating evidence the prosecution could use.

A couple days later a group called Texas EquuSearch arrived in Orlando for the express purpose of searching for Caylee. It was a group out of Texas run by a man by the name of Tim Miller, who started the organization to help search for missing people after his daughter had been kidnapped and killed. Miller was a well-respected individual who had been involved in the search for Natalie Holloway in Aruba.

I was at the Anthony house the night Miller came over. Miller is a small man, about 150 pounds, and he was there with his assistant. We were talking, and afterward I said to him, "Listen, I appreciate your coming down, but I represent Casey, and all I ask is that you do not attempt to speak with my client." He said he understood and would respect that.

It was my first meeting with Miller, but it would not be my last.

I DESPERATELY WANTED to be able to spend time with Casey—without anyone around eavesdropping. She had been placed under house arrest, and after meeting with the house-arrest person, it was arranged that the only places she could go were church, my office, and to check in with home confinement.

I told her, "Write down that every day you will be coming to my office for the whole day, and then you'll go back home," and that's exactly what she did. I needed to go over the discovery with her, and I needed her to get away from the distractions that continually popped up at the Anthony home. One time a security person from Padilla's group tried to talk with her. Another day Casey got into a loud argument with George, and everyone in the house could hear them yelling.

I just didn't want her around people and making statements, because each one of those people could be called as a witness to testify against her. As for the family members—based on what I was seeing—they weren't helping her at all. Her father and mother had both said very incriminating things about her early on in the process, and these comments were getting back to me. I did not want Casey speaking to anyone at home. I wanted Casey to understand that the only safe place to talk was with me and only in my office. As far as I was concerned, the less time she spent at home, the better.

Every day we sat in the conference room of my law firm, and I would read her the discovery. I have always been a strong believer in clients knowing as much as they can about the case, and that's what I wanted Casey to do. I wanted her to know the discovery backward and forward. We'd go over it together and strategize motions. And, of course, I was also building a bond between us so she would trust me, slowly but surely. I knew it was a process and I had the patience to wait for it to pay off.

While she was out on bond, it also gave us the opportunity to raise some badly needed money for her defense. In exchange for giving photos of Caylee and her to a national news organization, Casey was paid $200,000, most of which was used to mount her defense. Of course, when the media found out, she was roundly criticized for it—unfairly if you ask me. Whenever a person faces a serious criminal charge and the potential loss of freedom, that person sells whatever assets he or she possesses—their home, their car, expensive paintings, stocks and bonds—anything to mount a defense against the charges. And it's a darn good thing Casey was able to do this. Without that money, we wouldn't have been able to do a lot of the things we needed to do to fight her case. Without that money, we would not have been able to hire the experts that were needed to mount a viable defense against the barrage coming at us from the police, the prosecution, and the media.

About a week after Casey got out of jail, I received a call from a member of the media, a local television reporter. (I can't say who it was because he called me in confidence.) He said to me, "Hey, I'm hearing that Casey's going to be arrested tonight."

"Why would the cops tell you that?" I asked.

"Because it's true," he said. "The cops are telling everyone to go to the Anthony home, that something big is going to happen at the house."

"You've got to be kidding me," I said.

"Nope."

I immediately called Sergeant John Allen and said to him, "Listen, I've been told that you have plans on arresting my client tonight."

"No, that's not true," he lied. "I don't know where you got that."

"Are you certain you aren't going to go and arrest my client tonight?" I asked.

"Yes, I'm certain."

"Because the reason is, I would like the professional courtesy to surrender her if you are," I said.

The police almost always cooperate and let the client surrender because not only is it the custom, but it's also a major safety issue. It prevents incidents from occurring, and nothing could be a more dangerous location than the Anthony home with all those cameras, spectators, and protesters roaming around it.

When I hung up the phone, I said to myself, *This guy is lying to me. They're going to do it anyway.*

This was a case where everyone involved wanted as much publicity as possible, and in this case I believed the media over the cops every day of the week, and twice on Sunday.

As soon as I got off the phone, I faxed a letter to the Orange County Sheriff's Office. I wrote, "If you have any intention of arresting Casey Anthony, call me. I will be more than happy to surrender her and take her right to the jail so there will be no problems."

I strongly suspected this arrest was going to happen, so that night I waited in my office rather than go home. Around 8:15 P.M., *Nancy Grace* began recording live, using the Anthony home at 4937 Hopespring Drive as its backdrop. And sure enough, with the cameras rolling, eight unmarked police cars, sirens blazing, came riding onto the grass to arrest Casey for a couple of bad checks she had written during the thirty days when she was away from home in June.

The police went inside the home, and just as they were doing that, I received a phone call from Cindy. I had a moment to talk to Casey, and I told her, "Listen, just invoke your right to counsel. I'll find out what's going on and I'll come see you right away."

They arrested her, and as millions looked on, she was taken from her home with protesters screaming "baby killer" at her.

For the cops it was all a big show.

Why? I think it was to intimidate her and to show their power before the cameras. It served no purpose. They charged her with forging two checks, for which the bond was $1,000, and we posted it the next morning.

The cops held a press conference right after they arrested her, as they always did. They explained she was being arrested for economic crimes. The police said that Casey borrowed her friend Amy Huizenga's car while Amy was vacationing in Puerto Rico, found her checkbook in the glove compartment, and wrote several fraudulent checks valued at $644.

We posted bond, got her out, and went through the circus again, with all the media there. This time, however, I hired some security. I had hired two huge guys who had helped me move my office from Orlando to Kissimmee, Marvin and Little John, who wasn't so little.

"You want to make a little extra money?" I asked them.

"Sure," they said, and I hired them to help me pick up Casey from jail after we had posted her bond.

This exit went a lot smoother because no one wanted to mess with these huge guys.

I asked Casey about the phony checks.

"I couldn't go home because Cindy was there," she said. "I had no money. I was living either at my boyfriend's house or at another friend's house."

"What do you mean, you couldn't go home because Cindy was there?" I asked. "Both your parents were there."

"Oh yeah," Casey said. "That's what I meant to say. My parents were there and I couldn't come home without Caylee."

I wish I had pressed her then and there about her not wanting to go home because Cindy was there. I might have found out sooner what was really going on, but as they say, hindsight is always 20/20.

AFTER WE DROPPED CASEY OFF at her parents' house, I was royally pissed. I was steaming because I couldn't believe the cops were playing these stupid, unprofessional games. I went outside with Cindy and this time, in front of the cameras, I blasted the cops. I had a copy of my fax and explained, "These cops were so unprofessional. Look, I sent them a notice, and they lied to me point-blank." I really ripped into them.

CASEY WAS OUT OF JAIL for about a week when I got a call from Allen, who said, "We're going to arrest your client again."

"For what?" I asked.

"For two more bad checks," he said.

"You knew she wrote four bad checks the last time you arrested her," I said. "Why are you doing this again?"

"That's beyond my control," he said. "They decided to charge her with the other two checks she had written."

All they wanted to do was ride her through the carousel again, but this time they allowed me to surrender her. Of course, the cameras were there again. And each time the police arrested her, they tried to talk to her without her lawyer—which was the true purpose of this futile exercise. They read her her rights and asked her, "Would you like to speak?" and again Casey did as instructed.

"No, I want my lawyer present," she said.

We posted bond for a third time and brought her home again. That was it for the bad checks and the harassment.

RIGHT AROUND THIS TIME, Cindy and Casey were in my office when Cindy received a phone call from one of the cops.

"We need to speak to you right away," he said.

"I'm in Jose Baez's office," she said. "If you want, you can come here."

"We'll go anywhere but there," he said.

"No," she said, "If you want to meet with me, you can meet me here."

Two of them came to the office, along with a member of the FBI, and asked if they could speak with Cindy. I agreed. I let them use one of the other rooms, and that's when they told Cindy that an expert who worked for the University of Tennessee Anthropological Research Facility (also known as the "Body Farm") in Knoxville, Tennessee, had tested the carpet taken from Casey's Pontiac and determined that the chemicals released from the carpet were consistent with a "human decompositional event."

Said one of the policemen, "They came back saying it was human decomposition, and we believe Caylee is dead."

Cindy fell to her knees and wept. She was devastated, absolutely and completely devastated. She was so distraught she couldn't get up. I helped bring her to the couch and sat her there. Everyone in the room—the police, the FBI agent, myself, all of my employees—just felt horrible.

Casey had been taken back to the house, so she hadn't heard the news. Cindy lay on the couch in a fetal position, crying her eyes out, when she looked up at the police and asked, "Are you 100 percent certain that Caylee is dead?"

Nick Savage, an FBI agent, said to her, "Nothing is 100 percent certain." And I could see the blood rush to Cindy's face. She popped up almost instantly and said, "You mean to tell me you have the nerve to come here and stab my heart and take away my hope and tell me Caylee's dead when you don't know for sure?"

The cops started to stutter. They hadn't expected that response from Cindy. She turned to them and began to yell, "How dare you? Who the hell do you think you are to come in here and say something like that when you don't know for sure?"

It was as if she had risen from the dead and overpowered all of them. And it was at that moment that I felt a tremendous amount of respect for Cindy Anthony.

It turned out the reason the police were in such a hurry to tell her was because they had already leaked the results of the tests to the media. They didn't want Cindy to find out from the media.

Again, I couldn't get over their lack of professionalism. Their desire to try this case in the media overcame—inundated—their ability to conduct a proper investigation. And this was a perfect example of it. Here they had results from a highly novel type of test, in which they heated the carpet samples and studied the gasses that were released. It turned out the results were *very* preliminary (in the end they would reveal *no such thing*), but they released them because of their need to feed the media.

The media were a bigger priority than the investigation. Before knowing with certainty, the police were telling a grandmother her missing granddaughter was dead. In the end, it turned out to be true, but it doesn't take away from the lack of professionalism and the ridiculous way the police conducted themselves.

Put the pieces together: the ruse in the jail, the revolving door of arresting her, the leaks to the media, and the manner they were leaking information. These guys might just as well have been the Keystone Kops, but at the same time, the media were painting them as Super Cops. This bears repeating: *As far as the police were concerned, the Casey Anthony case was a reality show that the media were scripting, and the reason the cops got a free pass to do whatever they wanted to do was that the cops were trying to make their reality show come true.*

It was disgusting.

And that was just the beginning.

After Casey was freed, the craziness of the "Casey Anthony Reality Show" escalated. The cops, through the media, had declared that Casey was guilty of killing her two-year-old child, so once the public learned that she was out of jail, its outrage against her grew to the point where self-appointed crusaders demanding justice for Caylee began to camp out on the sidewalk in front of the Anthony home.

It started one day shortly after we had gotten Casey out when Ed Phlegar, one of my paralegals, came into my office and said, "The bloggers are saying they're going to organize a protest in front of the Anthony home. They're carpooling to bring in more people and asking those with vans and busses to volunteer their vehicles."

"Don't these people have jobs?" I asked Ed.

"Apparently not," he said. "You should see what they're doing."

I hadn't paid attention to bloggers before.

"You should take a look at this," he said to me. "These people are out of control."

I went online and started to read what these bloggers were saying and couldn't believe the anger and hatred that was developing against Casey and me. I also couldn't believe the number of armchair detectives out there who were trying to solve the case. There was a website called Websleuths, and in it they had gone through the public records and researched my entire career. The "sleuths" talked about me as though they knew me. Much of it was insulting, even cruel, and scary. The prosecution, through the media, was inciting these people to act out, and there was nothing that the Anthonys, Casey, or I could do about it.

Yuri Melich was even blogging—under the name Dick Tracy Orlando. I don't know if a lead detective in a high-profile case was ever caught blogging before, but this was certainly the case. I had every intention of cross-examining him about this in front of the jury.

I wondered, not for the first or last time, *What happened to innocent until proven guilty?* Apparently, in the age of social media, Casey's constitutional rights were being thrown to the wolves.

Every night, around ten trucks with long antennae sat up and down Hopespring Drive. The Anthony home became Orlando's second-most popular tourist attraction.

Some protesters brought signs. One day a woman brought her baby with her and had her hold up a sign that said, "Would you kill a baby like me?" Another lady brought her dog with a sign that said, "I would report my dog missing after 30 seconds, not 30 days." It was despicable, but the cameras were there to film them, and they could watch themselves on the local news. The more that these people got on camera, the crazier it would get.

Cindy, who could never keep quiet, became a star of the reality show outside the Anthony home. Incapable of just ignoring them, she would go out and argue with the protesters while the cameras filmed the mayhem. People would yell all sorts of nasty things at her, and she would yell right back at them, trying to convince them that Caylee was still alive and that the nanny had her. One day she went out and hammered "No trespassing" signs on her lawn. The TV crews were filming her, and she began yelling at the media with the hammer in her hand, which the media loved, as millions looked on.

Another time a woman got into an argument with Cindy. The woman had brought her young son with her, and during their argument the woman called Casey a "bitch." Cindy said to her, "If you call Casey a bitch again..." and in her anger the woman accidentally slammed her car door on her nine-year-old son. The little boy fell on the ground sobbing. His mother ignored him, more concerned with yelling at Cindy. They took the kid to the hospital. It made for some dramatic TV. The boy was fine, but this was some of the crazy shit that went on in front of the Anthony home.

One night protesters threw rocks at the Anthonys' windows and began banging on their front door. That's when the Anthonys started to lose it. Cindy came out of the house with a bat, and George pulled out a water hose and began spraying the protesters on the sidewalk. Five young adults—I hesitate to call them that—picked a fight with George, and they were pushing and shoving each other. From the living-room window, Casey saw the melee and called 9-1-1, a call that became big news. Leading the news that night was Casey's voice on a 9-1-1 call.

Every night outside the Anthony home it was as festive as the Florida State Fair. From inside the house, you could hear the protesters screaming, "Baby killer! Baby killer!"

Finally, the neighbors started to get angry because the commotion and the noise were ruining their peace and quiet. The neighbors wanted the protesters to go away, and fights would break out.

The cops just stood there, doing nothing. Around the same time, the son-in-law of Sheriff Kevin Beary had been arrested for domestic violence. I remember his statement, "We ask that you respect our pri-vacy," and I thought, *Who's respecting the privacy of the Anthonys?*

If the protesters had been outside the sheriff's home, you can be sure those people would have been thrown in jail in a heartbeat. But because this reality show in front of the Anthony home played into the public-relations plan of the prosecution—to poison the public's attitude toward Casey—the cops just let it happen.

CHAPTER 6

THE GRAND JURY INDICTS

I WAS SURE THE PROSECUTION was going to indict Casey for murder at some point. The prosecution's case was forming, and since every shred of evidence against Casey was being heralded in the media, I knew exactly what they would be presenting before a grand jury.

I knew they would parade Detective Yuri Melich in front of a grand jury to testify that Casey was lying through her teeth about her and Caylee's whereabouts, but they had no idea *why* she was lying, and quite frankly, it seemed to me that they really didn't care. Her story on its face was very odd. For two years she had talked of Zanny [Fernandez-Gonzalez], the nanny, a woman no one ever saw and who obviously never existed. She told everyone she worked a job when she didn't. Like clockwork, for two years, five days a week, Casey would get up, get herself and Caylee dressed, go to a job that didn't exist and drop her child off at a nanny's house that did not exist. And not a soul noticed. Clearly she was masking her web of deep, dark secrets that she was too afraid to reveal.

Here was a young person who seemed able to keep her secrets for a long time. Didn't the police and prosecutors want to know why she was keeping secrets? They didn't; the prosecution had made the determination early on that, because she was caught lying to them, Casey had killed Caylee, and they weren't interested in any facts or theories that might clash or weaken their main hypothesis.

I knew they'd march forensics experts to the stand to testify as to the smell in the car, a stain they said they found in the trunk, the positive reaction from a cadaver dog who sniffed in the trunk of the car, their scientific "proof" of decomposition, and one single long strand of Caylee's hair that their expert said showed "post-mortem root banding." Another expert would testify about the air samples in the car that had revealed the presence of chloroform. As a result, the prosecution's computer people checked to see whether Casey had looked up the term chloroform on the computer, and what do you know, they found two hits, proof to the prosecution she had intended to kill her daughter.

The cops' most damning "proof" that Casey had murdered her daughter were pictures they had of Casey partying at a nightclub, having a grand time, during the time Caylee was missing. They said this was evidence that, at best, Casey was insensitive and cold-blooded or, at worst, she was a remorseless killer. To the prosecutors and the public following the case, this "evidence" all added up to murder in the first degree.

They had paraded a lot of this before Judge Stan Strickland at the bond hearing, and the judge had hit Casey with a bond for $500,000. I had no illusions. Based on the same evidence, I knew Casey would be indicted.

October 14, 2008, was the day the grand jury convened. How did I know that? The prosecution announced it to the world, shockingly enough. Ninety-nine point nine times out of a hundred, the existence of a grand jury is kept secret because you never want your target to know it's being convened. But in this case, it was announced to the media, and on the twenty-third floor of the Orange County Courthouse in front of nineteen grand jurors, the prosecution marched six witnesses to testify against Casey Anthony: Melich, FBI Special Agent Nick Savage, canine handler Jason Forgey, FBI hair analyst Karen Lowe, computer forensics investigator Sandra Osborne Cawn, and Casey's father, George Anthony. You might wonder why a father wouldn't resist going before a grand jury to testify against his daughter. I certainly did. To this day we do not know what George testified to at the hearing, though we do know what he *didn't* say.

I have a theory why they convened this grand jury before finding Caylee's body. It was an election year, and it was the first time State Attorney Lamar Lawson was being challenged. It was three weeks before the election, and voters might have seen him as weak if his office hadn't indicted Casey by Election Day. So when I heard that the grand jury was convening, my first reaction was: *This has got to be a political move.*

That day I asked Cindy to bring Casey to my office. I was 100 percent sure the grand jury was going to indict her and that she was going back to jail, and I wanted to prepare Casey for that. What struck me as odd was that after she arrived, for some reason she kept holding out hope.

I told her point-blank, "You're going to be indicted and we need a plan to surrender you."

"Let's wait and see," she said.

I couldn't understand her optimism.

The media were beginning to mass in front of my office. Media trucks had followed her from the Anthony home. As it got later in the day, I could hear the *whap-whap-whap* of the rotors of the helicopters flying overhead. They all knew she was going to be arrested and wanted the footage for their TV news shows.

"Casey," I said to her, "Let's go early, and I'll turn you into the jail before this thing gets out of hand."

"No, I want to wait it out," she said. "I want to make sure this happens."

After George testified, he held a press conference with his lawyer present. It was on TV, so Casey and I were able to watch it. His lawyer did all the talking, but it was obvious he had testified against her.

When the press conference was over, I could see a change in her. She seemed deflated and defeated.

Looking back, knowing what I now know, she was thinking that her loving father would tell the police what he knew, and they would let her go. But I didn't know any of this at the time so I didn't ask her about it. What I do know for certain is this: After that day, Casey never wanted to speak to her father ever again. And from that day on, she never has.

I DECIDED WE SHOULD also have a press conference because I didn't want the last public images of Casey to be in jail clothes or behind bars. If there was going to be video footage of Casey, I wanted the public to see a free Casey. And that's what we did.

She stood by me while I conducted a press conference. I basically said, "She is innocent. We're going to fight these charges. She's the mother of a missing child, and she's someone's daughter, and she's human." Casey broke down and cried, and after the media left, we found out that the grand jury had indeed come back with an indictment.

I wasn't exactly sure how to handle this. I figured it would be best to turn Casey over to her bondsman, who would drive her to the jail, turn her in, and revoke the bond. That way she could just go straight to jail.

I began to drive to the bondsman's place to pick him up when I got a call to come back to the office. He called to say it was just as easy for him to meet us at the Orlando airport, where Casey would get out of Cindy's car and go with the bondsman. By switching cars at the airport, Casey would avoid the helicopters, which couldn't fly there because it would have been in violation of the airport's airspace. The bondsman would then take her to the jail.

I made a U-turn to go back to the office and could see a car following me, obviously a cop car. He wasn't a very good tail because I picked him up right away.

Back at the office, Casey left for the airport with Cindy, and I headed over there in my car. We kept in touch via cell phone. I saw Cindy pull up and could see the news vans drive up right behind her. I watched as Casey got out of the car and jumped into the bondsman's car, and they took off. I made a U-turn and followed right behind them.

It was a one-lane road, and I had news vans right behind me so I went really slowly to give the bondsman enough distance to lose the news vans, which made the people in the news vans go nuts. They were trying to get around me. They'd go to the left, and I'd swerve to block them, and then they'd try the right side, and I'd swerve back to block. I felt I was driving in a NASCAR race until something—common sense—overcame me.

I said to myself, *You're a lawyer. This is not what a lawyer does. If the media wants to follow her, that's their business. Your job is in the courtroom. You have to stop.*

I pulled off to the side of the road and let them all pass. I remember feeling ashamed that I had lost my dignity.

It was a very low point for me. I asked myself, *What are you doing?*

Just as I pulled off to the side of the road, Corporal Edwards of the Orange County Sheriff's Office pulled up and said, "That's some pretty fancy driving, counselor." A second police officer was in the backseat, and she looked over at me and snapped my picture, and they took off. To this day I have no idea what that was all about. Maybe she wanted a souvenir.

Soon thereafter the police pulled over the bail bondsman and arrested Casey on the way to the jail. They didn't even have the decency to let her surrender at the jail. They read Casey her rights in the police car.

"I don't want to speak unless I have my lawyer," she said. But on the way to the jail, she had a change of heart. She told them, "You know what, I do want to talk, but I want my lawyer to be there."

And I think what Casey was going to do at that moment was tell the police what she knew about George's involvement in Caylee's disappearance.

At the jail they told her, "We're not going to play any tricks. We're going to get your lawyer here and we're going to sit down and talk."

I was back at the office when the police called. I was told, "Your client is here. She has decided she wants to talk, but she wants you present."

"What?" I said. "What the... Put her on."

They put Casey on the phone, and she said, "Yeah, can you come here? I want to talk."

"Okay, I'm on my way."

I went to the sheriff's office. Edwards took me upstairs.

"Right now we have her in the interrogation room," he said.

"So this is going to be recorded?" I asked.

"Yes," he said. "If you want to speak to her privately before we all go in there, we'll put you in another room where there won't be a recording."

"I do want to speak to her before we all sit down," I said.

Even though they took us to another room, I still didn't trust that they weren't listening in and recording us, so I took out my cell phone, opened my iPod, and played Bob Marley's "Everything's Going to Be All Right" loud enough to drown out our whispered voices.

Casey walked in, and I put my finger over my mouth for her to keep quiet. I whispered in her ear, "What the fuck are you doing?"

"They want us to cooperate," she whispered, "and maybe we should talk to them."

I said, "Until you tell me what you want to tell them, you can't do this. You need to tell me first, and then we can talk about it and think about the best way to go about it, so we can protect you and your interests."

"I understand," she said.

"This is *not* the way to do it," I said. "I'll do whatever you tell me to do, but it's definitely *not* the way to do it. We need to make sure we sit down and discuss things thoroughly before we ever sit down and talk to them."

"You're right," she said. "I understand."

"So we're in agreement?" I asked. "You're going to go in there and tell them you're going to go into the jail?"

"Yes," she said.

I told the detectives, "She and I need to talk first. We're not going to say anything today. Please take her to the jail."

They were very professional and they did as I asked.

Later on, again looking back with much greater knowledge, I am quite certain that Casey was sure on that day that George would come clean and take responsibility for his role in Caylee's disappearance. When it didn't happen, she got agitated and angry and wanted to tell what she knew about her father's role in it. And for some reason, when she got back to the jail, she changed her mind and decided to stay mum.

The moment had passed. In the end, on that day at least, Casey couldn't bring herself to tell me about it.

Not yet.

CHAPTER 7

THE CAR

FTER CASEY WAS INDICTED and taken into custody, I knew, based on the bond hearing and some of the discovery that I was getting, that the whole case was going to revolve around evidence found in her car.

At this point, all the evidence was coming from the prosecution, and I knew I would need a good criminalist, and there's none better than Dr. Henry Lee, one of the stars of the O. J. Simpson trial. Lee, who has been involved in thousands of criminal cases over a forty-year career, has testified in most of the important criminal trials in recent American history. In addition to the Simpson case, he testified about the assassination of John F. Kennedy, the suicide of Vince Foster (Bill Clinton's close friend), the murder of JonBenét Ramsey, the murder of Martha Moxley, the murder of Laci Peterson, and the kidnapping of Elizabeth Smart.

I had gotten Lee's cell phone number from another forensic scientist. I called him and introduced myself.

"Dr. Lee, my name is Jose Baez."

He answered with a joke.

"So you're telling me you're biased," he said.

"Well, yeah," I said. "In a manner of speaking, I guess I am."

Lee knew about Casey's case. He had heard about it on the news and he was interested in meeting with me. Though his main office was in New Haven, Connecticut, he owned a home in Orlando and traveled to Florida often. He happened to be traveling to South Florida several days later, and we agreed to meet at a Chinese restaurant, of all places.

It turns out he's a big fan of Chinese food, and the people who work in Chinese restaurants recognize him and cook extra special dishes for him. Dinner was really a treat.

We started talking about the case. I had prepared a packet to give him, which included the discovery I had received from the prosecution as well as a videotape of law enforcement processing the trunk of Casey's car. Since the crime scene investigators had requested that the media film them, I was hoping that perhaps Lee might find something inappropriate that might backfire against them.

He said, "The best way of doing this is to inspect the car."

We set up a date for the car inspection. I started taking depositions to get more information, interviewing the employees of Amscot, where the car was abandoned, and the employees of the tow yard.

I didn't tell a soul that I had hired Lee. He was kind enough to sign onto the case for a $5,000 donation to his institute. The day came, and the media, which found out about our arrival through checking the public records, showed up. When I walked in with my paralegal and Lee, I could see the look of recognition on the faces of some of the reporters.

There's a long hallway that goes back to the forensics section of the sheriff's department, and we had to walk by a conference room where all the cops were sitting. Around the table joking and laughing were CSI Gerardo Bloise, CSI Michael Vincent, FBI Special Agent Nick Savage, Detective Yuri Melich, Sergeant John Allen, and Detective Eric Edwards. I'll never forget the look on their faces when I walked in with Dr. Henry Lee. Prior to that, I had just told them I was bringing an expert; I never mentioned a name. Their jaws all dropped. They sat up straight in their chairs. Early on, it was one of my finer moments.

"We're here to inspect the car," I said.

As Lee was getting on his protective gear, we went into the forensics area. Savage walked with me and said, "I have to tell you, Jose, I'm impressed. You got Henry Lee. What did you have to do, get a second mortgage on your house to get him?"

"Something like that," I said with a smirk.

The very first thing Lee and I did was walk over to Casey's car. It was sealed with yellow evidence tape. The doors and trunk were sealed. There was some black powder dust on the trunk, and I could see it had been dusted for prints. Why, I wasn't sure. Of course Casey's fingerprints were going to be on the trunk of her car.

When Bloise opened the trunk, I could smell something rotten. I had been to a morgue before and I had smelled dead bodies, and my first impression was that this smelled like a dead body, especially after hearing about it for so long.

I smelled something else in the air, a chemical-like substance, but I couldn't place it. It didn't smell like gasoline, but I could tell it had a gasoline base. If you took a good strong whiff, it almost hurt your nostrils.

Oh my God, I immediately thought. *This is not good.* I thought to myself, *This is not good at all. I'm going to have to talk to Casey about taking a plea.*

I was feeling low and watching Lee at work, looking for a reaction from him, because he had told me, "If there's something I need to tell you, I'll pull you aside and we'll talk about it."

He was looking at the contents of the trunk, doing his inspection, slowly and meticulously. After a while he stopped, and we left the area and went inside to ask for the trunk liner.

They brought it out piece by piece, and Lee took out his magnifying glass and began a methodical inspection. I watched him and couldn't believe just how meticulous he was. He went over that trunk liner inch by inch and then called me over.

"Do you see this?" he asked.

I could see a light hair.

"Do you see the shape of the hair?" he asked. "It's curved a certain way. That shows it's an animal hair. Not human hair."

I nodded as if this was exactly what we expected to find. Meanwhile, I noticed that Melich was taking photographs of everything Lee was doing. I guess he was documenting the examination. Lee resumed his exploration and then stopped. He called Bloise over and told him, "This is a hair. Collect it."

Bloise got out a pair of tweezers and did as he was told. Then Lee resumed his search and, after three hours of painstaking work, looking inch by inch, he finally completed his examination of the trunk liner. In the process he collected a total of fourteen hairs that had been missed by the searches of the Orange County Sheriff's Office and the FBI. Bloise, hard at work, collected each hair, one by one.

They then asked, "Do you want to see the contents of the trunk?"

We did, of course. I really had no idea what was in there. Prior to this I had heard Cindy talk about the pizza box so I figured there would be a small bag containing remnants of leftover pizza. Ten minutes later Bloise arrived with *two large boxes* filled with garbage. I couldn't believe how much garbage had been in the back of that car.

I said to myself, *This is where the smell came from.*

Prior to that, I was really feeling low. Once I saw this, my eyes opened up.

They started emptying the boxes piece by piece, and I could see that the contents had been dried; I was enraged.

The garbage they brought out had *no* smell. It was completely devoid of any smell whatsoever.

She had two large bags of garbage in the car and it doesn't smell? I said to myself. *What the fuck?*

"Where's the bag?" I asked, meaning the bag that must have held all the garbage. I wanted to know.

"It's not here," they said.

Well, where the hell is it? I thought to myself. *Perhaps they threw it away.* I left it at that. Little did I know that they had sent it to a lab to have it checked for bug evidence. Of course, they neglected to tell me that.

Lee started going through the garbage, pulling out three more hairs. He could see the trash no longer was soiled. In fact, there was an empty bottle with three or four ounces of dried spit from chewing tobacco in it.

I still worried that the smell I smelled was that of a human body. I too had heard what the cops always said: *Once you've smelled human decomposition, you never forget it.* Well, it was a pretty bad smell.

Afterward we broke for lunch, and I talked to Lee about what he had found. The first question I asked him was, "Does the car smell like a human body to you?"

He said, "It smells like decomposition. You never know whether it's decomposing garbage or a decomposing body. There's no way to tell, and for anyone to make that leap, it's impossible."

At that point I was *extremely* relieved.

We came back from lunch to find Angelo Nieves, the public information officer, outside the sheriff's office telling the press, "We're processing the car and it still smells like a dead body." Instead of reporting, which was his job, Nieves was making himself into a witness.

I'm going to call him as a witness, I told myself.

I chalked that up to just one more time when the cops overstepped their boundaries. I thought to myself, *They don't even know the* word *boundaries*.

We returned to the car and the garbage, and I continued to be amazed at the endurance of Lee. I was tired just watching him as he meticulously studied the evidence, hour after hour.

Later that afternoon, the police asked to talk to me.

Savage and Allen called me aside and asked, "What are we going to do to end this case?"

"The state hasn't made any offers," I said. "They aren't making any real effort."

"I'll make some calls," said Savage. "I'll make this happen. I think if you play your cards right you can get a great deal, and we can end this thing. The last thing I want to hear is ten years from now Cindy calling me, telling me she spotted Caylee at a high school football game, and that she's still three."

I told him, "I'd be delighted to explore any deals and listen to whatever the state has to say, but they haven't even approached me."

We were interrupted by Melich, who said, "They're about to open the cans."

Allen said, "You have to check this out. We want you to see this."

Of course they did.

We walked back over to where Lee was. Sitting on a table were metal cans that looked like small paint cans. They were sealed.

What they had done was cut out small pieces of cardboard from the trunk liner, put them in these cans, and sealed them. When you seal air, whatever smell there is gets magnified. I didn't know any of this. They opened one of the cans and said, "Smell this."

It reeked. I leaned over to smell it and just as I did, Melich snapped a picture of me.

"Why did you do that?" I asked him. He didn't reply.

What they were trying to do was catch me reacting to the smell. They wanted to either catch me making a prune face so they could use it against me in a motion or they wanted to leak the photo to the media to make me and my case look bad. There was no other reason for them to take a photo of me smelling the can than to try and use it against me in the media. It was pathetic. I didn't show any reaction.

I smelled it. Lee smelled it. My paralegal, Ed Phlegar, smelled it.

"Yeah, right, that's pizza," said Edwards sarcastically.

"What, you don't like pepperoni?" said Ed. "It smells like pizza."

We left around five after being there all day. On the ride back I asked Lee, "What about the cans? I'm concerned about the smell. That's pretty pungent."

"Look," he said, "the first thing they do is seal it. The gasses get caught in the can. They heat up the can, and it magnifies the smell. You can take your carpet from your office, throw it in one of those cans and heat it up, and you would have a stinky, smelly can just like they did. Don't read any more into that than what it really is."

He said, "They inspected the trunk, not once, not twice, but three times, and look at how many hairs I found after they were done. No one inspected that car more thoroughly than I did. There is nothing there." I was relieved. I had the very best man in the business telling me not to worry. That gave me strength moving forward.

When our experts came down to inspect all the evidence at the sheriff's department, Dr. Lee saw something about Caylee's shorts that no one had noticed. Her shorts were ripped. There were a couple holes due to the elements, but there were actual rips that we believe came from someone trying to fit too-small clothes onto her body.

In mid-October I drove to the FBI office in Maitland, Florida, and I met with Linda Drane Burdick, the lead prosecutor, Savage, Steve McElyea of the FBI, and Allen. Melich wasn't there. For some reason, whenever the cops needed to talk to me, Melich, the lead investigator, was never present. Either he hated me so much that he couldn't control himself or the cops thought Allen was my buddy and had a better rapport with me. Either way, his absence was weird. Savage had promised he'd make some calls to start the ball rolling on a plea deal and he was good to his word.

We sat around a table, and Burdick handed me a score sheet saying that if Casey, who had no prior criminal history, were to plead guilty to manslaughter of a child, the statutory recommended sentence would be thirteen years. If Casey ever was convicted of either first- or second-degree murder, she stood to spend the rest of her life in prison.

Burdick said to me, "In exchange for Casey telling us where Caylee's body is buried and telling us what happened, we might let her plead to count three, and she will only have to serve thirteen years."

Burdick was very specific with her words "we might let her plead," meaning this was not a formal offer but more like a "let's talk some more"–type offer. I think the reason she chose those words was because she didn't want the media reporting that they had offered Casey a plea deal.

Under these circumstances, I thought thirteen years was a phenomenal offer, and with some negotiating, I was sure I could have reduced that to ten years.

As her lawyer, I had the obligation to bring the offer to Casey, informal or not. Plus I always told Casey everything; it was her life, and I never played with it. I explained to her, "My obligation as a lawyer is to entertain all deals, and I have to bring this one to you."

"But I don't know where Caylee is," Casey said emphatically. And she would say it with such great frustration and anger that I believed her.

Over the course of the case, I brought up the offer more than once, and each time her answer was the same. I was convinced that Casey didn't know where Caylee was, alive or dead.

Since she couldn't lead them to Caylee's body, I couldn't make the deal, and it frustrated me, because I then didn't have anything to bargain with on her behalf.

Those negotiations never went anywhere.

It was my ethical responsibility to always discuss plea deals with my clients. My thoughts of innocence or guilt aside, as a lawyer I always had to explore the possibility. At the end of the day, I'm not the one facing jail time. I have had many innocent clients plead guilty because the calculated risk of going to trial, losing, and being sentenced to a long, long prison term was too much to bear. It's a screwed-up system, but it's the only one we've got.

Not that I think Casey ever would have accepted a deal, even if she knew where Caylee was. She was always very adamant about her innocence of the murder charge. Pleading guilty to murder was something she never would have considered.

CHAPTER 8

THE WACK PACK

THE FASCINATION OF THE CASE—as drummed up by the intense coverage of the media—drew all sorts of people to Orlando. Crazies came out of the woodwork. Psychics appeared. Colorful characters appeared left and right in search of fame and in a few cases, fortune. Ed Phlegar, my paralegal, would listen to Howard Stern in the office, and we would always listen to the cast of characters that Howard called the "wack pack." Soon we would have a wack pack of our own.

By early September Tim Miller had met with Orlando law enforcement several times. They went over Casey's cell tower records and looked at locations and wooded areas where the police hadn't searched.

Miller had honorable intentions, but, like a lot of people involved in this case, he was looking for publicity and he got it when he went on *Nancy Grace* and asked for volunteers—and donations.

To work for Texas EquuSearch, each volunteer had to pay twenty-five dollars. A lot of people joined. Most of the searchers were good people who were just concerned about Caylee and wanted to find her. Unfortunately there were also more than a few bad seeds, who were enticed by the attention given to the case by the media. They became obsessed by it. To me, they were like the groupies who followed The Rolling Stones or the Grateful Dead around the country. They volunteered because they wanted to be a part of the action. During the search to find Caylee, a number of these colorful characters came out of the woodwork.

One of the earliest "tips" came from a woman by the name of Kiomarie Cruz, who one evening took police to a section of woods near the Anthony home. She told the police that she was Casey's best friend during middle school and that she and Casey and a third friend, "Jessica Kelly," used to hang out in the woods a quarter mile down the street from Casey's house by the nearby Hidden Oaks Elementary School. She told police she and Casey used to bury their pets there. She also said that when Casey got pregnant, Casey wanted to give Caylee up for adoption, and that Cruz wanted to adopt Caylee, but apparently Cindy wouldn't hear of it. She would later testify that she sold her story to the *National Enquirer* for $20,000.

I asked Casey about Cruz, and she said she had known who she was, but they weren't good friends. Casey said Cruz's story that she had offered to have Cruz adopt Caylee was "complete nonsense."

When I asked Cindy about it, Cindy corroborated what Casey had said.

"That's a bunch of BS," said Cindy.

I didn't find Cruz credible because when I took her deposition, she didn't seem to know much about Casey and her life. She claimed that Casey, she, and "Jessica Kelly" were an inseparable threesome growing up, but when the police searched for Kelly, they were unable to locate her. Casey, it seemed, wasn't the only one with made-up friends.

Cruz stated in her deposition that she thought Caylee was alive, and she related how she had called Officer Appie Wells, and she and Wells went to the site where she and Casey used to go in the woods, in her attempt to see if Caylee was there.

"At ten at night?" I asked her.

"Yes."

"And you were hoping that Caylee would be there playing?"

"Yeah," she said, which took me aback. Why would a two-year-old be out playing in the woods late at night? Then Cruz said she never took the same route home because she believed that people were following her. She also claimed that Casey had called her during the thirty days in June to borrow money from her.

"Casey said she needed money for her child," she said. When police asked her for her telephone records, she said her fiancé didn't think it was a great idea.

She later told police that it wasn't Casey Anthony who had asked her to borrow money; it was another friend of hers named Casey Williams, an African-American girlfriend of hers.

She had gotten the two confused. And that's when I said to myself, *Here is yet another wack packer.*

Another of these colorful characters was a man by the name of Dominic Casey, who had emailed me, saying he wanted to work for me for free as an investigator. I was alone in this battle and was getting bombarded with an avalanche of leaks appearing in the media. I didn't have any money and needed help, so when I got a series of emails from an investigator who said he'd work for me pro bono, I jumped at the opportunity.

After I checked out Dominic's license, I called him and invited him to join me. When he came to meet me, he seemed capable enough, so I welcomed him to my team.

My first assignment for him was to look into whether a former fiancé of Casey's, a man by the name of Jesse Grund, might have abducted Caylee.

"Jesse met Casey while he was working in loss prevention at Universal Studios," I told him. "They began a relationship, and then he went to Florida State University in Tallahassee. Shortly after he left, Casey found out she was pregnant and she told him he was the father. They started seeing each other again, and he offered to marry her.

"Cindy didn't like him," I told him. "While they were dating, Jesse was at the police academy, and then he got a job working for the Orlando Police Department, and he was working there when Casey broke it off. Jesse underwent a DNA test to see if Caylee was his, and even though she wasn't his child, he still wanted to marry Casey and raise Caylee as his own. They were engaged, but after Caylee was born, they broke up because of Cindy."

I told Dominic that, according to Cindy, Jesse had been very possessive of Caylee, that he was jealous when Casey found a new boyfriend, and that Cindy suspected that it might be Jesse who took Caylee. (None of this turned out to be true, of course.)

"See what you can find out about Jesse," I said to Dominic.

About a week later, Dominic and I met in my conference room. I was curious as to what he had found.

"I think I've solved the case," said Dominic. "I've been doing some research, and the word on the street is that 'Zanny' is actually a code name for Xanax. I believe what happened was that Casey was giving Caylee Xanax to sleep. That's what she meant when she said 'Zanny the nanny.'"

I thought to myself, *Number one, that's not what I asked you to do, and number two, that could very well be the second-most ridiculous thing I've ever heard.* Number one, of course, was that there ever was a Zenaida Fernandez-Gonzalez in the first place. I also realized that this guy was not the type of investigator I wanted working for me on a case like this. But I had a problem. He was out there doing work for me, and if I let him go and the media found out about it, I couldn't trust him to keep his mouth shut.

At that point, I had lost complete confidence in him. I didn't think he was useful so I gave him menial tasks like running a license plate or standing outside the Anthony home and keeping his eye on the protesters.

"If something happens, give me a call," I said.

I just kind of blew him off, and he became increasingly frustrated with me because I wasn't including him in anything important. I really wanted to divorce myself from the guy.

It was tough, because I had never been in a situation with this amount of media scrutiny. Trying to keep things private was a major undertaking.

Dominic's full name was Dominic Anthony Casey. You cannot make this stuff up. Down the road, Dominic Anthony Casey would almost destroy me and my case.

Another of the colorful characters to come along was Gale St. John, who billed herself as a psychic dog handler, meaning she owns dogs which she claims are trained to find dead bodies. Her search team was known as "The Body Hunters."

On August 11, 2008, a man by the name of Roy Kronk called 9-1-1 to report seeing something suspicious in the woods near the Anthony home. On this same day, St. John was driving herself and a couple of her psychic associates when she videotaped herself pulling up to the Anthony home. You can see the media trucks on her tape, and she says, "I'm getting a feeling." Then she says, "Let's turn left over here," and she starts heading toward Suburban Drive. When she stopped there, she said, "My feelings are getting stronger." She pulled to the right, and on the tape you can hear the dogs breathing heavily.

St. John said the feeling she got that day was overwhelming.

"You get very sick to your stomach," she said. "You feel as though you've been punched in the stomach and something knocks the air out of you."

"I'm getting a feeling right here," she said, and everyone got out of the car. The dogs searched around and stopped at the exact spot where Caylee would eventually be found months later in December. Her dogs found no body.

I don't believe in psychics, but I had to give it to her. This was not the first beyond-bizarre experience in this case and would not be the last. She was right there, but the question we would later ask was, *Where was Caylee?*

AFTER SEVERAL DAYS of turning up nothing, people stopped volunteering to work for Texas EquuSearch, and it was then that Miller went on TV talking about how much money the company had spent. Orange County Sheriff Kevin Beary stepped up, donated $5,000 to the company, and asked Miller not to leave. Miller stayed a few more days, announced he would come back in November, and then returned to Texas.

Also going on the TV and making a name for himself was Leonard Padilla, the bounty hunter with the reality show who had dropped his bond on Casey when she was arrested on the bad check charges. I was able to get another bondsman to post the money, and Padilla, in search of a new path to publicity, joined Miller in the search for Caylee. Padilla and Miller announced that when they returned in November, they were going to launch the biggest search in U.S. history. In fact, they did come back and had a huge turnout—more than thirteen hundred volunteers—though no one ever found anything, including those who searched on Suburban Drive where Caylee would later be found.

One morning in November, I was eating my breakfast and turned on the news to find Padilla standing on the banks of a lake inside Jay Blanchard Park in Orlando. He had hired divers to search that lake because he believed Caylee's body was hidden there. Why, I was never sure, though perhaps it was because that was the park Casey had mentioned as the place where Zenaida Fernandez-Gonzalez kidnapped Caylee.

The reporters came in droves, and one of them asked him, "Mr. Padilla, are you going to search again today?"

He said yes.

"How many days do you plan on searching?" he was asked.

"We're going to stay until Tuesday," he said.

"Why Tuesday?"

"Because the flights are cheaper on Tuesday," he said.

I cracked up watching this. And then the reporter asked him, "Are you back out here trying to redeem yourself because you didn't find anything last time?"

"Fuck you," he shouted over the airwaves live across Orlando. "I don't have to redeem myself for anyone."

I almost spit out my cereal. I couldn't believe Padilla had said "Fuck you" on live TV. The commentator had to apologize for his language.

At any rate, Padilla and his divers went into the lake searching, and in the afternoon on TV there was breaking news. At the bottom of the lake he had discovered a waterlogged sack. Padilla was certain he had found Caylee's body.

After the discovery, he took a large roll of crime scene tape and cordoned off an area so no one could get close to him. There were hundreds of people crowded behind the tape, but not one of them crossed it, not realizing that Padilla and his divers weren't cops but civilian searchers.

The large bag was pulled out of the water, and the call was made to the police, who came out. I watched all of this unfold on television. As I said, everything about this case was televised. It was by far the most popular reality show on local, if not national, TV. This was huge, breaking news in the middle of the day, and everyone was looking in. The station broke into its regular programming, and talking heads were opining away about what was happening at this lake in Jay Blanchard Park.

As I watched the television, I could see Sergeant John Allen and Special Agent Nick Savage from the FBI pull up in their squad car. They walked over to speak with Padilla. Hovering above, helicopters were following their every move. I watched as the cops looked in the bag, walked back to their squad car, and left.

Later on Allen told me, "Oh my God, it was ridiculous. What a joke."

Inside the bag was a pile of rocks and a green Gumby doll.

At one point the police asked Padilla to stop his antics, but there was nothing legally they could do about it. And even though the effort was a wild goose chase, Padilla and the divers went on TV and gave interviews. It was all so absurd.

Later on, however, the event took on much more importance, because of what the commentators said about it.

When Caylee's remains were eventually found, the police took Casey into a room and recorded her reaction to the news coverage. She was close to hysterical and had to take a sedative.

After that happened, and the police leaked her reactions, one of the local commentators observed, "Casey didn't react that way when nothing was found at Jay Blanchard Park because she knew Caylee's body wasn't there. And the reason she reacted so strongly when they found Caylee's remains," the commentator said, "was because she knew they were Caylee's."

That wasn't bad enough. After he said that, the copycats on the other stations immediately repeated it like it was a fact.

The truth is that on the day they found the bag of rocks at Jay Blanchard Park, Casey didn't react because she never saw it reported on TV that day. She was locked in her cell for twenty-three hours a day, and when I went to see her that evening, she said, "The night before, they brought in an inmate who was screaming all night, and finally they took her out, so I slept all day."

It was late in the afternoon.

"So you just got up?" I asked.

"Yeah, I just got up a half an hour ago."

She never saw that news report.

The commentary "proving" Casey knew where Caylee's body was buried was an out-and-out fabrication by that news reporter, and it was the kind of nonsense that went on constantly throughout this case. It's an important story to tell, however, because the running commentary about how Casey didn't react to Padilla's discovery because she knew the body wasn't there is one of the huge misconceptions about the case.

It's weird to me how so many people can allow news reports and press reports to color their thinking. What people forget is that the media have a bias, and that bias is on the side of drama and effect. If it bleeds, it leads, as the saying goes, and controversy creates ratings. If there's no high drama, ratings fall. Nobody watches, so the way people get their information is not from an unbiased source, but rather from a business that needs to generate revenue by way of ratings to make money.

The common person doesn't give it that much consideration. Most don't think the media are that way; I didn't either until I got involved in this case. Before that, I never really gave it any thought. I would watch the news and thought I could rely on it. I never looked any deeper, the way I do today.

I NEVER BECAME INVOLVED with the searchers. I knew Texas EquuSearch was attracting a large group of people, including the groupies—like Dominic—who volunteered and followed the case. Dominic, as much as anything, was a groupie addicted to the Casey Anthony case. He followed the case on the TV and on the Internet, and after he left me, he offered his services for free to the Anthonys. He got in on the inside and stayed there. To my knowledge, he wasn't paid by anyone, but he stuck around. And in an odd way, he would end up being an important part of the story.

These groupies, I have to say, also included lawyers. The Anthonys were sucked into hiring a criminal lawyer by the name of Mark NeJame. An organization called the Never Lose Hope Foundation contacted the Anthonys and offered their help in finding Caylee. A member of the organization took the Anthonys to NeJame's office, where the charity organization allegedly paid $5,000 to NeJame to represent the Anthonys. Nejame hated me. He stood about five foot two in heels, and Casey would refer to him as "fun-sized." A witness, Krystal Holloway, called him "the lawyer who looks like a woman," and I've heard he thought I put her up to it. But I had never met her when she said that. I fear a lot of his animosity towards me came from that.

Cindy had called me on the phone one day and said that NeJame had offered to represent the Anthonys.

"What do you know about him?" she asked.

"I don't know a great deal," I said. "I only know his reputation and I'd rather not get into it." I don't like talking badly about other lawyers. It's unprofessional, and I don't do it. But I did tell her, "Cindy, it will look bad if you hire a criminal defense attorney. It will look as though you have something to hide. You have every right to do it and you should do what's in your best interests, but realistically, I don't think it's a good idea."

"You're right," she said. "It's a bad idea, and I'm not going to do it."

About three weeks had gone by when I heard on the news that the Anthonys went to visit a criminal defense attorney, and it was the same

Mark NeJame. Along with the report was another story that I was getting kicked off the case and NeJame was going to take over for me.

After that story broke, I went to see Casey.

"You know your parents have hired a defense attorney," I said. "If you're interested in someone else representing you, you let me know. I'll be more than happy to step down."

"Nothing could be further from the truth, Jose," Casey said. "As a matter of fact, I don't want that guy anywhere near me."

Again, looking back today, I can see why. She didn't trust her parents—especially her father—to look out for her best interests. I didn't know it then, but she was beginning to feel that her father was providing information to the police designed to take the spotlight off him and convince them of her guilt. That was why Casey was so adamant about her staying as far from her parents' lawyer as she could.

Now connected to the case, NeJame immediately went on a media blitz. He contacted national shows, which put him up in New York hotels so he could go on TV and defend the Anthonys and, in the process, bash Casey. What he was doing, I could see, was attempting to put distance between the Anthonys and Casey, portraying them as grieving grandparents, while delicately portraying Casey as a cold-blooded killer. And the only reason I say "delicately" is because Cindy would surely have fired him had he been more heavy-handed about it. NeJame's relationship with me was contentious from the beginning because of his relentless bashing of Casey.

There were a couple of important aspects of his being their lawyer. One day Cindy came to my office. This was during the period when Casey was out on bail. She told me, "We just left Mark's office and we took polygraph tests."

"Why's he polygraphing his own clients?" I asked.

She didn't give me an answer but then said, "I had to take another one, because the first one was inconclusive. And George did too."

"Really?" I said. And then I thought, *There's only one reason why a person takes a second one, and that's because the first one didn't turn out the way that person wanted. It's because someone failed the first one.*

The FBI had asked the Anthonys to take a polygraph test, and they had refused. The only reason to do so would be to release the results. But they never did.

The red flags kept going up. The first red flag flew when I was talking with George and Cindy in their living room, mentioned George and sexual abuse of Casey, and heard the deafening silence. This was a second one. I was quite sure Cindy didn't know anything about Caylee's disappearance. But George?

What's he hiding? I wondered.

And then, just before Caylee's body was found, the Anthonys fired NeJame. Cindy told me the whole story. She said, "Mark wants me to try and get Casey to hire him and fire you. He also keeps talking against Casey, and I'm not going to let him do it." She said she and NeJame got into a heated argument, and he went out and issued a press release that he was quitting because his clients wouldn't follow his advice.

I had never before heard of a lawyer disclosing reasons to the public as to why he was no longer working for a client. I don't understand why the Anthonys put up with it—they easily could have complained to the bar that he was giving away client confidences. But when this was happening, I thought to myself, *The reason they're keeping their mouths shut is because NeJame knows the results of the failed polygraph test, and there must be something incriminating in those tests.* I could have been wrong, but that was my logical conclusion. These tests have never been made public.

After NeJame left the Anthonys, he signed on as the attorney for Miller, the head of Texas EquuSearch. After Caylee's body was found, I wanted to see Texas EquuSearch's records, to see where and when they had searched. I wanted to interview those who had searched the area where Caylee was found but who didn't see a body. But Texas Equu-Search and NeJame refused to turn over any records. For months we had to fight to get those records. We finally got them but under very strenuous circumstances. Fighting us all the way was NeJame, getting his face in front of the camera.

NeJame later went on to become a TV analyst during the trial. In the end, the guy got the fame and attention he craved.

NeJame wasn't the only groupie lawyer in this case. Every time a witness came up, the witness would get a lawyer, and it was always a free lawyer. Someone would volunteer, "I'll represent you," and he'd donate his time and go on TV and make a statement. At every turn there was a new lawyer volunteering his services, speaking on someone's behalf, and getting his mug on TV.

I found these lawyers to be irresponsible and disgraceful to our profession. The role of the defense lawyer is so misunderstood, and when lawyers go on TV to bash another lawyer, it does the system and the public a major disservice.

And always, because it was the popular thing to do, and because the "Casey Anthony Show" script demanded that it be that way, the news that these lawyers generated *always* ran counter to the defense.

CHAPTER 9

THE DAY CAYLEE
WAS FOUND

As far as experts, I wanted the best. From the beginning, I thought to myself, *I have to be ready if Caylee is ever found deceased, and one of the people I will need is a forensic pathologist*. Right off the bat my first choice was the famed Michael Baden.

On December 10, 2008, I was in New York having dinner with Baden and his wife Linda Kenny Baden.

I had followed Baden since the O. J. Simpson trial and had always been a huge fan of his work. Geraldo Rivera knew Michael and introduced us. As we were having dinner, we were talking about different things, and I was getting to know him. My wife Lorena was with me, so this was a social situation more than business.

We also didn't have a body so our discussion was a bit premature, except that I wanted to be ready when I needed him—if I needed him. I didn't know for certain that Caylee was dead. I always hoped for the best and planned for the worst, so I was meeting with Michael. At the end of dinner, his conclusions were, of course, "You don't have a body so you don't need a forensic pathologist, but if you need any help, let me know, give me a call."

I flew home in time for a court appearance in Casey's case the morning of December 11. I arrived in court along with fifty other lawyers there to argue pretrial motions in other cases. The media were there, and all the lawyers knew who I was and whom I was representing.

When I walked into the courthouse, I could literally feel the chill from the other local lawyers. Not a single lawyer came up to me and said, "Hey, Jose, keep up the fight. You're doing a good job. If there's anything you need, here's my number. Don't hesitate to call." Not one said, "Hi, how are you? I'm so and so and I wanted to meet you." That would have been the norm in just about any other case; it's part of the networking that lawyers do.

Jose, you're on your own with this one, I thought to myself, and later on another lawyer told me, point-blank, that was the reality.

A pretrial hearing was scheduled in our case to get the parties together and to find out where everyone stood. If the defense needs a continuance, one will ordinarily be granted. If the defense and state are ready for trial, the judge sets a date within three weeks.

We were nowhere near ready. We were receiving mountains of discovery. I asked for a continuance.

A lot of so-called experts second-guessing my every move were sure I would announce, "Ready," in order to force the prosecution into trying the case immediately.

I never for a second considered doing that. I don't think any good lawyer would take that risk. That's like playing chicken, and you never play chicken with someone else's life on the line. So at that point I asked for a continuance. I stated we weren't ready and that we were still getting discovery.

However, by asking for a continuance, the defendant automatically waives her right to a speedy trial.

The judge granted the continuance.

WHENEVER I CAME into the courtroom, the media were always waiting for me, and I always said, "Let me do my work. When I'm done, I'll meet you guys outside." This was on the condition that they didn't follow me to my car and harass me with questions along the way. We had worked out this deal, so usually after I was done in court, I would speak outside the courthouse, go off in my car, and be done with it.

This day was no different. I walked out of the courthouse, got peppered with a bunch of questions, and then it was Tony Pipitone who asked me, "Jose, were you not taking a risk by asking for a continuance instead of trying the case immediately, since they don't have a body?"

"No," I said, "because we still believe Caylee is alive. We really don't have any evidence to the contrary."

I wasn't ignorant to the strong possibility she was dead. But if you're going to speculate, why not think positively? So I said, "We believe Caylee is alive, and hopefully she will be found before this case ever comes to trial." Just as I was saying these words, a man by the name of Roy Kronk, an Orange County meter reader, claimed to be relieving himself in the woods near the Anthony home when he stumbled across Caylee's remains. He called his bosses to say he had found Caylee's body.

When I left court that day, I didn't know anything about this. I went back to my office, and I was there maybe twenty minutes, when I received a call from Sergeant John Allen.

"Jose, do you know where I can find the Anthonys?" he asked excitedly.

"They're in California," I said. I knew they were there doing an interview on *Larry King Live*.

"Why?" I asked.

"I need to talk to them immediately because we just found Caylee."

"Are you sure this isn't another false alarm?" I asked.

"No," he said, "I'm about a quarter mile from the Anthony house right now. I'm looking at the skull. She had the same color hair, the same length of hair. It's a child. I'm quite sure it's her."

"I'll try to get hold of them right away," I said, "and I'll get back to you."

I called the Anthonys in California. They didn't answer the first time I called, but I got them the second time.

"Have you heard the news?" I asked Cindy.

"Yes," she said, "we're at the airport. We're getting ready to board the plane and come back." Then Cindy asked, "Do you know if it's her?"

"They think it is, Cindy," I said.

Cindy had been down this road before, so I don't know whether she was in denial or what. Under the circumstances she seemed pretty together.

I told her to call me after they arrived back in Orlando.

"I will," she said.

I told the people in my office that I was going to see Casey at the jail. I hopped in my car, and the first call I received was from Geraldo.

"Hey, I'm hearing that they might have found her," said Geraldo.

"I don't know if it's true or not," I said. "I'm on my way to see Casey now."

"All right, man," he said. "Good luck. I'll talk to you later."

On the way I called Michael and Linda Baden. Michael answered the phone.

"You're not going to believe this," I said, "but they found Caylee's body." Harking back to our dinner conversation of the night before, I said, "The moment is here. We didn't expect it to come this soon."

Michael and I talked, and he said, "Jose, I've done a large number of interviews on the case on Fox and other stations. You need to think twice about wanting me on your team."

"You're right," I said. "I need to look at it a little more closely. May I speak with Linda?"

He passed the phone to her. Linda has a vast knowledge of forensic science. She had just finished trying the Phil Spector case, and she had achieved a hung jury based mostly on science. In addition, she was an incredible lawyer.

"I'd like for you to get involved in the case," I said. "I'm on my way to see Casey right now. I need to act and I need to act quickly."

"We need to find a forensic pathologist," Linda said. "Are you authorizing me to make some calls and try to get some people together?"

I was. She made a three-way call and the first person she called was Dr. Werner Spitz, the dean of forensic pathology. He wrote the book that all forensic pathologists read. He works out of Michigan and has worked on huge cases. He testified at hearings on both the Martin Luther King Jr. and John F. Kennedy assassinations.

After he agreed to join us, I said to Linda, "We need more experts."

"Go see Casey," Linda said. "I'll work on that, and we'll talk after you get out."

I arrived at the jail and immediately noticed that something was weird. I was standing there, but they wouldn't let me pass the gate.

"I need to get in," I said. "I need to see my client. What the hell is going on?"

"We're sending the sergeant down to talk to you," said the guard.

I waited perhaps fifteen minutes when the sergeant came over.

"What we're doing," he said, "We're taking Casey to medical."

"Is she okay? Did something happen to her?" I asked.

"No, no, no, she's fine," he said. "We're doing that as an extra precaution."

"I still want to see her," I said.

"You can't," he said, "not until she gets back from medical."

"Listen," I said, "I am demanding access to my client. I want to see her—*now*."

"Sorry, you can't."

"I want to speak to your supervisor," I demanded.

"We'll have Captain DeFerrari come down and talk to you."

I knew they were stalling, but I didn't know why.

DeFerrari was a woman, first name Nancy, and she told me, "We took her to medical as a precaution. We're waiting until she gets out, and if she wants to speak to a psychiatrist, we're going to let her do that."

"No," I said. "I want to speak to her first. No one can speak to her until I speak to her." They were denying her right to counsel under the ruse that she was getting medical attention, but apparently there was nothing I could do to stop them.

"We have rules here," she said. "If someone is in need of medical attention, we're not obligated to let them speak to their lawyer first."

I had no choice, it seems, but to sit there and wait.

About thirty minutes later, I was let in to see Casey. I walked into the classroom, where Casey was waiting with two uniformed officers, and I could tell she was distraught.

I apologized to her for not getting there sooner. I asked if she was okay, and she said, "I'll be all right." Caylee was dead, and she was in mourning, and it was one of those moments where you just don't know what to say.

"This is what I know," I said, and I repeated what Allen had told me, and after I said that, one of the officers came in and handed Casey a sedative caplet with some water to swallow it down.

"I want to stay here and spend time with you," I said to her, "but you're going to need me on the outside more than you'll need me here."

"I understand," Casey said. "I hope this pill will make me sleep." She began to weep.

I called my associate Gabe and told him to come and stay with her.

"There are a lot of things we need to do," I explained to her, "and I need to be free to do them." After spending about an hour with her, I left.

It was only later that I found out why the police wouldn't let me see her when I first arrived at the jail. As soon as the police got to the site where Caylee's remains lay, Commander Matt Irwin, the head of the missing person's unit, came up with the bright idea of calling the jail and asking if there was a room where they could take Casey and video-tape her reaction to their finding Caylee's remains.

"We can take her into the medical unit," he was told. "There's a TV there. We can turn on the TV and record her reaction to their announc-ing they had found Caylee's remains and hopefully she'll say something, maybe flip out and confess."

This was the "medical care" I was told she was getting that prevented me from seeing her.

They sent someone to Casey's cell. They shackled her legs and hands in chains, marched her to the medical unit, sat her down where there were several correctional officers and a couple of nurses standing around watching her, and forced her to watch the breaking news that police had found Caylee's remains so they could record her reaction.

On the tape you can see Casey start to breathe heavily and start to hyperventilate, see her double over a couple times, and see she was in tremendous, tremendous mental and emotional pain.

For ten minutes they sat her there watching the horrible news made more horrible by the sensationalist media until one of the nurses said, "Okay, I think she's had enough." And that's when they took her back to the classroom.

Meanwhile, oblivious to what they were doing, I was outside trying to get in while they were torturing her. Clearly this was a violation of her right to counsel and what two of the correctional officers would later testify to be cruel and unusual punishment. It was another end around, where the police were trying to get something from her. In my opinion, it was one of the cruelest stunts I have ever seen the police pull on someone. They made her watch the worst tabloid channel—WFTV Channel 9, the local ABC affiliate—a channel so inflammatory it was just a notch below *Nancy Grace*.

To this day it was one of the cruelest and most disgusting things I have ever seen the cops do. After the trial was over, the video was made public on September 30, 2011. That day, the *Orlando Sentinel* reported that the jail's public information officer, Allen Moore, "said the decision to move Anthony was done by jail administration independently out of concern for the inmate's health and well-being." And Public Information Officer Angelo Nieves said, "Video was available to us. We availed ourselves to it, and it became part of the case file." Shamelessly, they were characterizing their actions as coincidental and not intentional. These public officials treated the public as if they were stupid. This is our government at work. They should be above this foolishness, but they are not. It's scary, and what makes it even scarier is that the media, the so-called "watchdogs," never called them out on it. They just kept taking the guided tour. It wasn't the first time and unfortunately it wouldn't be the last.

WHEN I LEFT THE JAIL, the media were in a feeding frenzy. It was nuts.

"What did she say?" they all screamed.

I refused to answer any of them. It was raining, and the reporters were getting in my way and getting aggressive. I wouldn't talk to them because it was none of anybody's business what her personal turmoil was at that moment, and that was all they wanted to know about.

All through the trial, whenever anyone asked me the question, "How is she doing?" my answer was always the same. I would say, "I'm her lawyer. She hired me to handle her legal case. I don't think it's my place to observe and comment on what she's going through. So unless I am specifically authorized by her, I'm not going to do it." And I never did. (Note: this is the first time I have ever publicly commented on anything that went on with Casey behind the scenes, and it's only because Casey has authorized me to do so.)

The media would hate me over that, but I wasn't in the business of public relations. I was a defense lawyer and I was just doing my job.

And as I was leaving the jail after seeing Casey, I again told them I had no intention of answering their questions about her reaction to the police finding Caylee's body.

That day the media were totally out of control, pushing me and trying to agitate me as much as possible. Ignoring them, I got in my car and drove away.

I wanted to find a place where I could have a little peace and quiet. I needed time to myself. Caylee had so quickly become a huge part of my life, and I didn't even know her. I was instantly overwhelmed with sadness and just needed a little time to compose myself, to say a prayer for the little girl who was my first thought when I woke up in the morning and my last before I went to bed. I also needed to make some important phone calls in private and I knew my office wasn't going to be that place because the reporters were all over there, and that was the last thing I wanted. I didn't want to have to go through that again.

I pulled into a gas station and as I was pumping gas, a media truck drove by and saw me. I could hear one of them shout, "There he is." They drove up to my car, and all I could think of was, *Oh shit.*

I stopped pumping the gas, put the gas cap on the car, got in, and drove off, with the media truck in hot pursuit.

You know what? I thought to myself. *You ought to go home.*

I live in a gated community and I figured if I beat them to the gate, they couldn't follow me. But I didn't want them to know where I lived so I tried to lose them. I sped off, but they managed to stay up with me.

Finally I gave in and pulled over.

"Listen," I said, "I have nothing to say so I would ask that you please respect my privacy and just let me go on my way, because I'm not going to say a word."

"You know we can't do that," said the reporter.

"Why?" I asked. "I'm not going to say anything."

"We'll lose our jobs," he said. "We just can't let you go."

It was as though I was placed under arrest by the media.

"Please, just go on camera with us for one minute," he said, "and then we can justify letting you go."

"Fine," I said.

I told him, "Yes, I saw Casey, but I can't tell you what she said. I can't tell you anything about that conversation. And that's it. I'm working."

"Is there anything else you can tell us?" he asked.

"No."

"How did she act?"

"I can't tell you."

"What are you planning on doing?"

"I can't tell you."

He asked five or six questions, and I wouldn't answer any of them. He said, "Thank you very much," and I got in my car and left. And they didn't follow me, so I went home.

I took a little time for myself and after I pulled myself together, I thought *my client needs me, so get focused and be a professional.*

I went back to work. I made my calls. I called Linda back. We started to talk about what we were going to do, and one of the things we wanted was to have immediate access to the crime scene—at least to be able to observe. We talked about making an emergency motion for a hearing, asking to observe the autopsy when it occurred, and asking to have immediate access to the scene.

I turned on my TV set to WKMG Channel 6, the local CBS affiliate in Orlando, in an attempt to closely watch what was on the news. And I watched as Sheriff Kevin Beary, a huge man, somewhere around six foot two and tipping the scales at around 350 pounds, was talking about the case while wearing full riot gear.

I said to myself, *Just in case they need him to swing into action.*

It was bizarre. Here was this huge guy with a bulletproof vest, a flashlight, and black hat. I kept thinking, *This guy has probably never been in tactical action in his life, but here he is, dressed up like it's Halloween.*

I could also see that Beary was crying. He was the police equivalent of Rams' football coach Dick Vermeil. Either he was hamming it up for the cameras, or I thought, *Maybe he's auditioning to be the weeping bailiff for the "Judge Larry Seidlin Show."* (Seidlin was the crying judge in the Anna Nicole Smith case.)

Meanwhile, the newscaster was saying, "Sources say that when the police found Caylee, she had duct tape wrapped all around her skull."

More leaks from the police flooded in about the duct tape. The police told the media, "When the results come back from the duct tape, it's going to be very bad for Casey." And the media took that to mean that Casey's fingerprints were on the duct tape. The police never said that, but the reporters made that leap of faith and printed it anyway.

AROUND 7:00 P.M. on December 11, I finally got a call from the Anthonys. They wanted to see me, and I wanted to speak to them as well. Because

the police were searching their home that evening, they were barred from going back there, and so a media outlet put the Anthonys and their two pro bono investigators, Dominic Casey and a man by the name of Jim Hoover, up at The Ritz-Carlton Orlando, Grande Lakes. I had heard Hoover's name before, and I always assumed he was Dominic's associate. Once again, Hoover turned out to be someone following the case, someone standing outside the Anthony home with the protesters until he approached Dominic and befriended him. Hoover was a licensed private detective, and they agreed to join together as the Anthonys' private security force. Hoover would later tell people he had run his own detective agency and had once been Howard Cosell's bodyguard. I chalked him up as just another wack packer in this case.

Hoover would later become important because he had filmed Dominic searching the area where Caylee was found only a month earlier, only to come up empty. That evening, he never mentioned a word of that to me.

I had a couple of errands to run before going to the hotel. When I arrived, the Anthonys and their investigators were at a large table in the back of the restaurant eating dinner. I felt as though I was walking into a dinner party. The mood wasn't somber at all, which I thought was strange. Here were the Anthonys eating at a five-star restaurant on the media's dime while crime scene investigators were on their hands and knees in the rain searching the woods for their granddaughter's bones. This family certainly grieved in a very different way.

I sat down and said hello to everyone. I didn't want to talk business at the table because of the presence of people who weren't part of the immediate family—Dominic and Hoover. I didn't think it was appropriate.

After dinner we went up to the Anthonys' room, and I met with George, Cindy, and Lee. Dominic and Hoover went back to their rooms. As I sat with the Anthonys, what I was anxious to see was their reactions, so when I talked to them, based on my conversation with Allen, I told them the police were quite certain it was Caylee.

Cindy, ever in denial, was not sold that the skeletal remains of a child found at the end of her block were those of her granddaughter. Apparently she thought there was another missing child who no one had reported missing on that corner, as insane as that may have sounded.

"I have reason to believe it's Caylee," I told them.

And then Cindy broke down, like the reality of the situation had finally gotten to her. And George just sat there. So did Lee.

Cindy, sobbing, walked into the bathroom and closed the door; George left to comfort her. I was sitting alone with Lee, and there was an awkward silence. Lee had the look on his face that told me *he knew* it was Caylee. And in the middle of the trial, I would find out why. At that moment, though, I had a really odd feeling. And just as I was thinking about Lee's lack of emotion, Cindy started to get angry. From inside the bathroom of the hotel room she was saying something harsh to George but not loudly enough for me to pick up what she was saying.

When they returned, I said to them, "I will pass on to you as much information as I know."

George then asked an odd question.

"What do the cops know?"

Again I was taken aback. I thought to myself, *When the hell are these people going to tell me what they know?*

Cindy asked me how Casey was doing.

"She's not doing well," I said. "Obviously."

And again, the only one crying in the room was Cindy.

I left them and drove home. The whole time, especially after listening to the "Zanny the nanny" stories, I had a strong feeling the poor child was dead, but I was like everyone else: hoping for the best while expecting the worst.

When I got the call from the police saying that they had found Caylee's body, I felt like I had gotten a kind of closure. I wanted her to be found, and now she was. I have a daughter and can only imagine the pain of losing her. I would see pictures of Caylee and imagine what she must have been like. We would sit around the office talking about her and it was fascinating to all of us that we had never met this little girl, but she had become such a huge part of our lives. I know everyone in our office grieved when Caylee was found dead, but, like a doctor working in an emergency room, we couldn't get emotional.

I am not, however, bulletproof. It really hurt.

CHAPTER 10

THE DAYS AFTER

I WAS REALLY DOWN. I hadn't wanted the six-month-long search to end up with the discovery of Caylee's dead body, even though I knew that was the likelihood. So for me December 11, 2008, was a very depressing day. I knew that in order to do my job, I should take my emotions out of it, but I just couldn't. I was very somber and depressed that day; I came home late and I was tired. I didn't even talk to Lorena about it. I was working more and more, and we were talking less and less. I was distant and disengaged, and it wasn't easy on her.

I should have known better, but I pressed on. I also knew I had to get up very early the following day to pick Linda Baden up at the Orlando airport at 7:00 A.M. for a court appearance.

After I picked Linda up, we drove immediately to my office. She was incredibly bright, a ball of fire, and I told her, "As soon as we start the hearing, I'm going to introduce you and let you take off with it."

We went to court with our motion to allow us to attend the autopsy and to be given immediate access to the area where Caylee was found.

Jeff Ashton, one of the three prosecutors in the case, was his usual abrasive and condescending self. He told the court our request was absurd because the body had not been identified and because the child buried there could be anyone. And because they didn't know who the child was, his argument went, we didn't have any standing to be present at the autopsy and couldn't have access to the crime scene. This was absurd. They were posturing as though there was another toddler missing in the Anthony neighborhood that no one had known about.

After Ashton sneered at us and made his argument, Linda stood and said, "Your honor, I'm going to address the issues. I'm not going to address the morass over there," and she nodded toward Ashton. I then thought to myself, *Yeah, I think we're going to work well together.* She made her points concisely and intelligently, and everyone could see she knew what she was talking about.

The judge ruled that we should go into the back room and try to work out our differences. Linda and I were met by Ashton, Linda Drane Burdick, and a female county attorney representing the sheriff's department.

Immediately we started arguing.

"We don't know it's her," said Burdick.

"Come on," I said. "Quit being ridiculous." And that was when from out of the blue Burdick said to me, "There's a unique way we think Caylee died, and if your client wants to plead out now, she needs to tell us first. We're withholding this information."

The hell they were.

"Are you referring to the duct tape that the police have already leaked?" I asked her.

"I don't know where the media are getting that from," she said. "It's not true."

I believe that was the first and only time that Burdick out-and-out lied to me. Then she said, "Obviously, the deal isn't the same as the deal we were talking about before. The situation is different now. She had her chance. The manslaughter discussion is off the table, but if she would come forward and tell us the unique way we think Caylee died, I will entertain something."

We were in a back room with the door shut, when a reporter for the *Orlando Sentinel* by the name of Anthony Colarossi put his ear to the door to listen in. We sensed someone was out there, and when I opened the door, I saw him standing there.

"Have a little decency and respect, will you?" I said to him.

Burdick and I were both angry about that.

While we met with the prosecution, Sergeant John Allen and FBI Special Agent Nick Savage returned from the crime scene. They came in and said to me, "We should be done processing the scene possibly by tomorrow, and then we can turn it over to you."

Based on their statement, I brought down a team of high-profile, world-renowned experts to examine the crime scene. We called in our forensic entomologist, Dr. Timothy Huntington. Werner Spitz flew in, as did Kathy Reichs, the prolific forensic anthropologist and novelist, and Dr. Henry Lee.

Linda suggested we hire investigator Pat McKenna, who is from West Palm Beach, Florida. McKenna knew Linda through other cases. McKenna, one of the private investigators for the O. J. Simpson murder trial, was the one who found the Mark Fuhrman tapes. Fuhrman had been an effective witness against Simpson, until McKenna found those tapes the defense played during the trial, on which Fuhrman used the N-word left and right. The mostly black jury took notice, and it was one piece of evidence that helped the defense acquit Simpson.

McKenna worked on many high-profile cases, including the William Kennedy Smith rape case. He's a topflight professional, and I was relieved to have someone like McKenna on board assisting me in the investigation. He quickly took over as our lead investigator.

We had the full team ready to go. All we needed was access to the crime scene and Caylee's remains.

Two days later, the prosecution and police still hadn't handed over the crime season, so while we waited, we went to the Anthony home. Huntington collected soil samples in the backyard, because we knew they'd do a geology sample comparison of the recovery scene and compare it to any dirt found either in Casey's car or on her shoes. We also checked out the backyard area and inside the home. We talked to the Anthonys, and while we were there, Dominic, who was working for George and Cindy, told me something I found odd: he said he'd been out only a month before in the woods in the area where Caylee had been found, and no remains had been found there.

I didn't really take this too seriously because Dominic often had a lot to say, but what he failed to mention was that he had a video of their visit to the site.

Dominic kept saying he had photographs, and I kept asking him for them, and he said, "Oh sure, no problem." It wasn't until several days later, when I saw on the news that Hoover (the Anthonys' other bodyguard) was trying to sell his video of the crime scene to different networks for $50,000, that I learned that Hoover had taken videos of their visit. Like so much other information in this case, I found out about it through the news.

Most of the time during the days following the discovery of Caylee's body, we sat in my office while we waited to be given access to the scene. Day after day, we waited for the call that would allow our high-priced investigators to go down to the recovery site.

The next day would come, and they would say they weren't finished, and then the next day, and then the next. They didn't turn over the crime scene for *nine days*, and when we arrived, we discovered they had demolished the scene, removed all the debris, took everything, and left it worthless for our purposes. Yes, they had turned it over, but the area they turned over was useless.

On December 16, big news flashed across the TV screens showing the three prosecutors, Burdick, Ashton, and Frank George, going to the scene where Caylee was found. Four days earlier these same prosecutors were standing before the judge arguing we couldn't go there—we didn't have standing—because they weren't sure it was Caylee. And yet, without telling us it was Caylee, there they were, parading around the recovery site on TV.

We later found out that the prosecution had been told by the FBI DNA unit on December 16 that they were in fact Caylee's remains. They were supposed to tell us immediately, but they didn't because they didn't want us filing motions to gain access to the site.

On December 19, the prosecution and police announced they had found Caylee, trumpeting that duct tape had allegedly been found around Caylee's mouth and nose. They were announcing to the world that things were looking very bad for Casey and that they might consider changing their minds and seek the death penalty.

I SHOULD TELL YOU THIS: in every case, I've found that you will get a little bit of luck if you avail yourself to it.

"We're going to catch a break somewhere," I kept repeating to everyone on the team. I said that because the publicity had been uniformly negative.

Our break came on December 18, the day *before* the prosecution announced that the body belonged to Caylee. Linda, McKenna, and I were all sitting in my conference room watching the TV, because the police were scheduling a press conference, and this one was being touted as one that would break some *big* news. We were also waiting there because we continued to hold out hope that the prosecution would turn over the crime scene to us.

Angelo Nieves, the public information officer, came forward and made the announcement that the police were investigating three prior tips called in in August about the area where Caylee was eventually found.

There wasn't much of a stir until Mike DeForest of WKMG asked Nieves whether the person who called in the three tips in August was the same person who found the remains on December 11, five months later?

And Nieves answered, "Yes."

And as we sat around the conference table listening to this, our jaws dropped. I was seated, and as soon as Nieves said that, I stood up from my chair. We all began watching much more closely.

I thought to myself, *How could this be?* And then Nieves took our great fortune a step further when he stated that in August a police officer had actually come out to investigate the call by Roy Kronk, the tipster.

I couldn't believe my ears. I couldn't believe what we were watching.

"Oh my God," said McKenna. "They have major shit all over their faces now."

We all knew the problem the police now were facing: I said to myself, *How do you call someone out in August, a police officer comes out and investigates, and they find nothing, and five months later you go back again to the same spot and you find her body?*

It reeked of trouble for the prosecution, and all of the media went nuts.

I can't say I felt sorry for Nieves, but I saw him squirming up there trying to deflect some very direct questions by saying, "I don't want this to take away from the fact that these officers are scouring the area and doing an excellent job recovering here at the scene."

Though he kept trying to put a positive spin on it all, the entire media contingent was going nuts searching for answers. It got to the point where Nieves finally said, "I'm not answering any more questions. We are currently investigating. That's the end of the story."

The introduction of Kronk, the meter reader who found Caylee's body, was a major turning point in the case. I'll never forget, after the press conference was over, DeForest came on TV and said, "This incredible new development has now opened a major hole in the state's case in which the defense will be able to drive a Mack truck through it."

Which was exactly what we intended on doing.

CHAPTER 11

THE KRONK CHRONICLES

T HERE IS STILL an enormous amount of confusion in the tale of Roy Kronk. As a result, the events surrounding the discovery of Caylee Anthony's bones remain a mystery.

Kronk, a recent hire as a meter reader for Orange County, Florida, was reading meters in the Anthony family's neighborhood. He was accompanied by trainee Chris Dixon and his trainer, David Dean, who had also trained Kronk.

Finishing their rounds around 1:30 P.M. on August 11, 2008, the three decided that, rather than heading back to the office early, they'd park off Suburban Drive to relax and hang out before they had to be back around three. Suburban Drive was not a far-off location; it's only twenty houses down from the Anthony home.

They were hanging out, grabbing a smoke, when Kronk had to urinate. He walked into the woods so he couldn't be seen from the nearby elementary school. His fellow workers followed, and they joked that this would be a perfect place to hide a body.

"In these swampy woods, a body could decompose, and no one would notice," said one of Kronk's coworkers half in jest, half seriously. And why shouldn't they have been discussing this? Caylee had been missing since June and there was no bigger topic of conversation around these parts than the mystery of little Caylee's whereabouts.

"This would be a *great* place to stash a body," said one of the others. Kronk agreed.

Kronk decided to have a look around and do his own investigation of the area. As he was standing there, he told his coworkers, "Hey guys, I think I see a human skull." Immediately they laughed him off, saying he was being ridiculous.

"No, no, come and look," he said. They started walking toward him, but were startled by the sight of a lifeless six-foot-long diamondback rattlesnake lying in the grass. Blood oozed from its mouth. Kronk surmised that it had been hit by a car, slithered into the woods, and died. They started freaking out, and at that point, according to Kronk, he came out of the woods and started talking about the snake. He changed the focus away from the skull and concentrated their attention on the dead snake. The topic of the skull did not come up again in conversation. The three then took photos of the large snake with their cell phones.

After putting the snake in their truck, they drove back to the office and showed fellow employees passing by in the office parking lot the snake they had found. You'd think Kronk would have said something about the skull he saw, especially since they had just been talking about Caylee's disappearance and how that spot would be a perfect place for a body. But he didn't. The location of the skull wasn't more than a quarter mile from the Anthony home, but by his account, he said nothing more about it until he returned home after work.

Once home, Kronk mentioned the skull to his girlfriend, Michelle, who was following the case closely on TV. Kronk says it was she who insisted he call 9-1-1.

"There's a gray bag down there," he told the woman at the other end of the phone. "I don't know. I'm not saying it's Caylee or anything of that nature." They then talked about the neighborhood, but Kronk was unable to tell her exactly where it was.

He told the dispatcher about the snake and said to her, "Right here, behind one of the trees down there was a gray bag, and then a little further up, I saw something white. But after I saw that eastern diamondback rattlesnake, I wasn't going back in there."

"Okay, thank you," said the dispatcher. "Good-bye."

The call was assigned to Deputy Adriana Acevedo. It came at night, and she really didn't know where to look. She drove down Suburban Drive and then called in, "I don't see anything."

The next night, August 12, Kronk called again. He told the dispatcher, "I went down there, and behind one of the trees was a gray, vinyl-like bag." Obviously he has been close enough to the bag to be able to identify what it was made of. He said, "It's like a pool cover or something like that. I didn't touch anything." And then he said, "A little bit further up someone ran across with a mower, but the weeds were still very high in that area." Again, he's giving details about the area, and here he's talking about the grass line, where they cut the grass along the woods. There's no sidewalk, but there's grass, and the city cuts it to keep the foliage attractive. That's what he was referring to. Then Kronk said, "There's a fallen tree that looks like someone has tried to cut it at one point, but there was a white board hanging across the tree, and there's something round and white underneath it." Obviously he was describing Caylee's skull. He said, "I don't know what it is, but it doesn't look like it should be there." Kronk and the dispatcher then discussed directions, the nearby elementary school, the snake, and his phone number. They told him he should call Crimeline.

"I don't want to," he said. But in the end he did and when he did, the dispatcher typed out everything that Kronk had said. She typed, "Caller was assigned as a meter reader to the Anthony residence. On the way back down to Suburban, passing the Anthony's street, there's a swamp with a six-foot-high fence. Caller stopped and looked down and saw a single metallic thing that looked like a vinyl bag and a little further up there was a little white, round object. Caller was not sure what it was. Behind the tree there was a six-foot diamondback rattlesnake. He wasn't interested in going to see any further."

Then it said, "There was a break where the tree had fallen over. That is where the caller saw it." So again, Kronk mentioned the tree.

After this 9-1-1 call, the Crimeline tip was investigated by Detective Jerold White, whom I found to be extremely professional and well organized. When the tip was assigned to him on August 14, it was marked, "Area has been searched." I would later find out that White had gone to Detective Yuri Melich and had asked him about the area. Melich told him he didn't need to follow up on that, because that area had been searched.

Kronk's call to 9-1-1 was assigned to Deputy Sheriff Elizabeth Collins on August 12. She called Kronk and talked to him on the phone. She was driving with her night light, which she shined into the woods, but she said she couldn't see anything. She suggested that Kronk call again after he got off work, and an officer would meet him at the site.

The next day, August 13, there was a third, brief 9-1-1 call. He told the dispatcher where he was standing as he waited for the police to arrive. Kronk met with Detective Richard Cain and a second officer, Deputy Kethlin Cutcher. According to Kronk, "The deputy [Cain] shows up. He gets out of the car. I told him what I had seen. I also told him that the day before that we had seen a six-and-a-half foot eastern diamondback rattlesnake right there. He pulled his expanding metal baton. I showed him in the area where it was. He took two steps into the woods. He basically slid down the hill. He came out, and told me the area had already been searched. He told me I was wasting the county's time and basically told me I was an idiot. He just started belittling me, and I left. When I get that kind of treatment from people, I'd just rather not deal with it anymore, okay?"

In no situation could I envision a scenario in which an officer is dispatched after someone calls the cops and says he had found a dead body, shows up, and comes back empty-handed, without really looking.

And we have a discrepancy, because Cain's story of what happened on August 13 is very different. Cain said that after he arrived at the scene, Kronk took him into the woods, stood right behind him, and showed him a bag that was full of leaves and sticks. There was no evidence of bones or body parts. Cain said he inspected the bag with his baton, saw that there was nothing to Kronk's call, and left.

Four months passed. Then on December 11, 2008, Kronk, again reading meters in the area of the Anthony home, returned to the site and this time he absolutely, positively found Caylee's skull.

In his written statement of December 11, Kronk said that this time he went into the woods to urinate, saw a black plastic bag, and hit it with a stick. He said he heard a thud, and that it sounded like he had hit plastic. He said when he felt it, it felt round, so he pulled on the bag with the stick, the bag opened, and a human skull with hair and duct tape around its mouth dropped out.

It was Melich and Detective Eric Edwards who pulled Kronk aside to take his statement. This was the biggest case of their careers. They had invested hundreds if not thousands of man-hours trying to find this child, and Kronk finds her body. But, they interviewed him for exactly *three minutes*.

Note that Kronk said "in it." Here he's clear that the skull was inside the bag.

"Did you open it? Was it open?" he was asked.

"No, it was closed," he said.

"Okay, so what happened next?"

"I saw a round dome," Kronk said. "It kind of looked like something, so I took my stick and I hit it, and it sounded like plastic or hollow bone or something. And then I took my stick, which is curved for pulling meter reader boxes, and I grabbed the bottom of the bag and pulled it. And I pulled it a second time, and then a human skull dropped out with hair around it and duct tape around the mouth. And I went, 'Oh God,' and I immediately called my supervisor that I had found human remains and I needed the police."

Kronk told the police he didn't touch anything. He reinforced that, and after they asked for his stick, with reluctance he told them where they could find it in his truck. He talked to the two detectives about his supervisor, and then Melich asked him a key question: "So is there anything else, the bag, or how you found it, or anything you wanted to tell us that you think is important?"

After Kronk again said he didn't touch anything, Melich asked him to raise his right hand.

"Do you swear what you told me was the truth?"

"Oh yeah," said Kronk.

THERE ARE A NUMBER of problems with Kronk's story, a few of which you may have noticed already.

First, Kronk calls 9-1-1 in August saying that he saw a skull twenty houses down from the Anthony home in the midst of the biggest case in recent memory. He knows where the skull is, but he can't seem to successfully get the police to see it. Doesn't this seem odd?

Melich and Edwards conducted a follow-up interview with Kronk on January 6, 2009. They were in a bind. If Kronk saw a skull in August and called the police, the police would have egg all over their faces for not following up and finding it. So Melich and Edwards went back to the question of what Kronk saw back in August.

"What do you think it was?" asked Melich.

"I thought it was a human skull," said Kronk.

"No question?"

"No."

Then Melich asked him, "If someone were to ask you why you didn't call that afternoon, while you were standing there, if you thought it was a skull and your reaction to that would be?"

"Well, it looked like a skull to me," Kronk answered. "I was ninety nine point nine, nine, nine percent sure it was a skull, but Dave tells me I'm crazy, and honestly, it was a hot day. I just wanted to go home. I wanted to take a shower. I wanted to, you know, drink a soda, relax in the pool."

And what was the cops' reaction to such an obviously ridiculous response?

"Um hum."

Which left open the answer to the very important question that Melich asked, but that Kronk ducked: *When Kronk first saw the skull, why didn't he persist until the police came and found it? Why didn't he go to the media?*

Second, when Kronk finds the body in December, he seems to claim it was just a coincidence that he's back there. In his statement on December 11, Kronk told them, "I've read this route before." It was the first thing he said to them. "And I know the area over here in the woods. It's a safe place to urinate." But he never said, "Because the last time I urinated here, I saw a skull." Instead, he said, "So I parked my truck with my yellow lights on, to make it appear I was actually doing something. I grabbed my meter stick out of the back of my truck and I went into the woods to urinate. When I finished, I noticed a black plastic bag and saw a dome in it." *Isn't it very strange that he doesn't mention the first sighting of the skull?*

And he and the police both downplay the August call to an extent that strains credulity. Recall that in the December interview Melich asks him a key question: "So is there anything else, the bag, or how you found it, or anything you wanted to tell us that you think is important?"

The natural answer would have been, "Yeah, assholes, I called you four months ago, and the cop came out and said I was wasting his time." But instead he said, "I just noticed there was white material like clothing or a pillow or something, but I really didn't stare at it too long."

What I found incredible was that there was nothing written in the report about the fact that he had called the police about the bag and skull back in August.

I found that to be a glaring omission.

When we launched an investigation into Kronk's background, we learned that when he was living in Tennessee fifteen years earlier, he had called in a tip to the police, telling them that there were stolen guns hidden in the woods. The police went out and searched, but found nothing. I found it both shocking and relevant that two times in this man's life he had called the police about something he saw in the woods and the police found nothing. How many times have you done that? This guy did it twice!

In a sworn statement on January 6, 2009, Kronk for the first time said he had told police on December 11 that he had made three calls in August about finding Caylee's body. In a conversation on January 6, 2009, Kronk also mentioned that he was told by the police not to say anything about the August calls. I interviewed all the officers in the case connected to Kronk, and everyone said the same thing: "I never told him not to say anything." Every police officer denied it, even though Kronk's statement was that he was told not to mention the earlier calls because "it would make the department look bad."

So the question then arises: Who was lying? Was it Kronk, or was it the cops? The police brushed Kronk's, "They told me, 'Don't say anything about the August calls'" statement under the rug, saying Kronk was making a joke. Internal Affairs came up with a cockamamie story that that conversation took place between Kronk and a coworker at the scene on December 11, not between Kronk and the police.

I don't believe that explanation for a minute. I don't see how you can confuse the two. In fact, to say it was a conversation between Kronk and a coworker strains credibility.

Third, Kronk changes his story about whether the skull was in the bag or outside it. He told the detectives in December that he found a bag with the skull in it. Back in August when he first found the skull, he said it was outside the bag. He told Crimeline that he was in the woods, stopped, and looked down, saw the vinyl bag and a little further up saw a little round white object. Obviously he's describing a skull.

This change was downplayed by both Kronk and the police. Kronk said, "I really didn't notice anything else, because obviously once I discovered what I discovered, the bag was minimal to me anymore. It really didn't matter."

Then Edwards said to him, "So the image that's being portrayed through the media is this skull rolling out of the bag and..."

Kronk replied, "No, I, no."

"So that never occurred?" asked Edwards.

"That never occurred," said Kronk.

In my view, we were watching Edwards get Kronk to change his statement of December 11, where Kronk told Deputy Edward Turso, the first officer on the scene, "A human skull rolled out of the bag." He also told Deputy Pamela Porter, the second officer on the scene, that it rolled out of the bag. So this wasn't something the media had made up. This was something Kronk had told *two* different police officers.

Now Kronk, with the help of "Eric the Masseuse," was saying it never happened. We had given Edwards the nickname "Eric the Masseuse" because he is an expert at massaging witnesses and their testimony. And the reason it was so important to the cops to get him to change his statement had to do with the initial investigation by Cain. If the skull had been outside the bag, why hadn't Cain seen it?

It also has a lot to do with subsequent actions by Kronk, as I noted earlier. If Kronk had seen a skull, as he initially told Cain and Kutcher, why didn't he go down the block and grab a media truck and show them the skull? If the skull dropped out of the bag, how did it end up that way? If he saw the skull, why did he wait four months to make sure the cops saw it? There are so many questions to be asked, if Kronk saw the skull in August.

It could mean one of two things. He could be telling the truth. If so, then the skull was outside the bag, and someone put it inside the bag and hid it while Casey was in jail. Or it tells us that Kronk was lying.

Other aspects of Kronk's story were also inconsistent. What I found most interesting was that Kronk told the Crimeline that he looked *down* at the round object. In all of the statements Kronk would make, he would say he saw it from a distance. Here he was saying, "I looked down and saw this round skull." To me that was an indication he was standing right over it. Another indication of that was the detail he was able to give about the type of bag it was, the cut on the tree, and the white board.

Fourth, as I noted earlier, there is some evidence that Kronk was coached by the police to get his story straight. The police claimed they weren't satisfied with Kronk's story, so they went back and interviewed him for a second time on December 17. I never did get a clear answer from law enforcement as to what prompted them to go back and talk to Kronk again on December 17. What they *said* was that they felt the evidence at the scene didn't coincide with his statements, so they wanted to go back and get a second statement to clarify some important points.

But, in my view, that's not what they were doing and I'll tell you why. Something law enforcement does too often is called "pre-interviewing." They interview the person privately, and after they are done talking to them and done getting the information they want, they go back and turn on the tape recorder and get the person to say what they want him to say. They can do this because the cops know beforehand exactly what the witness is going to say before the statements are recorded. And they do it so the accused and the accused's lawyers can hear only the conversation that was recorded and not the initial one. As I said, it's a technique often used by law enforcement, and I believe it was used all the time in this case. Often, the information given after a pre-interview isn't very reliable. The tactics are hidden. A slick detective can coach a witness, tell him what he wants to hear, tell him what he should say, and then they go on tape, and the witness merely regurgitates everything that he's expected to say.

The record provides evidence that Melich and Edwards pre-interviewed Kronk before interrogating him on tape on December 17.

From the transcript of their interview, Melich said, "Okay Mr. Kronk, we came down here to visit you at your house because we wanted to get a more detailed statement about the morning of the 11th, when you found what you found. Walk me through that morning *just like you did before* [emphasis mine], and then we'll kind of use that to go back to that earlier Crimeline tip that you mentioned."

This proves Melich and Kronk had talked earlier.

Kronk says, "Okay," and then he starts to talk about it.

Later in the interview Edwards said to Kronk, "Now, your description earlier when we first got here and did a little pre-interview, you had said it was almost like balding, like a male pattern baldness. The top was aha—"

"Okay, okay," said Kronk, and he gives them what they want. Here Edwards very clearly stated they had had a pre-interview.

Here's another example. Edwards and Melich were interviewing Kronk on December 17 and asked him whether he moved Caylee's skull.

"I mean I didn't move it as in physically move it...from one location to another," Kronk said. "I just kind of lifted it up a little bit when it..."

And Edwards chimes in, "Manipulated it some?"

Kronk then says, "Right. Yeah, manipulated it."

Clearly this was a coached term.

Later in the interview, Kronk was talking about being at the crime scene with his two coworkers and whether they talked on the radio to him. Then Edwards let the cat out of the bag. He said, "We discussed the radio transmission of, 'I told you she was there,' I think is what...."

And Kronk said, "Right, because, you know, because I gave them my theory that they thought I was insane at the time, or that it was a joke."

Edwards, of course, would argue that the technique is legitimate, just as Melich would say there's nothing fishy about a pre-interview. They would say, "We're not coaching him. He tells us what he tells us." But I don't buy that for a second. What they're actually trying to do is get Kronk to change his testimony.

It is inconceivable to me that events transpired the way Kronk described them. There are just too many inconsistencies. So what really happened? No one knows for certain, but consider what in all probability I believe did occur:

On August 11 Roy Kronk was taking a break from his meter reading with two coworkers when he had to urinate. He went into the woods, said to his coworkers, "Hey, I saw a skull," but after they saw the dead snake and got excited, he thought better of calling the police about his find, figuring, *Wait a minute. Why would I share the reward with these two other guys?*

So he returned later that day and hid Caylee's body, waiting for the size of the reward to go up, as it did, from $10,000 to $255,000. This is the evidence I believe backs up this theory.

Dave Evans, Kronk's attorney, rejected that theory, asserting that Kronk "immediately and repeatedly reported his find to local law enforcement."

But, consider this; on December 10, the day before Kronk "found" her body, his car broke down on his way to work. He was broke, needed a new transmission. He had to borrow $1,084.17 to fix it. The very next day, he called the police to report his find again. This time, the two police officers who arrived at the scene were Turso and Porter. In her deposition Porter told me that the first question Kronk asked was, "Do I still get the reward even though she's dead?" And the second question was, "Will my ex-wife find out about the money since I owe her child support?"

When Alex Roberts, Kronk's supervisor, showed up at the scene, Alex testified that Kronk told him he had just won the lottery, and that he was going to be rich because he was the one who had found Caylee.

Kronk also made his intentions known during his January 6, 2009, interview with Melich and Edwards. Kronk said to them, "And you notice I am still keeping a low profile as humanly possible, but you know what…"

"We really appreciate that," said Melich.

Then Kronk said, "But Roy has to eat too, so…" Basically he was saying he was going to go public, making the rounds of the reality news shows.

In the end, Roy Kronk ended up getting about $25,000, including $5,000 from attorney Mark Nejame.

For the record, here's what Kronk said when Edwards asked him why it took him four months to go into the woods and report Caylee's body:

"I had things on my mind. My car blew up. I had to replace it, okay? I had just started a relationship with my son again after eighteen years of not seeing him. All right, I got insurance to pay. I have to pay my parents back. I had to go out and find a car. I think we spent all Memorial weekend, all these days out trying to find me a car. I had real things to do, okay?"

After listening to the absurdity of his answer, did the cops say to him, "And all these things were more important than making sure we recovered this poor dead girl's body?"

No. Rather, they went on to their next question.

We would find out later that the police tried to bury any mention of Kronk's financial motives. Our investigators learned that Porter was ordered by Internal Affairs not to say anything about Kronk mentioning the reward to her. I was appalled by the report. But good cops, like Porter, don't always go along with what the other cops want. It's comical they changed the name from Internal Affairs to Professional Standards. These apparently are Orange County's professional standards.

There's more evidence beyond Kronk's clear financial interest in finding Caylee's remains. When he returned to the woods, at least one person saw him—Gale St. John. St. John, the psychic dog handler, told my investigator that she saw Kronk by that part of the woods that day. We believed her because she had a video of her and her associates there that day.

So (again, my supposition) he thought: *Shit, somebody saw me in the woods. I've got to do something. I'll call the cops, and when they arrive, I'll be able to say that I called them to show them what I found,* when in actuality he was doing nothing of the sort except creating an alibi for himself.

In his deposition, we asked Kronk why his cell phone would ping off nearby towers after he got home from work that afternoon. We didn't really have his cell tower records, so this was a bluff on our part. But he did not know that. He admitted returning to the general area and gave us a story about stopping at a store near the site where he saw the skull on his way home. This really sounded suspicious to me.

So Kronk bides his time. And then on December 11, after months go by and the reward goes way up, he cashes in his ticket.

Looking at the scenario backward and forward, that's the only explanation I can come up with. This is just my opinion, but can you think of a plausible alternative? There is significant evidence to support this theory.

AS PART OF OUR INVESTIGATION, the defense looked into the background of Kronk, and what we found wasn't pretty. Kronk was married twice, first to Crystal Sparks and then to Jill Kerley. They painted a picture of a man who was not only a habitual liar and fantasist but a violent abuser who was arrested for kidnapping an ex-girlfriend.

Kerley, a heavyset woman who suffered from Hodgkin's lymphoma, was married to Kronk for only four-and-a-half months. She divorced him because he was abusive. She told my investigator Mort Smith, "We were living in Maryville, this was after he got kicked out of the U.S. Coast Guard, and he packed a bag, put it in the car, and he told me we were going to the store. And the next thing I know, we went to his parents' house. He wouldn't let me call my mom and dad to let them know I was okay. And then he beat me in front of his father, because I wouldn't do what he asked me to do."

She told us of another time when he picked her up at the airport, and when they got home, he gave her a glass of wine.

"After I drank it," she said, "I passed out on the couch. I believe he drugged me and had every intention of having his way with me."

Kerley told our investigator that Kronk had a thing for duct tape. "He called it hundred-mile-an-hour duct tape," she said. "Nothing can get through it." She said that on two occasions he used duct tape to tie her down.

When asked about what went through her mind upon hearing that Kronk had found Caylee's body, she said, "That he had done it. The duct tape. A lot of reasons. I say that because of the abuse I went through. My gut told me he had something to do with it."

According to Kerley, Kronk enjoyed playing the game Dungeons & Dragons on the computer.

"He would believe he was one of the characters," she said. "It consumed him. I think if given the opportunity I think he would have killed me. I was very afraid of him."

Smith asked her, "Is he honest?"

She said, "I don't think he'd know the truth if it hit him in the head."

Sparks, who was in the U.S. Coast Guard with Kronk at the time they married, told a particularly chilling story of the day she received a call from Kronk's father. They had divorced, and she was working in the legal office of the U.S. Coast Guard when he called to say that Kronk was in jail.

"What happened?" she asked.

"Roy kidnapped his girlfriend," he said.

She wanted to know the details.

"The girlfriend, the nurse, they were living together and they had a breakup," the father said. "She went back to South Carolina, and Roy was upset enough he wanted to get her back. He rented a car, and he decided he was going to take her back to Key West. He used handcuffs, duct tape, and a plastic gun he got from a drugstore to hold her."

Sparks was asked by Smith why Kronk was estranged from his sister Susan and his niece Jessica. Sparks told him, "There was a concern that Roy wanted to be close to Jessica. In my heart I had concerns about it. There's concern about Roy being with young girls. Would he do something to his own niece? Someone would have to look at it with seriousness. Susan made sure Jessica didn't sit on Roy's lap."

Sparks told Smith about Kronk's violent streak. She said that after she divorced him, he often threatened to kill her.

"He was angry about the divorce," she said. "I pulled a fast one on him to protect myself, protect my child. I didn't want to be around the abuse, the violence, the alcohol. So he was angry. He made constant threats against me. He would say, 'I should have killed you when I had the chance.' I heard that all the time."

Sparks spoke of how relieved she was not to have Kronk in her life anymore. She told Smith that it had been years since she had heard from him when, out of the blue, a week before Thanksgiving, her son Brandon got a call from Kronk.

She said, "Roy said to him, 'Guess what? You'll see me on the news. I'm going to be a hero. I know where the little girl in Florida who's missing is. I'm going to go get her.'

"Brandon called me, and he repeated what Roy said, that he was going to get the body when the water went down." (Smith also interviewed the son, Brandon Sparks, who corroborated the testimony of his mother.)

According to Crystal Sparks, Kronk told his parents the same thing at the same time. This was in November 2008.

Sparks spoke at length about Kronk's proclivity for fantasy.

"Roy liked to fantasize," she said. "His world is a fantasy world. Make-believe. He loved Dungeons & Dragons. He would act out like he was the king. Roy was fascinated with the pretend. If he could inject himself into another world, and be that person, that was Roy. He believed in black magic, in wizards, fantasy, fairy tales, demons, vampires—that was his world."

"Is he a person who can be believed?" Crystal Sparks was asked.

"No. Absolutely not," she said. "I have to say that. Roy says so many untruths, and when he does tell the truth, you still don't believe him. Because everything in his head is made up. It's like a walking book, and he wants to make things up as he goes. The story you hear today will grow tomorrow. And he was known for that."

My faith that Crystal Sparks was telling the truth was bolstered when, during the second deposition on July 30, 2010, Kronk testified to something he had never said before. He said that at one point he stuck his meter reader stick into the eye socket of Caylee's skull and lifted it up. It came from out of the blue and when we heard him say that, our jaws dropped to the floor. This was after three 9-1-1 calls where he said he never touched anything, two statements on December 11, 2008, the follow-up December 17 "massage session" statement, two more statements on January 6, 2009, an eight-hour deposition on November 19, 2009. Almost two years after finding Caylee's body, he says he lifted her skull with a stick. This was exactly what his ex-wife meant when she said, "Roy's story would grow and grow and grow."

Kronk's propensity to exaggerate and to lie was, of course, relevant to our case. We wanted to show that his story couldn't be trusted, and that there was a very good chance that the crime scene was "staged," meaning that it had been interfered with by Kronk, and possibly others.

But Kronk was more than a liar. If the testimony could be believed, Kronk had a violent streak. Allegedly he was obsessed with duct tape, and there was even testimony that implied he had an interest in young girls. Now, ultimately, I never believed that Kronk had anything to do with Caylee's death. But I didn't tell the prosecution that. As you will see, the prosecution did everything they could to make it difficult for me to do my job. If I sent them down a few blind alleys, it was okay with me.

CHAPTER 12

A STAGED CRIME SCENE

I WAS SURE THAT THE KRONK SCENARIO would give us solid ground around which to build a defense. We started to investigate Kronk, listened to his 9-1-1 tapes, and read all his statements. I found it telling the way law enforcement handled the information. I said to myself, *They're going to try to sweep this under the rug and find a fall guy. We have to follow them and exploit that.* And that was exactly what they ended up doing.

The fall guy was Deputy Richard Cain. They made a decision that Kronk was going to be their prized pony, and they were going to ride him to the finish line.

On August 13, when Cain finally arrived at the scene, it's very likely that Kronk didn't show Cain the bag and Caylee's skull. Instead, it was a ruse.

I firmly believe that Cain was telling the truth.

The problem for Cain was that the prosecution's case depended on the veracity of Kronk. If Cain was telling the truth, by definition Kronk wasn't, and that presented a dilemma for the police and prosecution.

The issue of who was telling the truth, Kronk or Cain, came to the forefront on December 11, four months after Kronk first called the police in August, when Kronk again called to say he had found Caylee's remains.

When this four-month gap became public knowledge, the police department really looked incompetent. (That assumes there was a body to be found by Cain in August and that Kronk wasn't hiding it, which was possible.)

Unable to keep hidden the information about Kronk's August 9-1-1 calls, the sheriff's department must have felt it had no choice but to throw Cain under the proverbial bus.

Kronk informed them about the three prior August 9-1-1 calls on December 17, 2008, and the police brass now had a major problem. Kronk had been caught in a serious omission. What everyone wanted to know after the media got hold of the story was, *Why wasn't Caylee's body found when he called in August?*

They took Kronk's statement, but now they realized what they had to do if they wanted Kronk's story to stand up: Cain had to be the fall guy.

To verify whether Kronk was telling the truth, you would think that the police would have investigated Kronk's background. You would also think the first person they would want to talk to would be Cain, who came out to the area when Kronk called. You would think their first question to Cain would have been, "What happened? What did Roy Kronk say?" But they can't do that because they had already arrested their culprit—Casey—and charged her with first-degree murder.

Instead of investigating Kronk, they decided, *Let's investigate Cain.*

On December 17, they launched an investigation in which they questioned everyone *except* Cain.

After the cops talked to Kronk at his home in St. Cloud, Florida, for about an hour that evening, they were shitting in their pants. A few hours later they called in Officer Adriana Acevedo and asked her about Kronk's call back in August.

If you listen to the audio of the interview, you can hear how confrontational Allen was with her. All Acevedo did was respond to a call that night, and she told Sgt. Allen it was really too dark to see much. From listening to the interview, it's clear how unhappy Allen was, because he was getting aggressive in his questioning.

After talking to Acevedo, they interviewed Kethlin Cutcher, the officer who arrived with Cain on August 13 to meet Kronk. To repeat, they were *not* calling Cain. They talked to everyone else so they would have the facts and possible inconsistencies that they could use to attack Cain, no matter what statement he decided to make. It's something defense lawyers do before we cross-examine a witness. You interview all the other witnesses and get the facts so that you can arm yourself with questions and effectively confront and cross-examine the witness.

Cutcher was interviewed just after midnight on December 18, 2008, and then at 9:00 A.M. they called in Cain. It was clear to me that rather than go to Cain to find out if Kronk was lying that, they were questioning Cain for the express purpose of catching him in a lie.

Apparently, that was their plan: to catch Cain in a lie and set him up as the fall guy in order to sweep the major screwup in this investigation under the rug.

Detective Yuri Melich and Allen called Cain in for an interview, and as soon as he walked in the door, Allen became confrontational with Cain. He asked him, "Do you know who Deputy Rusciano is?"

"I know of him," said Cain. "I don't know him personally. I know him because he was fired."

They weren't being recorded—this was another of their pre-interviews, where they got their point across without being taped—and according to Cain, Allen began yelling at him, telling him he could end up like Rusciano.

Rusciano had had the bad luck to have dated and to have had a sexual relationship with Casey Anthony *before* any of this happened. When asked about their relationship, Rusciano, who was married and didn't want their tryst made public, told investigators it was a casual relationship and that he barely knew her. The investigators then impounded Casey's computer, found out that he knew her well and had been intimate with her, and fired him.

Beginning around nine in the morning, they turned on the tape recorder, and Cain told them what happened that day in August. He stated unequivocally that when he went to the scene after Kronk called 9-1-1, he did nothing wrong. He told them that he and Kronk walked together into the woods, and Kronk was standing right behind. Kronk showed him a bag that he described as "pretty heavy." Cain testified that he lifted up the bag with his baton, and that when the bag tore, leaves and sticks came spilling out. He said that he inspected the debris closely, that he didn't see a skull, and that he found the trip to be much ado about nothing at all.

It wasn't what the brass wanted to hear, and Allen, becoming frustrated, said, "Let me close the door a minute." After closing the door, he said to Cain, "You understand what we're doing here, right?"

"Yes, I do."

"And you understand the importance of telling the truth?"

"Yes, I do."

"You understand the importance of telling the whole truth, right?"

What Allen was really saying to Cain was, "Hey, you're not playing ball. Your story doesn't match Roy Kronk's story. And the cops who don't play ball, wink, wink, they get fired."

"Yes," said Cain, who naively had no idea his superiors were setting him up to get rid of him.

So Cain went to work, and he had some time to think about what Allen was saying to him: *Hey man, your statements have really fucked up the "Case of the Century" for this department.* Surely Cain said to himself, *If I don't change my story, I'm going to get fired like Deputy Rusciano.*

When Allen and Melich at three in the afternoon reinterviewed him, Cain did a complete one-eighty. Allen's warning probably was sufficient in and of itself, but it wouldn't surprise me if someone high up the ladder got to him during those six hours and told him, "Listen, you're going to need to play ball and go back and tell them the truth." Meaning, lie.

And that's what Cain did. In the second interview, Melich said to Cain, "It's been a couple hours, and I know that during that time you've had some chance to think about the call [from Kronk], and think about what actually happened. And I understand from the onset what you originally told us, it differs a little bit from what you told us now because you've had a little bit of time to think about it, correct?"

"Yes, yes," Cain said, and then this time he proceeded to say that he never saw a bag, and that Kronk stayed near the street and never went with him into the woods. He also said he might not have searched the exact area that Kronk had pointed out. All this so as not to contradict their star witness, Roy Kronk.

Allen said to Cain, "Earlier you indicated that you picked the bag up with your baton and sticks fell out, right?"

Cain said, "Right."

Then Allen said, "Okay, did that happen?"

Then Cain said, "I don't believe it was a bag. It was probably just... yard waste."

Allen asked him again, "Did you pick a bag up?"

Cain answered, "Not a bag," and then sighed, which I was sure was Cain saying to himself, *There goes my career.*

"Did you pick anything up?" asked Allen.

"Just yard waste," said Cain.

Allen, who was angry about the whole Kronk situation because there wasn't much he could do to salvage it, aggressively pursued the line of questioning and got Cain to admit it might have been a piece of a trash bag.

"It wasn't a whole sack," Cain said.

Allen asked, "Did it look like a garbage bag?"

"It wasn't a full-sized bag," said Cain, sounding uncomfortable.

Allen then said, "All right, name three other things it could have been besides a bag?"

Cain said, "It could have been a piece of dark clothing. It could have been, I don't know, a shirt. I don't know. It could have been a piece of something out of their yard. I don't know."

Allen asked him, "You never said to him, I don't see a bag in here. Show me what you're talking about?"

"No."

"Would that have been a reasonable thing to do?"

"Probably."

"What other ways to handle that call might have been reasonable?"

"Maybe ask him to go find it," said Cain.

"Okay. Did you do any of those things?"

"No."

Allen asked, "What do you think was going through your mind when you went back there, and this guy was describing there was a bag there, and you didn't see it? Did you say something to him about there's no bag there?"

"I thought maybe he saw something he didn't see," said Cain, still ignorant that his career was about to come crashing to an ignominious end.

After the second interview, Internal Affairs immediately launched an investigation of Cain to determine whether he lied under oath. They called a slew of witnesses, including the first responders, anyone Cain worked with, and Allen and Melich, and even though Allen and Melich both claimed they weren't hostile toward Cain, Cain said they were.

Cain *was* fired for lying. But, I believe he was set up for it. He appealed his dismissal, but before the appeal was heard, he resigned. He moved far away. He left Orlando and moved to Pennsylvania. We were able to take

his deposition before he left, but the internal investigation was still pend-
ing, so he was unable to answer the questions we most wanted answered.

Cain left in shame, sacrificed for the honor of the state's star witness,
fabulist Roy Kronk.

I later sent one of my investigators to find Cain, but he didn't want to
come back to Florida and testify. The poor guy just wanted to put it all
behind him and move on with his life, and I can't say that I blame him. I
would have loved for him to come forward and be brave enough to stand
up and own up to the truth.

I wanted to question him severely about his actions. I wanted to ask
him who he had spoken with between 9:00 a.m. and 3:00 p.m. I wanted
to ask him, "Did you feel pressured to tell your story?" And I wanted
to know, "Which of your stories is the truth, the morning story or the
afternoon story? Or is there an altogether different story?"

There was a time when Cain returned our calls, but we couldn't get
him to come to Florida to testify. We knew he wasn't cooperative, so we
elected not to bother calling him as a witness. Since the prosecution
didn't call Kronk during the trial, it also decided not to call Cain.

Instead *we* called Kronk, and when Cain didn't testify, the jury had
to wonder whether the prosecution was hiding something. The jurors
had to be wondering, *Where's the cop who showed up that day? What's the
prosecution hiding?*

They had to be thinking, *This is hardly a search for the truth.*

In any murder investigation, examination of the body is essential evidence. If the body is found as it was left by the murderer, then the position and condition of the body can be very revealing. If the body has
been tampered with then it's a staged crime scene, and one should be a
lot more cautious about drawing conclusions from the state of the body.

In the Casey Anthony case, the prosecution would contend that
there was duct tape wrapped around Caylee's mouth, and that Caylee's
mandible (the lower jaw) was found in the perfect anatomical position, meaning that the duct tape held the mandible in place. But if the
skull had rolled out of the bag, the duct tape would not necessarily
have remained where it was originally placed, and the mandible would

not have been in perfect anatomical position as it was found. This would have destroyed the integrity of the crime scene. The prosecution was intent on demonstrating that the cause of death was the duct tape, and that there was evidence that the duct tape had been wrapped around Caylee's face. But as we will see, the evidence did not show this at all. And if you allow for the fact that the body had likely been moved, it didn't show a thing.

After looking at all the inconsistencies, and even though there were still a lot of questions that remained unanswered, one thing was clear: we couldn't trust Kronk. What I eventually was able to convey to the jury and make absolutely clear was that we weren't accusing him of being Caylee's murderer, or being involved in her death in any way. What we wanted to convey was that because of Kronk's activities, the crime scene was so compromised that it couldn't be trusted. Because of the moving of the skull, the moving of the duct tape (the duct tape was stuck to some hair, but was otherwise loose, not wrapped around the skull as implied by the prosecution), and the different stories concerning the skull rolling, and Kronk's picking up the skull with his meter reader stick, we told the jurors that the clear conclusion was that this was a staged crime scene, and that they couldn't trust any evidence that came from Suburban Drive. In other words, if you can't trust the messenger, you can't trust the message.

This is the point of the whole Kronk saga. I needed to show that it was possible—actually quite likely—that Kronk had interfered with the body. And there was a great deal of evidence supporting me in this. The police and prosecutors needed to discount my evidence, even if it meant throwing Cain under the bus to do so.

But the weaknesses in Kronk's story were not the only indicators that Caylee's body had very likely been moved. The specific area where Caylee's body was ultimately found had been searched at least five times between August and December, but no one found a body.

On October 21, 2008, Keith Williams, an Orlando trailer park security guard, was found in the woods off Suburban Drive with a shovel in his hand. He was seen by the assistant principal of the nearby Hidden Oaks Elementary School, who asked the police to issue Williams a trespass warning. When we talked about Williams, we joked that the police attitude was, "Get out of here, kid. You might find Caylee."

When the police questioned him, Williams told them that he knew Casey because Casey used to play with his younger sister when they were kids. He said he was someone who was following the case on TV, that he had a lady friend who worked with him by the name of Charlie, and Charlie told him that her mom, who lived in Texas, was a psychic. Williams said he called the woman, who told him that Caylee had drowned and that she was buried in the woods not far from the road near the school. I don't believe in psychics, but I have to admit it's quite a coincidence. He said he had searched in the woods in the exact area where Caylee's body was later found, but all he could find was a bag of stuffed animals, which he took to the Anthony home. When told by Cindy that the toys didn't belong to Caylee, Williams said he went and threw the bag back into the woods.

We later found out while investigating Suburban Drive that in October a woman and her neighbor had called 9-1-1 after they heard a child screaming from the wooded area near the elementary school. The call was made to the Orlando Police Department, not the Orange County Sheriff's Department, and a massive search was undertaken in the exact area where Caylee's remains later were found. A helicopter flew over the area, they brought in dogs, and performed an exhaustive search. No child was found, but after searching the records of the Orlando Police Department, we could verify that the site where Caylee was found was the area where they searched for the child who allegedly was screaming in the woods.

Two intensive searches in that area also were undertaken by Tim Miller and his EquuSearch team, one in September 2008 and one during the weekend of November 8, 2008. Records show the searchers tramped all over the area around Suburban Drive, but nothing turned up during either search.

In addition, Laura Buchanan, an EquuSearch volunteer from Kentucky, had given us an affidavit saying she too had searched that area, but there was no body there.

And finally, there's the saga of Jim Hoover and Dominic Casey, bodyguards for the Anthonys. During our visit to the Anthony home in December after Caylee was found, that evening we brought our forensic team over to take soil samples and to do some tests, Dominic revealed that he and his sidekick Hoover had searched the exact area where

Caylee's body had been found a few days earlier. We would later discover that they had videotaped their traipse through the woods, because Hoover attempted to sell the film for $50,000 to any national news media that would pay him. When I interviewed Hoover, he told me the following:

On November 14, Dominic had asked Hoover to come into his office and take a seat. When Hoover sits down Dominic tells him, "I know where Caylee is." Dominic doesn't say anything further, and Hoover thinks, *Well, fine, let's go get her.* Then Dominic adds, "She's dead." Dominic tells Hoover that he got a tip revealing the location of the body.

They went to the woods on Suburban Drive to find her. Hoover said that Dominic brought a small garden tool with him for the purpose of digging up her body. Once they were in the woods Dominic told him they were looking for three flat pavers in the woods and a large black trash bag. He said Dominic had gone into the woods earlier and had already removed three wooden two-by-fours, which, he said, the pavers were under. Hoover said that Dominic was intermittently talking to someone on his cell phone during the time they were in the woods. He said Dominic talked to the person on the other end of the phone about six times. He said they found a dirty blanket with a rose on it under the pavers, but no Caylee.

From his testimony, it was clear to me that Hoover and Dominic had looked for the burial site, but Caylee was nowhere to be found.

So that's at least five searches of the area where Caylee was ultimately found. The prosecution had its own theory. It was determined to prove that the body hadn't been found by these other searchers because heavy rain had flooded the area, thereby keeping her hidden. The prosecution was hot on proving this because it was afraid we were going to parade all these people before the jury and tell them about the fruitless searches in the general area where Caylee's body had been found by Kronk.

To this end the prosecution hired a hydrologist from the University of Florida to run tests about the water levels in the area. He did a really sophisticated study to calculate the rainfall and to measure the amount of rain. Unfortunately for the state, his conclusion was that in the area where Caylee's remains were found, it was wet only ten days during those six months, and it wasn't during the critical period when the searchers had been out there.

This was significant evidence that multiple searchers had looked in the area where Caylee was found on December 11, but had failed to find her. This was making the prosecution very nervous, and when these prosecutors became nervous, there was no telling what they would do.

They went after Laura Buchanan, accusing her of presenting false evidence in a capital case. Of course, they leaked what they were doing to the media. They conducted controlled phone calls, in which people would call her and have her talk about what she did. They also had a fellow searcher call her and say, "You know, if you tell the cops that someone from the defense put you up to this, or told you a lie, they will probably leave you alone."

I was lucky. Buchanan, like Pamela Porter, was a stand-up woman. Her response was, "I know I could do that, but I'm telling the truth." If she hadn't said that, they would have come after me.

Her lawyer, Bernard Cassidy, called me on the phone and said, "Sergeant [John]Allen called me and told me they were going to charge Laura with a life felony unless she gave you up." Meaning they wanted her to testify that I had put her up to her testimony. If she didn't, he said, she was told she would be looking at life in prison.

I was livid. It appeared they were so desperate that they were going to charge this woman and then use her to take me out. I planned on using this at trial, so I listed Cassidy as a witness. This is certainly one of those moments where you ask yourself, *Is the fight worth the effort? Would I go to jail for Casey? I had a wife and child and a practice, everything I needed. Why should I risk it for someone I don't know?* These are the risks that defense lawyers take every day across this country, as long as prosecutors and law enforcement are allowed to investigate defense lawyers who they have cases against.

As Albert Krieger, a great defense lawyer, says, "A defense lawyer is literally in harm's way. If you ignore this and do not have your guard up, you are skydiving without a parachute." My family will tell you that I was stupid for not getting out. But I had meant it when I took that oath to be a lawyer. I thought I was being brave. Maybe I was a little of both.

And here's the funny part. After the trial was over and the prosecution had lost, the police held a press conference. I've never seen prosecutors and cops hold a press conference after losing a trial. They were trying to save face and one of the statements they made was, "There is still an ongoing investigation." Meaning they were still investigating Buchanan. Their actions were so disgraceful, but apparently they wanted their pound of flesh.

LET ME TELL YOU what we found later on: The police and prosecution had taken complete control of the area and then destroyed it before we had our chance to look at it. All we had to go on were the hundreds of photos the police had taken of the site. When Dr. Henry Lee came down in late December, after our failure to get access to the crime scene, he started looking at the crime scene photographs. When Lee began studying the photos and saw the large tree at the site, the tree that was removed before we were allowed to visit, the first thing he said was, "That tree that's fallen there was used to hide the body."

A group of us were seated around my conference table in my office, and when he said that, we all got up to take a look. That made complete and perfect sense; if you want to hide a bag containing a body, you either bury it or put it underneath something. There was something else we found interesting about that tree: it was apparent in some of the crime scene photos, but it was missing in others. We later learned that the photographer had it moved in order to take better pictures of Caylee's remains.

We learned from a report written by one of the crime scene investigators that Stephen Hanson, who worked for the medical examiner, and another crime scene person picked up the tree and moved it. In other words, the person who hid Caylee under that tree had to be pretty strong to lift it up in order to place the bag and body under it. Did anyone think 105-pound Casey had the strength to be able to do that?

I spent a full week, eight hours a day, looking at each and every one of those photos. I sat in my office with my door closed, flicking back and forth from photo to photo. It's grunt work, but very important work because the crime scene photos are the first images. They can tell you a great deal about the crime scene. And one of the things I noticed was the lack of the white board that Kronk had described in his 9-1-1 call. It had apparently disappeared, as though it was never there. In my opinion, the purpose of that white board was to be an X marking the spot. I don't know who put the white board there and I don't know who removed it. Even today I don't know for sure whether someone put it there with the intention of using it to help relocate the bag and the body at a later date, or whether it had been placed there by whoever put the body there.

FROM THE VERY BEGINNING the police decided that Casey Anthony was guilty and decided to only focus on evidence that supported this theory. They arrested her prematurely, as I noted earlier, and decided to collect the evidence later. This is not the way to run an investigation. The police work was sloppy throughout.

When Kronk reported finding a body on Suburban Drive, Melich would later say that that area had been searched, but that wasn't so. The EquuSearch people didn't begin searching until September, so there's no way EquuSearch could have searched that area. Chalk that up to more brilliant detective work by Melich.

Yet Melich, to my knowledge, never caught any flak for sloppy police work. He was always portrayed as being thorough. In fact, before we went to trial, he was nominated for detective of the year by *America's Most Wanted*. That was just and appropriate, if you think about it, because reality shows are about personalities, fame, and show business, not being a good detective. Deputy Richard Cain would take the fall, but nobody gave any shit to Melich for ignoring Kronk's tip in August.

Later I would ask for all the paperwork of all the searches by law enforcement around Suburban Drive prior to Kronk's trip. They gave us nothing, claiming they never searched there. But here was White saying, "That area has been searched."

This could have meant one of two things: the police searched there and hid the search records, and all the evidence from the defense, because they didn't want us to be able to claim, "You searched the area, and the body wasn't there. Casey was locked up in jail, and therefore she couldn't have done it."

In fact, we did argue that very thing for a long time.

Choice number two: the police were totally incompetent. No reports of searches exist. Why? I want to know why. Why wouldn't you search the closest wooded area to the Anthony house? For any police department, that would have been the *first place* to look. For one thing Kiomarie Cruz, who had claimed to be a close childhood friend of Casey's, said that's where they played as kids, and where Casey would eerily bury her dead pets.

I still have a hard time believing the police didn't search the area, but maybe they didn't. Everything at trial is open to interpretation, so here's my interpretation: they were grossly incompetent, they were lying, or, something more sinister than lying, they destroyed records, *and* covered it up.

Despite all of Kronk's crazy stories and his inconsistencies, and his love of duct tape, the police never thoroughly investigated him. To my knowledge, they never pulled his phone records to see if he had any contact with the Anthonys. He could have known Casey, or George, or Cindy. But they didn't do that.

They could have confiscated his computer. Who knows, maybe it might have led to maps he had of the woods, or maybe he had shopped for something incriminating. Or there might have been things he had researched or searched for on his computer. But they didn't do that, either.

They could have taken his DNA when it was discovered later that there was foreign DNA on the duct tape. But they didn't do that.

They didn't take his hair samples, which would have come in play when later on an unidentified male hair was found near Caylee's skull. But they didn't do that. Nor did they take his fingerprints.

One can only speculate why they didn't do any of this. Perhaps, if they had done any of this and found Kronk to be involved, it would have ruined their case. Kronk muddied the waters something awful, yet the police left him alone. They didn't open any unmarked doors. Was it because they were afraid of what they might find?

The police didn't interview Kronk's ex-wives. We did that.

I don't chalk that up to incompetence. No, to me it looked like a deliberate effort to keep the truth at bay, or hide it.

What's even more shocking: the prosecution never called Kronk to the witness stand during the trial. We had to call him.

You would think the first witness—if not the key witness—for the prosecution would be the guy who found the body. The prosecutors never called him, because they knew we'd destroy him on cross-examination. We called him and interrogated him using direct examination, which isn't nearly as powerful a tool.

Another thing that shocked me was that it wasn't until the prosecution's closing argument that Jeff Ashton finally admitted that the prosecution didn't believe Kronk.

Unfortunately, it came after I had closed my case and sat down. If I had had the opportunity, I would have stood and said, "When you're asking for the death penalty, it takes a lot of nerve to show the jury a crime scene and evidence from that crime scene when the person who gave it to you is, in your own opinion, dishonest."

To me, the prosecutors are supposed to be ministers of the truth and justice. I won't say it was prosecutorial misconduct, but it was certainly deliberate on their part not to call him. I'm sure their response would be, "We didn't call him because we didn't believe him, but we don't believe the scene was staged or anything like that, so we presented everything in good faith."

I have a different point of view. To me, what they did was scandalous.

CHAPTER 13

THE ANTHONY
FAMILY SECRETS

O N JANUARY 22, 2009, I started getting a series of text messages from George Anthony. The texts were saying in effect, "I'm sorry. Please tell Casey I love her." These were obvious, "I'm checking out" kinds of messages. Clearly George was intending to kill himself. Frantically, I called his cell phone several times, but kept getting his voice mail.

He then left me a voice message. He didn't admit anything, but he wanted me to apologize to Casey for him.

I couldn't understand what he was trying to tell me.

Apologize for what? I wondered.

I kept calling him and calling him to no avail. Later that day I got a call from Cindy that George had driven to Daytona Beach, Florida, rented a room at the Hawaii Motel, and swallowed enough pills to kill himself. An alarmed Brad Conway, the Anthonys' third lawyer, called Sergeant John Allen, and through George's cell phone pings, the police found him in his motel room. He was taken into custody under the Baker Act, and the rescue squad rushed him to the Halifax Medical Center in Daytona Beach. He was held there for a couple of days before being evaluated and released.

I wondered, *Why did George Anthony try to kill himself?*

There was always something hard to understand about George's behavior. Nine days after Caylee's disappearance, George called the police. Not to report Caylee missing. Rather, he called to report the theft of gas cans from his garage. George knew that Casey also used these cans, so their disappearance wasn't exactly a major mystery. So why did he report them missing? George had once been a cop and knew reporting stolen gas cans to the police wouldn't amount to anything. There was no Gas Can Task Force to solve that crime. He knew all that would happen was that police would come, take a report, and that would be the end of it. No detective would be assigned to the case. I would later ask the jury, "Who in the world would report twenty-year-old gas cans missing?" And if you like coincidences, the officer who responded to the call was none other than Deputy Richard Cain.

George's suicide attempt was very upsetting. I had loved George. I had thought him to be a phenomenal guy. I even bought him a birthday card and wrote some really kind things about how much I respected him as a father and as a man. And I don't usually buy anyone a birthday card. It's just not me.

But I never gave it to him. Something held me back—maybe it was the day I had mentioned sexual abuse in the living room and the place went silent. Or maybe it was the business with the gas cans. Or possibly it was because of my staff's research on George, which had started to reveal some character issues.

George had grown up in Warren, Ohio; when he was a young adult, he joined the Trumbull County Sheriff's Office as a deputy. He was an officer for approximately ten years, working mainly in auto theft, narcotics, and homicide. Then suddenly, he resigned.

Cindy said the reason was that after Lee was born, she persuaded him to quit because the job was too dangerous. But I had also heard from one of the Anthonys that he quit because he was involved in a car accident in which two people were killed. My investigator, Mort Smith, interviewed a survivor in the crash, and apparently George was responding to a call when he went through a red light and crashed into another vehicle. Two passengers in the other car died.

I've never heard of a cop simply quitting after ten years, especially to become a car salesman. We wanted to find out if perhaps he had been fired, but unfortunately the building that housed the records had burned down, and all the records were destroyed. The police chief had gone to the academy with George and was a friend, so we got nowhere talking to him.

George was married to another woman before he was married to Cindy. We interviewed her. She told Smith that George was nothing short of a pathological liar. She said, "George couldn't tell the truth to save his life." She said he was a compulsive liar. I had only heard those words used to describe one other person—Casey.

After leaving the department, George went to work for his father in the car sales business, which apparently didn't go too well. George was married to Cindy by this time, and Cindy's brother, Rick Plesea, said that George got into a huge argument with his father and threw him through a plate-glass window. After that George took out a second mortgage on their home and went into car sales on his own. He opened Anthony Auto Sales, but the business went under, and George and Cindy lost their home. In 1989, when Casey was three, they relocated to Orlando, where Cindy's parents had moved. From then on George bounced around from job to job.

"George was collecting unemployment and worker's comp," she said. "George could have worked. He didn't work because he didn't want to work."

George had worked in distribution and as a security guard for the *Orlando Sentinel*. He had also worked as a fumigator, and then he worked in security as a guard. That's what he was doing when we met him. He was working the 3:00 P.M. to 11:00 P.M. shift.

George, Cindy, and Casey arrived at the home of Cindy's brother, Rick, the day before his wedding. Rick was surprised to see Casey was obviously pregnant. In his sworn statement, he told police, "She had a tight-fitting top on and her stomach was protruding. Her belly button was sticking out at least a half inch."

Rick invited them all in. He hadn't seen the Anthonys in a long time, and he said to George and Cindy, "What's up with Casey? You got something to tell me? What's going on here?"

According to Rick, their response was, "What?"

"She's expecting?" he asked.

"They looked at me like I was crazy," Rick said.

Rick looked over at his wife, who rolled her eyes at their answer.

"Cindy," her brother said, "She looks like she's pregnant. Come on."

"Oh no," said Cindy, "she's not. She's just putting on weight."

"Cindy," said her brother. "I've seen a lot of pregnant girls. I'm not an expert, but man, she looks pregnant."

Everyone on his wife's side of the family wanted to know, "Who's the pregnant girl?"

Rick said he told Cindy that his mom and dad also thought she was pregnant.

Commented Rick, "Cindy's a nurse for crying out loud. She can't see it?" So he said to Cindy, "You're kidding me. Now tell me, is Casey pregnant?"

And Cindy, either in denial herself or lying, said to him, "Casey told us that she'd have to have sex first in order to have a baby and that she did not have sex with anyone."

Thought Rick, *If that's not a baby, it's a tumor, and she only has a short time to live because it's big.* It was June, and she was more than seven months pregnant.

In an email to Cindy, Rick wrote, "You guys will go down in history as the stupidest parents in the universe."

Someone was keeping secrets. I knew I was on to something.

Every time I would see Casey in jail, she would be happier than a pig in shit. She was almost ecstatic to be there, and for a long time I couldn't understand why. When you go see a client in jail, they may be happy to see you, but inevitably the client is angry to be in there. But unlike all my other clients, Casey was happy in jail because she had structure and she was safe. A couple times she even said to me, "I feel safer in here than I do out there," and I thought to myself, *That's a weird thing to say.* She even said it to her parents during one of their early visitations. I also picked up on it when she told Detective Yuri Melich the first night the police were called that she had gone to her boyfriend's house because she felt "safe." At the time I asked myself, *What does that mean?*

The prosecution made a big deal of the fact that there were searches on her computer for chloroform and neck breaking, but they were among a slew of searches on topics like self-defense for women and how to use household items as weapons for self-defense. These searches were indicating someone who didn't feel safe at home. The neck breaking search had to do with the art of kung fu, used for self-defense.

I was asking myself, *These searches indicate someone who doesn't feel safe at home. Why is she so afraid of being home? Why does she feel safe somewhere else? Why does she feel safe in jail? Why is she making these searches?*

Another interesting thing I learned: once Caylee was born, both Lee and George moved out of the house.

Lee moved out, I was told, because one more person in the house was too much for him. That was also around the time George and Cindy separated. I would later hear that George left at the insistence of Casey. Eventually George worked his way back home, but that was one more event I found suspicious. *Why was the man being kicked out of his own home? Why were Lee and George moving out?*

THE MYSTERIES WERE PILING UP. Why did George attempt suicide? Why was he apologizing to Casey? Why did he report the gas cans missing? How did he know to bring a gas can to pick up Casey's car at Johnson's Wrecker Service? Why did Casey feel unsafe at home and safer in jail? Why did Casey leave every day for two years to an imaginary workplace, taking Caylee to an imaginary nanny? Why did Lee and George leave when Caylee was born? Why was the family in denial about Casey's pregnancy?

Eventually, the answers began to come together.

We received some shocking information from Jesse Grund, one of Casey's former boyfriends. Jesse was Casey's fiancé at the time Caylee was born. He was around the Anthony family a lot and noticed that after Caylee was born, Casey was careful never to leave Caylee alone with Lee.

Jesse asked her point-blank what the deal was with Lee.

Casey told Jesse that when she was a teenager, Lee would touch her inappropriately. She said she didn't want him doing that to Caylee. We began to wonder if Lee was actually Caylee's father.

Casey's critics in the public and in the media have said she made up these charges to get herself acquitted of murder charges, but nothing could be further from the truth. This was no recent fabrication. The conversation with Jesse took place *two-and-a-half years before* Casey was charged with murder. These allegations were made *long before* anything ever happened to Caylee. Casey had also told her most recent boyfriend, Tony Lazzaro, about Lee fondling her as a teen.

There was further testimonial evidence of the sexual abuse. Casey had befriended one of the inmates at the Orange County Jail, and the two had exchanged letters. In one of those letters, Casey had stated that

Lee had abused her and that she was starting to feel her father had abused her too. The inmate had kept the letters and given them to prosecutors in the hopes of getting a reduced sentence for herself. We were able to read the letters through discovery.

I became even more suspicious because when the FBI asked Lee about the incest with his sister, the FBI said his response was, "We'll talk about it when the time is right." (Why the FBI accepted this answer without following up, I don't understand.) If true, I could not believe this response. It was a tacit admission in my opinion. I don't know a brother in the world who would give an answer like that unless the charge was true, and that's why I started my discussion about Lee with Casey. I had learned that Casey had told Jesse about Lee abusing her. I figured if she could tell Jesse, maybe she'd feel comfortable enough to tell me about it. I figured it may have been too soon to ask her about her father, but perhaps she'd tell me about Lee.

"Casey," I said, "I understand Lee sexually abused you."

Hesitantly, she began to talk about it, saying that Lee had fondled her, touched her, felt her up.

But Casey had stayed away from home for thirty days because she feared someone at home, and Lee didn't live at home. There had to be more to it. I didn't think the abuser was Cindy. I had seen her in interactions with Cindy, and I didn't feel that Casey feared Cindy.

"Where do you think Lee learned it from?" I asked her.

"Well, what do you think?" she said sharply.

I said to her, "Tell me about the first time your father touched you."

She slouched in her chair.

"I don't want to talk about it," Casey said. She was embarrassed. What girl was ever comfortable talking about having sex with her father?

"Listen, all of our experiences in life make us who we are today," I said. "I am who I am because of my past mistakes, my past life, the way people treated me." I told her about some of the things that happened to me, including my long quest to become a lawyer.

"I'm a persistent person," I said, "and I'm the type of person who doesn't give up, because that's what life taught me. And I can tell you're the same, that you're a fighter.

"You have to confront your demons. You have to confront what's there."

"He touched me," Casey began, "and then it went a little bit further than touching."

That was the first conversation. A little bit came out at a time. Slowly she would tell me more and more, how it first started with inappropriate touching when she was eight years old, then he made her touch his penis, and then he made her jerk him off. She said he even named his penis "Baldy" and used to tell her to play a game called "pet the bald-headed mouse."

"Pet it until it sneezes milk," he would say to his eight-year-old daughter.

When she was eight, Casey said, her father started having intercourse with her, three or four times a week, until she was twelve. I assume he stopped the habitual abuse at that age because she had gotten her period and he was afraid of getting her pregnant.

I began to loathe George, but I couldn't let my emotions get the better of me. I didn't want to push Casey too much or ask her too much, as I wanted the mental health professionals to get an unfiltered version. I knew all I needed to know. From that day on, the entire defense team called George "Baldy," a constant reminder of the child molester and rapist we *believed* him to be.

During the summer of 2009, the defense team had a retreat off Cape Cod in Massachusetts, and to the amazement of all, our computer expert found the pictures taken on the day Caylee was born. Casey delivered Caylee by natural childbirth at the hospital, and standing right there on the receiving end, as the baby was coming out, was none other than her father, George. We all thought it was disgusting. I have a daughter who's an adult and I would never consider putting her in that situation. Tell me, how many women have their fathers attend the birth of their children?

Now we wondered, *was George Anthony Caylee's father?* Casey had said that Caylee's father had been a man by the name of Eric Baker, but I never believed that. Her story was that Baker, whom she said was married and had a son, came over for a one-night stand, got her pregnant, and then went back with his wife. She said he and Casey agreed he would not be part of Caylee's life. Then conveniently, Baker tragically died in an automobile accident.

The cops verified that a kid named Eric Baker did die in a car accident, but no one who knew Casey knew who he was. No Eric Baker had been part of Casey's life that anyone could recall, so I never bought that story. If I couldn't verify the story, I didn't believe her. I was convinced that Baker, like Zanny the nanny, was another of Casey's many imaginary friends.

As we looked at the birth pictures, we could see that everyone was happy and smiling about the new addition to the Anthony family—everyone but George, that is. That's when Smith, our investigator, quipped, "Look at George. He's pissed off. It's like he's saying, 'Goddammit, I'm my own son-in-law and I don't even like him.'"

We all laughed, even though it wasn't at all funny.

CASEY'S ALLEGATION of sexual abuse at the hands of her father wasn't out of the blue. It actually explained a great deal. It was the reason Casey left the house every day for two years, letting her parents think she was working at Universal Studios when in fact she was unemployed. She didn't want to leave Caylee alone with George. She said she feared that George would molest her daughter, as he had molested her. Recall that at this time George was working the 3:00 P.M. to 11:00 P.M. shift.

It explained why the family was in denial about Casey's pregnancy. It explained why George and Lee left the home after Caylee's birth.

After Caylee was found, law enforcement took DNA samples from the entire Anthony family, but they delayed giving us the results. We had to file a motion to get them, and Judge Stan Strickland gave the prosecutors twenty days to comply. It was right around the twentieth day that George made his suicide attempt. I thought, *he must have tried to commit suicide because he feared the test would prove that he's Caylee's father.*

Casey had told a psychiatrist who interviewed her that George had had sex with her when she was eighteen, and she felt there was a good possibility he was the father. She also told the psychiatrist that she actually *told* George he was Caylee's father.

The DNA test came back after George's suicide attempt, and it turned out that neither George nor Lee was the father. But even if George wasn't the father, his suicide attempt in close proximity to the DNA test was proof enough for me that he had been having sex with Casey. But how would we be able to prove it? That would be our biggest challenge, especially given Casey's history for lying.

The incest would also explain why Casey had such a love/hate relationship with George. It would also explain so much of her behavior and her promiscuity. Like most victims of sexual abuse, Casey didn't know the sexual boundaries with men. I could see that with the men she was dating. It was all about sex. For the most part, the relationships were superficial; I didn't see any deep love for these individuals. I could have been wrong, but when she spoke of them, she didn't speak highly of them. It's as if they all reminded her of her father.

I had gotten to know Casey through two ways. One way was through talking to her in jail. I really thought very highly of her. I thought she was a kind and gentle person and just wasn't buying the murder accusations against her.

The other way was through discovery—reading the testimony of others.

I was reading what her parents were saying about her, what her boyfriends were saying, and what she was saying about Zenaida and her other imaginary friends, and I began to see classic signs that she was leading a double life, something victims of sexual abuse often do. They don't want to face their reality—it's far too painful—so sex abuse survivors learn to lie to cover up the truth. They also put on a facade in an effort to hide their pain and compartmentalize their feelings. And that's what I was seeing with Casey. We were truly in a "What came first, the chicken or the egg?" position. Was she lying about being abused or lying *because* she was abused?

Later, when we got the letters that Casey had written to inmate Robyn Adams, we got the judge to give us fifteen days before releasing them to the public. That is when co-counsel Cheney Mason and I decided this would be a good time to speak to George and confront him about the sexual abuse.

We were in Cheney's office. He was behind his desk, and George and I sat in chairs next to each other. We told George about the letters in which Casey wrote to another inmate whom she befriended about the abuse.

"Casey said she's been sexually abused by you, George," I said.

George sat there for perhaps forty seconds, his head bowed. He didn't say a word. We certainly noted that he didn't deny it. Cheney and I looked at each other in wonderment.

"Oh my God," is what George finally said. He slapped his leg with his hand and he asked, "What else did she say?"

After he left I said to Cheney, "Did you hear him deny the sexual abuse?"

"No," he said, "I didn't."

"I have a daughter who's an adult," I said, "and if anyone had ever accused me of having sex with her, I'd have gone nuts. I would have lost it. But this guy just sat there."

Several days later George wrote Casey a letter.

> Casey Marie,
> Where do I begin???
> Well, met with Jose & Cheney Mason on Wednesday March 24th.
> Jose in Cheney Mason's office delivered me disturbing news & ask me 2 heartbreaking questions?
> You know what 2 questions he asked, and I am <u>num</u> . . . . .
> Why, why also destroy Lee. . .
> Why, why also destroy Mom. . .
> Why, why also destroy me, your family. . .
> Why, why also destroy Caylee Marie. . .
> After all I have tried, sacrificed, continued to love you, my daughter, why???
> Continually coming to court, continually wanting to see you, why???

Read it and ask yourself: how would Casey know what the two secrets were unless the two of them shared those secrets? The two questions were, "Was Casey sexually abused?" and, "How did Caylee die?"

I hadn't told Casey I was going to confront George. She wouldn't have known what the two questions were—unless George knew the answers to both those questions.

Second, there was yet another nondenial from George. If he wasn't an abuser, he would have written, "What are you talking about, Casey? I never abused you. Why are you telling these lies?" He didn't do that, did he?

The rest of the letter is a total guilt trip to make it seem as if it was all her fault, which is another characteristic of a sexual abuser.

> Thursday
> March 25, 2010
>
> Casey Marie,
>
> Where do I begin ???
>
> Well, I met with Jose & Cheney Mason on
> Wednesday March 24th
> Jose in Cheney Mason's office delivered me
> disturbing news & ask me 2 heartbreaking
> questions?
> You know what 2 questions he asked,
> and I am numb.....
>
> Why, Why also destroy Lee...
>
> Why, Why also destroy Mom...
>
> Why, Why also destroy me, your family...
>
> Why, Why also destroy Caylee Marie...
>
> After all I have tried, sacrificed, continued
> to love you, my Daughter, Why ???
> Continually coming to court, continually
> wanting to see you, Why ???

Toward the end of the letter he writes about how gracious he had
been to show up in court to see Casey. He then writes of his continually wanting to see Casey. What a trooper he was, considering he had
refused to post her bail and help her out in any way financially.

But George never saw himself as the bad guy. Instead, as is common
with abusers, he saw himself as the victim of Casey's treachery.

And like most abusers, he also was a coward. After the letter was made public, George never again came to court to see Casey.

When the trial was over, George and Cindy gave an interview with Dr. Phil McGraw. McGraw asked George about the first time he heard that Casey was accusing him of sexually abusing her.

His answer was that he learned of it when he read the letters that were released in discovery. That was a lie. I guess he forgot about us confronting him and also forgot about the letter he wrote Casey. Even after the trial, George continues to lie and gets a pass every time.

CHAPTER 14

WHAT HAPPENED ON JUNE 16, 2008

(THE EVIDENCE NO ONE EVER TOLD YOU ABOUT)

BEFORE CASEY OPENED UP TO ME and told me what happened on June 16, 2008, I felt horrible for her. One thing about her that I found shocking was that she didn't have a soul in the world who was there for her. Not a single friend came to me and said, "I'm Casey's friend. I appreciate everything you're doing for her, and if you ever need anything from me, I'm here."

One afternoon I was in the office talking to members of my staff about this. "This girl doesn't have a friend in the world," I said.

That's so unusual for a girl of twenty-two. Girls that age usually have tons of friends. Casey knew a lot of people, but she wasn't close to one of them.

And her family? Her very own family was throwing her to the wolves. To this day I find it incredible that not a single member of the Anthony family ever handed me a check and said to me, "Please use this to try and save Casey's life."

Despite all of the Anthonys' showboating for the media about Casey's innocence, they never put their money where their mouths were. Yet they sold pictures of Casey and Caylee to CBS for $20,000 and took that money and went on a lavish cruise. Not a penny was spent to save their daughter, who was facing the death penalty. I have clients who are migrant farmworkers who don't have a decent place to live but who each week, like clockwork, come in and hand me fifty bucks in cash, or even twenty, to help a family member in need of legal help. This was truly a first for me.

Early on, after seeing she was fighting this world all alone, I decided I would be there for her.

I'm not going to abandon her, no matter what, I told myself.

Slowly, but surely, she began trusting me. I never take a client's trust lightly, especially Casey's. She could have hired any lawyer in the country and her parents were encouraging her to fire me. But she remained loyal. Unbelievably loyal. For a girl who never had anyone show her any loyalty, she was incredibly loyal to me.

We were sitting in the jail one day when she said to me, "I have something to tell you."

"Okay," I said, bracing myself, because I had no idea what she was going to say.

"I've been thinking about this for a long time," she said. "I want to know if you'll do me a favor. I'd like you to be my godfather."

"Wow." I was so touched.

Casey wanted to have some connection to a person who was always there for her, and while I was flattered by the request, I could never cross the attorney-client relationship. She needed an attorney *way more* than she needed a godfather.

I had spent months visiting her in jail trying to gain her trust, which is the key to the attorney-client privilege. You always hear about how defense lawyers hide behind it—that's certainly what the prosecution in this case kept harping upon—but it's a false argument. What's so important about the attorney-client privilege is that it allows the client to tell things to the lawyer, knowing that information won't go any further than their conversation. Without the attorney-client privilege, the client has no one at all to trust. Guiding the client through the legal system and protecting their interests, while doing it within the confines of the law, helps defense lawyers truly evaluate their clients' cases and assist them in determining if they should plea bargain or take their case to trial. It protects the system as a whole, and without it, individual rights cannot be protected and the system does not work.

Several times I had asked Casey what she knew about Caylee's disappearance, and always she talked about Zenaida the nanny. I knew it would be quite some time before she would trust me enough to tell me the truth. It began when I sought to eliminate the existence of Zanny the nanny.

When I was in college, I worked as an investigator for a loss-prevention company. The company sent me to a school for interviewing and interrogation, and one of the things I was taught was when you're interviewing someone, you prevent them from lying by cutting them off, because once a person lies, the guilt of knowing that they lied prevents them from coming forward and telling the truth. You stop them from telling the lie, thereby removing the guilt.

So there came a time when I never allowed Casey to deny that Zanny the nanny was a fictional person. It became a foregone conclusion.

"Even if this nanny does exist," I told her, "I don't want to hear about her anymore." I made it clear to Casey that I didn't believe that Zanny existed. In fact, one day I said to her, "That's it, no more, don't mention her to me ever again."

There were a couple of times she slipped up and started to say "Zan..." but I would stop her in her tracks, until finally she stopped mentioning her name, and we got past it.

If Zanny didn't exist, then what happened to Caylee? Who took her? Where was she? Seemingly this was a riddle without an answer, and a number of strange events occurred around this question.

In early 2009, after I learned that Dominic Casey and Jim Hoover had been searching in the woods on November 14, 2008, at the spot where Caylee would be found a month later, I stopped seeing red flags and realized I was on red alert. Meaning, *What were the two private investigators working for George and Cindy doing in the woods where Caylee's body was found?* This activity was beyond suspicious.

I wasn't buying Dominic's stories about being sent there by a psychic, or the fact that he was investigating whether that was a teenage hangout of Casey's. Sergeant John Allen said it best when he asked, "Why would you think you would find a teenage hangout when Casey is no longer a teenager?" I was beyond buying stupid reasons as to why they were there. When discussing this video with George and Cindy, George said something that took me to the point of no return.

"You know, during those six months that Caylee was missing, I was down on Suburban Drive too!" George said.

WHAT THE HELL? I screamed to myself. What was *he* doing there? And why in the world would George admit to walking around near where Caylee's body was found? I thought about this and decided, *Forget red alert, I am now swimming in a sea of red!*

Linda Baden and I came to the conclusion that there was only one reason George would say that: to create an alibi for himself. If a witness were to come forward and say he saw George in the woods, George could then say, "I already told you I was down there."

This had already happened once before—three months earlier. On November 5, 2008, nine days before Dominic and Hoover searched off Suburban Drive, a news station reported that someone saw George in a wooded area in east Orlando. It was not Suburban Drive, and when I asked George about it, he said he was scouting an appropriate area to put his kid-finders tent, where he passed out flyers for Caylee. I remember thinking, *What a strange place to put a tent*, but at the time I had no real reason to think it was suspicious.

But *now* my head was spinning. The imagined scenarios were endless. *Did George move Caylee's skull there and then send Dominic to Suburban Drive to search? If so, why? Was this the area where Caylee was originally hidden and then moved to Suburban Drive to be found? If so, then how does Roy Kronk fit into all this? Is that why Officer Cain couldn't find her?* I thought about it so much my head hurt.

But since I didn't know the exact location, I couldn't send our investigator out there to search for clues as to what was going on.

For months I wanted to get George to make this statement on tape, but I couldn't take his deposition without tipping off the prosecution as to my thinking. I had to sit on this information until just before trial, when we met with the Anthonys and their lawyer, and I finally got George to admit being near the wooded area off Suburban Drive. We recorded it, so if he lied about it on the stand, we could impeach his testimony.

I knew I needed Casey to tell me what happened on the day Caylee died.

Casey and I had discussed her sexual abuse, and I felt it was only a matter of time before she would tell me the truth about what happened to Caylee.

The day I had a major breakthrough with Casey came in the early months of 2009. I had set it up a couple days before when I said to her, "You know, Casey, I've never pressed you about what happened. I never asked why you didn't trust me. You had no reason to do so. But time is running short, and I need to know. You and I have to have a serious conversation about what happened. And I promise you that I will not tell a soul unless you allow me to. There's so much out there that I could be doing, and I'm not doing it because you're not allowing me to.

"Do you not trust me? Do you feel I'll walk away?"

"No, no, no," Casey said, "I don't feel that way."

I surmised at this point that she didn't want to disappoint me. As we sat in the jail, she began to tell me what happened the day Caylee disappeared.

"Let's start from the moment you woke up," I said. "What happened?"

"On the 16th [of June] I had fallen asleep," Casey began. "I dozed off, and when my father woke me up, he started yelling at me, 'Where the hell is Caylee? Where the hell is Caylee?'

"I got up. Usually I locked the bedroom door, but on this morning the door had been ajar. Caylee usually slept in my bed, but on this morning I was alone. I'm a light sleeper, but I couldn't recall Caylee leaving the bedroom. My father and I started looking around the house. We looked in all the rooms, and she was nowhere to be found. We went into the garage. She wasn't there either. Then we both went outside. I looked to the right. My father looked to the left, by the pool. At the end of the house there's a path, which leads to a shed. I walked down around the corner and looked down the path toward the shed. I didn't see her. When I walked toward the pool, I noticed that the pool ladder was still attached. Caylee and my mom had been swimming the night before. I couldn't believe it was still up. Caylee loved to swim, but once she got into the pool, she had no way of getting out, so I always made sure someone was there with her.

"I turned around and started to walk toward the house when I saw my father carrying Caylee. I could see Caylee was dripping wet. I could tell she was dead. She had passed away. You could tell she had been in the water a long time."

Tears flowed from Casey's eyes. I'd never seen her break down like this.

I had my eyes locked on her. I didn't take a single note.

She said, "My father started yelling at me, 'It's all your fault. Look what you've done. You weren't watching her. You're going to go to fucking jail for child neglect. You weren't watching her, she got out of the house, and look what happened. It's all your fault. Your mother will never forgive you, and you'll go to jail for the rest of your life.'"

Casey said she just cried the whole time he was yelling at her.

Casey said her first reaction was to blame her father. Why hadn't he kept an eye on her? She said she went so far as to ponder whether he had molested her and then killed her.

Maybe he was doing something to her and he tried to cover it up, she thought.

Casey said she went inside the house and laid down on her bed. She said her father walked into her room and told her, "I'll take care of her." Those were words he had often said to her. "Don't worry. I won't tell anyone. I'm taking care of it. Don't say a word of this to anyone, especially your mother," and he walked away.

Casey said that after George went to work later in the afternoon, she remembered he called her on her cell phone and told her, "I took care of everything." And again he warned her not to tell her mother.

Casey said she was frantic and did not know what to do. After pacing and crying for about an hour, she said she could not hold it in any longer and wanted to tell her mother and began to frantically call her. She tried Cindy at work and when she couldn't get ahold of her there, she tried her cell.

"I desperately wanted to tell her and I called her a bunch of times, but she didn't answer." Casey said. When she couldn't get hold of Cindy, Casey said she just "went to Tony's house and acted like it never happened."

Casey's phone records would show that she was telling the truth. She had called her mother a total of six times in a matter of four minutes. And the call from George was there at 3:04 P.M., exactly when he would have arrived at work. One thing you should know is that during the months of June and July 2008, Casey and George spoke on the phone a total of two times—June 16 and July 8. This struck me as extremely odd, given that his daughter and granddaughter were missing and not living at home, as they had all their lives. By comparison, in March 2008, they spoke a total of thirteen times. When looking at these records, it seemed clear that George was avoiding Casey as much as she was avoiding him. (Casey never had a copy of her phone records in the jail—they were too voluminous—nor did she ever have access to them when she was out on bail, so she could not have tailored her story to match the phone records.)

Finally, I had what I believed to be the truth. I wanted more, but then she said that was all she could remember about that day.

After arriving at Tony's apartment, they later went to Blockbuster, but she said she had no memory of having done so. She said she remembered going to Tony's house, but otherwise it was all a blur to her. She said that during the thirty days she stayed away from the house when her mother was there, most of it was a blur. I would ask her specific questions about her activities, and most of the time she would say, "I don't remember."

"Casey," I said, "that's not good enough. We need to explain why you went to a nightclub. We need to talk about that."

"We can talk about it all day," she said, "but the fact of the matter is, I don't remember who that person is [meaning herself], or what that person was doing."

I believed her. It all made sense. The prosecution's contention that Casey had killed Caylee was made from whole cloth. Casey had loved that child. Her whole life revolved around her and protecting her from abuse from her family. But I still couldn't condone how she acted during the thirty days.

Prior to that time I had gone into Casey's room, and it was a shrine to Caylee. Casey took so many pictures of Caylee and put them up on the wall that the room oozed of her love for her daughter.

When I saw it months earlier, I had said to myself, *There's no way this girl murdered her daughter.*

When she was done telling me the whole story, I kept telling myself, *It all makes sense.* And I told myself something else too: *The reason the prosecution has no proof that Casey murdered Caylee is because the charges brought against her simply aren't true.*

The key question everyone asks when they hear this is, *Why didn't either George or Casey immediately call the police?*

The answer has everything to do with the screwed-up dynamics of the Anthony family. Why didn't George call the police? There are several possibilities.

Did he fear the police would find out he was abusing Casey? Was he afraid an autopsy would show that the child had been abused? Another possibility: if George called the police, would it later come out that he was Caylee's father?

What if George called the police, and Casey was arrested for child neglect? Let me throw out this family dynamic: Casey and George had a love/hate relationship. What if the police arrived and Casey said Caylee drowned because George should have been watching Caylee, and he wasn't. George surely would have pointed the finger at Casey and accused her of the same thing. Since both were home, it would have been he said/she said. George might have anticipated that Casey would be angry that her daughter had died because her father had been negligent, so George would have feared that Casey would tell the police that he had been sleeping with her since she was eight years old. If I were George, I surely wouldn't have wanted the police to find *that* out.

If abuse had been revealed, George would have faced charges for sexual battery on a minor, a penalty that would have far exceeded any negligent homicide charges that Casey would have faced.

Whatever the motive, George seemed to do everything he could to hide his involvement in what happened and to make sure that if any blowback came from Caylee's death, the onus would rest entirely on Casey's shoulders.

When questioned about June 16 by law enforcement, George spun the story that would be repeated over and over in the media, a story that would become a "truth" in the reality show chain of events repeated over and over. George said that Casey had told him that she was taking Caylee to the babysitter, Zanny, that she was going for a meeting at work, and that she might stay over at the babysitter's. He said she told him that Casey would also stay there because Casey didn't want to come in late to wake them up.

George said Casey left the house with Caylee at about ten minutes to one that day. He said he knew the time because he was watching one of his favorite TV shows, *Diners, Drive-ins and Dives* on the Food Network.

"I was watching it," he said, "and I remember Casey and Caylee, you know, leaving and the last time I saw Caylee."

"I walked with Caylee and Casey out when they left to get into their car and go." He said he held the door open while Casey buckled Caylee in the back passenger seat, and "you know, just blew her a kiss, told her I loved her and, you know, 'Jo Jo' will see you later." Numerous times he also told us that as Casey and Caylee left, he checked his watch to see how much time he had left before he had to get ready to go to work. He was certain of the time they left.

His cover story went so far as to describe exactly what Casey and Caylee were wearing. He said Casey was wearing gray slacks and a white shirt, and Caylee was wearing a backpack with monkeys on it, a pink T-shirt, and a denim skirt with her hair in a ponytail.

"She said 'Bye, Jo Jo,' and that's the last I saw her," he said.

It was the story that cops bought, and the media spread throughout the blogosphere, and none of it was verified. Or true.

Why was George able to describe in detail exactly what Casey and Caylee were wearing when they walked out the house on June 16? The way he told it, he didn't know that would be the last time he would see Casey and Caylee, yet he remembered exactly what they were wearing? It didn't make sense.

Later I would ask him what Cindy was wearing that day, and he couldn't remember. And then I asked him what Cindy was wearing last week, and he couldn't remember. I didn't find his testimony to be truthful.

The shorts were for a 24-month-old child, and Caylee was already a 3T, and you know how fast kids grow. In the trial Cindy testified that Caylee hadn't worn those shorts in almost a year. This was a critical piece of evidence. But there was more.

Whoever dressed Caylee after she drowned ripped those clothes as he was putting them on her. And that's what Dr. Lee was going to testify to.

No one knew about that, and it never came out in the case. That was a piece of evidence we were really looking to smack them with.

Our problem was that Dr. Lee quit our team about ten months before the trial. He informed me he just couldn't continue. The prosecution was going to require him to take his deposition, and he had to submit reports, and he was catching a lot of pressure from his friends in law enforcement for being involved in this case.

When Dr. Lee said he couldn't continue, I was so distraught about that I actually flew up to Connecticut to try to get him to change his mind. I went to his institute, and we sat down and we talked.

"Quite frankly," he told me, "I just didn't need the aggravation. And then he recommended that perhaps I should drop out too.

"You really should consider quitting," he said to me. "You don't need this aggravation either. It's more trouble than it's worth."

So Dr. Lee never testified to the rips in the shorts. But it was clear that Caylee's body was found wearing shorts she had stopped wearing long ago, which confirms Casey's version of events.

THE HARDER AND MORE IMPORTANT question was: *why didn't Casey call the police after she saw that Caylee had drowned?*

One reason certainly was the guilt Casey felt that she hadn't been able to protect her child. She had been up most of the night before texting and talking to Tony, knowing she had to watch Caylee in the morning. She had also been on the computer early in the morning, just before seven, figuring Caylee would be okay with George for a little while, and when it turned out she was wrong about that, the guilt ate her up.

And then there was George telling her that she was going to go to jail for child neglect. People get arrested all the time for not watching their children who get injured or die. Casey must have felt scared about the possibility of going to jail for Caylee's death.

Here's another important question: *Was there negligence in Caylee's death?* There's some probability that there was. The real question is, *Who was neglectful? Was it Casey or was it George?* Given the circumstances and the timing, you have to take a strong look at the concrete evidence we had.

George said he was having breakfast with Caylee around 7:30 A.M. There were no safety locks on the doors for this child, and Caylee had the ability to open the sliding door to the pool. (We have a photo of her doing so.) She also loved to swim and would sometimes wake George up in the morning and say, "Jo Jo, swim. Jo Jo, swim."

While George was with Caylee, Casey was on the other side of the house in Lee's old room, working on the computer. In looking at the computer records, someone was on the computer that morning from 6:52 A.M. to 7:52 A.M., with visits to Yahoo!, AOL Music, Facebook, and Myspace. Forensic computer experts will always tell you the most difficult thing to do is put a face behind a computer. But you can speculate, based on the type of searches made, creating a profile. The searches that morning fit the profile of Casey, who could spend hours on Facebook and Myspace. The records show that from 9:00 A.M. continuously until 10:59 P.M. she was on Facebook and Myspace. She was researching outfits worn by shot girls in clubs, going to Victoria's Secret, Frederick's of Hollywood, and other sites featuring sexy outfits, shot girl outfits, and Tila Tequila. Tony was a promoter for Fusion nightclub, and Casey was helping him out by managing his shot girls. The shot girls are pretty girls who walk around the club selling shots. What she appears to be doing here is legwork for Tony in trying to find the cutest outfits for the girls to wear on the nights he was a promoter.

These were not the searches of someone out to kill her daughter.

If Casey was on the computer, who was negligent when Caylee wandered toward and into the pool?

George himself gives us the answer.

According to the computer records, at 1:50 P.M. someone got on the computer and signed into AOL Instant Messenger. George had an AOL Instant Messenger account. George's user name was george4937. Right after someone logged in to instant messenger, the first search was to Google. Then someone typed in "foolproof suffocation." It was misspelled, and George was a poor speller. Google automatically corrected the spelling, and the first link that was clicked was "venturing into the pro-suicide pit." It appeared that someone was thinking about killing himself.

"Venturing into the pro-suicide pit" is a blog discussing websites that talk about suicide. Shortly thereafter, the person at the computer went to a page that said "heat can melt disposable breathing circuits." And then a little later, someone visited a link that appears to be a gardening website (George was an inveterate gardener): ten ways to kill a rhododendron.

I suppose you could argue these searches were made by Casey, but AOL Instant Messenger had been used on the computer, and this occurred more than an hour after George said she had left the house with Caylee. It wasn't Cindy. She had left the house and Lee didn't live there anymore.

There's further concrete proof that George was on the computer, not Casey. We checked Casey's phone records, and at the time these suicide-related searches were being made, Casey was on the phone talking with Amy Huizenga. When we interviewed Amy, she couldn't recall anything special about the conversation. Would Casey have these morbid thoughts about killing herself at the same time she was talking on her phone with her friend? It didn't make any sense. Casey's cell tower records also support her claims that she was at home. The records show her in the vicinity of the home until 4:18 P.M., when she left for Tony's house. While it was never conclusive evidence, it does support her statements and contradicts George's testimony. Because they knew it hurt their theory, it's no wonder that the prosecutors didn't admit the cell tower evidence during the trial.

Again, not exactly a search for the truth.

It appears suicide had long been on George's mind, so much so that he tried it on January 22, 2009.

So who was negligent in Caylee's drowning? By looking at the websites being researched, all concerned with suicide and death, it certainly appears that the one who felt the blame was a guilt-ridden George Anthony.

When it came to evidence concerning George and Casey's computer use on June 16, the police really pulled a fast one. You would think if you were investigating the Anthony computer—very important evidence—that you'd look into and list the computer searches on the day Caylee died. But the police didn't do that, as my computer expert, Larry Daniel, discovered.

Sandra Cawn, who did the computer investigation for the police, reported that she had conducted a search of the computer on June 16 and 17, 2008, and in her report she showed that there was NO COMPUTER ACTIVITY between the hours one and seven A.M., and then she said "for the nine o'clock, noon hour, and between three and eleven on the 17th of June, there was NO COMPUTER ACTIVITY."

She gave zero evidence as to what the computer activity was. And for a while I couldn't comprehend what she had done. But by telling the public what time Casey wasn't on the computer that day, she was hiding the truth: she (or someone connected with the police) had deleted the computer evidence that would have shown that George's story was a lie and that Casey was telling the truth.

George said Casey left at 12:50. And yet someone was on the computer over an hour after that time. It had to have been George on the computer because he said Casey was gone, and he was the only one out there trying to kill himself. But Cawn's report says nothing about his computer use.

If you look at the discovery you will find that the Anthony computer was in use practically non-stop on the days prior to June 16. If you search June 16, there is only one entry. Where are the other entries?

There was nothing there. It was gone. It mysteriously disappeared. When I looked at this I was stunned.

If you go to the cookies, there is not one cookie listed for June 16th. Here was the supposed "unfiltered version" of what was on that com¬puter, filtered by the police.

When I came across this information, I wanted to find out whether the prosecutors were aware of this. It was possible that the police did this on their own and kept it to themselves.

To find out, I initially put Larry Daniels on my witness list. I planned on him testifying to the omissions and ramming this down the state's throat at the trial.

I also hired another confidential computer expert, Josh Restivo from St. Louis, and he verified the same thing that Daniels had found.

CASEY'S REVELATIONS about what really happened on June 16 were, for me, a major breakthrough in the case. It was what I had been waiting for all along—the truth, not some story about people who didn't exist. But I immediately realized a *major* problem. Her testimony was almost useless. I say this because Casey had lied so many times and for so long that I knew no one would believe her. She was the girl who told lies. I realized very quickly that if we were going to use this information as a defense, we were going to have to find evidence to corroborate what she was saying. But how do you prove a secret? I knew it would be difficult, if not impossible.

I decided it was time to reread all of the discovery and do another walk-through of the evidence, but this time my goal was to try to disprove what Casey had told me. While her story made perfect sense, I wasn't so quick to jump on board, especially given her prior proclivity for lying. I was going to be her harshest critic, because I knew if I couldn't buy it, I couldn't sell it to the jury.

I then reviewed all of the evidence in the case, including phone and computer records, an effort which took weeks. I made a column for and against her story and the more I reviewed the evidence, the more the column in her favor began to stack up. I'm a visual person and knew with so many facts in this case, it was exactly what I would do to sway the jury.

It began with the pool ladder. Casey told me it had been up. I checked it out.

On June 16, 2008, the day Caylee died, Cindy said she came home from work and found the pool ladder up against the pool. This alone caused Cindy to be alarmed; when she went to work the next day, she told her coworkers about the ladder being up.

"Somebody has been swimming in my pool," she told them.

"That's what pools are for," replied Cindy's coworker Debbie Bennett.

"No, you don't understand," said Cindy. "The pool ladder was left up, and the gate was open, and we *never* leave the ladder up. It must be kids in the neighborhood."

We later found out that Cindy and Caylee went swimming the night before, and while Cindy never admitted it, she may have been the one who left the ladder up when they got out of the pool that night. I found this conversation with her coworkers to be odd. Why would they even have this conversation? For a long time I suspected that Cindy might have known all along that Caylee was dead. But Casey never told me that was the case, and I had no other evidence to support that.

The mystery I couldn't solve was what would George do with Caylee's body if he found her wet and limp in the pool? I reread all of George's statements to the police and found a bombshell on July 24, 2008. Without his realizing it, George made a very damning statement to the detectives about his involvement.

George had met with law enforcement and told them about the smell in Casey's car and in doing so he said the following: "I know that as a fact. I've been around that. I mean the law enforcement stuff that I did, we caught people out *in the woods, in a house, and in a car.* So I know what it smells like. It's a smell that you never forget."

There were three places where we knew Caylee had been dead. The first was the *house* where she died. The second was a *car* in which she was transported, and the third was in the *woods*. This was six months *before* Caylee was found in the woods.

George didn't say, "I smelled bodies in a Dumpster, in an alley, and in a morgue." His statement only mentioned the places where her body had actually been.

What I found shocking was that he made this statement long before Caylee was found in the woods. I know this is subjective, but I didn't think it a coincidence and I was going to question him severely about this at trial. I couldn't wait to ask him, "How did you know she would be found in the woods?"

If that statement doesn't impress you with being damning evidence, consider this: what if Casey had made it? I guarantee you the prosecution would have trumpeted that statement to the media as being her tacit confession.

Another small piece of evidence that suggests Caylee died at home was the fact that when Caylee's remains were recovered, she didn't have on socks or shoes. According to all of George's statements, Caylee never left the house barefoot. So where were her socks and shoes? This was just another piece of the puzzle that began to form.

Next was the most damning piece of evidence: the duct tape. Recall that, while Caylee was missing, George had inexplicably called the police to report the loss of two old gas cans. When the police searched the Anthony home they found the same brand of duct tape as that found with Caylee's remains. They found it in only one place—*on one of the gas cans George had reported to the police stolen.*

To me, George calling the police and reporting the gas cans missing was the biggest red flag in the case. Reporting them would only do one thing: it would document the incident. He knew Casey had taken the gas cans, and by calling in the theft of the gas cans, it would point away from him and directly to Casey.

George did something else in what I believe was an effort to try to pin Caylee's death on Casey. He recounted how, when he sought to retrieve the gas cans from the trunk, Casey ran ahead of him ostensibly to keep him from seeing what was in the trunk.

And then, after the duct tape was found near Caylee's remains, he did all he could to make the prosecutors believe he hadn't been the one to put the duct tape on his gas cans. More likely, any evidence pointing to him they blithely ignored because it didn't fit the reality show script that was supposed to end in Casey's conviction.

Prosecutor Jeff Ashton asked George during his deposition, "It's your recollection today that when she gave the [gas cans] back to you, the one did not have the duct tape on it?"

"Most definitely," was George's response. "I'm positive."

"And you testified before that, in doing that, you would have put duct tape over the vent, since it was gone?"

"Yeah, if I would have used that particular can. Yeah," said George. He said he would have done so to keep the vapors inside the can.

"I would have done a neat job with it. I wouldn't have done what you showed me in the photograph."

"Sure," said Ashton.

"I wouldn't have done that," said George.

"And that's the can you would use for gas for the mower, the round one?" asked Ashton.

"Yeah. That's the one I used to use. Yes."

But George's story goes back and forth. Then George told Ashton that when he gave the police the gas cans on August 1, 2008, the cans *did not* have duct tape on them. He seems to be implying that the duct tape was applied while the cans were in police custody.

Extremely agitated, Ashton asked him, "So is it your testimony now that when they took it on August 1, that it did *not* have duct tape over the vent?"

"Didn't have duct tape over the vent," George replied. "And when it came back to me, or the last time I saw it, now it has duct tape on it. And I did not put that on there."

Asked Ashton, "So then explain to me, if you will, how it's possible that you used this can to get gas for your lawnmower sometime between June 24 and August 1, would have put duct tape over the vent in order to utilize it in your car, but then it wouldn't have duct tape on it on August 1st."

"That's a mystery to me, too," said George.

Ashton wasn't buying his story.

"Did you take the duct tape, put it on and off again?"

"No, sir. I did not do that," said George.

Replied an exasperated Ashton, "But your testimony here today, under oath, [he needs to remind him that he is under oath] that you have a specific recollection that when the police officers took this from your home on August 1, 2008, that this piece of duct tape was *not* on this can?"

"Uh-huh."

"Please answer out loud 'Yes' or 'No.'" (Ashton wanted to lock in his answer.)

"It was not on the can," said George. "Yes. It was *not* on that can."

George was saying that he wasn't responsible for the duct tape that was on the gas can. In his own inimitable way, he was saying that the police had planted the duct tape. He feared the police were going to use the duct tape evidence against him, but George was trying to use the duct tape evidence to pin Caylee's death on Casey.

As hard as he—and the police—tried, and as often as they boasted they would, they couldn't link Casey to the duct tape because the truth was she had never been anywhere near it. Proof of that was, even though the duct tape on the gas can hadn't been exposed to the outdoor elements and was still completely sticky, it didn't have Casey's fingerprints or DNA on it. Not a single trace on any of the pieces of duct tape could be linked back to Casey.

Something else to think about: Whoever put that duct tape on the gas can while leaving no trace had to possess knowledge of and skill in police investigatory techniques. Only one member of the Anthony family had been a cop, and that was George.

A couple months later, the media would deliver the final blow to the ridiculous theory that Casey had put duct tape on Caylee's mouth. They did this by finding a hidden video of the same duct tape on a poster of Caylee at the command center manned by George. For all of their bashing of Casey, it was the media that would put the prosecution's "murder weapon" in the hand of George Anthony, three weeks after Casey was arrested and in jail.

After the media uncovered the duct tape at the command center manned by George, police began to question people who worked there with him. One of those people was a woman by the name of Linda Tinelli, who told Detective Eric Edwards and Sergeant John Allen that one day the wind was blowing the tablecloth off the volunteer table.

"I have something that will fix that," said George.

He then went into his car to grab some tape. She couldn't remember what kind of tape it was, but a video obtained by the media made it clear that it was Henkel duct tape, a unique brand with the logo clearly visible, that police were saying had killed Caylee. Another media outlet, WKMG, would obtain video showing almost an entire roll of the duct tape behind the donation jar. Four months later the entire roll of duct tape had disappeared after last being seen with George Anthony.

This occurred three weeks after Casey was arrested. This had to make the cops nervous. Could they have arrested the wrong person? Edwards asked Tinelli if she would wear a wire and go and speak to George, but she refused. They were so desperate they asked her twice. Again she refused. On one of those occasions Tinelli told Edwards that he reminded her very much of George.

Edwards immediately responded, "The only difference between me and George Anthony is I have a job and my kids are still alive."

After the police spoke to the volunteers at the Caylee command center, several people suggested that they should speak to a woman by the name of Krystal Holloway. People were whispering that there might have been something going on between George and Holloway. Holloway initially denied the affair to police, but then came clean and admitted it. She didn't want to be dragged into the spotlight and the never-ending media circus of the Casey Anthony case.

In her statement to law enforcement, Holloway dropped a major bombshell. According to Holloway, George, in a moment of weakness, had told her about what happened to Caylee. She said that while with him in her apartment one day, the two of them shared a quiet moment when Holloway asked him if he had seen Casey or spoken to her.

George said no, because of all that's going on. And then he said to her, "You know, I've always respected you because you've never asked me once whether you thought my daughter did it or not."

"Well," said Holloway, "I don't know her. But I can tell that two people like you wouldn't raise someone who would do something like that."

"Thank you," George replied.

Holloway began to cry, and George said to her, "It was an accident that just...snowballed out of control."

"I know what's that like," said Holloway, "because I've been through that myself." George was on the couch, and she was sitting on the floor. She got up and gave him a hug.

"I felt so bad," said Holloway. The admission took Holloway aback because she now knew that Caylee was dead, and this searching for George's darling granddaughter was only a ruse.

Holloway's testimony was very important, because she was the only independent witness who showed that Casey's version of the events on the 16th was correct. She had no obvious reason to lie, and she was a reluctant witness, not wanting to get involved.

We needed to make sure that Holloway was credible. She wasn't without her problems. She had an alias of River Cruz. And she sold her story to the *National Enquirer* for $4,000.

But Holloway wasn't a kook. Apparently she had a stalker and used the other name to get away from him. And she needed the money because she said that she had loaned George close to $5,000, and he never paid her back. George told her he wasn't working and that no one would hire him because of the case. According to Holloway, Cindy didn't know George wasn't working, so every day George would get dressed and pretend he was going to work and would instead go see Holloway. (Sound familiar? For two years Casey had dressed and pretended to go to work.) I know I've already used the "apple doesn't fall very far from the tree" expression, but I just can't resist.

Another thing that gave Holloway's story credibility was that she lived in a gated community with a guard, who testified that he had seen George coming and going from her apartment several times during that time period. Being in the news every day and driving a PT Cruiser plastered with Caylee's posters all over it, George wasn't hard to spot. George had also sent Holloway a text message after Caylee's remains were found that read, "Thinking of you. I need you in my life."

When co-counsel Cheney Mason and I confronted George about the sexual abuse, we also confronted him about Holloway's statements.

"George," I said, "we have statements from Krystal Holloway that we got from the police. It came through discovery, and it hasn't been released yet to the media. There are some things you need to know that are in there."

"Krystal says you told her that Caylee's death was an accident that snowballed out of control." I said to George, "Your daughter's life is on the line here, and if you saw an accident, it will save her life. I have to tell you, what Casey says is irrelevant, because nobody believes her, so I need to find corroborating evidence for everything she says. So, George, please, if you saw something, we can find a way of working this all out. 'Cause if you saw an accident, it will save your daughter's life."

He answered quickly and defensively.

"You know what?" George said. "No. The last time I saw my granddaughter alive was at 12:50 P.M. when she walked out the door on June 16."

My mouth dropped, and George could see it. I was saying to myself, *He's lying.*

"Did you see how defensive he got after I mentioned Krystal Holloway?" I asked Cheney. "You know what? I've seen that before, when Casey lied in defiance." It was the same body language and the same attitude.

A number of things came together for me at this point. "This man hates his daughter," I said.

"I have a daughter too," said Cheney, "and I agree with you."

There's no way I wouldn't fall on my sword for my daughter. I realized that George Anthony was in a tough position, but he had the perfect opportunity to free his daughter. Here was his chance to throw his daughter a lifeline, to stand up and tell the truth, or even to lie, and he wouldn't even consider it.

"This guy's a monster," I said. And Cheney agreed.

After meeting with George, I went back to Day One to find further proof that George knew Caylee was dead and listened to Cindy's first 9-1-1 call on July 7. There's a moment when Cindy says to George, "Caylee's missing."

And George softly says, "What?"

Cindy says, "Casey says the nanny took her over a month ago." And all you hear is dead silence. I'll never forget as I was listening to that, I said to myself, *George, you son of a bitch.* Because George knew. And I would argue this to the jury. When you listen to that 9-1-1 tape, you hear his silence as loud as could be. He doesn't scream, "What do you mean Caylee's missing?" Rather, he is dead silent. How do you not go nuts or ballistic over the fact that your granddaughter has been missing for more than a month?

During the trial we asked several police officers and Casey's brother, Lee, about George's behavior when Caylee first was reported missing.

"Did George ask any questions?" I asked.

"No, he didn't ask any questions. He just stood there."

And that's the biggest question of them all, and only George Anthony can answer it: *Why?*

When I connected the dots, every dot fell into place. The gas cans. The duct tape that George had used. The statements about Caylee's death being an accident. The fact that Caylee was found so close to home. She was placed there—not to be hidden, but to be found—until someone else found her and hid her under a heavy tree. It all made perfect sense.

I was being a lawyer here and needed the information, but now that I had it, I had to figure out what to do with it. Do I try to cut a deal with the prosecutor? Do I let them know what I had learned? I didn't know. I asked myself, *If I tell the prosecutors, will they be sympathetic toward Casey?* I knew they wouldn't. We were at the point of no return.

The prosecution had filed for the death penalty when this clearly was not a death penalty case. From the perspective of the prosecution, this case was all about winning, not justice. The prosecution wanted to kill the most hated woman in America. However, she was steadfastly maintaining her innocence, and the evidence was starting to prove she wasn't guilty, which only made them dig in their heels harder. I knew they would destroy her—*and me*—to win this case if they could.

What was I going to do? I remember the day I confronted this dilemma. I closed my eyes, took a deep breath, and said to myself, *All I can do and all I will do is fulfill my oath.*

CHAPTER 15

MAKING UP A CAUSE AND MANNER OF DEATH

ONCE CASEY FINALLY TOLD ME what really happened on June 16, it was clear to me that the prosecution's case—that Casey had killed Caylee with duct tape, put her in the woods, and lied to cover it up—contained a series of serious leaps of faith without evidence to support them, based on their main argument that Casey didn't act right.

But until that day finally came, months after Caylee was found, I had been deeply concerned that what they were saying was true.

On December 12, 2008, the day after Caylee's remains were found, I ran into FBI Special Agent Nick Savage. He had seen that I had hired a group of well-known experts to process the crime scene and said to me, "With all the evidence we've got, I don't think if you had Jesus Christ on the defense team you'd be able to save her."

If Savage said that to intimidate me, he certainly succeeded.

I didn't know the full story then, so my first reaction was to feel the icy fingers of fear run down my spine. I felt badly for Casey on various levels. One, I felt horrible that her darling daughter had been found dead and not alive. Two, if found guilty, Casey was the one who was going to fry for this. As a lawyer, even if you represent someone who may be guilty, you get to know them and you learn to have sympathy and empathy for them.

I do this work for two reasons. One, because not everyone who gets arrested is guilty. Human error in the justice system is extremely prevalent, much more so than people realize. And second, just because a person makes a mistake doesn't mean he or she should pay for it for the rest of his or her life. I believe in forgiveness, I believe people can change, and I believe in redemption. And I know that's because of my own experiences in life, not because I was a bad person, but because I did some stupid things growing up, and even as an adult I've done some stupid things. But I don't think that makes me a bad person. I'm much more than that, and that's what I think my clients are. They are *much more* than just criminal defendants. There is a basic human dignity that everyone has; everyone is capable of loving and being loved and contributing to life as a whole. And if you don't think that way, you cannot do this job effectively.

All I could do was stand back and wait and see what he was talking about. What was all this evidence he was boasting about?

I remember when I was watching the TV news coverage of their processing the crime scene, I could see how happy and excited the detectives and law enforcement officers were when they were there at the scene. They were smiling and laughing and joking around not twenty feet from Caylee's remains.

We're going to have to look at what the cause of death is going to be, I said to myself.

We were very anxious to see what Chief Medical Examiner Dr. Jan Garavaglia's autopsy was going to show, and on December 19, 2008, Garavaglia spoke at a press conference. She got up and said, "With regret I am here to inform you that the remains found off Suburban Drive are that of the missing toddler, Caylee Marie Anthony."

Garavaglia (who gained fame as "Dr. G" from the Discovery Health Channel show, *Dr. G: Medical Examiner*) then announced that the cause of death was "undetermined," and the manner of death was "homicide."

"What the hell does that mean?" I asked Linda Baden.

"Hell if I know," she replied. "That's a first for me."

We knew right there that something was *very* fishy.

What that means in plain English is that they don't know how she died, but they know it was murder. They were going to try to say they knew the who, but not the when, how, or why. None of it made any sense to me, and I knew if I had trouble with it, so would a jury, so that's where the center of our attack of the prosecution's case would begin.

Chief Deputy Medical Examiner Dr. Gary Utz, who initiated the autopsy for the state, determined that there didn't appear to be any trauma on the body. There was no indication Caylee ever had a broken bone, or even a prior injury. There was no indication of any violence to Caylee's body.

We knew then and there that Garavaglia was going to have a problem justifying why she called Caylee's death a homicide. Her report, after all, gave no reason for it.

Later we would find that Dr. G gave three nonmedical reasons for calling it that, specifically: (1) Caylee's disappearance was not reported to the authorities immediately; (2) her body was hidden in a wooded area; and (3) duct tape appeared to be applied to the lower face.

These aren't medical facts, I said to myself. You don't need to be a doctor or a scientific expert to come up with these reasons. It was all in an investigative context.

Our conclusion: these were the facts the cops were talking about.

We would later find out that when Caylee was found, Dr. G was at the airport and heading out of town. Everyone in the medical examiner's office was on high alert, waiting for the call, and when it finally came, she called in and assigned the case to Utz, a board-certified forensic pathologist who had done many, many autopsies. He was fully qualified to do it.

When Garavaglia returned from her trip, she took Utz off the case and replaced him with herself. Dr. G was the big name in town. Because of her TV show on Discovery Health, she is well-known throughout the community and the nation.

Utz had begun the autopsy, and when we asked him his opinion as to whether he agreed with Garavaglia declaring the manner of death a homicide, his words were, "You'd have to ask Dr. Garavaglia about that...It's her opinion. It's not my opinion. "

When we pushed Utz further on the subject, he refused to tell us what his opinion was. That struck me as odd, and I immediately was given the impression he disagreed with his boss's opinion and moreover, he was not at all happy about being pushed aside on the biggest case of his career just because Dr. G had a good relationship with the cops.

When I asked Utz why Dr. G took over the case from him, he said, "Because it's a high-profile case and because of her relationship with law enforcement."

When I heard that, my jaw dropped.

I thought, *She took the case back because it's high profile? And because of her relationship with the police?*

The medical examiner is supposed to render an independent opinion. Utz gave us a clue that Dr. G's opinion wasn't without prosecutorial bias.

We knew we could benefit at trial over the two medical examiners dueling over the issue of the cause of death, and I decided to put that one in my back pocket and use it later when needed.

We immediately began researching Dr. G's past. Casey said that Caylee had drowned accidentally, and my co-counsel, Dorothy Clay Sims, discovered that Garavaglia had written a book in which she stated that the most common cause of death of young children in Florida was drowning. I couldn't wait to ask her about *that* at trial.

The next question was obvious. If the medical examiner was going to call this a homicide, then how did Caylee die if there were no evidence of foul play?

How was the state able to mount a case for murder, other than offering evidence that Casey was a liar, that she neglected her daughter when she went out dancing a couple times at a club during the thirty days when she was "missing" (we knew for the first time she wasn't missing; it was more of a coping issue than evidence that she was glad to be rid of Caylee), and that she was promiscuous and had a lot of boyfriends?

Basically, the police and prosecution made up—invented—the cause of Caylee's death. They had no idea what actually happened to Caylee, who took her, or who put her in the woods. There was no physical evidence whatsoever that Casey was involved in Caylee's death, but because the police had focused their attention solely on Casey, her activities, and her car—and no one else—they blindly went ahead and took what they believed to be the next logical step: accusing Casey of putting duct tape over Caylee's mouth and nose and smothering her to death.

For the many months before I learned the truth about what really happened on June 16, the duct tape evidence was the most troubling piece of evidence I had to deal with. I stayed up many nights and labored many hours over the photographs of the duct tape found near Caylee's skull, wondering how I was going to attack this piece of evidence.

What I found shocking was that *no fingerprints* were found on the duct tape. None. Not any. If there's anything that lends itself to fingerprints, it's duct tape. There was also *no DNA* on the duct tape. If the duct tape had actually been wrapped around Caylee's face to suffocate her, as the prosecution alleged, you would think the odds would be 100 percent that Caylee's DNA would've been all over that duct tape, especially if you consider the force necessary to apply it. If someone had put duct tape on Caylee, why was no saliva, mucus, and as she decomposed, all of the decomposition liquid, found on the tape afterward? It just didn't seem possible at all.

To counter this obvious truth—that there was no evidence that duct tape had been used to kill Caylee—I was sure a desperate prosecution would use the argument that the outdoor elements off Suburban Drive degraded the DNA so much that none was left.

Three things destroy DNA. One is heat, the second is moisture, and the third is law enforcement. I can tell you that more often than you'd think, law enforcement will contaminate a piece of evidence because it's so easy to do. They certainly did it in this case.

When the FBI processed the duct tape, his first move was to send it to fingerprints first and not the DNA section. That was a critical mistake. Second, after the duct tape left the fingerprint section, when they were searching for what they described as a fragment of a heart-shaped sticker, the supervisory forensic document examiner, a lovely woman by the name of Lorie Gottesman (I found her to be such a pleasant and nice lady because she was extremely polite and honest) contaminated the duct tape. As I said, it's easy to do. When the duct tape was examined, *her* DNA was found on it. When she placed the duct tape on what is called a Video Spectral Comparator, a machine that uses lights and filters to view items that are not visible to the naked eye, her DNA could have been on the machine and transferred to the tape. She could have contaminated it by speaking while handling it, or by placing the duct tape on her desk and allowing it to touch something on her desk that had her DNA on it. If Gottesman could get her DNA on the tape so easily, why in the world wasn't Caylee's DNA on it?

Or Casey's for that matter, since she was the one accused of using it to kill Caylee.

There was further proof that someone else handled the duct tape. There was a low amount of DNA on the sticky side of the tape. Now, in order to identify whose DNA it was, you have to match thirteen different markers. But to prove that it *doesn't* belong to someone, it's enough to have just one marker to eliminate that person. And the one marker that was found excluded Casey and Caylee. Because the police never got a DNA sample from Roy Kronk, no one will ever know if it excluded him as a possible contributor to the DNA on the duct tape.

That should have been enough to cast major reasonable doubt into the case, but what the prosecution did was argue that the DNA had been contaminated from another law enforcement person. It just didn't know who.

I was determined to identify the culprit.

I needed to find an expert on what is called Low Copy Number DNA, which is the analysis of DNA when only minimal amounts are present. Europe has many of the leading scientists in DNA. An Englishman, Sir Alec Jeffreys, discovered DNA fingerprinting in 1984, and he was the first to use it in a criminal case. The first person ever to admit DNA in a courtroom in the United States was none other than my adversary, Jeff Ashton.

I wanted the top expert in the field, and so I traveled to the Netherlands to meet with Richard Eiklenboom, the best when it came to LCN.

Before I began Casey's case, I had planned on taking Lorena to Egypt. We had it all planned, and I had to put it off because of the case. I still had the ticket vouchers. I came home one day and said to her, "Lorena, I have phenomenal news. We're going to Europe."

She was very excited.

"The bad news," I said, "is that we're going to a DNA lab."

I spent two weeks in Richard's lab and learned all about LCN. I learned about DNA from A to Z, from recovering it at a crime scene, to the way it's processed. I learned each step at the lab—the way the statistics run, how it's amplified—and became a complete expert. I even went through Richard's certification program and got certified in trace recovery and DNA analysis.

I knew that when the time came, I'd be able to fight Ashton toe-to-toe on the issue of DNA. I also hired Richard's wife, Selma, who was a knowledgeable fireball of a woman.

I was out of money, so I asked the Eiklenbooms if they would come work on the case pro bono, which they did. They provided me with insight and so much knowledge. Richard and Selma showed me the example of a burned body that had been thrown in the water and how they were still able to find DNA. He showed me the case of a person who had died twenty-five years before, but from whom they were still able to recover DNA on a pair of underwear from touch, not blood or semen.

He talked to me about the duct tape, and what it meant that there was no evidence of DNA on it.

His conclusion was that the duct tape was *never* wrapped around Caylee's face.

The photographs of Caylee's skull and the tape nearby backed up his conclusion. I found numerous photographs that showed the duct tape in a completely different position from ones in other photographs.

I knew that if I presented this photographic evidence at the trial, it would be tricky, because I would have to show the jury photos of Caylee's skull, and it was going to require a delicate type of examination to be effective. But the evidence was too important not to put before the jury.

In addition I also had the evidence that Dr. Werner Spitz pointed out at our autopsy of Caylee's remains, in which we found scientific proof that the skull had been moved from its original location. In other words, she didn't decompose the way she was found. The decomposition residue inside her skull proved she had been lying on her side.

The fact that I kept reading the 26,000 pages of discovery over and over again allowed me to find a needle in the haystack. I found an FBI email that gave us some disturbing news. The email said:

From: MARTIN, ERIN P. (LD) (FBI)
Sent: Friday, February 06, 2009 10:10 AM
To: LOWE, KAREN K. (LD)(FBI); CARROLL, BRIAN J. (LD)(FBI); FONTAINE, ELIZABETH K. (LD)(FBI)
Subject: Tape from Caylee case

UNLCASSIFIED
NON-RECORD

Hello.
   Nick Savage called in and they have been getting requests for info about the tape from skull. The prosecutor would like to know if any of you had taken pistures (w/scale) of the tape as it was received to show the full length and width of tape pieces before they were separated. They are esp interested in the width info.

   They want to know if it would be possible for the tape as it was to cover both the mouth and nose areas - they would need the measurements/photos w/ scale in order to do some computerized re-creation images of the skull w/tape. The ME's office only took initial photos of tape on skull w/o scale and they didn't measure it because they thought the full measurements would be done by us.

By "scale," they meant ruler measurements.

The reason they wanted such pictures was to show that the tape was wide enough to cover both Caylee's nose and mouth and to suffocate her. What this email shows is that the prosecutor (most likely Ashton) is forming his theory of death by duct tape.

There are two problems with this cause of death: first, this isn't coming from the medical examiner's office—it's coming from the prosecution. A prosecutor does not get to make up a cause of death based on what he or she *thinks* may have happened.

Second, this email was dated February 6, 2009, *before* the prosecution changed its position and decided to seek the death penalty. I would argue that the prosecution was also locked into using it in deciding whether to take another human being's life. It was disgusting and reprehensible.

After the trial I heard Ashton make the claim that it wasn't his decision to seek the death penalty, and that he never felt there was a likelihood that Casey would get it. He claimed it was the decision of his boss, Lawson Lamar. Ashton was trying to give the impression that he didn't support seeking the death penalty against Casey. I am here to tell you that nothing could be further from the truth. We tried multiple times to get the death penalty taken off the table, and the biggest opposition always came from Ashton, who was the "death penalty lawyer" on the prosecution team.

The prosecution hired Dr. Michael Warren, a forensic anthropologist from the University of Florida, to get on the stand and show a video superimposition of a photograph of a smiling Casey and Caylee that would morph into a vision of a piece of duct tape covering Caylee's nose and mouth with her little skull in the background.

The medical examiner's pictures lacked scale, so they invented evidence. It was disgusting. Judge Belvin Perry admitted it over our objections, even though it was ridiculously prejudicial and served only one purpose: to try to inflame the jury, to get the jurors angry so they could render their verdict with their emotions, not their brains. It's an age-old prosecution technique, an attempt to get the jury to hate the defendant, ensuring that a conviction will follow—the evidence be damned.

Throw in Kronk's crazy testimony, and the prosecution had a complete and total mess. Death by duct tape? Only in the mind of Ashton.

But, the theory played well to the media which was always hungry for a "let Casey Anthony die" angle.

Once we went to trial, my method of attack had one focus. I was going to show the jury that only one reasonable conclusion could be reached about the duct tape found near Caylee's remains. Using the photos and evidence at the crime scene, I would show it was a staged crime scene.

There were two other pieces of duct tape evidence. There was an identical piece of duct tape on one of George's gas cans. Another piece of the identical duct tape had been used to put up a poster at the command center manned by George. The evidence showed that this was George's duct tape, not Casey's.

By this time our defense was beginning to take shape, and we didn't just have Casey's word; we now had solid forensic science backing up her story.

CHAPTER 16

THE PROSECUTION'S EVIDENCE WAS GARBAGE

NUMEROUS TIMES I heard this case being referred to as a circumstantial case, but I never thought of it that way. I always looked at it as a forensic case rather than a factual one. The reason is the only real, factual witnesses who were relevant were George and Cindy. Even Lee wasn't particularly relevant to exactly what happened to Caylee.

All the other evidence in the case came down to science.

Science was the key factor in determining Casey's guilt or innocence—it always has been and always will be.

To better understand the prosecution's case in terms of the forensics, the best and clearest way is for me to break it down into two strands. The first strand has to do with the information the police investigators gleaned from going over Casey's car after it came back from the tow yard.

The second strand comes from the recovery site of Caylee's body off Suburban Drive. (I'll present that evidence in the next chapter.) But first, let's talk about Casey's car, and why what was in the trunk was so crucial to the prosecution.

The prosecution based its entire case on a theory that after Casey killed Caylee, she dumped her into the trunk of her car for a couple of days and drove her to the woods where she disposed of her body.

Shortly after Casey was arrested, Deputy Charity Beasley went and picked up her car. She secured it with evidence tape, made sure everything was sealed, and followed the tow truck to the forensics bay.

With the car in hand, the prosecution had to somehow prove there had been a body in the trunk and that it was Caylee's. Since it was Casey's car, the link was obvious. But knowing what I know now, it's interesting to see the lengths to which the prosecution had to go to make its case.

The areas the prosecution dealt with to try to prove its case that there was a body in the trunk had to do with cadaver dogs, a stain, hairs, and the air in the trunk of Casey's car.

Their first line of "evidence" came from the dogs, who, the prosecution contended, alerted to the trunk of the Casey's car and in the backyard of the Anthony home.

Deputy Jason Forgey arrived with his dog, Gerus, who supposedly alerted to human decomposition in both the trunk and the backyard. Later that day, Forgey went to the Anthony home and deployed Gerus, who again alerted in the backyard. He then called in another cadaver dog by the name of Bones. Bones went to the backyard and alerted as well.

The next day the crime scene investigators returned with their two cadaver dogs and found—*nothing*. This time neither dog alerted. How do we account for this? What's the explanation? How can a dog find evidence of decomposition one day and nothing the next?

There are several reasons, all having to do with the nature of cadaver dogs.

The first reason is that a cadaver dog can be inconsistent. Cindy told me that, according to a police officer at her home, the reason the police brought Bones in was because Gerus was not being consistent in his alerts.

Here's another example of just how unreliable these dogs can be: after Caylee's remains were found and most of her remains had been recovered, there were still a few bones missing, so the police recruited Forgey and Gerus to help find them. Gerus was deployed to the woods off Suburban Drive, where there was a *100 percent certainty* that a dead body had been.

After sniffing around, Gerus did not alert in the area.

The second reason cadaver dogs can be inconsistent has everything to do with their training. Studies have shown that there's a tremendous amount of unreliability when it comes to dog handlers, because often they cue their dogs. I did extensive research on cadaver dogs and the kind of training they receive, and I learned that cadaver dogs are most reliable when using double-blind testing.

How does double-blind testing work?

Dogs are very smart and can read their handler's body language, so it's crucial when deploying a dog to a vehicle for the dog to have to choose among *several* cars, not just the target car. Thus, it's important that *the handler* not know which car belongs to the suspect.

The police didn't do this when they inspected Casey's car. In this case Gerus was only given one car—Casey's car—to explore, and he alerted. Forgey testified there were two cars for his dog to sniff when he deployed Gerus on Casey's car. However, every other witness said there was only one car for Gerus to sniff—Casey's.

The second piece of evidence had to do with evidence concerning a stain found in the trunk. Crime scene investigator Gerardo Bloise processed the trunk by spraying it with Bluestar Forensic, which is very similar to luminol. It can identify human stains not noticeable to the naked eye using an instrument called an alternating light source (ALS). It works like a black light, so that if you wipe away a bloodstain, the ALS will reveal it anyway. The police got a slight reaction in the trunk, but eventually the stain they found was determined not to be human.

The third piece of evidence had to do with hairs in the trunk—actually *one hair* that belonged to Caylee.

When the crime scene investigators were about to start processing the car, they advised the media that if they parked across the street behind the gate, they could film them inspecting Casey's car. This was at night, and they opened the garage doors so the film crews could get them on camera working. They did this strictly for publicity, and you could argue they also did it to intimidate us. Or both.

While they were processing the trunk, they found some hairs. It's not uncommon to find hairs in the trunk of a car, not only the car owner's but others. Our bodies shed more than a hundred hairs a day. They found Caylee's hair, Casey's hair, and dog or cat hair. They took a mini vacuum and swept up the rest of the evidence for later inspection.

Early on, the prosecution sent the hairs it had found to the FBI lab at Quantico, Virginia. The FBI lab would find *one lone hair* of Caylee's that had a darkening band around the root end of the hair.

Around this one hair, the prosecution decided to build its case against Casey.

I needed an expert on post-mortem root banding and reached out to the man who basically discovered it, Nicholas Petraco. He wrote the first peer-reviewed article on it about twenty years ago. It was important to bring him in because this was going to be a key issue.

Many times after someone dies, scientists will find a dark band around the root of the hair. They call this the "death band" or "the dead man's ring," but the scientific term is post-mortem root banding.

Now the thing about post-mortem root banding is that nobody knows where it comes from. We don't know how it's caused. We don't know if you only get root banding from a dead body. We don't know when it begins to turn black. We know very little about it, except that it's been seen on dead bodies.

As for the one hair, there was no way for anyone to know how long the hair had been in the trunk. It could have been there a year. And no one knew the condition of the trunk, what else was thrown in there, what chemicals were in there, how often the trunk was open, whether any moisture got in through the rain. The banding of the one hair could just as well have been caused from environmental conditions as from post-mortem root banding.

There have been two studies to see whether hairs from *live* people also develop root banding from being left out in the elements. One study was done by a grad student at John Jay College of Criminal Justice in New York. She found this was the case. A second study conducted by FBI analyst Steven Shaw, who actually worked on our case and did the study subsequent to my taking his deposition, found that hairs from live people left out in the elements developed these so-called "death bands."

Shaw's team performed a blind study where examiners took hairs from living people and exposed them to the elements like being out-doors, in a trunk, etc. His team then took hairs that came from dead people and asked the examiners to determine which ones came from dead people and which did not. Two FBI analysts studied two different hairs that came from a live person and called it post-mortem root banding. The end result is this "science" isn't very scientific at all—it's completely subjective, relying on the opinion of the examiner.

There was another issue connected to the root banding, and that had to do with the questionable actions of prosecutor Jeff Ashton.

Ashton was the liaison between the state attorney's office and the FBI. It was my understanding that the FBI didn't trust him.

When the results of a new FBI hair banding study was released, to their credit, the FBI held a conference call and made sure we were on the call. This ensured we had equal access to information.

Despite any lack of scientific certainty, the prosecution stubbornly stuck to its guns when it talked about the post-mortem root banding, arguing the hair had come from Caylee's dead body, when the evidence was neither proven science nor verifiable. Of course, when the prosecution alerted the media to its "find," the public was convinced of its probity as well, despite the weakness of the evidence.

I ask you: If Caylee's body had been in Casey's trunk, bouncing along, decomposing, wouldn't investigators have found more than *one* hair displaying root banding? The root banding issue really posed more questions than it answered, though the most likely scenario was that the single strand of hair had been in the trunk a long time, and moisture, heat, and other environmental conditions caused that hair to look very similar to post-mortem root banding.

So after all that posturing, the prosecution had no body, a negative confirmation for the stain in the trunk, and one hair that it was determined to show came from a dead Caylee.

The prosecution had one last chance at a conviction. One of the few shreds of "evidence" the prosecution had left was the smell in the car. According to the prosecutors, this terrible smell was proof Casey had kept Caylee in the car while her body decomposed and started to smell. After Casey dumped her daughter's body in the woods, they contended, her car retained the foul odor of death.

To win its case, the prosecution had to prove that the terrible smell in the car came from a dead body.

There was only one problem: Casey had left a large bag of garbage in the trunk of that car for three weeks in the hot sun. If the smell came from the garbage and not Caylee's body, then the prosecution had *no case*, because it really had no other way to tie Casey to her daughter's disappearance and death.

Was it a body, or was it garbage?

That was the $64,000 question.

George was the first person to say the car "smelled like death." However, once we began to investigate this, the "evidence" lost most of its effect. First of all, not a single police officer who responded to the Anthony home the night of July 15, 2008, noticed "the smell of death." The car was parked in the garage and the garage door was open—the police went in and out of the house and past the car through the garage door many times that night. Add into the mix that George was telling them that the car smelled like a dead body, then that really makes you wonder. George said he had opened the trunk expecting to find a dead body. Instead, he had found moldering garbage.

The tow yard manager took the bag of smelly garbage from Casey's car and threw it into his trash bin. The police sent an officer to retrieve the bag and bring it to the forensics bay. A woman from CSI testified that the trash smelled horrible. The police then emptied the bag, looked at all its contents, and then did something very unusual: they set out to destroy our argument that the garbage was causing the bad smell by deodorizing it. They literally put it in what they called an air room where they separated the trash and aired it out, thereby drying it. The smell disappeared after a short period of time. And what was the reason for their doing that? With the smell gone, it would be a lot harder for a clever defense lawyer to argue that the smell from the car trunk came from the trash.

We only got to see to pictures of the trash when it was initially brought in. We could see this moist wet bag of trash, which I was told had meat and other food products in it, and the next picture taken showed it to be completely dry with no food whatsoever. I have a hard time believing that three college kids had such clean trash with not a drop of leftover food in it.

When we looked at the photos of the trash when they got it, and then the trash afterward, they couldn't even be compared. When their anthropologist, Dr. Arpad Vass, asked for air samples from the trash, they sent him samples from *after* it was aired out. They also took samples from the forensic bay—six weeks later. You might ask, *What kind of science is this?* My answer: garbage science.

The prosecution knew it had a bad smell in the trunk. They also knew they had a smelly trash problem. So it was something of a leap to accept that the smell came from a body in the trunk, rather than the trash bag. Clearly, any decent defense lawyer was sure to argue the point. If you have a bag of moist trash in a trunk of a car for three weeks in the hot sun, you can expect it to stink—perhaps as much as a dead body.

The prosecution's argument that the smell of the car proved Casey's guilt would have gone nowhere, except that one of the CSI personnel had heard there was a scientist at the Oak Ridge National Laboratory who was studying the odor of human decomposition. So they contacted anthropologist Arpad Vass.

I called it "fantasy forensics." Vass's experiments were, in my opinion, no better than a high school science research project.

Vass is a forensic anthropologist who studied at the University of Tennessee Anthropological Research Facility. The facility was given the nickname the "Body Farm" by author Patricia Cornwell. This is a place where people donate their bodies to science so students can study how a body decomposes in numerous settings, including being buried underground, wrapped in a blanket, and in the trunk of a car.

Vass studied the chemical compounds a body releases after dying. In his study he buried four different bodies at different levels, one at two feet, one at six feet, and so on. He then stuck tubes just above the bodies; above the tubes he placed Tedlar gas sampling bags that caught whatever chemicals flowed from the bodies as they decomposed. He would then take the bags and run them through a machine called a gas chromatograph–mass spectrometer (GC-MS) to obtain the chemical breakdown of the chemicals caught in the bag.

What Vass did was create a database that would attempt to determine the chemical signature of the bodies at different states of decomposition.

In 2004 he published the first of two peer-reviewed papers that explained his results. He then repeated the study in 2008, adding a couple of bodies, and concluded that there was still no signature for human decomposition and that the chemicals coming from decomposition are varied. He wrote that they are also affected by numerous factors such as soil and weather.

Vass wasn't able to come down and personally take air samples from Casey's car, so the prosecution called upon Dr. Michael Sigman, a chemist from the University of Central Florida. Sigman took air samples and then ran the chemicals in the Tedlar gas sampling bag through the GC-MS at his lab at the University of Central Florida. He also sent additional samples to Vass.

Sigman concluded that the main component in the trunk was gasoline, and while he found levels of chloroform, he said that they were at *very low levels*. Vass labeled the results "useless." He then asked the Orange County CSI unit to cut a piece of carpet from Casey's trunk liner and send it to him.

He heated it up in a Tedlar gas sampling bag at 130 degrees—a temperature that he said he assumed was the same temperature as the trunk of a car in summer in Florida. His associate Dr. Marcus Wise, a chemist, then ran the results through a GC-MS and reported that the main component was chloroform.

This is crucial: with a GC-MS you can run a qualitative analysis, which tells you which chemicals are present, or you can run a quantitative analysis, which tells you *how much* of the chemical is there. All Dr. Wise did was a qualitative analysis. So they knew that chloroform was there. What they didn't know was *how much* was present. Was it a lot or was it a trace amount? The answer was critical, and no one had any idea.

Wise sent the results to Vass, who reported to the prosecution—without any evidence to back up his statement—that there were high amounts of chloroform in the trunk of the car.

It's important to note that Vass's study, since it gave no amounts—he had no idea how much chloroform was in that trunk—was weak, if not useless, as evidence. It meant nothing because chloroform is a very common component found everywhere, including in household products, degreasers, and even drinking water in very small doses. It might have been significant only if he had found chloroform in large, concentrated amounts.

So the question was, *How much chloroform was there?* Vass just made the assumption it was in *large* amounts because it was the *main* component, but in science you can't make assumptions. You have to verify, or else, as in this case, you can be very wrong. The best way I can describe Vass's experiment was shooting from the hip. It was junk science at best. And with a woman's life at stake, at worst it was negligence.

Based on this flawed information, the police performed an investigation into Casey's computer at home to see whether she had done any searches looking for chloroform. If Vass hadn't irresponsibly, in my opinion, stated there were high amounts of chloroform, the state wouldn't have had any case at all.

There was a day when Cindy called me to say that Sergeant John Allen and Melich were at the house and they wanted to know if I knew why Casey would be searching for information about chloroform on her computer.

"Chloroform?" I said. I thought it was the most ridiculous thing I had ever heard. There might be a million ways to kill a child, but using chloroform would be number one million and one.

I thought the death by chloroform assumption by the prosecution was so ridiculous I couldn't believe it.

Understand, with this information, the prosecution had a theory it was more than willing to share with their adoring public: Casey had chloroformed Caylee before she suffocated her. The state had a murder weapon, a cause of death, and an argument for premeditation, something they could hang their hat on when asking for the death penalty. Because of Vass, now they were *really* into this ridiculous chloroform theory.

And sure enough, the prosecution released the report on Casey's computer usage and found she had made two searches for chloroform.

Those occurred in March 2008, *three months before* Caylee disappeared. Casey's boyfriend at the time, Ricardo Morales, had posted on his Myspace page a photo of a man and a woman entitled, "Win her over with Chloroform." The man is giving the woman a kiss on the cheek while taking a facial tissue and getting ready to put it over her mouth to subdue her.

Casey, who was twenty-two at the time, told me she had no idea in the world what chloroform was, but after seeing her boyfriend's post about chloroform, she searched online for "chloroform" to find out what Morales was talking about. By sheer bad luck, Morales had given some credence to the prosecution's utterly ridiculous theory of premeditated murder via chloroform. I would later write in a motion that this whole chloroform line of argument was one of the biggest frauds ever pulled on the American public.

To this day I can't understand how so many people ended up buying the chloroform argument. Even now people think chloroform had something to do with this case. The cops said it, and the media regurgitated it. In this age of reality television, where news is entertainment, we question neither the authorities nor the media.

The waters became even muddier when Vass's colleague, Dr. Neal Haskell, a forensic entomologist expert, suggested to Vass that the fruit flies from the trash in the trunk of Casey's car, "might be coffin flies." Haskell volunteered that he would be more than happy to take a look at them. (If you've ever left a doggie bag in your car, or thrown out old trash from your home, you know what these fruit flies look like.)

Vass emailed Orange County Sheriff's Department Crime Scene Investigator Michael Vincent. He wrote, "Mike, forgot to mention something in my last email. I finally got a call back from Dr. Neal Haskell, my entomologist friend, and he said that the 'fruit flies' may really be coffin flies and that might be significant. He said that if you still have them to please send them to him at the following address and he will check them out."

Haskell did check it out, and he concluded that the flies recovered from the garbage bag were *Megeselia scalaris*, a species from the family of flies known as Phoridae. Coffin Flies, *Cornicera tibialis*, are from the same family, but are from a different genus. There are more than two hundred genera and three thousand described species within the family of Phoridea, which is why this doesn't make any sense. If you took high school biology, you know that's like saying an orangutan is the same species as a human being. No matter. In his report, Haskell went on for two or three paragraphs talking about coffin flies, and how they are known to get into areas such as car trunks. The police, of course, let the media in on their little secret. This "information" gave the media more fuel to say Caylee's body was in the trunk.

"Coffin Flies Found in Trunk of Casey Anthony's Car," was the headline.

As it would turn out, there were *no* coffin flies. Not one. Did the media report "Not One Coffin Fly Was Found in Casey Anthony's Car" in a future headline? Of course not.

What's most important for me to note here is that the flies they found didn't come from the trunk of Casey's car. They came from the *garbage bag* that was in the trunk. These flies are commonly found in garbage and are not specific to human decomposition.

With the coffin fly theory at a dead end, Haskell was struggling to find a way to tie the smell in the trunk to Caylee's body, so he came up with yet another half-baked theory about how the decomposition in the trunk could have been Caylee, not the garbage found inside. This time the evidence concerned a blowfly, or rather the *leg* of the blowfly.

The most common fly associated with human decomposition is called the blowfly, but they are also commonly found most everywhere. Check your windowsill and you might find a dead one. When a person dies, blowflies are early colonizers to the corpse. They come by the hundreds to lay their eggs on and feed off it.

Haskell reported that investigators found a *leg* of a blowfly attached to a napkin in the trash. The napkin was sent to Vass, who found that the napkin contained what are called fatty acids, which, he said, were commonly found with human decomposition. What Vass conveniently didn't mention was that fatty acids are also commonly found in cheese, meat, and other normal food products like *pizza*, which is what Casey and her boyfriend had eaten before throwing the box in the trash bag that lay moldering in Casey's car for three weeks.

The far-fetched conclusion reached by both Vass and Haskell was that there was a body in the trunk because of the chemical composition (chloroform) and the fatty acid on the napkin.

Here's how far they went in trying to tie Caylee to Casey's car: The prosecution's scenario was that because blowflies don't travel at night as frequently (this was a weak attempt to try to explain why there was only one), Casey had opened the trunk, tried to clean out the decomposition with a napkin, and accidentally caught the leg of a blowfly as she was cleaning up. Then she threw it all in the trash and immediately closed the trunk so no other flies or insects could get into the trunk. This is another huge leap, but somewhere out there is a blowfly missing a leg that knows the true story.

This was the state's case as it related to Casey's car.

I needed help and proceeded to seek out experts in the various fields to disprove their "science." I knew I needed to find an entomologist, a bug expert. I had never worked on a case with entomological evidence before.

Linda Baden knew Haskell, but obviously he was working for the prosecution. Nevertheless, they were friends, and she asked him who he would recommend. Haskell touted one of his former students, Dr. Timothy Huntington, the youngest of the fifteen board-certified entomologists in the country.

I liked Tim right away. He's a tall, thin, and honest guy from Nebraska.

"All I want from you is the truth, whether it helps or hurts," I told him.

"Great," he said, "because that's all you're going to get from me."

He took a look at the evidence, everything Haskell was saying, and the very first thing he told me was, "I can't believe Neal is taking these tremendous leaps in his report." He had a lot of respect for Haskell, but he couldn't go along with his conclusions about the flies coming from a dead body.

Tim said to me, "If I go outside to my backyard, and I see shit in the grass, why would I assume it's the neighbor's kid and not my dog?"

What he was saying was, *If you find flies that are normally found in trash, and you find trash in the trunk, why would you assume the flies come from a dead body and not from the trash?*

I NEEDED TO HIRE SOMEONE to combat this "air science." I called Vass and asked for a referral, which he offered, and was someone who lived in Belgium. I then did some research and consulted with Dr. Lawrence Kobilinsky, an expert in DNA from John Jay College of Criminal Justice. He looked up who had done work in the area and advised me to hire Dr. Ken Furton, an expert in chemical compounds as it relates to dead bodies. He used the chemical compounds as training aids for canines in finding dead bodies. Furton, a member of the faculty at Florida International University in Miami, did a lot of work for the FBI.

These scientists are really dedicated to their field, and when cases come along that offer interesting issues, they want to be involved. When I called Furton, he said he was shocked that the FBI hadn't called him to look into their air issue because in fact he had done more work in that area than Vass, the prosecution's expert.

"Well, my friend," I said, "Here's your chance to get involved."

We also consulted with Dr. Barry Logan, chemistry director at one of the largest private labs in the country, NMS Labs. Logan was a toxicologist who did extensive work in forensics and ran the forensics division in his lab. We asked him to talk about the different protocols and methodologies of the prosecution's scientific studies as they related to this case.

With Logan and Furton, we mounted a double-barreled attack on Vass's "evidence." Furton would attack the actual chemistry, and Logan would attack his methodologies, comparing Vass's research to what was done at other forensic laboratories.

Logan confirmed for me that the prosecution's case didn't even rise to the level of junk science. At trial he said the tests "lacked organization and planning, [were] poorly documented, and did not follow even minimal standards of quality control."

Step one, collect the samples. Step two, put it in a Tedlar bag. Step three, do this, and so on.

We did find written protocols that Vass used in another case he worked on just four months before he got involved in our case. That case had to do with the Charles Manson murders back in 1969. After cadaver dogs had alerted in several areas at the Barker Ranch, the police called Vass to see if he could collect samples and check his database to see if there were dead bodies buried there.

Vass ran soil samples and concluded, based on his database, that there were dead bodies buried at several locations. The investigators then used ground-penetrating radar and performed an excavation. They found no dead bodies.

In this case, when sending law enforcement written instructions (or protocols) on how to collect the samples, Vass warned them not to collect samples anywhere near—drum roll, please—garbage and gasoline! The reason Vass gave for these instructions was that even something as small as a can of soda could contaminate the sample, creating a false reading.

I argued that Vass violated his own protocols. Furthermore, according to Logan, Vass had zero quality control for something as volatile as chemicals, which could be exposed so easily to contamination.

In one experiment, the goal was to identify the chemicals inside the trunk of Casey's car. Furton said that Vass went to a junkyard in Tennessee and collected carpet samples from other cars and tried to compare the chemical makeup among the carpets. They found chloroform in one of the other trunks. Once again, they were out to prove that the chemicals in the trunk came from Caylee's dead body and not from the garbage.

Vass claimed there were 484 chemicals that come from human decomposition. In one of his papers, he narrowed it down to thirty important ones. In the carpet sample from Casey's car, only five of those thirty were found. And, said Furton, if you excluded overlap from chemicals found in the garbage as well as in the air and gasoline, only three of the chemicals in the top thirty were found.

And despite all of this, it was Vass's conclusion that the chemical signature from the carpet sample from Casey's car was consistent with a human decompositional event.

I asked Furton to review Vass's findings. Furton compared Vass's work with key publications that contained the study of chemical compounds of human decomposition. There were fifteen in all, which isn't a lot, but it tells you this is a new area of study. Further, as reported by ABC News (and others), Vass's "emerging research had never been used in a criminal trial before." Furton made a chart and listed the compounds that each study associated with human decomposition. To his amazement, he discovered that each study listed different compounds. While there was no apparent consensus on the subject, Vass had proclaimed that certain compounds could determine the presence of decomposition—something he did in this case—but as Furton explained it to me, "Dr. Vass has no scientific basis for his conclusion."

Furton's research concluded the opposite of what Vass concluded: there was no uniform signature for human decomposition.

What was masterful about Furton's work, as it related to our defense, was that all the chemicals that Vass found, as they related to the carpet samples from Casey's car, were *also* found in garbage. Vass had concluded that the chemicals in the trunk proved that Caylee had been in there, but that wasn't at all scientifically accurate. Rather, it was bullshit.

The evidence showed, said Furton, that the chemicals in the trunk proved only that *garbage* had been in Casey's car.

So why was it so important for Vass to find that those chemicals meant that a body had been in the trunk? Because of the "signature of human decomposition" evidence, we redoubled our investigation. We investigated Vass and discovered that he was listed on a patent disclosure as an inventor for a machine ("The Labrador Patent") that analyzed burial remains and decomposition odor. The machine looks like a metal detector and uses the database that Vass created in his studies to determine whether human decomposition is present. One thing we discovered was notable: he didn't put the patent application on his CV, though other patents he applied for afterward were listed.

Vass and his partner were going to sell this machine to police departments all over the country. But in order to sell his machine, he needed to have the results admissible in court. If they weren't admissible, his machine was toast. So for the very first time in the United States, the database was admitted into evidence. I asked Vass if he had a financial interest in this case, to which he replied, "Not in my opinion." So much for pure science.

Vass had a financial motive for finding what he inevitably found. After the trial was over, I found a brochure that showed the estimated amount of revenue they could make by selling it to law enforcement in the U.S. market was $486 million. Did that influence him? I don't know.

We tried our best to preclude his "junk" science, but of course we were unsuccessful. We made a motion to exclude the "evidence," arguing that to admit it would be a "miscarriage of justice." The testing was done unreliably, we argued. We showed that the chemicals—common chemicals—were not from a decomposing body but from garbage.

As much as we discredited it in front of the judge in what is called a Frye hearing, our motion to exclude it from coming before a jury was denied. I thought we were most persuasive, but the judge let it in anyway.

He let *everything* in, but it didn't matter. We had the science on our side.

LO MEJOR DEL MIAMI FASHION WEEK 2008 EN TARGET STYLE

HISPANIC

TARGET

La Primera Revista de Negocio   ados Unidos

EL DEFENSOR

JOSÉ BÁEZ , THE BAEZ LAW FIRM

A diario defiende los derechos de hispanos en el centro de la Florida.
Es criminalista y afirma que se discrimina a los latinos.

NEGOCIOS: LOS 20 ERRORES | LOS HISPANOS Y LA POLÍTICA.

Despite the English-speaking media's attempt to paint me as completely
inexperienced, I was actually well-known in the Orlando area, especially in
the Hispanic community, long before I took Casey's case.

Me at age 17 in the navy.

CASEY'S IMAGINARY FRIENDS

Jeffery Michael Hopkins

- first appeared in 2006
- 2-4 yrs older than Casey
- trust-fund baby
- former co-worker at Nickelodeon
- 24 yr old widower from Jacksonville
- had son named Zachary, 2 yrs older than Caylee, mother is deceased
- the Anthony's invited him to numerous BBQ's and dinners but he never showed

Zachary Hopkins
- son of Jeffrey Hopkins

Jewels Hopkins
- Jeffrey's mother
- battling cancer
- got married suddenly in late June or early July
- was supposed to meet Cindy and Casey for girls day at the mall

Tom Manly
- Casey's boss at Universal

Thomas Frank
- Casey's boss at Universal

Zenaida "Zanny" Fernandez Gonzalez

- first appeared in 2006
- former girlfriend of Jeffrey Hopkins
- very attractive, "perfect 10"
- had long black hair, but got it cut several times over 2 yrs.
- had great smile
- lived in same complex as Jeffrey
- drove a Ford Focus
- parents were wealthy and connected lived in NewYork, Carolina's and Miami

Eric Baker
- Caylee's father?
- Died in motorcycle accident
- Had a son / Caylee's step brother

Samantha Fernandez
- Zanny's older sister

Gloria Fernandez
- Zanny's mother
- struggling with heart issues

Juliette Lewis
- Zanny's roommate
- Casey's co-worker from Universal
- had a daughter named Annabelle, same age as Caylee Zanny would also watch Annabelle
- Cindy and Casey once waited in a parking lot for 1.5hrs but she never showed

Annabelle Lewis
- daughter of Juliette Lewis

Racquel Ferrell
- Zanny's roommate
- co-worker at Universal

Casey had close to a dozen imaginary friends, complete with fantastic detail created over the course of years. If there ever was a girl that had built up a fantasy life to escape from reality, it was Casey. Above is the original diagram presented in court explaining her relationship with each.

Casey and Cindy at Rick's wedding. In how much denial do you have to be to not see that she is pregnant?

There is no evidence of any kind that Casey was anything than a loving mother to Caylee. I kept a copy of this picture in my suit jacket throughout the trial as a reminder of that love.

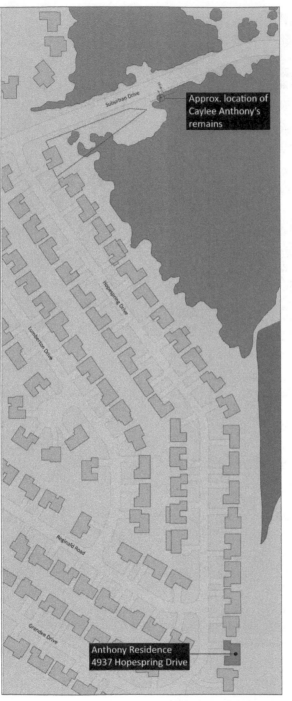

Caylee's body was found a stone's throw from their house and 19.8' from the road, yet the prosecution maintains that it was there undisturbed for six months, despite at least five searches of that specific location.

The area where Caylee's body was found after law enforcement excavated the area. An arrow points to the exact spot. Present are (from left to right): me, Linda Baden, Pat McKenna.

The only piece of evidence linking the crime scene to the Anthony home.

The duct tape was found one other place—at the Caylee command center, manned by George Anthony, three weeks after Casey was put in jail.

In front of the DNA lab, known as the Crime Farm, in Holland.

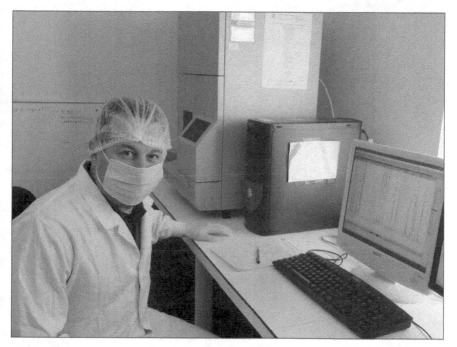

Studying Low Copy Number DNA in Holland.

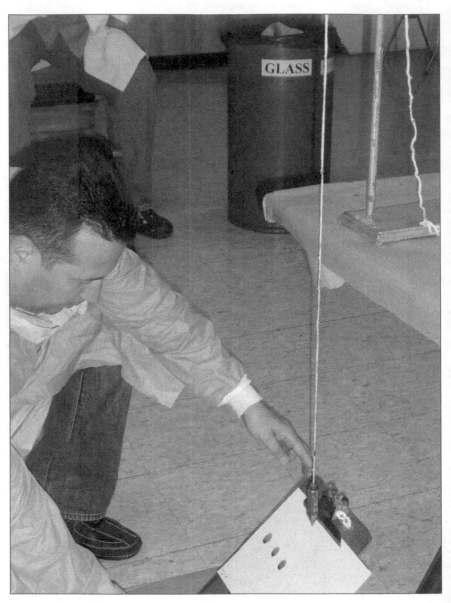

Me at blood spatter school in Corning, NY.

At blood spatter school, channeling my inner Dexter.

The picture posted on Myspace by Casey's boyfriend, Ricardo Morales, that led to Casey's search for the term "chloroform."

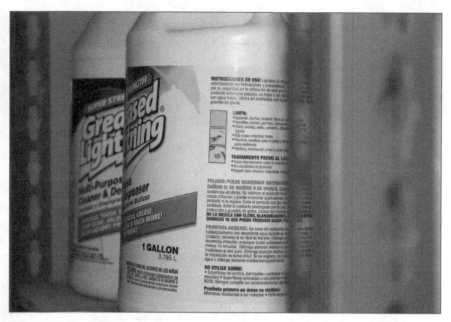

Bottles of Greased Lighting, which contains chloroform, in the police forensic bay, where the Casey's car was kept. Chloroform was found in minute quantities in the air in Casey's trunk, but this could be the result of contamination. They were not happy when I took this picture.

The wet, smelly garbage in Casey's trunk after three weeks in the Florida sun.

The sanitized garbage after the police investigation.

Trunk of Casey's car that the prosecution claims had a decomposition stain.

Trunk of car with decompositional fluid.

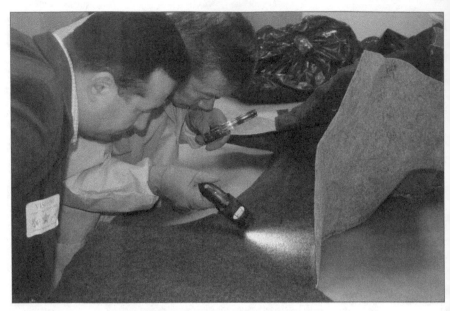

Dr. Henry Lee's meticulous examination of Casey's trunk.

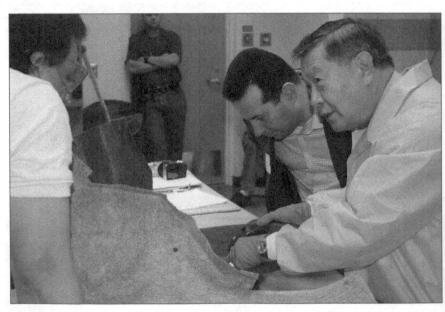

Dr. Henry Lee points out to Orange County CSI's Gerardo Bloise one of the 14 hairs he found that the police department missed.

My team of experts at work (from left to right): Henry Lee, Cheney Mason, me, Richard and Selma Eikelenboom, Timothy Huntington, Nicholas Petraco.

The team of experts (from left to right): Timothy Huntington, Richard and Selma Eikelenboom, me, Cheney Mason, Henry Lee, Nicholas Petraco, Michelle Medina.

My staff (from left to right) celebrating at a private party right after the verdict: Sallay Jusu, Jeanene Barrette, Michelle Medina, Shakema Wallace. Behind them on the right is Robert Haney, who provided security at the trial. You can see the verdict being replayed on television and Jean Casarez, a reporter, talking on the phone.

With William Slabaugh and Michelle Medina, two lawyers in my firm.

With Geraldo on his sailboat.

Nancy Grace and I kiss and make up.

I kept a picture of David on my phone to keep my spirits up. The big guys don't always win.

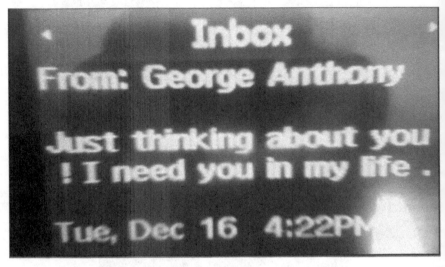

George Anthony's text to Krystal Holloway.

The photo of Caylee's smiling face used in the prosecution's despicable video superimposition.

Caylee was fully capable of getting to the pool on her own. This picture was taken six months before her death.

The pool with the ladder down.

The pool with the ladder up, as it was the day of Caylee's death.

I created a number of set pieces for the jury to help them follow the complex evidence, thanks to Legal Graphicworks. (Used with permission of the *Orlando Sentinel*, copyright 2011.)

LEVELS OF CHLOROFORM

Dr. Marcus Wise

"So in the sample where we found chloroform, it was not quantified in any of the samples because that would have been a meaningless number."

Dr. Michael Rickenbach

Q   And it's not what you would call shockingly high levels of chloroform, would it?

Dr. Arpad Vass

"The reason we progressed is because the chloroform was shockingly high, unusually high."

Dr. Michael Sigman

"In those samples, the three compounds that we just talked about; chloroform, tetrachloroethylene and dimethyl disulfide were present, but they were at low, they gave very low responses in the instrument."

Dr. Kenneth Furton

"It's my opinion that using, um, that those five compounds are not unique to human decomposition because two of those compounds,

I also created a number of charts to help the jury keep track of the complex and conflicting testimony.

Jeff Ashton and Linda Drane Burdick, after the verdict is read. Behind them are the defense team, celebrating. (Used with permission of the *Orlando Sentinel*, copyright 2011.)

Congratulatory texts stream in to my phone right after the verdict.

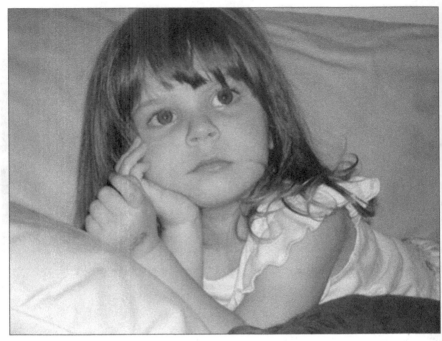

Caylee Anthony. Despite all the hatred directed at us, we knew that we were fighting for justice for her, as well as for Casey.

THE PROSECUTION'S
FANTASY OF FORENSICS

WE WEREN'T SURE when we were going to get Caylee's remains. Finally, the prosecution released her body to us on December 23, 2008, a full twelve days after Caylee's body was found. I called Dr. Werner Spitz, our pathologist, and told him apologetically, "We have the body now. I am so sorry to ask this of you, because I know tomorrow's Christmas Eve, but can you come down tonight?"

He laughed.

"Jose, are you stupid?" he said. "I'm Jewish. It's not a problem."

The medical examiner's office apparently tipped off the media as to which funeral home Caylee's body was being sent, so when I arrived there was a pack of media trucks parked outside. Spitz hadn't arrived as yet, so we decided we would wait until after the eleven o'clock news, knowing they'd pack up and go home after the news was over.

Spitz didn't arrive until close to 1:00 A.M. on December 24. We walked into the funeral home and saw a big silver box sitting on a table. Caylee's remains came in the silver box; it looked like a Christmas present.

Her skull was wrapped in paper inside the silver box.

"The skull has not been opened," said Spitz. "It doesn't make any sense. How could the medical examiner not open the head?"

Opening the skull is standard protocol in any autopsy of skeletal remains. Examiners open the skull to get the best possible view of what's going on inside. Spitz went on and on about the skull not being opened.

Spitz had assumed that Dr. Jan Garavaglia, the medical examiner, would follow standard protocol and open the skull, so he did not bring a saw.

"Do you have a saw?" Spitz asked the funeral director. "I need a saw. Any saw."

The director returned with a rusty old saw.

Spitz sawed and sawed, and after about a half an hour, he gave up.

"This saw doesn't cut," he said.

"We're going to have to buy a saw," I said. The only store open at three in the morning was Walmart.

"Come on, Pat," I said to our investigator, Pat McKenna.

When we entered the Walmart, the place was virtually empty. There were only a handful of employees. This was perfect. I figured we'd be able to get in and out quickly without anyone noticing us. (Media interest in the case grew exponentially after Caylee's body was found.)

McKenna and I split up in our search for a saw, and just as I began my search, a bus from a home for the mentally challenged dropped off its passengers so they could shop with the least amount of hassle. I'm looking for the saw, and one of the ladies from the bus (she had Down's syndrome) saw me and began shouting, "Baez, Baez, Baez." She followed me throughout the store, pointing at me and yelling, "Baez, Baez, Baez."

McKenna found a saw, and I yelled to him, "Let's get out of here." We trotted to the checkout counter and noticed the tabloid magazines, each featuring a horrible story about Casey. One story trumpeted, "Casey Anthony's Drunken Party." Another proclaimed, "Secrets and Lies," and yet a third featured a story headlined, "Caylee's Mom Did It: She Fed Tragic Tot to Alligators." I was looking at all these headlines, while waiting to pay $4.99 for a saw to cut open Caylee's skull, when the woman with Down's syndrome found me and again began yelling, "Baez, Baez, Baez."

It was surreal. I couldn't believe why I was there and what was happening. We paid and hurried out the door.

We returned to the funeral home, and Spitz went through the bones, looking for trauma. Spitz sawed Caylee's skull in two in a matter of minutes, and we found something we hadn't expected: there was decomposition residue on the top left-hand side of her skull.

"This is evidence she was laying on her left side," said Spitz.

We hadn't yet received the photos from the crime scene. When we got them, they showed that the skull was upright, not lying on its left side. Caylee had been moved. This ended up being an important piece of evidence that helped us win the case.

Opening the skull gave us another extremely important piece of evidence. The prosecution was contending that Casey had killed Caylee by using chloroform and putting duct tape over her mouth—basically suffocating her. If a person dies of suffocation, many times there is bleeding behind the back of the ears because blood vessels pop; there can also be some discoloration behind the area of the ears. But you can't know this unless you open the skull. The prosecution's theory was that Caylee suffocated, but the medical examiner's office never took the necessary steps to confirm that. Spitz found no evidence of discoloration. There was zero evidence that Caylee had been suffocated.

I suspect the reason the prosecutors didn't check was they were too busy looking for chloroform and other drugs like Xanax to back up their other theory that Casey drugged Caylee before killing her. We were sure that the prosecution's case was made up of whole cloth. Additionally, all toxicology results were negative for chloroform and all drugs. Now we had the evidence to prove the incompetence of the autopsy performed by the prosecution and the evidence to show that Caylee didn't die of suffocation by duct tape, the way it said she did.

That was huge for us. Dr. Garavaglia was later featured in a documentary on the case and tried to explain away some of the criticisms directed at the autopsy. As far as I was concerned, she never answered them. Spitz called Dr. Garavaglia's autopsy shoddy, and that's exactly what it was. Michael Baden would always tell me, "If you're sloppy in low-profile cases, you're going to be sloppy in high-profile cases." I was beginning to see just how right he was.

The next piece of evidence trumpeted by the prosecution was the remnants of a heart-shaped sticker supposedly found on the duct tape. According to the police, after duct-taping Caylee's mouth to suffocate her, Casey put a heart-shaped sticker over her mouth as a sign of affection. Can you even picture something that ridiculous? As I've been saying, the prosecution all along treated this case like a reality show and it was the one writing the script.

The police then searched the Anthony home for more heart-shaped stickers, and wouldn't you know it, they found some, along with stickers of Mickey Mouse, Pluto, stars, and bears—stickers you would typically find in any two-year-old's home. Police also found a heart-shaped sticker attached to a piece of cardboard in the wooded area off Suburban Drive.

In order to search the home, Detective Yuri Melich issued a sworn affidavit when applying for a search warrant to the Anthony home. Melich swore under oath, "While processing the duct tape at the FBI lab in Quantico, the latent print unit noticed residue in the perfect shape of a heart. The heart was not hand drawn and residue appeared to be consistent with the adhesive side of a heart-shaped sticker. It appears that the sticker was put on the duct tape intentionally." But that wasn't what Elizabeth Fontaine of the FBI laboratory in Quantico testified to in her deposition.

Question to Fontaine: "Did you ever communicate to anyone, quote, 'It appears that the sticker was put on the duct tape intentionally?'"

Answer: "Never."

She was next asked: "Why were you so firm when you said that?"

Answer: "I could never say that it was a heart-shaped sticker to begin with."

She would later say, "I could never and would never jump to the conclusion that something was placed intentionally or that it even was what I thought it was."

Fontaine said that she saw "something" in the shape of a heart but she continued processing the tape. No fingerprints were found on the tape, and then when she went back to look for the heart, it was gone. *It had disappeared.*

We called this the "phantom heart-shaped sticker."

What they did then was give the duct tape to another examiner in the document section, who used several devices to do her testing, including one that looks at paper with different light reflections to allow it to pick up the minutest impressions. She found *no* sticker fragments. She found nothing in the shape of a heart on the duct tape.

Nevertheless, the prosecution went with its theory anyway, also discussing the sticker found attached to the cardboard thirty feet from the skull. In that part of the woods, there were all kinds of things—tires, a toilet seat, trash, pens, paper, etc. It was across the street from an elementary school, which was probably where the sticker came from. And to make matters worse, the sticker they found on the cardboard looked *nothing* like the stickers they said they recovered from Caylee's home. In fact, they weren't even close.

But the prosecution, desperate and out of real evidence, tried to feed the story of the phantom heart-shaped sticker to the jury anyway, contributing to what we called, "the fantasy of forensics."

CHAPTER 18

SLINGS AND ARROWS

THIS CASE INTRUDED ON MY LIFE in so many unpleasant ways. I went home early on December 24, 2008. It was Christmas Eve, normally a most festive evening, especially in the Hispanic community.

That evening Lorena and I had a get-together at our home. We invited family and friends, but I wasn't much in the mood to party. That day the defense had conducted Caylee's autopsy, and my thoughts were wrapped up in the case. While everyone else celebrated, I was on the phone talking strategy with Linda Baden.

Linda and I discussed our need for a botanist, because we figured forensic botany would play a role in the case. Caylee was found in the woods, and there might be possible evidence of soil or weed growth. It's a specialized field, and neither Linda nor I knew anyone, but she said she'd make some phone calls. Meanwhile, Lorena was getting more and more upset because I was on the phone talking business when she wanted me spending the Christmas holiday with my family.

That night our home was filled with tension. Everyone struggles to balance work and family, but it's even harder when the whole world's watching and criticizing your every move. I lost focus for a long time.

About a month later Lorena and I had dinner at a Mexican restaurant, and by the time I got home, I wasn't feeling well. I was up all night vomiting, and my stomach hurt so much that we got in the car and went to the hospital.

The staff treated me with kid gloves. They put me in the Intensive Care Unit to make sure no one would notice me. The doctor was concerned the pressure of the case was getting to me, but after running some tests, the doctor came in and said, "This is just a case of some bad Mexican food."

My visit to the hospital made it into the media the next day. I was fine by the morning and even flew to Colorado for a forensic meeting, but every TV news program that morning reported that the stress had gotten to me, and that I had had a heart attack. I will never forget sitting in the airport that night, watching as Nancy Grace did a news report about my stress-related hospital visit. She followed that with a video of George Parnham, the lawyer representing Clara Harris, a Texas woman who was accused of driving over her husband twice in her Mercedes and killing him. The video showed Parnham, who had actually had a heart attack, being taken by stretcher into an ambulance.

I thought to myself, *She's comparing this guy to me? Is she nuts?*

But even Nancy Grace couldn't have anticipated the stress that I would be feeling a short time later.

I got a call from Dominic Casey, to whom I hadn't spoken in months, and he told me, "The police want to talk to me." I explained to him that his information, whatever it was, was privileged. They wanted to talk to him about what he and Jim Hoover were doing in the woods off Suburban Drive a month before Caylee was discovered.

"It's as if you're a lawyer," I said. "You should not be talking to the police, especially about the time you were working for me. And if you do talk to them, I want to be present."

Of course, Dominic did whatever Dominic felt like doing. I had zero control over him, and he went and spoke to the police anyway. I filed a motion to prevent it, but I filed it too late. So he went in and talked to them and was represented by Brad Conway, the Anthonys' pro bono lawyer. During the conversation the police asked him, "If you had found the body, did anyone ever tell you to do anything other than call 9-1-1?" The tape was paused before he answered, and after the tape was turned on again, he said, "Yes, Jose Baez told me if I found Caylee, call me first, not 9-1-1."

There are major problems with that. The first is that every time we spoke, it was about finding Caylee alive. And secondly, it was a complete and total lie; we never discussed anything of the sort. Dominic had a way with stories.

But even if it were true, it still wasn't unethical. Say I represent a client, and the client says to me, "I killed somebody and I put the body in the woods." I don't know whether that's true or not and I would not be able to negotiate his surrender to the police, or even his cooperation, until I verified he actually did what he said he did.

If I said to him, "Go over and check the body. Don't touch anything. And let me know," there would be nothing at all unethical about that.

But on the basis of this allegation by Dominic, Judge Stan Strickland, who certainly seemed to have it in for me, filed a bar complaint against me, accusing me of obstruction of justice and charging me with not just an unethical act but one that was criminal.

That was bad enough, but what disturbed me more was that he never had the decency to call me aside to ask me about it. He would have gotten a better picture if he had taken me aside and said to me, "I have these concerns. What do you have to say for yourself?" He didn't call me in and tell me, "I feel obligated to do this, and this is why I'm doing it."

No, I had to find out about the bar complaint from my lawyer, who was told about it. And the Florida Bar didn't tell him the nature of the complaint, so all I could do was imagine the worst. Remember, I was the guy who was denied admission to the bar for eight years. I was the guy they deemed not to have enough character to join the bar.

For two weeks this bar complaint hung over my head without my knowing the basis for the complaint. And I will never, ever forgive Strickland for that.

The day I learned of Strickland's action, I was scared shitless. I didn't know what to do. I drove home, walked into our bedroom, and took refuge in the walk-in closet where I kept my clothes. I took off my suit, sat down, and was suddenly overcome with a terrible feeling of doom. After all my success, after all the work I had put into the Casey Anthony case, all of it was going to come undone—I was going to be disbarred and disgraced in front of the world.

I fell into a deep, deep depression. I didn't want to talk to anyone. Lorena would say to me, "What's wrong?" But I didn't want to talk about it. I shut down. I couldn't sleep, and my stomach would often be in knots. I walked around like a zombie because I knew the cops were investigating me, and I knew the judge filed the complaint. I thought to myself, *I'm not a big shot. People get wrongfully accused of things all the time. How are they going to give you a pass?*

The depression grabbed me by the gut, and I walked around in a fog for the two weeks I waited to find out what I was accused of. I did my job working on the case, but I derived little joy from my work.

The day arrived when I learned what the accusations against me were. When I found out, I was so furious I could barely stand it. It turned out that when Strickland heard Dominic say, "Jose Baez told me if I found Caylee, call me first, not 9-1-1," it was proof I was obstructing justice.

How could he have believed the guy? This was the guy who believed the psychic who told him Caylee's body was in the gas tank of Casey's car. This is the guy who believed the postal service was involved in her disappearance. This was the guy who believed that "Zanny the nanny" was a code name for Xanax.

I thought to myself, *This clown has zero credibility, and I'm going to have to prove that.*

I knew it wouldn't be difficult because, luckily, I remembered an email exchange between Dominic, Cindy, and me, in which Dominic said that he had information that Caylee was flown to Puerto Rico on a private jet, then held there until she was flown to Colombia and taken across the border in Venezuela. He said his associates were closely watching the kidnappers and to not release the information to law enforcement until extraction was in play.

Once the bar saw this email, the Dominic Casey debacle was over.

It was still not a happy time. Until I could clear my name, I felt very low.

Lorena became pregnant that same month. She was elated, but I was so depressed, I couldn't express any joy about anything, and she felt I wasn't displaying the proper amount of joy over her pregnancy. What she didn't realize was how much this case was affecting me. I told her initially, but after that I clammed up. She really didn't know how much this case was bothering me.

Meanwhile, Casey was taking a pounding from the prosecution and its attack dogs in the media. Casey had photos posted on Facebook, pictures of her when she was eighteen years old. Among those pictures were ones of her drinking, partying at clubs, peeing in public, and mooning one of her friends, her ass bare to the wind. She was a kid, but in the prosecution's attempt to enrage the jury pool, it sought to portray Casey in the worst possible light by leaking the photos to the media. Those photos were spread around the country through the tabloids and the newspapers that chose to act like the tabloids.

I tried to block them, but Strickland overruled me once again. The photos were released, and everyone following the trial began referring to Casey as "the party girl."

When the prosecutors talked about Casey to the cops, they would say, "Her daughter was missing, and she partied for thirty-one days." They knew it was improper. Worse, they knew it was bullshit. They didn't care.

They also questioned Casey's boyfriends about her sex life and made the testimony public.

The cops actually asked, "What was she like in bed?" "What was she like afterwards?" "Was she cold, a wham-bam, thank-you-ma'am type, or was she warm and cuddly?"

The boyfriends were asked, "Did you wear a condom?" "Did she tell you she had any diseases?"

There wasn't much we could do about that. It had absolutely nothing to do with how Caylee died, but the cops were trying their best to paint Casey as a slut, to show she was sleeping with different men. I wanted to scream from the rooftop, *I hate to break it to you, but Casey's sex life has nothing to do with her guilt or innocence.* But suddenly her sex life became a focus of discovery.

This served one purpose: they believed if a juror thought she was a slut, that juror would look at the evidence with a different perspective and vote against her.

The next up to take a shot at me was the *Orlando Sentinel*, which ran a two-part hit piece on my background. The paper brought up my issues with the bar, my prior bankruptcy, and basically dug up every negative thing it could find about me. On a positive note, as a result of the *Sentinel's* story, I met Cheney Mason in April 2009.

Apparently, Cheney read the story and wrote a letter to the *Sentinel*, suggesting that the paper try balanced reporting and look into Jeff Ashton's history of being named in appellate cases for improper conduct. He even cited the capital cases that had to be retried. The *Sentinel* thanked Cheney for the letter and promised to be fair and do a piece on Ashton.

It's been three years, and the paper still hasn't written so much as a blurb, while I got blasted on the front page of the paper two days in a row.

I drove to his office in downtown Orlando and thanked him. Cheney was old school. He was a country boy with a Southern drawl. Prior to meeting him, the only person I knew who spoke that way was Florida State University football coach Bobby Bowden. Cheney, the former president of the Florida Association of Criminal Defense Lawyers, practiced law the way I was taught.

Whenever I had problems or issues, I would hop in the car and go see him. Anytime I needed help, Cheney was there.

Finally, he said to me one day, "Jose, do you want me to try this damn case with you?"

"I have no problem with that," I said. I talked with Andrea Lyon and Linda Baden, and both agreed.

By the fall of 2009 I had become the Snidely Whiplash of jurisprudence. I couldn't turn on the TV without hearing that I was covering up for a killer and that I, the inexperienced, bumbling defense attorney, was subverting justice by muzzling Casey and preventing her from admitting her evil deeds.

Knowing how cruel and mean the media could be to me, I took every measure to protect my family from suffering the same fate. When Lorena was pregnant, I did all I could to keep it under wraps from everyone. I knew that one slip by the wrong person would unleash the media upon us, so during her pregnancy, we didn't invite family or friends over to the house. The only people who visited us at home came from my office. We had a very sympathetic doctor, and anytime we went to see him, he let us in the back door so none of his other patients would see us.

The day came for Lorena to give birth. Our doctor called the hospital to let them know I was coming. Lorena was admitted under the name of Sabrina Philips. I entered through the front door and was recognized by a few people, but fortunately no one said anything. Our son, Jose Sebastian Baez, was born on September 1, 2009, at 11:45 P.M.

I was grateful to everyone at the hospital who respected our privacy and didn't say anything to anyone. One time I was standing in the common area, and a woman gave me the dirtiest of looks, as if I was there to kill some babies. A part of me wanted to be angry, but another realized that people were going to be ignorant, and I chalked it up to complete and utter ignorance on her part. I moved on.

A couple of months after Jose was born, I finally told Cindy. That same day I received a call from an NBC news reporter sending his congratulations; I can only assume it was Cindy who told him. I asked him not to say anything, and he swore to me he wouldn't, but I had to hold my breath until the next day, when no reports surfaced on TV. Later, one of the cops congratulated me. Turns out he was told by one of the jailhouse snitches. When you achieve celebrity, you become instantly recognizable; unfortunately, you give up your personal privacy as well.

It was disappointing we couldn't celebrate Jose's birth the way we would have liked to.

By 2010 CASEY'S FUNDS had run extremely low, even though she had received donations from people who were outraged over how unfairly she was being treated. The cost of fighting the case was exorbitant, and coupled with the weakness of the economy, which affected my law practice significantly, we were hurting financially. I was also spending so much time on the case that I didn't have time to network and bring in new business.

I had to cut corners, and the first move I made was to hire interns from Florida A&M University College of Law instead of secretaries. I had run through five secretaries because they weren't used to the high stress of the job. I had taught a course at the law school in 2008, and the school invited me back each year to talk to the students. Many wanted to come work with me, and it was great to be around the law students because of the energy and enthusiasm they brought to our office.

Then there were a couple months when things were so tight that I couldn't make the payroll. Some of my staff came to me and said, "I can get paid next week." Everyone at the office made sacrifices, and I am indebted to them all. Luckily, the doors stayed open, and my staff was able to work on Casey's case as well as other cases.

During the three years I represented Casey, I conducted three jury trials. Two were homicide cases, and one was a rape case. All three defendants were found not guilty, though you didn't read about any of those cases in the newspapers. I did get one local news story on News 13, but no one else picked it up. I was angry that the media didn't cover those cases. Of course, my winning didn't fit into the media's story line of the "incompetent lawyer."

When I was in court, everyone knew who I was, and when the jury came back in the rape case, I saw two reporters waiting to learn the verdict. When it was "not guilty," they turned on their heels and left. Had I lost the case, I guarantee you they'd have jumped on the story and reported it. I apologize if I sound a little bitter, but really, how could I not be?

By 2009 I had also lost faith in both George and Cindy Anthony. I was aware that George was leaving clues for the cops as to Casey's guilt, but I always thought Cindy would be loyal. Then there came the day when Casey hadn't seen Cindy in four months, and we had a court appointment to air a motion. It would have been Cindy's first chance to go see Casey in a long, long time.

Casey was looking forward to seeing her, but Cindy instead traveled to Tampa to see Meredith Viera.

"Is my mother here?" Casey wanted to know.

I told her the truth. Clients want you to tell them straight.

"She didn't come," I said. "Your mother is having lunch with Meredith Viera instead."

Just about every month, it seemed, the media would spread rumors about my demise. It started when the Anthonys hired a lawyer, and after that the rumors never ceased: Casey was going to fire me, or the judge was going to hold me in contempt, or the bar was going to take away my license, or another big-shot lawyer was going to take the case away from me. Those rumors, coupled with the digs about my competency, made me realize that the prosecution had poisoned the atmosphere of this trial by doing all it could to convince the public of Casey's guilt. As a result, the media wanted Casey jailed and wanted me to fail. It always bothered me, but I got more and more used to it.

Sometimes a rumor started because another lawyer joined my team, like Andrea or Cheney, but as often as not, it started with no basis— they were all baseless, actually—simply because they felt like starting a rumor.

There were times when the media would ask the Anthonys, "Are you satisfied with Jose representing Casey?"

In what other case does a question like that ever get asked?

As soon as the prosecution announced that it was going to seek the death penalty, all the amateur legal experts knew that I would need a death penalty expert to defend Casey because I wasn't qualified to do so. You have to have tried two death penalty cases and you also have to have a certain amount of credits to be qualified. Most people who are charged with the death penalty are poor people, so unless you're a veteran public defender, and really, almost a lifer in the public defenders' office, chances are you're not death penalty–qualified.

I'd say 95 percent of lawyers are not qualified to try death penalty cases, but in my case, whenever the press wrote about me, they said it was because of my inexperience.

The other thing they ruminated about was that Andrea was going to replace me as Casey's lawyer. I don't know why, except that it fit the media's image of me as an inexperienced, rookie Latino lawyer.

Later in the case I was unable to pay my mortgage, and my house went into foreclosure. I was about to leave the house when I saw the helicopters flying over. I looked up, and I knew what this was about. I couldn't leave my house. I didn't want them to film me leaving. It was humiliating, never mind putting my family at risk, something for which I will never forgive them. The media took that to mean I was going to quit the case.

"He can't afford to stay on the case," was what they wrote.

But I never considered quitting, not for a second. I told myself, *I will try this case out of a cardboard box before I quit.*

CHAPTER 19

THE SHRINKS

INCEST HAS BEEN CITED as the most common form of child abuse, with estimates that between ten and twenty million American children have been victimized by parental incest.

Incest is considered by experts to be a particularly damaging form of sexual abuse because it is perpetrated by an individual the victim trusts and depends on. The victim feels great pressure to keep quiet because of her fear of the family breaking up over her revelations.

Father-daughter incest is most common, though mother-son incest does happen. It's difficult to assess just how prevalent parental child abuse is because of the secrecy that surrounds it. Experts say that many young incest victims accept and believe the perpetrator's explanation that this is a "learning experience that happens in every family."

As a result, it remains one of the most underreported and least-discussed crimes in our nation because its victims can't bring themselves to come forward because of guilt, shame, fear, and social and familial pressure. There's another more practical reason: incest victims feel that either no one will believe them, or they will be blamed or punished if they report the abuse. As in Casey's case, more often than not, they're ridiculed for coming forward.

Casey had been courageous enough to tell me about the incest she had endured. But because of the compartmentalization, and all the discredited lies she told to the police at the beginning of this case, we knew no one would believe her. She was the girl who cried wolf.

One of the problems I knew we would have with Casey's account of what occurred on June 16, 2008, was how to present what really happened to the jury.

We knew putting her on the stand would be risky, so instead we decided the best way to get her testimony admitted was to have psychiatrists interview her and put them on the stand.

We debated this for six months. Casey's death penalty lawyer, Ann Finnell, kept saying, "How are we going to get this in without her testifying?" Cheney Mason talked about a case he had in which he was able to get it in. In fact, Cheney said he submitted a video of his client making the statement without subjecting him to cross-examination.

This was not a case where we were pleading not guilty by reason of insanity. We did the research. We knew we were on very thin ground, but we still wanted to hire psychiatrists to talk to Casey.

One of the first names to come up was Dr. Jeffrey Danziger. A graduate of Harvard University and the University of Miami Miller School of Medicine, he was an associate professor at the University of Florida and had a thriving practice in psychiatry in Winter Park, Florida.

At the behest of the court, Danziger had interviewed Casey and had made a competency evaluation. In his report, Danziger wrote, "Casey Anthony does not fit, in my opinion, into any of the categories of maternal filicide. The history is not consistent with an altruistic or mercy killing, a mentally ill or psychotic mother, the accidental death of a battered child, spousal revenge, or an unwanted child."

He noted what a "doting, loving, devoted" mother Casey was.

He quoted Cindy saying, "Casey bought safety door handles and outlet covers. She carried an extra key for the car, for what if she locked the child in the car by accident. She was very safety conscious. She called me if the child had a sniffle, the child never had a diaper rash. She cooked her food, healthy food, vegetables."

He explained her behavior during the thirty days she was away from home by citing a "pathological level of denial."

Danziger wrote, "Denial is a psychological mechanism in which the existence of unpleasant realities is disavowed, and one keeps out of conscious awareness any aspects of reality that if acknowledged would produce extreme anxiety." He said she was acting the way she was because of a "refusal or inability to recognize reality."

In his initial competency hearing report, he wrote about how normal she seemed in the face of such stress, calling it a clear indication of her compartmentalization.

Danziger seemed a perfect person to examine her for the defense. I thought he would carry a lot of weight not only with the judge but also with the jury, in part because he had been called by the court to evaluate her the first time.

When we talked to him, Danziger seemed excited at the opportunity. "I'm glad to not have to sit on the sidelines for this one," he said.

We were ecstatic to have him. We thought we had ourselves a great psychiatrist.

Danziger went to see Casey several times, and each time we talked to him, he indicated to us that he was certain she had been a victim of sexual abuse. He said that while she didn't have any symptoms of mental illness and didn't have any diagnosable issues, she did show classic signs of sexual abuse, such as lying, compartmentalizing, and pretending nothing was wrong.

We're going to be super strong with him, I thought.

We only had one reservation about Danziger: normally when he testified in court, he was a witness for the prosecution.

We also hired a psychologist, Dr. William Weitz. He was referred to us by a friend of Andrea Lyon, who had a colleague that used him in another case. The background of Weitz, a graduate of the University of Miami with a PhD in clinical psychology, had to do with post-traumatic stress disorder. He had once trained at the Walter Reed Army Medical Center (now called the Walter Reed National Military Medical Center) in Washington, DC.

What I wanted to talk to Weitz about was the sexual abuse, of course, but equally important, I wanted to be able to explain Casey's behaviors during the thirty days after Caylee was found in the pool by her father, behaviors that the prosecution and the media had trumpeted as shocking proof that Casey killed Caylee: partying at the nightclub Fusion, getting a tattoo, and ostensibly staying away from home all that time, as the prosecution described it, to party.

I wanted to ask him how someone reacts after going through a stressful event, such as the one Casey underwent. I wanted him to analyze her behavior during the thirty days after Caylee was found in the pool by her father.

Weitz, like Danziger, was extremely excited to be part of the case.

I always had my reservations about Weitz, but I couldn't put my finger on it. But he went to see Casey and reported the same thing as Danziger. He said she showed classic signs of being a victim of sexual abuse.

"I couldn't be more certain that Casey was sexually abused by George," he said.

After getting their reports, we made the determination that we were going to put them on our witness list. We weren't sure how this was going to play out, but the trial was right around the corner, and we needed to make a decision, so we decided to go with them. After all, we could always decide not to call them if we so wished.

We filed their names on the witness list, and the prosecution took its depositions, and the day Danziger was to show up for his deposition, I felt a shiver down my spine that something was very wrong because when I arrived, Danziger was already in a room in the state attorney's office with Ashton and Linda Drane Burdick, the prosecutors.

What's going on? I asked myself.

I would soon find out.

His testimony was certainly promising and would have helped us tremendously with the jury. In his deposition with Ashton, Danziger described Casey's ambivalence toward her father. He said Casey talked about finding emails from women on his computer, and how when her mother found them, her father blamed Casey, saying Casey had been the one setting him up.

Danziger said Casey hated the fact she could still love him, that she was a little girl wishing he could be her dad.

"I can't figure out why I don't hate him," Danziger quoted Casey. "Years of anger, frustration, hurt and pain, finally openly speaking about it, but it's painful and distressing."

Danziger related that Casey's great fear was that her father would sexually abuse Caylee, the way he had abused her. He said that was why she always locked her door at night, why Caylee ordinarily never went outside by herself, and why she had Caylee shower with her.

Danziger then recounted Casey's events of June 16, how she saw her father carrying Caylee's limp form, and how George had said, "I'll take care of it."

He also quoted Casey as saying she didn't think it was an accident. She posited that her father had held Caylee underwater and drowned her. He quoted Casey as saying her father's suicide attempt was his way of trying to force her to take the rap for Caylee's death.

But the jury, I knew, would hear none of this, because toward the beginning of his deposition, Danziger began by backpedaling furiously.

"Jeff, let me just say something parenthetically here," he said to Ashton, who was doing the interrogation. "And this is something that has caused me great distress and places me in a bit of an ethical bind and concern.

"In my meetings with her, with Casey, she said things that accuse others of criminal behavior. I am deeply troubled, and I don't know how to handle this. I realize you're entitled in the deposition to know what she said to me, but I am very troubled about being a vector by which statements she made may accuse others of crimes past and present. I don't know what to do."

He continued, "I am very nervous and reluctant to say things she told me [knowing] what the media would do with it. [I'm not sure] I am ethically doing the right thing by reporting things she said that accuse others of crimes that may never have happened. I don't know what to do, and I've expressed my concern about this."

He concluded, "I am just deeply worried that I'm doing the wrong thing."

Added a smug Ashton, "We are equally concerned with unsupported allegations of criminal conduct being thrown around in this case." The irony of his sanctimonious statement by the guy who had been bashing Casey without remorse for the last three years almost knocked me over.

I couldn't believe what I was hearing. I couldn't believe Danziger was behaving this way. He was a professional. He had a reputation to uphold. If he was going to in effect recuse himself, why didn't he at least have the decency to call me and let me know beforehand. There would have been no point to his testifying.

As I was listening to him, I became so angry that I wanted to jump up and punch him. How could he tell me one thing and then get up there and testify in a deposition to the same thing, but put so many qualifications to his answers that they were worthless? It was disgusting. He was making it clear that there was no point whatsoever for us to put him on the stand.

After his testimony, we told Ashton to take him off our witness list. When we arrived back at my office, Cheney, Dorothy, and I talked about why he did what he did. We decided it was remotely possible that his conscience got the better of him at the last minute, but that didn't make any sense. He knew the topics of conversation. He knew the parameters of the testimony. We were certain that Danziger did his about-face because he gets most of his work from the prosecution, not from defense lawyers. We figured that someone had threatened him and said something like, "If you testify for Casey Anthony, you can forget about getting more business from us."

Of course, we didn't have any proof of that, but that's certainly what we thought. He'll deny that, but that's his business. It turns out I couldn't have made a worst choice.

I could only hope I'd have better luck with Weitz, an older gentleman who had retired from private practice.

His deposition turned to the subject of incest.

"She told me that her father had physically and sexually abused her back to the age of childhood," Weitz said. He said that took place from the time she was eight until she was twelve.

"What sort of physical abuse was described to you?" asked Ashton.

"She described physical touching and involvement all the way to sexual intercourse," Weitz said.

"When you say physical, do you mean striking her?" asked Ashton.

"No. I would say . . . physical, sensual. More of a sexual assault or sexual—in a sexual connotation."

"To include fondling and intercourse?"

"Yeah, fondling, touching, hugging, kissing, all the way to intercourse, correct, on multiple times."

When asked how frequent the incest was, Weitz said Casey had told him her father had raped her "a few times a week" over the course of four years, from the time she was eight until she turned twelve. And when he stopped, Weitz said, Casey said her brother Lee, who was four years older than she was, began coming into her room at night while she lay in bed, and he would fondle her breasts. Weitz said Lee did this from the time she was twelve to when she turned fifteen.

Weitz testified that years later Casey tried to tell Cindy about Lee's sexual abuse, and that her response was to call Casey a whore. Rather than protect her from Lee, said Weitz, she attacked Casey. She was getting no nurturing from her mother, she told Weitz.

According to Weitz, Casey indicated that sex with her father continued on a less frequent basis up to the time she became pregnant with Caylee. Casey was twenty. When Weitz asked her who was the father, she told him she thought it could have been her father, but she said she also could have gotten pregnant at a party with coworkers from Universal Studios, during which her date drugged her drink, she passed out, and he raped her.

Said Weitz, "She only had two beers yet she felt kind of woozy and drugged, and basically she doesn't remember when she woke up the next morning. She doesn't recall what happened the previous night."

Weitz said she wasn't dating anyone regularly at that time. She didn't have a romantic interest at that time.

"As the discussion comes up," said Weitz, "she's not sure of the biological father. She believes she could have been impregnated at that party."

Her father was also suspect, but as I said, he was ruled out as the potential father after the discovery came out in the case and her DNA didn't match his.

Weitz cited a couple of examples of George's questionable behavior.

Weitz said Casey told him that both her parents went to the hospital with her when she gave birth, and her father was in the delivery room with her when she gave birth.

At Caylee's funeral, the tape of which Weitz watched, he noticed that when George got up to talk about Caylee, he talked about the sweet smell of his granddaughter, the smell of her sweat.

"That is not, in my estimation," said Weitz, "descriptions that grandfathers make of their granddaughters."

"Meaning?" asked Ashton.

"Meaning it had a sexual connotation," said Weitz, "in my professional opinion, based on thirty-five years of study as a psychologist, and based upon my experience, training, and knowledge and education as a psychologist."

Weitz said Casey described to him, from the time Caylee was born, her fear of leaving Caylee in the house alone with George. He said she feared he would molest Caylee the way he had molested her.

"She never felt comfortable and wouldn't leave her—if at all possible—leave her alone with George," Weitz said. "She felt George was a threat to her daughter."

Weitz said that sometimes Casey would be "mad and angry," and sometimes she'd be "sad and overwhelmed."

Later Weitz testified, "According to Casey, her father had sexually assaulted her many times over a number of years; that she felt that he was highly impulsive, erratic; that...he could lose control over his behavior easily, and so she feared him and feared for her daughter's safety." When asked what he meant by "poor control" over his behavior, Wise replied, "Poor impulse control."

Ashton then had the gall to say to Weitz, "I did not hear anywhere in your recitation before that about any physical abuse by the father."

When I heard that, I almost lost it. Cheney chimed in.

"Just one second," Cheney said.

"Mr. Mason, is there something that you wanted to..." said Ashton.

"Yeah," said Cheney, "for you as a prosecutor to think that sexual assault is not violent is pretty bizarre."

"So is that an objection or just a..." said Ashton, refusing to answer.

The two then bickered for a while before moving on.

Weitz quite rightly told Ashton, "The whole culmination of any kind of sexual assault would be seen by her as physically violent."

According to Weitz, Casey was normal in every way, except for exhibiting behaviors associated with being a victim of sexual abuse. Weitz listed the mental illnesses and diseases and dismissed them one by one. She wasn't antisocial, he said, nor did she have borderline personality disorder, histrionic personality, narcissism; she didn't have avoidant personality disorder, nor dependent personality disorder; she didn't have obsessive-compulsive disorder; and most importantly, her test scores showed no signs of malingering, meaning she wasn't lying.

She has "no mental disease or defect," he said. Rather, he said, she suffered from post-traumatic stress disorder. Weitz testified that Casey's behavior was consistent with being a victim of sexual abuse.

He said when she talked to him about the abuse, "she was almost in a kind of a daze or fog" and that, "she could present it as information but with no real facial response, any kind of nonverbal behavioral response showing any kind of anxiety or disturbance or upsetness and stripped of emotion."

He said that during the thirty days she was away from home after Caylee died, "She was basically still in emotional shock and traumatized, and she was basically functioning in denial, suppressed mode. Essentially she was dealing with, one way or another, the loss of a child she loved."

He said, "She basically talked about being numb."

He explained why Casey lied to her mother and to the police. He said Casey used lies as a "protective measure," a way to dull the pain of the death of her daughter.

He said she lied to protect herself.

"She's acknowledging to me that she tells untruths, that she lies, and she's aware of some of that, and she sees it as using it for her protection," said Weitz.

Ashton asked him whether she believed what she was saying when she was telling people that Caylee was with Zenaida the nanny.

"I think she wanted to believe it," said Weitz. "I think she was in total suppression and denial. Denial, as you're aware, is an unconscious process, and people who are in denial basically can act as if certain things never took place. So I think she wanted to believe that her child was alive, I mean, on a certain level. But I think that the behavior's explained, in my professional opinion, by suppression and denial."

He said that Casey's reaction to her pregnancy was to deny it was happening.

"She was pregnant, and she was showing and everything, and even the parents, everyone was in denial about that she was in pregnancy; that they didn't think she was pregnant even though she was well into term."

Weitz said Casey told him of a wedding she had gone to, and though she was showing, her parents were making excuses for her.

Late in the deposition Ashton asked Weitz "if Miss Anthony would have had the same behaviors of denial and compartmentalization if she had killed Caylee."

Weitz said it was possible. However, it seemed unlikely given that she showed "absolutely no motivation to want to do that in any personal, behavioral, or emotive capacity."

He continued, "To do that it would almost suggest if she did kill her child and there was nothing more than what currently is on the plate, then I almost would be tempted to think of some psychotic reaction. Because I can find and see, professionally, no motive, no baseline for why, given the nature of the relationship, her behavior, the responses of people about her being a mother and how she interacted with her child, no underlying motive for doing so.

"So therefore to answer your question, rather than being in denial and defensive, I would almost think that for her to kill her child, she would almost have to go through a psychotic episode."

Ashton pushed Weitz to get him to say that it was possible that Casey killed Caylee. But Weitz wouldn't buy it. He told Ashton, "There is nothing that I could see in this case that would suggest that your hypothesis about her acting in that way comes to merit. Okay?"

"Okay," said Ashton, but of course for him, it certainly wasn't okay.

"I don't want to overstate what you're telling me," said Ashton toward the end of the questioning. "Your opinion is that every untruth she said about Caylee between her death and the police being notified, that thirty-one days, every untruth she said about Caylee was not a deliberate untruth?"

Answered Weitz, "I can say to you that since Caylee's the most threatening, traumatizing, potentially overwhelming issue that would confront her, anything that had to do with her daughter or her daughter's death would be the most likely suppressed or that she'd be in denial about, so information around her would more likely be not accurate."

Later on, under his breath, Ashton called Weitz an asshole.

I heard him say it. Michelle Medina, one of my associates, also heard him say it.

Ashton denied saying it, and Burdick denied hearing it.

But he said it all right. Weitz was taking apart his case, point by point, and Ashton, the quintessential bully and sore loser, didn't like it.

One of the most important things Weitz said had to do with a refutation of another of Ashton's nonevidentiary-based (fantasy) accusations that Casey had killed Caylee because Caylee was a burden, something getting in the way of her partying.

Nothing could have been further from the truth, said Weitz. After she became pregnant, said Weitz, she never once considered having an abortion or putting the baby up for adoption. Even though she thought she might have been impregnated through rape or incest, she was very clear she never considered an abortion.

"She wanted the child," said Weitz.

Weitz said definitively that Casey did not consider Caylee a burden, something to be discarded like old luggage because she interfered with social relationships, romantic relationships, job opportunities, or travel, as the police and the prosecution so callously and wrongly declared.

"Having that child for some very specific reasons was very important to her," said Weitz. "Having a daughter was important. It was significant to her. She said, 'I loved her at first sight, and that child was the most meaningful part of my life for three years.' That to me is important."

Casey was a loving mom, a very protecting mother, said Weitz.

Said Weitz, "She immediately had love for her child. Her child meant everything to her, and the three years were the best that she ever had and she never regretted not having an abortion or adopting."

Does this sound like a mother who killed her baby because she wanted to go out and party?

Moreover, said Weitz, she was never the partier the prosecution contended she was, but a mother who spent most of her time at home taking care of Caylee.

The prosecution made a big deal out of the fact that Casey got tattoos while she was away for the thirty days, but Weitz said that the tattoo on her shoulder that read "La Bella Vita" was actually a tribute to Caylee.

"It was obtained…after her daughter passed away," said Weitz. "She told me La Bella Vita would mean the good life or the wonderful life. She said she contrasted that with the way her life had turned, the juxtaposition of how lousy her life had become. She said her life had been relatively normalized, moving in the [right] direction, and then it had catastrophically changed, both in terms of what had [happened] in her life legally and also the loss of her daughter.

"She represents it to be the irony in how her life had transpired," he said.

There had been some talk that Lee might be the father, because Casey named her daughter Caylee, but Weitz said that was not the case at all.

Weitz explained how Caylee got her name.

"She said it has nothing to do with Lee," said Weitz. He said Casey wanted to name her after herself and with a similar meaning. She wanted a name that sounded Irish, that she had considered Riley, but that she decided against it because she wanted her child to have the initials C.M.A. Her mother had that, and she wanted to pass it on to her daughter.

Originally, she was going to spell it K-A-Y-L-E, but finally she changed it to Caylee.

"And then she says it was the greatest thing that ever happened to her, and George took her from her," Weitz said.

"Meaning George killed Caylee?" asked Ashton.

"It is the perception of Casey that her father had something to do with the death of her daughter," said Weitz. "She believes that George either harmed and/or took the life of Caylee."

Later Weitz said, "She believes George took Caylee out of the bed, had a sexual—some sort of sexual experience with her daughter, and in order to cover it up killed her."

All of a sudden I had a problem. As soon as Weitz said that, I knew I couldn't put him on the stand. Weitz became far too defense-oriented on how Caylee died, and it made me uncomfortable. I don't like witnesses who try too hard, even if they are for the defense, because I don't think they are credible. During Weitz's testimony, I kept hearing things that I had never heard Casey say before. I just didn't think the jury would find him believable.

In his deposition Weitz seemed hell-bent on pinning a murder on George. I never for a second believed George murdered Caylee. My belief was that Caylee accidentally drowned in the backyard pool. After Weitz's deposition, Ashton and the media made a lot of comments about how Casey said that George killed Caylee, but that's not what she said.

I want to be clear about this: Weitz was trying to pin a murder on George, and I didn't believe that to be the case.

Here's what he was conveying: he was saying that he felt George may have drowned her because his shirt wasn't wet, and he felt Casey might have been drugged at the time Caylee died, because Casey's normally a light sleeper. And he also was saying, "Oh, by the way, George was sexually abusing Caylee," but that part of the testimony was lost when the press got ahold of the murder accusations.

The fact was that Casey didn't know what happened to Caylee. All she saw was George carrying away her limp body. And after she was arrested, she knew that she was being thrown under the bus by her father for something she didn't do. So she could think the best—that Caylee's death was an accident—or she could think the worst—that he killed her. She was in a position where she was facing the death penalty. She was sitting in prison and slowly came to the realization that her very own father was out to have her killed to save his own scalp. When that happens, you think the worst, so I can see how Casey might have said to Danziger and Weitz, "He did it intentionally." But it was never anything she *knew*. It was always something Casey *felt* might have happened, and she felt that way because she was so hurt by and angry with him. That anger was what motivated her to think the worst.

Because Danziger and Weitz were out, Casey taking the stand became more of a reality.

There were times during our three years on this case when my associates and I talked about whether it might be possible that George killed Caylee to cover up sexual abuse, but eventually we backed away. If George had been messing with Caylee and maybe even sexually abusing her, we felt that might have been the reason George didn't call 9-1-1 when he picked her up out of the pool. An autopsy clearly would have shown that she had been sexually active, an investigation would have ensued, and George would have gone down big time.

Or maybe he thought he was Caylee's father and didn't want that revealed. Or maybe he was afraid his incestuous behavior with Casey would come out, as it eventually did. We thought of different motives, but we didn't say them because we didn't have any evidence of them. I could have thrown those suspicions out there, but what I wanted to be able to do was look the jury in the eye and say, "As much as we'd like to be able to say that somebody murdered the child, the fact is there is no more evidence that Casey murdered this child than there was that George did it."

And that's the truth. If you look at all the evidence compiled by the state—the prosecution and the police—even if you believe everything they say about the smell in Casey's car, it doesn't tell you *how* Caylee died. It only tells you whether she was transported in that car or not.

The prosecution had no confession and no statement. It had *nothing* to tie a murder to Casey. And that was because the accusations as invented by the police were so absurd. And that was the approach I decided to take at the trial. It was, after all, the more conservative one, even though I've been criticized for it. I didn't want to go too far, because I thought it would affect the credibility of our case. I don't believe in making accusations without any evidence to support them, despite accusations to the contrary.

I will respond to their criticism in this way. Not only did Casey tell me she was sexually abused by her father, but there was plenty of other evidence she had told other people about that abuse. There's evidence this was a young woman who had her periods since she was twelve years old, but who never once went to a gynecologist until she became pregnant at age nineteen. Why? There may be two or more reasons for this, but the most plausible is that a gynecologist would have noticed the evidence of sexual activity—especially when she was a preteen. It would have raised questions about possible sexual abuse.

And then there's plenty of evidence of her compartmentalization, the way she pretended nothing was wrong in the face of such horror. She lied to fashion a story that soothed her. How her pregnancy was hidden for more than seven months, not only by her but by her family as well. The fact that she told two boyfriends about the abuse prior to Caylee dying refutes the charge of it being a "recent fabrication." Moreover, she didn't have sexual boundaries with men. All these are signs of sexual abuse. And all of that came to play a role in the trial. So when people say I never submitted any evidence of sexual abuse, they are *very* mistaken.

Here's another thing: If Casey had walked into the state attorney's office on June 15, 2008, and said, "I'm a victim of sexual abuse. My father has been abusing me since I was eight years old. I've been afraid to come forward, but I'm doing so now," I guarantee you they would have arrested George and filed felony charges. And the only reason she didn't come forward? Victims of sexual abuse almost never do. They are too afraid that their parents will be arrested, that their families will be broken up, that the parents won't love them anymore, and most importantly, *that no one will believe them.*

Sexual abuse—incest—is the most underreported crime in the world and if people who are abused cannot come forward and can't expect a process that is helpful to them and makes it easier to speak out, it will *never* get reported. I find it so hypocritical the way people approached Casey in that regard.

But the fact remains, despite the headlines, this case was *never* about sexual abuse. I never meant to make it so and didn't try. It was a low priority.

But her sexual abuse was an explanation for why she acted the way she did during the thirty days she was away from home after Caylee disappeared.

The fact is, how she acted during those thirty days should have been irrelevant to the question of whether Caylee was murdered. If the judge had precluded any discussion of her behavior during those thirty days, there never would have been a discussion around the topic of George's sexual abuse. If the prosecution had really wanted to make this trial about the first-degree murder charge, *none* of these things should have been allowed into evidence. They prosecuted this case by discussing everything but a murder. And this was the end result.

If you are outraged by our approach, you really aren't looking at it from a logical perspective. As I said, whether or not Casey was abused is irrelevant to the question of how Caylee died, but so is her behavior during the thirty days. The prosecution made a big deal of her clubbing and partying. What does that tell you about whether there's been a murder? These are all irrelevant facts, but what made them relevant was the prosecution's approach, not ours.

If you can understand that, you can understand it all.

CHAPTER 20

YOUR HONOR

PERHAPS THE HARDEST ISSUE I had to face in 2010 was Judge Stan Strickland's clear prejudice against Casey. He had made public remarks such as, "It appears that the truth and Ms. Anthony are strangers." And most telling, whenever we made a motion, he always ruled against us. It got to the point where we just couldn't win in the courtroom.

When the case began, we were buoyed by Strickland's reputation for fairness. *He's defense-friendly*, we were told, which is why, for a long time, we took our defeats and swallowed hard.

Then came the issue of Casey's bad check charges that stemmed from her stealing Amy Huizenga's checkbook during the thirty days after Caylee died. They were written for a total of $644, and if this had been any other client, Casey would have been put in a pretrial diversion program and asked to take a course and repay the money.

Instead she was overcharged with thirteen counts by an overzealous prosecution. We made a motion before Strickland to reduce them significantly because of double jeopardy.

"We should withhold adjudication on all of these," I argued. Strickland got around my argument by saying, "I've never withheld adjudication on so many counts" adding, "Who knows? If we try this [check] case and I hear the facts, I could sentence her to prison." Basically he was saying, *You'd better plead her guilty, or I'm going to sentence her to prison for $644 in bad checks.*

Needless to say, Strickland ruled in favor of the prosecution on the double jeopardy issues.

Everyone knew we were going to plea out the check charges, and we asked to continue that portion of the case until after the murder trial. After all, the checks were written after the supposed murder, and if only for judicial economy, we thought it was a no-brainer.

Under most circumstances an economic crime would be tried after the more serious crime because the economic crime becomes substantially less important if a client gets the death penalty. The rules are different, however, when you have the most hated woman in America on trial.

The always scheming, ruthless prosecution, however, was out for blood. Though these were mere economic crimes, it refused to offer us a plea deal because it wanted a trial—a tactic unusual and unconscionable in itself. And the prosecution wanted the check charge trial to go first because it wanted to have convictions in the check trial in case Casey took the stand in the murder trial. That way the jury would know she was a convicted felon. Also, those convictions would be considered if she was found guilty of murder and a jury had to consider the death penalty.

In a calculated move on its part, the prosecution overcharged her. Instead of charging her with uttering a forged instrument, three counts, it stacked the charges by adding fraud and grand theft to each count. So it was three felony counts per check, which is never done. And the prosecutors had her dead to rights. They had her on video writing the checks and had a complaining witness saying she didn't have permission to write them. She was facing thirty years, even though normally a judge wouldn't sentence anyone to prison for $644 in bad checks.

This prosecution, continuing to overstep its bounds, refused to allow us to plea bargain on the check fraud charges. I argued to Strickland, "If she gets convicted of first-degree murder, I'll be more than happy to plead her guilty to all of these economic charges. She'll be doing a long prison term, and these will be insignificant. Why do this when it'll cost so much money to change the venue and go to trial? It just doesn't make any sense."

At first Strickland seemed to agree, saying it was the logical thing to do, but then the prosecution became insistent and kept pushing.

"No, no, no, this is something we really want," the prosecutors argued. In the end, the judge denied our motion to have the check charges heard after the murder trial.

Ironically, had Strickland listened to me and granted the motion, Casey would have been facing thirty years on the check charges after her murder acquittal. My belief is that Strickland's successor, Judge Belvin Perry, would have slammed the book on her and sent her to prison for many years. In the end, Casey didn't have to do any time at all on the check charges because the prosecutors were overaggressive and shot themselves in the foot.

As Strickland liked to say, the irony is indeed rich.

There were numerous times when we thought of trying to get Strickland recused, but I was reluctant to do so unless I was sure we would win. I'm a strong believer in the metaphor, "If you're going to shoot the king, shoot to kill." Instead, we waited for a situation where we could show without a doubt that Strickland was biased and Casey was unable to get a fair trial.

It'll come, I told myself. *You can set your watch by it.*

One day after a hearing before Strickland, co-counsel Andrea Lyon and I left the courtroom. After we were gone, Strickland asked an officer to go and get one of the members of the audience. The person he called up to see him was Dave Knechel, a blogger who went by the name of "Marinade Dave." I first learned of their meeting because one of Andrea's students had been in the courtroom when Strickland called him forward.

I can tell this story because Marinade Dave wrote it on his blog, and one of my investigators got him to confirm it.

According to Marinade Dave, Strickland called him up to the bench and said to him, "I want you to know I've read your blog, and I think you're really fair. I wanted you to know how much I enjoy reading your blog."

Marinade Dave's blog was naturally called Marinade Dave, and on it he wrote such fair and unbiased articles as, "Casey Anthony Must Die," and, "Premeditated and Pretty Stupid."

Cheney and I wanted to handle it quietly and delicately, so one day after a hearing we approached the bench and asked if we could meet with the judge.

Cheney said to him, "We need to speak with you about a matter."

Strickland said, "No, we can't talk in private because the press will want to be involved. I don't feel comfortable about it."

We hadn't asked to meet privately with him; we just wanted to talk to him in his chambers and ask him about Marinade Dave.

"What's this about?" the judge wanted to know.

"It's about us asking you to recuse your self," said Cheney.

We had wanted to do it quietly so Strickland could quit on his own, sparing him from both embarrassment and the firestorm the media surely would ignite. But Strickland refused to meet with us.

We were struggling about what to do. We met with the prosecutors about Marinade Dave and the judge; true to form, they were no help.

"We don't know if it's true or not," they said.

"We'll investigate," we said. And that's what we did. Marinade Dave told our investigator everything, including the fact that he had been in the hospital, and that Strickland called him to see if he was feeling better.

Then the media got into the act and interviewed Marinade Dave. It turned out that he and the judge had met for lunch to discuss the case. After lunch Strickland took him to the court's back area, showed him around, and even gave him a law book.

We filed our motion. We had ten days to do it and finished on a Friday. The story was blasted all over the news. Strickland accused us of waiting until 4:00 P.M. on a Friday afternoon so he wouldn't be there to respond, and for maximum media impact.

We had no such plans. That had *nothing* to do with it. How were we supposed to know he left early on Fridays? He was the one who had the media on his mind, not us.

In the end, Strickland had no choice but to recuse himself. If he had stayed on, we would have appealed his decision to the appellate court, and it was clear we had made a strong case for him to step down.

It was a question of his fairness, and he was unable to stand up to the storm of criticism that came from the media when they learned of his relationship with Marinade Dave.

Rather than just step down, Strickland wrote a scathing order in which he ripped me and worse, ripped the defendant. Under the law this man was supposed to be impartial. When we saw his comments, we were appalled and knew we made the right decision.

Cheney refused to take it lying down. He filed a motion to strike his comments and added his own commentary, arguing that a judge should not have any relationship with the media, including bloggers. It was inappropriate, he argued. The two of them went at it.

After the not-guilty verdict, Strickland became a commentator and one of our strongest critics. I was on a plane watching *Nancy Grace* and couldn't believe that he was her guest. It turns out that Strickland and Nancy Grace were classmates at Mercer University School of Law. He also granted an interview with a local TV station in which he said he disagreed with the verdict.

I couldn't believe what he was doing. Strickland's appearances caused a major stink in the local legal community. I was getting calls from lawyers who threatened to complain to the Judicial Qualifications Committee (JQC), which regulates Florida judges. They wanted the JQC to know what Strickland was doing. Shortly thereafter, he resigned as a judge. My suspicion is that he resigned because of those complaints.

When Strickland stepped down, Cheney, who had been on the circuit a long time, had a strong suspicion that the judge who was going to replace him would be Judge Belvin Perry. He was the chief judge of the Ninth Judicial Circuit Court of Florida and didn't have any active cases. Perry had more of an administrative role. He filled in for trials and presided over some of the more important cases. He was a former prosecutor who had tried death penalty cases. His father was the first African-American police officer in Orlando. Cheney had a wonderful relationship with Perry; the two of them were old colleagues, and Cheney considered him a friend.

We thought we had finally caught a break. We had important motions coming up, motions Strickland was sure to shoot down. We were optimistic that Perry wouldn't hold the same strong prejudices against us that Strickland had held.

We were also more confident about Perry's expertise in criminal law; Strickland had mostly been in workman's compensation during his career, and we wanted someone more sophisticated and more fair.

Initially, I really liked Perry. My first interactions with him were extremely positive. When we had our first sidebar, I felt relaxed. He was very pleasant, and I sensed he was going to listen to both arguments and make his decision based on the law, despite what everyone in the media was saying about him.

Hard-nosed, no-nonsense is what the press said. Some local lawyers were calling my move to recuse Strickland a "huge mistake." One said it was "the dumbest move Jose Baez ever made."

Just before Perry came on board, we made a motion to declare Casey indigent. It was necessary because we could no longer pay for the experts we needed to defend her, and if she were declared indigent, then the expenses would be borne by the state. Our motion was granted by Strickland, and we were gratified when Perry gave us most of what we were asking for.

Going into the trial, I felt relieved. *Finally*, I thought, *I have a shot at a fair trial. Wow, we're finally on a level playing field. We're going to be able to make things interesting.*

I was about to find out I couldn't have been more wrong.

As time went by, the media kept portraying Perry as a no-nonsense judge, saying he wasn't going to put up with Jose Baez's crap. The media was setting the stage as it waited for me to do something that would incur Perry's wrath. I don't really know whether that had anything to do with the way he would treat me, but I felt it was certainly a strong possibility.

In hindsight, I should have left well enough alone. We were hoping the new judge would be a breath of fresh air, but at the end of the day, the verdict would have been the same. It's just that I would have been spared a lot of humiliation and distress.

There had been a lot of criticism that the case was taking a long time to get to trial. The critics, however, don't know the first thing about murder trials. On average it takes two to three years for a murder case to go to trial. If it's a death penalty case, it's closer to three years, and can be even longer, depending on the circumstances.

As hard as I was working, I still wasn't able to accomplish all that needed to be accomplished. There were depositions of my experts I had to take. I had to depose law enforcement. The prosecution kept piling on more and more discovery, knowing I was short-handed. There were depositions relating to forensics, and we had a slew of pretrial motions we had to prepare.

When Strickland was presiding over the case, the prosecution had suggested that he set a deadline for taking depositions and filing motions. Based on those suggestions, Strickland set a trial date of May 9 2011. It was more than a year away.

When Perry took over and announced he would enforce the deadlines, trial preparation jumped from first to fifth gear. If I had been under pressure before, now I was under the gun to do the impossible.

The average complicated case has about a thousand pages of discovery. This case had *26,000* pages! It had more than three hundred hours of audio and video. Given the limited resources we had, I didn't think there was any way this case could have gone to trial in three years. It did, but I was working seven days a week, fourteen hours a day to prepare for it.

It's a lot harder to defend a case than to prosecute one. The work is much more intensive. At times I would get so frustrated, I wanted to pull my hair out. If I have any regrets, it's that I didn't come forward and tell the court I was being ineffective because we were pushing so hard and moving so quickly.

For Perry to push us that hard was borderline sacrificing Casey's right to a fair trial and competent counsel.

The other problem I had was that the prosecution knew I was short-handed, that my financial resources were severely limited, and prosecutor Jeff Ashton, an admitted street fighter, did everything he could to make my job as difficult as possible. One thing we had to do was go through the prosecution's witness list and take depositions. Ordinarily the list is broken into A witnesses (the important ones), B witnesses (less important), and C witnesses (those who probably won't be called). But the prosecution had a policy where it rated every single one of its witnesses as an A. The prosecutors refused to tell me which ones weren't going to be called, increasing my workload considerably.

I regret not going before Perry and telling him, "Listen, I'm being ineffective because I'm working seven days a week, fourteen hours a day, and I just can't do it anymore." I know he would have taken control of my calendar, asking me who I was interviewing and what I was doing.

But I have an ego and didn't want to look bad. I didn't want to be honest, and looking back, I'm ashamed of myself for it. I didn't stand up and say, "I'm being borderline ineffective here. I'm cutting corners, and it shouldn't be that way."

THEN ISSUES dealing with discovery arose. The whole no-nonsense judge theme carried out by the media gave Ashton, the prosecutor in charge of the forensic evidence, an opening. It created an advantage for him that was really sneaky, but brilliant. He kept filing motions claiming we weren't living up to our obligations in discovery. In essence, he wanted Perry to think that we weren't following his orders. He filed a motion asking the judge to make us give him a list of each expert, the expert's field, and what opinions he or she was going to render at trial.

It seemed reasonable on its face, but in Florida we take depositions, which provides for a lawyer to put a witness under oath with a court reporter and ask the witness questions before trial. Using depositions, a lawyer can prepare for trial with no surprises. If the witness testifies differently at trial, the lawyer can impeach him with the testimony from the deposition transcripts. It's a great tool and prevents a trial by ambush.

If the prosecution wanted to know what my experts were going to testify to, all Ashton had to do was take their depositions.

Instead, Ashton cleverly made a motion asking that we provide him with an outline of what my experts were going to testify to ostensibly so he could *prepare* for their depositions.

And Perry made my life immeasurably harder by granting that, just as he would grant almost all of the prosecution's motions.

Understand, this isn't ordinarily what happens. In a common criminal case, you take the deposition, file your motions, and have your hearings—end of story. What Perry did by issuing that order was to create new rules of procedure for the Casey Anthony case.

It all added to our already overwhelming workload. I was drowning in an avalanche of work. Now I had to sit down with our experts and come up with an outline explaining who they were, what their fields were, and what they were going to testify to.

I thought it was a ridiculous request, but I did it anyway because I was ordered to and had no choice. The information I provided was very general; I certainly wasn't going to do Ashton's work for him.

After I handed in the information, Ashton filed a motion saying it wasn't good enough, that I hadn't explained enough. Perry issued another order, granting his motion to make me explain even more.

Here's what Ashton wanted from me: *Tell us the questions you're going to ask them and tell us what they're going to say.*

I said to Cheney, "Help me out here. I'm not going to give Ashton our entire direct examination," which was essentially what he wanted.

Unlike a movie, a trial is not a scripted event, and I wasn't about to hand over a script to him when I didn't know what may or may not happen in the trial.

Cheney and I took one more crack at giving Ashton what he wanted. I emailed it to Cheney and said, "Look it over and let me know if it's okay, because this is what I'm going to send them."

"Have you ever run into something like this?" I asked him.

"I've been trying murder trials for forty years," said Cheney, "and I've never heard of such a thing."

I sent it to the prosecution. It was much more detailed. And of course it still wasn't good enough for Ashton, so he filed a motion to hold me in contempt.

By now I was so angry I couldn't see straight. I knew Perry was probably at his wit's end, but I knew that, rather than order the state to take the experts' depositions, he was going to order me to do something more, fine me, or hold me in contempt. I thought if Cheney handled the motion, arguing with his experience that this motion was a first for any defense lawyer, that Perry might understand the unreasonableness or the laziness of Ashton's request.

It didn't matter. Perry fined me $600 for the hours it took Ashton to file the motion and ordered me to produce something even more detailed. And then Perry went further.

He said, "I order that all your experts file reports. And I'm going to order them to be handed in within a certain period of time. And any opinions not in the report or deposition will not be testified to in trial."

Essentially, by doing that he was narrowing the defense.

I was livid, of course.

I went back and wrote it up again, adding very little, because there wasn't much left for me to write. It wasn't all that much more than what we gave the prosecution in the first place. And this time it was acceptable to Ashton, which led me to believe this was all gamesmanship on his part.

I still had to go back to each of my experts and ask them for reports, even though ordinarily this isn't something they're obligated to do. Now I had to ask these people, the top people in their field working for minimum wage, to submit reports under a hard deadline. It was difficult, but we had to do it, and we did, on top of all the other things we already had to do. Perry was putting my feet to the fire to get in these reports.

What Ashton was doing on his part was very clever. I had to give him that. He knew he held a winning hand and he kept playing it. He knew if he kept it up, Perry would get angrier and angrier with me. The judge would think I was thumbing my nose at the court, not paying attention to his orders, when nothing could have been further from the truth. I was working around the clock trying to get it all done and I was over-loaded with work.

Then Ashton did something that can only be characterized as sneaky, underhanded, and calculated. Since my experts had hard deadlines to get their reports in, they were not as long and detailed as they could have been. I had told them all that I really just needed to get the broad strokes of what their opinions were.

"The state can go into further detail with you during your deposi-tions," I said.

But Ashton intentionally didn't take depositions of a lot of my experts that produced reports. I believe he did this so he could hold the judge to his order that stated, "If it's not in the deposition and it's not in the report, they aren't testifying to it." Throughout the trial, he kept bring-ing up the fact that we were in violation of his order because there were no depositions, even though it was Ashton who had failed to take their depositions, not me. I had taken the depositions of every single one of the state's experts.

Many judges never would have put up with that. They would have said to Ashton, "You're asking me to make the defense do all of your work. I'm holding you in contempt for wasting this court's time and for being lazy and underhanded."

But that lifeline never came. Ashton would keep pushing that enve-lope until he pushed me nearly to my breaking point.

CHAPTER 21

PREPARING FOR TRIAL

THROUGHOUT THIS CASE I always felt the obligation to do what I could to remove Casey from the shadow of the death penalty. I never felt this was a death penalty case, even before I heard the truth about what really happened to Caylee. Having to go to trial with your client's life on the line is a huge and awesome responsibility, so I constantly focused on the goal of getting the death penalty removed. It was a big concern, to say the least.

Around the time I was considering calling the two shrinks who examined Casey to the stand, or at least listing them as witnesses, I came up with an idea that I thought might get Casey out from under the death penalty shadow.

I knew if we listed the psychiatrists as witnesses that the prosecution was going to take its depositions and ultimately know what our defense was going to be anyway. So I offered Linda Drane Burdick a deal: if she would consider taking the death penalty off the table, I would let her know in advance our defense strategy, and she could hear it from Casey herself.

Another reason to make the offer was that if the prosecution agreed, then there wasn't going to be a death-qualified jury. A death-qualified jury is generally more conviction-prone because if she were found guilty, they would be able to proscribe the death penalty.

The prosecution had no clue what our defense was going to be and was desperate to hear it. This was the perfect opportunity for it to find out. The deal made sense. We'd get something, and the prosecution would get something. At first Burdick seemed eager to do it, but she faced strong opposition from Jeff Ashton. As I said earlier, Ashton strongly opposed taking the death penalty off the table. The reason for it, I'm convinced, was that he was in charge of the death penalty part of the case. If the death penalty were taken off the table, he would have had a much smaller role in the trial.

So at the end of two weeks of negotiations, the prosecution came back to me and said, "We won't take the death penalty off the table, but if you tell us what your strategy is, we'll consider it."

Ashton was asking me to trust him, and even though he thought otherwise, I wasn't that naive or stupid. '

We said thanks but no thanks.

As we started accumulating all the evidence that backed Casey's version of events, there was a real possibility that we were going to have Casey testify at trial. We knew she would still take it on the chin for her numerous lies and we knew putting a client on the stand is always a risky move. And even though we were constantly looking for ways to admit evidence about her in without having to call her to the stand, I also knew we'd call her if we had to.

As I noted earlier, one way to get the information about Casey's abuse into the record was to put the psychiatrists on the stand and let them testify. We had to submit reports from each of our experts. However, we were concerned that one shrink's report might not be submitted in time because we added him to the witness list later than the others.

We had a closed-door meeting with Perry. I was in chambers with Ashton and Ann Finnell, my death penalty expert. This was a last-minute meeting; Burdick, Frank George, and Cheney Mason had already gone home for the day, so we called Ashton in to discuss the issue in front of Perry.

Ann told the judge the report of one of the psychiatrists might be a couple of days late. She said she didn't want there to be any misunderstandings.

"Not a problem," said the judge.

And then Ashton asked, "So what is the doctor going to testify to?"

Ann didn't say anything for a few seconds.

Ashton said, "Just tell us. We're going to find out tomorrow anyway when we take his deposition."

"She's going to testify that the child died by accident, and her father covered it up," Ann said.

That was the first time the state had learned what our defense was going to be. And I'll never forget Ashton's bizarre reaction: he started to jump up and down in his seat like a little child. He burst out laughing, sounding like a hyena, and kept on jumping up and down in his chair as he laughed. We were talking about the death of a child here.

Ann and I looked at each other, and we looked at Perry, who had a deadly serious expression, and then the three of us looked directly at Ashton as he engaged in his celebration dance in his chair.

"Is that all?" asked Perry after Ashton finally calmed down.

"Yes, that's everything," we said, as we watched Ashton run out the door to pass on the exciting news to Burdick.

I turned to Ann and I said, "So what do you make of that reaction?"

"I think he's mentally disturbed," she said. "And I mean that in all seriousness."

AFTER THE PROSECUTION took the depositions of the two psychiatrists, both sides agreed they should be sealed because they contained medical information as it related to Casey's mental health, and because there were issues of sexual abuse by George and Lee, which was protected under state law. Perry immediately sealed them, saying that he wanted to review them before deciding whether they should remain sealed.

A couple of days later Cindy called me to say she and George had an appointment the next day at the state attorney general's office to discuss the depositions of the shrinks.

I lost it. I smelled the skullduggery of Ashton and immediately contacted Perry, telling him that the state was planning to meet with the Anthonys to discuss the information that he had sealed.

Perry had a clear response: "Sealed means sealed." Despite this clear message from the judge, the prosecution went ahead and had its meeting anyway. That was the arrogance of Ashton, whose attitude was, "I can do anything I want because I can get away with it."

And get away with it he did.

To me the prosecution's actions should have subjected it to a contempt citation. The prosecution argued that it didn't show the Anthonys the depositions, but rather told the Anthonys' lawyer the information from the notes prosecutors took during the depositions. The clear purpose was for the lawyer to pass the information to the Anthonys, which he did. The benefit to the prosecution by making sure the Anthonys found out what was in the shrinks' depositions, of course, was that when the Anthonys found out that Casey was revealing George's sexual abuse, they would turn on Casey, no longer support her, and became state-friendly witnesses.

I thought Cheney was going to have a heart attack. "This is the clearest case of witness tampering that I have ever seen," he said. Cheney always would say, "These prosecutors always feel they have to have the advantage. They can't play on a level playing field. Nothing makes them angrier than playing on a level playing field."

He was absolutely right, and I heard that expression constantly in this case because they would abuse the system time after time.

How do you get away with that? I asked myself.

When we told the judge what the prosecution had done, Perry said he'd reserve his ruling, but instead he put it on the back burner and never did rule, not even after the trial. Once again, Ashton was allowed to get away with—dare I say it—murder.

With the trial coming up, I began to think of the strategy for our defense. I envisioned a five-prong attack on the state's "evidence."

The first prong was what I called "good mother" defense. One of the strongest and biggest advantages we had was that, as much as the cops went through Casey's life with a fine-toothed comb, speaking to anyone and everyone who knew her and Caylee, there wasn't a soul who could give a single incident that Casey had been anything but a loving mother. To me this was huge because it bolstered Casey's testimony that Caylee's death was an accident and contradicted the prosecution's theory that Casey had deliberately killed her daughter.

I've said this before, but in cases of real child abuse that leads to death, you almost always see a progression of abuse. You see a bruise, a black eye, or a visit to the hospital with a broken arm. The child will be malnourished and often neglected. There are always numerous documented incidents as the abuse progresses, until the actual death of the child.

That was *never* the case here. Caylee always was well taken care of and loved, and you could see it throughout her home. I can't tell you how many people testified about what a wonderful mother Casey was.

I really wanted to ram this home because it not only bolstered the accident theory but also counterbalanced all the outrageous behavior Casey was accused of exhibiting during the thirty days she was away from home after Caylee died.

The second prong was going to be all about George and "Baldy." We were going to go into the sexual abuse of his daughter and all the other things we discovered about George: his lies about the gas cans and the duct tape, his affair, his proclivity for making statements that pointed the finger at Casey, and his lies to law enforcement. I felt we had a very strong case against him.

Ashton, after his underhanded trick to inform George and Cindy what Casey was going to say against him, was sure George would turn on her and be a star witness for the prosecution.

But that didn't entirely explain Ashton's giddiness. Here's one reason he was so giddy: because George was his witness, Ashton would take a larger role in the trial.

The other reason he was giddy was that he was sure George was going to make a great witness. George had always been a media darling, and Ashton was sure that because George had experience as a law enforcement officer, he would come across well on the stand. But I knew George a lot better than Ashton did. I had spent nearly three years with the Anthonys in their home. I didn't think George would come across as credible on the stand and I was sure I'd eat him for lunch.

Ashton thought he was gaining a strong ally through his machinations, but he would be sadly mistaken come trial time.

The third prong was the information about Suburban Drive. Caylee's body had been discovered on August 11 and then found again on December 11. What's important to know is that when her body was found on December 11, she was found only nineteen feet from the road. Her remains were not found deep in the woods, as it was often described. As far as I was concerned, nineteen feet was by the side of the road. I intended to explain that and show how many people had been in that area between August 11 and December 11, with no one finding her body. It was incredible how many people had searched that area in the months before she was discovered and had not found anything.

My initial plan was to call thirty different people to the stand to testify that they had searched the area and that her body wasn't there. But the problem was that by the time the trial came around, we faced tremendous obstacles from EquuSearch and such hostility from the media that the majority of the volunteers who worked for EquuSearch had no interest in helping us with our case. These were people who, inflamed by the media, expressed outrage at Casey's behavior. The other problem was that anyone who became involved in the case became the subject of scrutiny and harassment from the media, which would go so far as to follow them to their homes. They were automatically thrust into the limelight, whether they wanted the attention or not. This made it even harder to find defense-friendly witnesses because no one wanted to be skewered in the press for helping us out.

Even in the mitigation, which is part of the death penalty defense where you go back into the defendant's life and try to humanize the person facing the death penalty, we faced terrible opposition. Our mitigation specialist had the door slammed in her face by Casey's third-grade teacher! Casey was a child when they interacted, and all we wanted to know was what she was like back then. Some sicced their dogs on our legal team; others threatened them. It was a most hostile environment, anathema to a defendant getting a fair trial, and all because of this Frankenstein-like persona the media had built about Casey that turned the public into a lynch mob with pitchforks.

I couldn't believe how hostile these searchers were to the defense. The ones who weren't hostile appeared to be fame seekers, and we weren't looking for them either. Then came the attempted public destruction of Laura Buchanan whose arm was twisted to lie so the police could charge me with a crime. When she bravely refused, she was publicly castigated by the police and the press. The police made it known they were investigating her. Didn't anyone find it strange the police were advertising their investigation? It was really nothing short of intimidation. Again, the prosecution was out to win its case, no matter what the tactic.

Without witnesses to testify that they had searched the area before Caylee was found and had come up empty, we still had other convincing evidence to prove our point. Before entering the woods on Suburban Drive, there is six feet of grass; when I visited the scene, I noticed that the grass had been mowed. It occurred to me that someone had to have mowed it between August 11, the first time Roy Kronk reported seeing Caylee's remains, and December 11, when he actually turned over the body.

You mean to tell me, I said to myself, *that for five months people came here and mowed the grass and no one saw or smelled a body that lay only nine feet away?*

My investigator tracked down the manager of the lawn service who had the contract from the county. The manager said that his company had on average ten workers cutting the grass in that area—a couple guys with weed trimmers, one with a blower, and a couple on lawn mowers—and would cut the grass twice a month. On ten different occasions these men were walking around the area where Caylee was found on December 11, and none of them had seen or smelled anything.

Not only that but there was an elementary school across the street, and people in the neighborhood walked their children past the spot to the school every day. No one saw her body or bones?

Pat McKenna, my investigator, went door to door canvassing the neighborhood, but because of what was reported in the media and because of the intense media spotlight, no one wanted to speak with us. No one wanted to get involved. No one wanted any part of the Casey Anthony circus.

All we were left with was the measurement of how close she was to the street and the testimony of the grass cutters. We also knew of other searchers who had been out there and didn't find her, but it was one of the weaker parts of our case. I really thought it would be stronger, but in this case we just couldn't beat the influence of the media.

Prong number four was Roy Kronk, who discovered Caylee's remains, and the suspicious circumstances surrounding when and why. I knew this information would be very interesting for the jury as we sought to cast reasonable doubt on the contention that Casey had put her daughter in the woods after killing her.

The fifth prong was the science. We strongly felt that every piece of forensic evidence favored the defense. Of course it did. The prosecution's case had been a fantasy of forensics, and because of that, there was not one shred of evidence to prove its woefully weak and fantastic charges.

But that didn't mean a not-guilty verdict was in the bag. Not by a long shot. The prosecutors had the power of the state behind them, and I could not imagine what sort of treacherous pitfalls they had in store for me during the trial.

CHAPTER 22

THE SIDES ARE DRAWN

WHEN I FIRST SIGNED ON to represent Casey Anthony, I had no idea what I was getting into. It started as a case where I thought Casey was keeping her daughter away from her parents because they had had a spat of some sort, and it wasn't long before the case went from a missing child case to a case of murder in which the prosecution was asking for the death penalty.

I didn't have to be a rocket scientist to see that to win an acquittal I would need help making a case for the defense.

The first person I recruited was Linda Kenney Baden, the wife of the famed forensic pathologist Dr. Michael Baden. Linda was a lawyer, and she was nothing short of brilliant. Linda was in charge of the forensics, and she and I worked extremely well together. What made her so valuable to me was her willingness to teach me and work with me. She wasn't one of those lawyers who did the work, turned it in, and went home. She was always willing to share with me what she was thinking and she wasn't shy about letting me know the different ways I could improve as a lawyer.

Linda was able to stay on for three wonderful years, but we ran out of money (flying her back and forth from New York to Orlando was expensive), and she could no longer afford to pay for the trips out of her own pocket. Though Casey was declared indigent, the court won't pay for a lawyer's legal fees or travel expenses. In fact, when the trial was moved to Clearwater, Florida to pick a jury, I had to pay for my own travel expenses.

I really enjoyed working with Linda and I hope to again in the future. However, she introduced me to a lawyer from California by the name of Todd Macaluso. I liked Todd from the start and nicknamed him "Macko the Wacko" because of his great sense of humor and larger-than-life personality. Todd was a civil lawyer with a heavy interest in criminal law. He had a lot of experience dealing with expert witnesses and was a great help to me. Unfortunately, his brother had passed away a year earlier, and he barely spent time in his practice. As a result, his office bounced a trust check; he was suspended and had to withdraw from our case. I was really sad to see him go.

The next lawyer to come on board was Andrea Lyon. I brought her on after the state changed its mind and filed to make this a death penalty case. Andrea had tried more than 120 homicide cases and was the nation's leading death penalty lawyer. She was the first woman to try a death penalty case.

I wanted a woman as my death penalty lawyer because this case was filled with women's issues and I wanted someone who would be sensitive to them.

I met Andrea in Orlando when she was speaking at a death penalty seminar and thought she was extremely engaging. I knew this was the person I wanted.

Todd and I flew to Chicago and recruited Andrea. She was a beast of a lawyer—extremely well organized, thorough, and very aggressive.

Andrea ran a death penalty clinic at DePaul University College of Law, so she was able to recruit dozens of law students to do a lot of our grunt work. She also had her own investigator and mitigation specialist. Andrea was a perfect addition to our team.

Unfortunately, she ended up having the same problem as Linda. She was in charge of funding for her clinic, and our case didn't bring in any money for her. When her clinic began suffering financially, she had to withdraw.

After Andrea left, the lawyer who replaced her was Cheney Mason, a local Orlando legend.

Cheney and I were so different. We were generations apart. I was young and Hispanic; he was older and white. I spoke with a Northeast accent; he spoke with a drawl. They used to call us "Chico and the man;" the bloggers would call us "the sleazer and the geezer." And yet we saw eye to eye as to how a defense lawyer should conduct himself and how the case should be tried.

Our lives had taken similar career paths. We both had dropped out of high school at a very young age. We both entered the military when we were seventeen. He went to Vietnam, came back, and went to school. I went to college under the GI Bill.

Cheney was old school and had a wealth of experience, though one of the biggest reasons I respected Cheney was that he never once questioned my authority as lead counsel and never once overstepped his boundaries.

What I loved most about Cheney was that he was totally committed to the cause. We worked so well together. Though he was well respected in the Orlando legal community, once he was named co-counsel in the case the media began disrespecting him, and some local lawyers would criticize his work. Cheney was a former president of the Florida Association of Criminal Defense Lawyers and had earned the Robert C. Heeney Memorial Award, the highest honor given by the National Association of Criminal Defense Lawyers.

But again, this was not real life, it was the media's Casey Anthony reality show, a show that depended on name-calling and controversy for television ratings. Everyone was fair game, including Cheney Mason.

One day Cheney and I were driving back to Orlando from Gainesville after deposing witnesses, and I thanked him for all the work and time he had put into the case.

"I really believe, while I'm not religious," I said to him, "that God put you in my path to be here with me."

Cheney was my rock. After the departure of others who worked with me, Cheney would say, "Jose, come hell or high water, if it's just you and me trying this case come May 2011, we're going to do it. And what's going to surprise a lot of people: you're going to be able to answer the bell and come out swinging."

He could say that because he too could see how the case was developing. He started to see the gaping holes in the prosecution's mostly made-up case. He believed in our case as much as I did and he was a reservoir of strength to me throughout the whole exhausting trial.

The other great reservoir of strength came from Dorothy Clay Sims. I knew mental health issues would come up during the trial, and that was her specialty. A world-class lawyer, she knows the subject backward and forward.

Dorothy is a throwback to the '60s. Her children served in the Peace Corps. She has traveled the world and hasn't owned a television set for twenty years. She heard about the case listening to the TV in a coffee shop.

I had seen her at a death penalty seminar giving a lecture on performing background checks on expert witnesses and how to depose those witnesses. She was phenomenal and when she joined our team, we loved her instantly.

She is the ultimate giver. Dorothy did a great deal behind the scenes helping me prepare and making sure we had all the information we wanted on the experts and on the jury. When it came to work, she was a machine, and equally important, she too totally believed in Casey's innocence. Fifty years from now Dorothy and I will still be friends because she's such a beautiful person.

The final person to join our team was Ann Finnell, who took over as death penalty counsel after Andrea left the team. Ann was quiet, but had an enormous sense of humor. She also had a wealth of experience; there was not a female lawyer in the state of Florida that had more death penalty experience than she did. With a wealth of talent and experience, our team was complete.

There were also three important people on my office staff whom no one knew of, no one talked about, people who never spoke in court except for perhaps a minor time or two. The first was Michelle Medina, my right-hand woman in the firm. From A to Z, you name it, she did it. She helped keep my practice afloat while I was trying the Casey Anthony case, working hard at what sometimes seemed like an impossible task. She was our one-woman nerve center. No one outside of my own family has remained more loyal or hardworking than Michelle, and I will forever be in her debt.

Michelle was truly the unsung hero of the case.

Another was a recent law school graduate by the name of Lisabeth Fryer. She came on board in 2010, when she started interning through Cheney's office. I used to call her "E-less," because of the missing E in her name; she quickly became our legal guru. In her midthirties, she is an incredibly brilliant and bright woman. She had been on law review a

Barry University Dwayne O. Andreas School of Law in Orlando, and she earned the highest score in the state of Florida on the bar exam.

The first time she would speak in court as a lawyer would be during jury selection in the Casey Anthony case. She was ready. One day she will end up on the state appellate court; that's how brilliant she is. I loved having her as a resource.

The third was William Slabaugh, a law student when the case began. William was one of my students when I taught at the Florida A&M University College of Law. He interned for about a year and a half, volunteering his time and working for me while he was studying for the bar. After he passed the bar, I gave him a job, putting him in charge of the 26,000 pages of testimony and the exhibits.

William was a hard worker and extremely committed to the case. Whenever I needed a transcript relating to the case, I called William, and he was always able to find it for me.

We were in court on the day William learned that he had passed the bar, so we asked Judge Belvin Perry if he would swear Will into the Florida Bar. Perry said he would.

I leaned over to Casey and said, "Judge Perry's going to swear in Will." Casey knew Will had been working on the case for two years and she was really happy for him. When I told her that, she looked over at him and smiled—as we all did—as he was getting sworn in.

Of course, the media took a million photos of Casey smiling in court, and the next day the leading headline was, "Casey Laughs While on Trial for Killing Daughter." All she was doing was supporting Will and being grateful for all the work he was doing.

The truth, as always, was less interesting than the accusations.

There were numerous other people who claimed to be on the defense team who really weren't, but I'm not going to write about them. The list of imposters involved with the case is too long already.

Our opposition—the prosecution representing the state of Florida— consisted of three individuals: Linda Drane Burdick, the lead counsel, Frank George, and Jeff Ashton.

Burdick had the reputation for being thorough, extremely professional, and tough. During the three-and-a-half years that we worked on the case, she lived up to each and every one of those qualities.

The prosecution case was extremely complex. It had a stream of witnesses and a daunting amount of evidence. Organizing it all was a major task, and Burdick was in charge of it all.

She took copious notes at every deposition. She documented everything, both the interesting and the mundane; of all the lawyers, I could see that easily she knew the most about the prosecution's case. I qualify that by saying "on the prosecution's side;" I was determined to know the case even better than she did. That was my biggest challenge because Burdick was a hard worker and was committed to the task.

It drives me nuts that so many people think that Ashton was the lead prosecutor when he wasn't. He was second chair. It was Burdick, not Ashton, who really put the nuts and bolts of this case together for the prosecution.

Burdick and I got along. There were times, of course, when we disagreed and butted heads, but we always showed respect for one another. I don't know how she truly feels about me, but I can say how I feel about her: I thought she did a fantastic job both before and during the trial.

She excelled because of her thoroughness. She was a machine in that regard, though I felt it backfired somewhat during the trial. She lacked, well I don't want to say personality, but when you're mechanical as an advocate, you lose a little of the personal touch. I knew that while the jury would take in everything she said, she would be monotonic in her argument and in her case presentation.

If Burdick had a chink in her armor, it was her extreme overconfidence in the state's position. She didn't for a second believe she would lose the case, though I can say at times she had a very realistic view of what the case was all about, including its weaknesses. She was the only one of the three prosecutors who acknowledged their case even had weaknesses, and she wasn't as quick to jump the gun the way George and Ashton did.

Of the three prosecutors, George was the most personable. He had a great sense of humor; he and I got along very well. We would both use humor to break the tension of the long hours, and I felt that it was George who kept the state's team together emotionally.

I never believed that Burdick and Ashton got along. I could see numerous times the two of them were at odds about how to handle the case. When Burdick got angry, her face would flush. I know this because she sometimes turned that anger on me. There were also times when it was directed at Ashton. I think they put up with each other more than they got along.

The proof of that was after the trial when she backed her boss for state attorney rather than Ashton, who was running against him. After working closely with someone for so long, you would think there would have been more of a connection.

As evidence of her lack of respect for Ashton, after he wrote his book *Imperfect Justice,* Burdick quipped that the book title should have been *Imperfect Memory.*

That leaves me with Ashton. When the trial was over—a trial that I won and he lost—the last thing I wanted to be was unprofessional to my colleagues on the prosecution side and rub their faces in it. I would be trying more cases, and there was no reason to spike the ball in their faces and act inappropriately. And I made sure that I didn't do that.

My posttrial press conference was very subdued. I complimented the prosecutors on their work, thinking, *Let's leave it at that.*

Even before the verdict came back, I went up to Ashton, shook his hand, and told him I thought he tried a very strong case. And after the trial was over, I never gave Ashton a second thought. We were never going to be friends; he was insignificant to me. He had opposed me in a trial and treated me poorly, but the trial was over. As far as I was concerned, it was time to move on.

I was hoping that even with all our battles and our head butting and his lack of fair play, perhaps it would be the end of this nonsense.

But I was wrong.

In his book he did nothing but bash me. It's no secret he still harbors ill will against me; even after the publication of his book, he never misses a chance to go on television and take a cheap shot at me.

It never bothered me that much because I learned through the trial to grow a thick skin, and now under my blue suit I have alligator skin. What bothered me was not what he said, but how much his words hurt my family.

When I first met him, I thought, *Okay, this guy is just a standard lifer prosecutor who has a way about him, believing that everyone is crooked but him. And whatever needs to be done, he believes the ends justify the means, no matter how unconstitutional or underhanded.* But I have to tell you, there are prosecutors like Ashton in district attorneys' offices across the country.

I was shocked by how emotional he could be. It's one thing to be passionate, but it's another thing to be so emotional that it hurts you and your case. And from what I saw, he was emotionally unstable. When Ann remarked that Ashton was emotionally disturbed, I didn't know what to say. I'm not a mental health professional, but I noticed that during the hundreds of hours we spent together, there were times when he would become just plain silly and act like a petulant child.

For example, he filed a motion to find out how Casey was able to afford our famous experts, even though she didn't have a job. He was accusing me of having a conflict of interest and of selling her story. He was accusing me of something unethical without any evidence whatsoever. But that was par for the course for him. Like a lot of his theories, it came from thin air inside his head.

We had a closed-door meeting with Judge Stan Strickland on the motion, who found there was no conflict of interest. When we were back in open court, I requested that Strickland keep what was said in chambers private because of all the leaks that were coming from the prosecution.

I could see Ashton getting red-faced and angry. I looked at him in pure amazement and then leaned over and said, "Are you all right?"

"No, I'm not all right," he started to scream. He just lost it completely, all on national television.

The judge stepped in and scolded us both.

I knew right then and there I could get under his skin whenever I wanted to. It was like playing with a child. That's how easily I could do it; I did it intentionally many times during depositions and court hearings.

The defense team joked that we should officially name Ashton as our fourth chair because his childlike behavior was doing us a world of good.

We knew that come trial time, the longer the trial went on, the more I was going to be able to get under his skin and make him look like a complete jerk in front of the jurors. And true to form, that's exactly what happened.

After the trial one of the jurors said to a network reporter that Ashton was nothing but a "cocky asshole." Another juror, the foreman of the jury, went on *On the Record with Greta Van Susteren* and said that the jury didn't appreciate Ashton's attitude. He said they didn't like the fact that when he was questioning our bug expert about Caylee's remains, he made a joke about "a pig in a blanket." He was talking about a dead child, cracking jokes, and the jurors didn't like it. They didn't like his attitude and they certainly didn't like his inappropriate laughter.

I knew going into the trial that Ashton would be his own worst enemy. I also knew that going into the trial I would also benefit from the overconfidence of Burdick and the rest of the prosecution team.

What the prosecution had, and what I didn't have, was the media on its side.

What I had, and what the prosecution didn't have, was the evidence on my side.

My defense team was ready to do battle.

It was time to go to trial.

CHAPTER 23

PICKING A JURY

B EFORE JURY SELECTION, I filed a motion for a change of venue. There was no way Casey could get a fair trial in Orlando. I was hoping the trial could be held in Miami or Broward County, where I felt jurors would be less likely to be poisoned by the publicity surrounding the case.

Rather than move the trial, Judge Belvin Perry ruled that we were going to travel to another jurisdiction to pick a jury, bus them to Orlando, and then sequester them. That way we would not have to take the Casey Anthony Show on the road. The show would come to us. What Judge Perry wouldn't do was tell us where we were to go to pick jurors. He was afraid the news would leak, the media would taint the area, and the end result would be we'd have to pick yet another area.

Judge Perry, I have to say, derived a great deal of enjoyment from keeping this secret. He refused to even tell us, the lawyers, until a week before jury selection was to begin. We were frustrated because if we felt his choice of location wasn't suitable, we wanted to be able to make a motion with some valid research behind it to show *why* his choice wasn't valid.

Judge Perry didn't buy our argument.

The day finally came when he told us. We had to hand him a list of everyone who needed to know—and he made us responsible for them—and so anyone not on that list who found out would be in violation of his order and would suffer his wrath.

A day or two before, Judge Perry was spotted taking a tour of the courthouse of West Palm Beach. The media reported it, of course, but none of us bought that we were going there. Judge Perry was tightly keeping the secret, and we didn't think he'd let it out of the bag that easily. It appeared to me that this was a decoy.

Too bad. As I said, we wanted South Florida to contain the jury pool. No one cared about Casey Anthony in Miami, Broward County, and even as far north as West Palm Beach. We just didn't think the case was that big a deal down there.

Even before we found out where we were going to pick a jury, I was feeling strong. I walked into the court administrator's office in Orlando, and I remember her telling me, "Jose, everyone here is going nuts, getting ready for this trial, but not you. You look so relaxed."

I had my second wind, working seven days a week, sixteen hours a day, practicing my opening and closing arguments. I started with the closing argument; I believe in doing that first because that's where the journey ends. It's where I want to get. I start with my goal, and I work backward.

I had spent literally hundreds of hours on that. I had begun work on my opening statement, and I was confident.

Then we were told of the location of the jury pool—St. Petersburg/Clearwater, which was only an hour and a half away. The media market overlapped with Orlando.

Wait a minute. That's just too close, I told myself. *This is no good.*

I went to see Cheney Mason. We discussed it and decided to file an objection.

Judge Perry called us into chambers. He was not happy. He had gone to a lot of trouble to pick this location and didn't appreciate the defense causing trouble.

We had told him earlier that the one place we did not want to go was the Jacksonville area. It's a very conservative circuit, not to mention they had just had a missing child case where a child was found in a Dumpster. They caught the guy, and the whole community was outraged.

Judge Perry said to us, "Well, if you're not happy with St. Petersburg/Clearwater, then the only other place I'm going to be able to take you to is Jacksonville. So what I'll do is start making arrangements for everyone to go there."

Checkmate. We withdrew our motion.

THE DAY WAS SET for our caravan to travel to Clearwater. We had to pay for our own hotel rooms, and we didn't have much money, so we stayed in a Quality Inn. The state stayed at a Marriott, a much better accommodation. We couldn't afford much. We brought office equipment rather than buy new. Our law student interns packed together in a couple of rooms.

We had Richard Gabriel, one of the best jury consultants in the country working with us, but a couple weeks before the trial Richard, who was from Los Angeles, had to resign. He had another trial about to begin, a paying job, and he couldn't afford to work for us for nothing. Judge Perry said it would only take a week to pick a jury, but we knew it was going to be a lot longer than that.

Richard said he would help us from afar, but unless a jury consultant can be in the courtroom, looking at the jurors face to face, he can't be of much help, especially since the jury selection wasn't going to televise the jurors' faces.

Days before jury selection, we began a search for a last-minute replacement. All the best ones had prior commitments, but then we found a woman by the name of Amy Singer, who from her website appeared to be a very reputable jury consultant. She agreed to do the job, but she had a conflict and couldn't come down herself.

"I'll have one of my associates come down," she said, "His name is Jim Lucas."

Jim hadn't been on the original list I handed to Judge Perry, so I couldn't even tell Jim where to go. He lived in West Palm Beach, so I told him to start driving north. The embargo was lifted at nine, and I called him on his cell and told him to drive to the courthouse near the St. Petersburg/Clearwater airport.

He arrived in time. The first day we knew he wasn't going to be of much use, so we told him to go to the back of the courtroom and take notes, and we'd discuss at the end of the day.

That evening I asked him, "How many death penalty cases have you worked on?"

"None," said Jim. "I'm a trial graphics consultant. My company just does trial exhibits. I'm not a jury consultant. Amy asked me to come down here to take notes."

What the...was my first thought. My co-counsels, Dorothy Clay Mills and Cheney Mason, were flabbergasted, but I was always trying to make lemonade out of lemons. *He's a graphics expert. That's perfect. We could really use someone like that for this case. He might even be better than a jury consultant.*

And the way it turned out, he was, big time.

WHEN I FOUND OUT that Jim wasn't a jury consultant, I said to myself, *The heck with it. I'm going to do my own market research.*

That night I said to Dorothy and Jim, "Let's go get some oysters." We drove around, away from the busy part of Clearwater, and went to a local seafood restaurant on the beach. We were asked if we wanted a table, but I told them I wanted to sit at the bar.

While Dorothy was getting to know more about what Jim did, I turned to the lady on my left and struck up a conversation. We talked about everything, and then we finally got around to the trial.

First of all, she didn't recognize me, which I thought was wonderful. And I asked her about the trial, and she said, "Oh yeah, the Casey Anthony trial is here."

"How much do you know about the case?"

She said she was a crime junkie. She watched all the court TV shows and the *Law and Order* shows, and she followed the news. But as much as she followed it, as much as she proclaimed herself to be a trial junkie, she didn't recognize me.

I asked her what she knew about the evidence in the case. All she could tell me was, "The kid was missing for thirty days. The mother didn't call the police. She went out partying. The meter reader found the little girl in the woods."

She was there with her boyfriend, who was into the beach scene, and he didn't know much about the case at all.

I was shocked. I thought, *I'm not getting the dirty looks I was getting in Orlando. Even though it's only an hour and a half away, these people have lives to live. They're not following the case the way the people in Orlando are.*

I thought, *This is actually a better area than I thought it would be.*

About twenty minutes into the conversation, she finally said, "Wait a minute. You're the lawyer, aren't you? I knew you looked somewhat familiar, but I couldn't place you."

Every time we went out to dinner, I did the same thing. I'd go to the bar and strike up a conversation with people, trying to get a feel for the Clearwater area and what kind of people comprised the community. I found them to be somewhat liberal, and I loved it. They were like the Key West people I knew, but Key West is more conservative because of issues related to alcohol.

I couldn't believe the gold mine Judge Perry had found for us.

Jury selection took three weeks. Going into the trial we had a general idea of what kind of jurors we wanted. We didn't want any young mothers, especially single mothers, because they would be comparing themselves to Casey saying, "I never would have reacted that way."

We wanted to shy away from women in general because we thought they'd be more critical of Casey. We wanted males over the age of forty-five, closer to fifty and sixty. They would look at Casey as a young girl, and they'd have sympathy for her.

The thing about generalizations: they're weak. My experience after forty-five jury trials tells me that you always have to look at the individual characteristics of each juror. They always trump your generalities.

At this point Dorothy, our secret weapon, took over. Dorothy set up her research team at the Quality Inn that resembled Gene Hackman's team—all those people doing research—in *The Runaway Jury.* Except we were doing it *ghetto style,* which means on a budget.

Dorothy and seven interns from the College of Law at Florida A&M used social media to do their research. We would get a list of jurors in the jury pool in the courtroom, and the second it was handed to us, Dorothy would type in the names and biographical information into her computer and send it to the nerve center back at the hotel. The interns would spring into action, checking all different websites, review sites, LexisNexis, etc., in order to accumulate as much information as possible on each potential juror.

What they found was amazing. They did criminal background checks, and we'd know if a juror was lying when asked if ever arrested for a crime. They'd find books a juror reviewed on Amazon. They'd find items they purchased, and they'd read websites if they had them, look up domain names, and find car registration. We even searched social media websites. We certainly live in the information age.

We were really on top of things, rocking and rolling with the seven volunteer law students cooped up in a hotel room with Dorothy leading the way.

It's a good thing we were able to find the criminal records of the jurors, because at the start the prosecution was not sharing that information with us. Usually the prosecution runs background checks and shares that information with the defense. Not in this case. It was waiting until *after* the questioning of the juror was done, and only then would they bring it out. It didn't matter. Thanks to Dorothy and her interns, we had the information ourselves.

During the first couple days of jury selection, we were working around the clock, questioning potential jurors individually. Hundreds were excused for hardship, meaning they couldn't be sequestered in Orlando and leave their homes for two months, or leaving their job was a financial hardship. We had to be in court at eight thirty in the morning, and we would not stop until seven at night. The process seemed endless.

By the time we got back to the hotel, it was eight at night, and then we held meetings to discuss what had happened that day, what jurors we liked, what jurors we didn't like, and what our plan was going to be for the next day. And when our meeting was over, I'd grab a bite to eat, and then I'd meet with Jim and his partner Tyler Benson, and we'd go over designing graphics for my opening statement.

I had planned out my opening statement, but now that I had a graphics expert at my disposal, I had to start from scratch, because I now could incorporate a visual presentation that was going to make the opening so much more persuasive and impactful. We had to pull photos and other exhibits to make a complete visual presentation.

We'd finish around two in the morning, and then I'd go to bed, and I had to be up at seven so I could be in court again at eight thirty.

After a couple days of this, I began to get sick from exhaustion.

After a session in court, we took a break, and I started to feel nauseated. I went into the bathroom and started vomiting. Cheney came in to see if I was all right, and I almost passed out.

"That's it," he said, "We have to stop."

He saw I couldn't continue.

Cheney went and told Judge Perry. I was able to straggle into his chambers, and Judge Perry was very, very considerate—surprisingly considerate. He took one look at me, and he canceled court for the day right then and there.

Casey was having lunch, and she was brought back to court. I told her that I wasn't feeling well. The media wasn't told anything.

I took a little medicine and got into bed. I awoke a couple hours later, and decided, *I'm just going to stay in bed all day.*

After a couple more hours, I turned on the television to see what was on the news about the case.

It was pure madness. One station speculated that I was driving to the appeals court to appeal one of Judge Perry's rulings. Another was replaying a video of Casey talking to me at the defense table. The reporter, trying to read her lips, decided what she was saying was, "Get me a plea." They were sure our objective now was to get Casey a plea deal. A third television station stated unequivocally that I had quit.

What the hell, I said to myself.

I sent texts to a couple reporters I dealt with saying, "None of the rumors are true. We ended court today on a private matter. Jury selection will resume tomorrow."

That then made the news, accompanied by commentary that went something like this:

"He's lying."

"Do we believe him?"

"Maybe he's not telling the truth."

Jesus, I said to myself, *why did I even bother?*

When I got back to court the next day after being sick, Judge Perry took me aside, and he was very gracious and nice. He asked me if I was feeling better; it was truly the nicest he had ever treated me.

I always wanted him to like me, and at times I felt he did, but unfortunately more times than not I had the feeling he hated me. I still don't know why.

The hardest part about jury selection for me was the fatigue. There was even one point when I was selecting the jury when I made a Freudian slip and asked to use one of my peremptory challenges to remove Judge Perry, who got a chuckle out of it. But the reason that happened was the fatigue. Once the trial itself began, I was fine. But until then, I was working around the clock picking the jury and redoing my opening argument. It was almost too much to bear.

In PREVIOUS HEARINGS, Casey was an excellent client in the courtroom. She did what she was told. She took notes. She didn't make facial reactions. She didn't speak out loud. She didn't do anything.

The moment we sat down to do jury selection, Casey just broke down in tears. It was as if the reality that this case was going to trial had finally come.

Judge Perry read his instructions, "You're here for the *State of Florida versus Casey Marie Anthony*. The state has elected to seek the death penalty." When Casey heard this, she broke down crying.

The prosecutor asked for a sidebar, complaining about her crying.

We were pissed.

"She's on trial for her life," I said. "What do you expect her to be doing? Laughing?"

"I can't prevent someone from crying," said Judge Perry wisely.

I WAS AMAZED at how many jurors we felt to be stealth jurors, meaning people who wanted to be on the jury for reasons having nothing to do with justice. Either they wanted to be famous, or they planned to write a book, or they wanted to be on the jury so they could find Casey guilty. We looked for any signs, and we were especially wary of those who wanted to be on the jury too badly.

In addition to the stealth jurors, we struck a few others. There were several potential jurors who had been arrested and didn't put it on their sworn questionnaire.

Dorothy and her researchers discovered that one potential juror had gone on Amazon and bought a toy action figure sitting in an electric chair! He had also written a couple of pro–death penalty blogs, but on the stand he was giving all the right answers as it related to the death penalty. Fortunately, this guy had also had a DUI, and he neglected to put it on his questionnaire.

THE INSANITY NEVER WENT AWAY. One day the court was questioning a juror when a heavyset woman with blonde hair by the name of Elizabeth Ann Rogers got up from her seat in the gallery and began shouting, "She killed her child, for Christ's sake. She killed her child."

She was arrested immediately, and Judge Perry held her in contempt. He threw her in jail for two days.

A prospective juror wanted to get out of serving, so he walked up to a news reporter and asked how he could get out of it. He found out quickly. Judge Perry held him in contempt and fined him a couple hundred bucks.

Then there was Patricia Young, the sixty-five-year-old EquuSearch volunteer from St. Petersburg who appeared on the jury list. We had her on our witness list as well. We wanted her to testify she had searched the area months before Caylee was found and never saw a thing. She had also been a protester outside the Anthony home. Because we listed her, the experts speculated we were going after George, because one evening George came out of his house and pushed her, which the media captured on tape.

Young was in the jury room, and she was telling people, "I volunteered for EquuSearch, and I wonder if this is for the Casey Anthony case."

Linda Drane Burdick was the one who recognized her name. She brought it up to me and said, "Do you think this is her?"

"It could be," I said.

And then the judge called her into chambers, and wouldn't you know it, it was the same Patricia Young. She was the only woman from Clearwater on the witness list. What were the odds?

WE WERE ALLOWED ten peremptory challenges—in other words, challenges without cause—for the twelve jurors, and we were given a couple more for the five alternates. In most criminal trials, the judge also would give the defense a few extra peremptory challenges just to eliminate any issues on appeal as it relates to jury selection issues.

Here's the thing about jury selection: In order for you to preserve any right of appeal for being denied striking someone for cause, you have to first exhaust all your peremptory challenges. Thus ninety-nine point nine, nine, nine percent of all trial lawyers will exhaust their peremptory challenges, and then if there is a juror you feel should be excused for cause, you then ask for an additional one. The judge always gives it to you, because he knows exactly what you're doing—creating a record for an appeal. This is especially true if the reason for excluding that juror is borderline. To eliminate that, the judge will say, "Okay, we will give you another one." At a certain point, if you object, and your reason isn't very good, he will then say, "Denied," and then you are left with a weak appealable issue.

This case was very different. Judge Perry gave us *not one single extra* peremptory challenge, which shocked me. But what could I do? I preserved the issue and moved on.

WHEN PICKING THIS JURY, my first priority was choosing jurors who were good as they related to the death penalty. Step one for a defense lawyer in a capital case is always to save the client's life. Step two is to find good jurors for the guilty or innocent phase. Many times you come across jurors who are really good on the guilt or innocent phase but bad for the penalty phase, and you have to get rid of them. As a result, you end up with plenty of jurors you really like, but if they are proponents of the death penalty, you must get rid of them. This is the reason why death-qualified jurors are so conviction-prone.

In the end we ended up with twelve jurors and five alternates. Even though their names have been released, I refuse to publish their names for the purposes of this book. They have a right to their privacy, and I will do what I can to keep it that way.

Juror number one was an elderly Caucasian woman, sixty-seven years old, and a retired nurse. We liked that because nurses are generally nurturing people. She was extremely pleasant, mild-mannered, and didn't feel very strongly about the death penalty.

When I was questioning her, she made the statement that trials fascinated her because a trial was about solving a mystery. At that point I wanted to make clear that she understood that a trial is not a two-sided affair.

"This is the prosecution's show," I said to her, "and if we sat back and did nothing and if the prosecution failed to deliver the goods, you cannot convict."

During my entire jury selection I wanted to educate the jurors about the burden of proof and about what it meant to be certain of guilt beyond a reasonable doubt. While questioning them, I wasn't looking for answers as much as I was educating them about the fact that the defense didn't have to prove anything.

Juror number two was a forty-five-year-old African American male who worked as an IT person for Pinellas County. His wife was a registered nurse, which we liked. We also knew we were going to bring the jury technical evidence with respect to computers, and we felt it would be good to have his expertise on that jury.

I also liked the fact he wasn't big on the death penalty, but one time when I was questioning him, trying to educate him, he made a really bad facial expression, and I became really angry at myself because I knew I had pissed him off.

I really liked him as a juror anyway, but I worried about the face he made; it turned out he would be the last holdout for a manslaughter conviction, until he finally gave in.

And so while I liked him, out of all the jurors, he was the one I was concerned about most.

Juror number three was a thirty-two-year-old Caucasian female, a Democrat who had no children. What we really liked about her was she was a volunteer at Camp Torreya, a camp for lesbian, gay, bisexual and transgender (LGBT) teens. That told me a lot about her. It told me she was compassionate, and it told me she understood the nature of discrimination.

For me, this juror would be critical to us as to how this case was going to be tried. I knew the prosecution was going to try to get the jury to discriminate against Casey by citing the decisions she made and the lifestyle she led. I knew this because the prosecution didn't have any evidence of a murder.

You might wonder why the prosecution didn't know and why they didn't ask to remove her. I don't think they knew. Having Dorothy and her staff of crack researchers really did give us a big advantage in this regard.

Juror number four was a fifty-four-year-old African American woman. She was a Democrat, and she was married, and she made the comment that she didn't like to judge people, a comment the prosecution jumped on, using it to try to exclude her. She was using it, it turned out, in a religious context.

The prosecution tried to exclude her with one of its peremptory challenges, and I objected, noting that this was part of a pattern on their part to exclude all African Americans from the jury.

We asked the prosecution to give us a race-neutral reason for excluding her under *Batson v. United States*, but the reason they gave wasn't satisfactory to Judge Perry, and he refused to remove her from the jury.

The next day the prosecution asked the court reporter to transcribe her answers, and they renewed the motion to kick her off the jury. We renewed our objection, and the judge again denied their motion.

The reason the prosecution was trying to kick all the African Americans off the jury is because, as a rule, African Americans have been victims of discrimination for a long time, and they are less trusting of it.

And because they realize the finality of the death penalty, African Americans are generally against it. Prosecutors know this, so in death penalty cases they systematically exclude them. The end result is that whites make up the death case juries, but in my opinion this by definition makes the death penalty unconstitutional in its practice. In theory, the proponents of the death penalty say it's not unfair, that it works; in practice, it does not. This was the one occasion that having an African American judge may have helped. Even the conservative Judge Belvin Perry Jr. must have felt discrimination in his lifetime, and if the prosecution was going to exclude potential jurors because of their race, it was going to be harder than usual to do that with Judge Perry on the bench.

We loved juror number four. She wasn't too crazy about the death penalty. On a scale of one to ten, for us she was a ten.

Juror number five was a seventy-one-year-old Caucasian woman who was retired. She was also a Democrat. She didn't own a computer, so I knew she wouldn't be affected by the hate on the blogosphere. She was just a nice laid-back lady. She wasn't crazy about the death penalty either, and what we also liked, she didn't have young children. We knew she'd be fair.

Juror number six was a thirty-three-year-old Caucasian male, who worked as a chef. His only downside was he had two young children living at home, but we liked him because he appeared to be fair, and we thought that since he was a chef, he'd bring an artistic quality to the jury. Even though he was a Republican, we felt he'd be on the liberal side. We figured if we were going to get a parent with small children, it should be a male. This juror didn't grade high, but for us he was adequate.

Juror number seven was a forty-one-year-old divorced Caucasian female. She was another Democrat, an executive assistant and a youth counselor, so she was another person who we felt would be tolerant, wouldn't be so judgmental. We did the research on the place where she worked—this was where Dorothy and her crew were so phenomenal—and their mission statement said, "We base our concepts on a belief in God, and the uniqueness and inherent worth of each individual." Not exactly pro-death penalty there.

Juror number eight was a sixty-year-old Caucasian woman who was a service representative at Verizon Wireless. She was middle of the road for us. She had had prior jury service, and we noticed that a few times she smiled at Cheney. I even told him, "Flirt with her. She likes you." She didn't have any small children, of course, and we had a good vibe about her. Also she was not very pro-death penalty.

Juror number nine was a fifty-three-year-old Caucasian male. He was unemployed, I assumed because he was retired, but he once had been a logger. He was very laid-back, seemed like a very nice guy, and again he wasn't too pro-death penalty. For a short while we had a concern he might be a stealth juror, but we didn't feel that strongly about it, so we kept him on.

Juror number ten was a fifty-seven-year-old Caucasian male who also worked for Verizon Wireless. He was a customer service representative, and we were concerned that he knew juror number eight. He didn't. I went to a sidebar with him, and I found him to be a nice gentleman.

During a trial there is usually one juror with whom you make the most eye contact, and for this trial it was this juror. Most people avoid eye contact, but he was the type of person who would look you in the eye. I felt a very good connection with him.

Juror number eleven was a thirty-eight-year-old Caucasian phys-ed teacher at a high school. He was a Democrat, a very good-looking guy who some in the media called "George Clooney." Burdick certain-ly seemed smitten by him. We also liked him because he wasn't crazy about the death penalty.

I remember liking him immediately because of something unique that he said.

During the questioning he was asked, "Did you think when you saw the media coverage that Casey was guilty?"

"I suspected something," he said, "but guilty of what?"

During the three weeks of our picking a jury, no one gave a better answer.

"Guilty, yeah, but of what?"

It was the basic definition of our case. We weren't going to parade Casey up there as being completely innocent, but we certainly weren't going to let them say she was guilty of murder. This was somebody who wanted it proven to him, rather than his just assuming it.

There was another thing we liked about him. While he was initially okay with jury service, the next day he came back to say the school he worked for had a course they were offering him, and he wasn't sure he would get that course if he had to leave to be a juror. Basically he didn't want on, which made us like him even more, because we then knew he wasn't a stealth juror.

He ended up serving, and from the first day of the trial he was the one who took the most notes, and we all knew he was going to be the foreman.

And then there was **juror number twelve**. She was a sixty-one-year-old Caucasian female who worked for Publix supermarkets as a cook in the deli department. She was the only juror who was strongly in favor of the death penalty, and the reason she made the jury was that Judge Perry didn't give us any additional peremptory challenges, and we couldn't strike her. Even so, I felt, *Eleven out of twelve isn't bad at all.*

In fact, when we were done, I thought to myself, *This is a phenomenal jury—fair and impartial. I don't think I've ever picked a better one.*

CHAPTER 24

A FLOWER IN THE ATTIC

I HAD A COUPLE OF DAYS before the start of the trial to fine-tune my opening statement. I estimated it was going to be about two hours long, and my biggest challenge was how to keep the jury's attention for that length of time, especially after sitting through two hours of listening to Linda Drane Burdick.

My idea was to keep them alert and awake through the use of different types of visual aids. The idea was to blow up whatever point I wanted to make. This is where Jim Lucas was so creative. I used the standard trial exhibits which sat on an easel, and in addition Jim created a magnetic board for me to put up information as I was making a point; I had a hand board—smaller-sized exhibits I could hold in my hand—giving me the opportunity to get closer to the jury to better create a bond with them; I used a standard PowerPoint so the jurors could use the television screens in front of their seats; and I used a standard whiteboard that I could write on. The purpose of these different types of visual aids was to stimulate the jurors' visual perspective in different ways to keep them interested.

I also brought with me a tape measure to demonstrate how close Caylee's remains were to the street. I wanted to show that she was on the side of the road to be found, not in the woods to be hidden.

I was ready. I knew the facts backward and forward. I had gone over my opening countless times. My detractors always talked about my swagger and my cockiness, but my confidence came from being prepared. It was nothing more than that. I knew going in that I knew the case better than anyone in that courtroom, and it was only through hard work that you get that way. One of my favorite expressions is "Opportunity favors the prepared mind."

One of the things my mother always said to me was, "If you want to be the best, study the best, and become better." The week before the opening statement I would turn off the sound of the ballgame and read Clarence Darrow's autobiography, *The Story of My Life,* and read his closing arguments in the Leopold and Loeb case. I watched trials of the old masters like Johnnie Cochran in the O. J. Simpson murder trial. I watched Roy Black during the William Kennedy Smith trial. I watched Gerry Spence, any of the masters, to see what made them persuasive. I had studied them before, but they always served as a great refresher.

I knew this was going to be my moment, that if I did it right, someday people would watch me.

THE TRIAL DAY CAME, and I wasn't nervous. Rather I was anxious, like a race-horse ready to burst out of the gate. I had the feeling, *I can't wait to go.* As usual, I drove to Cheney Mason's office opposite the Orlando courthouse and parked in his garage. We'd meet in his office and walk across the street together. That day I was carrying Clarence Darrow's autobiography with me, intending to read a passage or two during breaks in the proceedings.

From across the street in front of the courthouse, I could see the media vultures getting ready to pounce. As soon as we crossed, they attacked us, and it was far more chaotic and hectic than I had ever seen before, except for the first time when we got Casey out of jail. The crush of media was overwhelming, but we kept walking forward, and I felt like a boxer surrounded by his entourage getting ready to walk into the ring.

They threw questions at me left and right, but I didn't answer any of them. I was determined not to speak to the media during the course of the trial.

I remember hearing one question from a reporter, who said, "Jose, you look like you have a little extra bounce in your step. Are you expecting to drop some major bombshells today?"

Oh shit, I thought to myself, *you better calm down. I don't want to come across as overconfident.*

I didn't answer her.

When we reached the courtroom, I couldn't believe how packed it was. There was real tension in the air, and for the first time in my career a little nervousness crept in. I knew my entire defense team was looking for me to start this trial off with a bang.

In a trial, you always want to start strong. The opening statement is critical because it gives the jurors a framework from which they will look at the evidence. If you don't set up the framework at the outset, it becomes very difficult to make them see it in the middle of the trial.

After we walked in, in came the prosecution, Frank George, Jeff Ashton, and Linda Drane Burdick, who was wearing a red jacket. In the three years I had known her, she had never worn anything but gray or blue. Nothing flashy. Nothing bright. Plus she had had her hair done, and she looked very nice. It was as though she had gone on one of those television shows and had had a makeover.

She got up and began her presentation. She began with something like, "The time has come to tell a story of a little girl named Caylee," and right away I knew the prosecution was going to do exactly what I was sure it would do: appeal to the jury's emotions.

Who's going to be able to overcome the death of a beautiful little girl? Let me grab your hearts and keep them.

Her approach was no surprise. The prosecutor's number-one card, one that they always play, is to try to appeal to the jurors' emotions, trying to get them angry about the crime. After all, isn't that what the television news does all of the time? That's why the prosecutor and the TV news reporters work so well together.

While the prosecution was appealing to the jurors' emotions, I knew that I was going to have to appeal to their intellect. Of course, if I could grab their emotions here and there, it wouldn't hurt.

One thing I've noticed about prosecutors: They always have themes and expressions, which are usually ridiculous. In this case Burdick's theme revolved around Day One, Casey did this, Day Two, she did this, Day Three, she did this, until she went through the entire thirty days when Caylee went missing. The mistake she made was that thirty days is a *long* time, and the jurors got bored. In fact, they had to take a break right in the middle of her opening statement.

She started talking about the events of Day One, and then Day Two, and then Day Three, Day Four, and so on. While she was recounting Casey's activities for the thirty days, ten times she must have said, "Where's Caylee?" But she left out the key question, which was not, *Where's Caylee?* Rather the most important question—and my focus— would be, *What happened to Caylee? How did she die?*

My mentor, Rick DeMaria, taught me to take the prosecution's ridiculous theme and bring it up again and again to make it seem as ridiculous as it is. And that's what I did with Linda Burdick's Day One, Day Two, Day Three, Day Four recitation. Over and over I told the jury, this case isn't about Casey's actions during those thirty days.

No, this case is about one thing and one thing only: *How did Caylee die?*

I WAS ALSO A STUDENT of Steve Jobs. He would give brilliant presentations; I would study his Apple product releases. I saw how when Jobs spoke he always told his audience at the outset exactly what he intended to say in his talk. I did that in my opening statement. I wanted to explain to the jury what I was going to tell them.

I broke it down into five areas.

"First off," I said, "I would like to tell you what happened. We sat through almost two hours. There was Day One, Day Two, Day Three, Day Four, and so on and so on, but no one ever told you what happened. But today you will be the first people to know exactly what happened to Caylee Marie Anthony."

The second area of focus was Roy Kronk. I told the jury that his was a name not mentioned in Burdick's opening statement. I told the jurors that his role would be crucial in deciding their evaluation of the case.

The third area I was going to discuss was the investigation by the police. I told the jurors that the police were very thorough when it came to investigating Casey, but that their investigation was directed at one person and one person only.

"At what point do we stop speculating?" I asked the jury. "At what point do we stop guessing? At what point do we stop being so desperate?"

The fourth area I was going to focus on, I told them, was Suburban Drive, where Caylee's remains were found.

"There are numerous suspicious circumstances surrounding that location," I said, "and I want to make sure it's brought to light to you.

"I want to make sure you understand what was there, who was there, and for how long."

And then I said we were going to talk about Casey's car.

"The evidence, or the lack of evidence, or the confusion of the evidence that surrounds this car," I said, "will probably double, if not triple, the length of this trial." I said that by the end of the trial they would be asking themselves whether the evidence about the car would have any relevance at all.

Then I talked about the fantastic nature of forensic evidence. I told them the state's case would be more science fiction than science. I didn't spend a lot of time discussing the forensics because they hadn't been educated yet about it. I was going to wait until the closing arguments to discuss the finer details that made the forensics so powerful for us. Then I explained how Caylee died.

"Now, everyone wants to know what happened," I said. "How in the world can a mother wait thirty days before ever reporting her child missing? It's insane. It's bizarre. Something's just not right about that. Well, the answer is actually relatively simple. She never was missing. Caylee Anthony died on June 16, 2008, when she drowned in her family's swimming pool."

I told the jurors not to be distracted by emotion. This was a theme I would come back to over and over. I said the levels of distraction might even reach the bizarre, but that they should never forget that this is a first-degree murder case.

"They want to take someone's life," I said.

But then I told them, "This is not a murder case. This is not a manslaughter case. This is not a case of aggravated child abuse. This is none of those things. But you can't be distracted."

I then made the point that the Anthony family was extremely dysfunctional. This, I knew, would make them sit up and take notice.

"You will hear about ugly things, secret things, things that people don't speak about. Things that Casey never spoke about."

I invited the jury to come with me to Hopespring Drive, what looked like an all-American home.

"You never know what secrets lie within," I said. "You never know what's going on."

I began to give them a look at the evidence that would explain her strange behavior after Caylee's disappearance.

I told the jury, "On June 16, 2008, after Caylee died, Casey did what she's been doing all her life, or most of it. Hiding her pain. Going into that dark corner and pretending that she does not live in the situation she's living in. She went back to that deep ugly place called denial to pretend as if nothing was ever wrong."

And I told them they'd hear evidence of this and that and in the end, they would conclude that something was not right with her.

I then gave them information that they didn't hear from the prosecution: that Casey was an excellent mother.

"The child never went without food," I said, "never went without clothing, without shelter. You won't hear a single person come up here and testify how she was neglected or abused. There are no broken bones, no trips to the hospital, no moment that would help you determine that this child was abused or anything but loved by all the members of the family."

"Especially her mother."

I then began to talk about the abuse.

"You see," I said, "this family must keep its secrets quiet. And it all began when Casey was eight years old and her father came into her room and began to touch her inappropriately, and it escalated and escalated."

"What does a sex abuse survivor look like? Do they have a tattoo on their forehead? We can be sitting next to a sex abuse victim and not even know it. These things are kept quiet. And these ugly secrets slowly will come out through this trial."

I told them that by the end of the trial they would come to know why Casey acted the way she did, and why she acted as though nothing was wrong.

I gave them subtle evidence that Casey hadn't committed a crime.

"She didn't run," I said. "She didn't move to California, to New York. She didn't say to her parents, 'Sorry, you're never going to see your granddaughter again.'"

"That would have been the easiest thing for her to do."

"Instead," I said, "she acted as if it never happened."

I THEN TALKED ABOUT how Casey pretended she had a job and how she pretended she had a nanny.

"Is that normal?" I asked. "Is that what normal people do? They pretend they're going to work? They have fake emails from work?"

I told the jury there was a reason she did this. I told them she did it to protect Caylee from abuse, as she had been abused.

"Anything Casey could do to protect her child she did," I told the jury, "including living a lie, making up a nanny, making up a job. That's what Casey had to do to live. She forced herself to live in a world that she wanted, not the one she was thrust into."

I told the jury how when she became pregnant, the family hushed it up. I told them about the wedding she went to when she was seven-and-a-half months pregnant, and how Cindy and George denied she was pregnant. The exclamation point was when I showed them a picture of a pregnant Casey who was clearly showing, less than two months from giving birth. The jury had to wonder: why did the Anthonys claim they didn't know she was pregnant?

"The entire family wanted to keep it quiet," I said. "And if they hid this child, this beautiful child, in life, you can best believe that they would hide her in death."

I told the jurors, "They hid this child like a flower in the attic." I said it on purpose. We had seven women who would decide Casey's fate, and most of them were old enough to remember the movie or the book about four abused and mistreated children who were the product of incest, and I could see a look of recognition on some of their faces. It was an important moment where I could feel we had made a connection.

About an hour and a half into my opening, I asked the jurors if they wanted to recess, because I knew they were tired around that time when Burdick was speaking to them. Also we had a few smokers on the panel. I stood three feet from them, and I asked them, "Do you want to take a break?"

None of them did, and it wasn't *what* they said as much as *how* they said it. I could see in their eyes they were saying, *No way. Don't stop now. I want to hear more.*

I knew at that point we were on the right track.

I TOLD THE JURORS how Casey's brother had molested her, how Lee had started to follow in dad's footsteps. I told them the FBI had tested Lee to see whether he was the father. I told them he hadn't denied the abuse when confronted with the evidence.

"You're going to hear all kinds of bizarre family behavior that just doesn't make sense," I said.

I them told them about how George was making statements incriminating Casey for Caylee's murder.

I told them Casey was the way she was because of who raised her. I became more graphic. I told them, "Casey was raised to lie. This child, at eight years old, learned to lie immediately. She could be thirteen years old, have her father's penis in her mouth, and then go to school and play with the other kids as if nothing ever happened. Nothing's wrong."

I told them this information should help them understand why no one knew her child was dead.

"Sex abuse does things to us. It changes you," I said. "Some people are fortunate to live with it. [Meaning survive it and move on.] Others are not, and in this sad tragedy, it had to happen to Casey."

Then I described to them—and to the public—how Caylee died, and I did something the prosecution couldn't do. I had photos of the house, of the sliding door leading to the pool, and of the backyard and the pool, and I was able to help the jurors visualize the scene.

I told the whole story of June 16, how George woke Casey and started yelling at her, "Where's Caylee?" How they searched the house, the bedrooms under the beds, the closets, in the garage, and then they went outside.

I talked about the above-ground pool and the ladder that was up, and how Casey saw George holding Caylee's body, and how she cried and cried.

Then I told them how George had yelled at her, "Look what you've done," and "Your mother will never forgive you," and "You'll go to jail for child neglect."

I told the jury that Casey should have been stronger, that she should have called 9-1-1.

"Casey should have done the right thing," I said, "and that's what she's guilty of." We always wanted to acknowledge Casey's bad behavior. I never felt we should shy away from it. Instead I wanted her to own it, to fall on the sword and give them nowhere to go with it. That way we could focus on the big question of murder.

I KNEW THAT THE KEY to winning the case was one key question: how can you call it a murder if the prosecution doesn't know the cause of death?

I knew that because a couple months before jury selection, I got a call from CBS's *48 Hours Mystery*. They said they were curious about whether Casey could get a fair trial, so I suggested that they do a focus group to determine what people were thinking and how they were analyzing the evidence. We selected Orlando because we wanted to get the most tainted jury pool possible.

48 Hours Mystery hired a dozen "jurors," a good cross section of the community, and they had them fill out juror questionnaires, just like a real jury would. Our trial consultant, Richard Gabriel, spent an entire day with them, discussing only the prosecution's case. They talked about air samples, the cadaver dogs, the duct tape, and Casey's behavior after Caylee disappeared, and while they were talking, I was able to sit behind a two-way mirror and watch and listen to them interact.

I was fascinated. I learned they really didn't believe the air sample bullshit the prosecution was trying to sell. They also put very little weight on the cadaver dogs. Also, they had real problems with the fact there was no DNA on the duct tape.

What they did put significant weight on were the computer searches, and from that, I knew those computer searches would be critical, and that I would have to take great pains to explain *why* Casey was looking for chloroform.

The biggest problem with the prosecution's evidence, I learned, was that these people could not understand how this could be a murder if the prosecution didn't know the cause of Caylee's death.

"How can you say it was murder if you don't know how she died?" said a forty-nine-year-old woman in the focus group.

And that was *huge*. Most of them said they figured it was some kind of accident.

None of them liked Casey. They didn't like her at all. But in the end they just couldn't envision her committing murder just so she could go out and party. None of it made any sense to them.

And when they took the vote on first-degree murder, Troy Roberts, the correspondent for *48 Hours Mystery*, asked everyone to stand up who would acquit her. Ten stood to acquit. And that turned out to be the exact same number for the first vote of the real jury.

The focus group was very helpful. I had such an accurate preview from the community that hated her the most. I also learned they didn't like the media coverage.

But from that focus group, I learned there was one key question that the jury needed the prosecution to answer: "How did Caylee die?" Our entire defense was built around that question.

I REITERATED THAT this was not a murder case and not a manslaughter case. I could just as easily have said, "This was not a murder case," and left it at that, but the lesser offense of manslaughter carries a significant penalty, and you don't want to ignore it. I learned that lesson in the Nilton Diaz case, where Nilton ended up getting hit with a manslaughter charge. I didn't want that to happen again.

I told the jury, "This is a sad tragic accident that snowballed out of control." I used the confession that George had made to his lover, Krystal Holloway.

I asked the jury why George hadn't called 9-1-1. My answer: because the police never investigated him at all, we will never know. I went on to ask why, after Cindy Anthony told the police that the ladder to the pool was still up, they completely ignored her. Why were no questions asked? Why was there no information gathered? Why were there no forensics?

I knew the answer.

"Because they had murder on their minds," I said. "An accident wasn't sexy enough for them. There was this bizarre girl lying to them, telling them outrageous stories, and the media was eating it up, and so they continued to pursue their murder theory."

I told the jury what I felt lay at the heart of this whole case.

"They were more concerned about the public than they were in doing their jobs," I said.

I TALKED A LITTLE about George, and his gas cans, and the duct tape and how the same duct tape was found where George was handing out flyers. I told the jury that Casey had been in jail when the duct tape was found.

I said, "Follow the duct tape, and it will point you to who put Caylee's remains where they ultimately ended up. Or maybe not." But I made it clear that though the prosecution's contention was that Casey was the only one who had access to that duct tape, it was a contention that wasn't true at all. If anyone had access to the duct tape, it was George.

My conclusion to the jury was, "The *only* physical evidence that you will find in this case that connects Caylee's remains to anyone at the home is this duct tape."

I then told the jurors about George's affair with Holloway.

"He has denied, and he will deny on this stand, that he ever had a relationship with her," I said, "but he couldn't get around the guard at the gate where she lives. Because that woman saw him coming and going many times at her home. And Krystal Holloway will tell you they had a conversation, and George began to break down and cry, and she asked him, 'What happened to Caylee?' And he said, 'It was an accident that snowballed out of control.'"

I said, "This was before Caylee was ever found. This was while he was passing out flyers asking for donations to help find his missing granddaughter."

Then I told the jury about George's attempted suicide on January 22, 2009.

I said we had no intention of accusing George of murder, or that he had anything to do with Caylee's death.

"It was an accident that snowballed out of control," I reiterated. "This is not a murder case. This is not a manslaughter case. This is a tragic accident that happened to some very disturbed people."

Before I wrapped up, I turned to the story of Roy Kronk. I told the jury I wasn't accusing Kronk of murder either. But I did say Kronk used Caylee's remains as a meal ticket. I used my tape measure to show how close to the road she had been left. I asked why none of the EquuSearch people had found her. I talked of the thousands of people who had searched for her and came up empty.

I recounted how Kronk had found her on August 11 and then again on December 11. I recounted the confusion.

At the very end of my opening, I drew a big V on the board, and I said to the jurors, "At the end of the day, when you go back home, after this case is over and you go back to Clearwater and you're sitting around your dining room table, and someone asks you, 'Why did you find Casey Anthony not guilty?' you're going to say, 'Because they couldn't tell me what happened to Caylee. They couldn't tell me how she died.'"

And again, I repeated, "It's not a murder case, not a manslaughter case, and definitely there was no child abuse." Which was true. And not to give it all away, after the trial was over, all the jurors said the same thing, "We found her not guilty because they couldn't tell us how she died."

In my opening statement, I was challenging the prosecution to do something I knew it couldn't do. I challenged the prosecutors to tell us how she died, and they couldn't do it. The jurors looked to the prosecution for answers, and it never delivered.

Then I drew an A and a line to Z, and I said, "A prosecutor is supposed to give you their case from A to Z to prove their case beyond a reasonable doubt. If they don't know what happened to her" and I put a big question mark in the middle, "that's a huge gap, and if A is George Anthony being the last person to see Caylee alive, you're going to have doubt, and if Z is Roy Kronk, who found Caylee Anthony, you're going to have even more doubt."

"So what are you left with? Nothing."

And that's how I concluded my opening statement.

I sat down, and when I came back to the table, my team was very complimentary. I can remember leaving the courtroom to go to one of our offices and walking past a reporter from *People* magazine.

He looked around to make sure no one was listening, and he leaned over to me and said, "Jose, that was fucking brilliant." And in the hallway I could hear the buzz, because I had revealed evidence that had never been revealed before. Everyone was describing my opening as "turning the case upside down." But I knew this was no easy task. I was facing a prosecutor desperate for a conviction, a judge who hated my guts, and a disbelieving media. I didn't for a second think that things would get easier. To the contrary, I knew that I was going to have to scratch and claw my way through this trial; but I had no intention of letting up.

This was not going to be a sprint. This was a marathon, and I was too well aware that I'd be running a route covered with sharp nails in my bare feet.

CHAPTER 25

THE FOCKERS

FTER MAKING MY OPENING STATEMENT, I felt really good, but it was only three in the afternoon when the prosecution called their first witness. I was sure they were going to call Cindy Anthony. I felt she would have been their strongest choice.

Instead we were thrown off guard when they called George. It was at the same time the prosecution's best—and worst—move.

The purpose of the prosecution's calling him was to deflate and reject the sexual abuse charges that we had made against him. George took the stand, told his life's history, how he worked as a police officer in Ohio, quit the job to work with his father in the car business, parting ways after they didn't get along, and then how he and Cindy left for Florida to start over.

When Jeff Ashton asked him if he ever sexually molested Casey, he said no.

When Ashton asked him if he was present in his home when Caylee died, he said no.

When Ashton asked him if he disposed of Caylee's body, he said no.

He denied everything, displaying the usual, "I'm the victim here. Feel sorry for me."

What was interesting was that during direct examination Ashton asked him if he had seen the ultrasound of Caylee, and he responded by saying, yes, he had seen the pancake—Caylee's vagina—and so he knew it was a girl. That was creepy enough, but Ashton then brought out that George had been in the delivery room when his daughter gave birth to

Caylee. Everyone on the jury and in the courtroom was a little creeped out by that fact. By itself that piece of information took away some of the effectiveness of George's testimony.

The reason Ashton asked him about that was because he knew I was going to bring it up on cross-examination, and he wanted to steal my thunder.

Ashton did a decent enough job on his own in direct, and when he was finished, I got up to cross-examine George, and I began with a question about the day Cindy's brother accosted him and Cindy at his wedding wanting to know if Casey was pregnant. George had denied she was. He said he thought she was getting fat when in fact she was seven-and-a-half months pregnant.

He continued to insist he hadn't known.

I asked him whether during the final two months of her pregnancy he ever asked Casey who the father was, and he said no.

I said to him, "For two years Casey dropped Caylee off at a nanny who you never met. Is that right?"

"Yes."

I brought up the marital problems he and Cindy were having at that time. I mentioned that he had moved out after Caylee was born.

Ashton got up to object.

"Relevancy?"

"He moved out because of molestation issues with Casey," I said, "not financial issues that he claimed."

Ashton said that the breakup was over fights between George and Cindy over money Casey had stolen.

When George testified, he denied he left because Casey didn't want him around. He said it was because he had been gambling on the Internet and because he had lost a lot of money to a Nigerian bank scam.

George again said that Casey and Caylee left the house on June 16 at 12:50 P.M.

I changed directions and started to ask about the gas cans. I wanted to ask him whether he had put the duct tape on the gas cans.

Ashton objected.

"The question is beyond the scope of the direct examination," Ashton said.

Judge Perry: "Sustained."

I asked George about the duct tape.

"Objection. The question is beyond the scope of the direct examination," Ashton said.

I asked George why he had hired a lawyer within twenty-four hours of his calling the police.

"Objection. The question is beyond the scope of the direct examination," Ashton said.

"Sustained."

I asked him if he put the duct tape on the gas cans.

"Objection. The question is beyond the scope of the direct examination," he said.

"Sustained."

I asked him about the smell of decomposition in Casey's car.

"Objection. The question is beyond the scope of the direct examination," Ashton said.

Judge Perry: "Sustained."

The prosecution had made a decision to call George up to the stand multiple times during the case, thereby trying to limit some of my cross-examination. But there is a case called *Blue v. State* that says it's an abuse of discretion for a judge to restrict cross-examination if it's reasonably related to the defense. All of my questions had been reasonably related, even if they were beyond the scope. Judge Perry should not have sustained Ashton's objections, and I was somewhat thrown off by this. I had never heard of not being able to go after a witness.

Casey was on trial for her life, and I should have been allowed to attack George the way I wanted to, especially with his being the focus of our defense. But it was another one of those moments where I had to adapt. We were playing by new rules, and I was going to have to change the way I played the game in order to adjust to them.

This is like starting a game and changing the rules in the middle of it, I thought to myself.

I sat myself down and gave myself a talking to.

I'll have time to regroup and really come after George harder, I decided. And this is why I say calling George first was the prosecution's best move, but it was also its worst move, because I knew this was going to be a long trial, and I would have many more shots at him. As a result, I wasn't too concerned I wasn't able to follow the fireworks of my opening statement with a boom.

Afterward I heard all the boo birds.

"Doesn't Baez know Law School 101? You don't go beyond the scope."

"He kept trying to go outside the scope. What does he think he's doing?"

The haters were saying, "He did a great job during the opening, but he really flopped during his cross of George."

The truth is, those people didn't know what they were talking about. They hadn't a clue.

The jurors would forever have the opening statement as a map of where this case was going to go, and that was the biggest impact of the day—not George's denials, for I would have multiple shots at him.

And that was the prosecution's biggest mistake.

If it had put George on at the beginning of the trial and only given me one shot at him, I probably would have scored a few points, but they would have gotten lost and forgotten as the case went on.

What the prosecution did was make George the central part of its case, and he was a *horrible, horrible* witness. The state called him a bunch of times, and we called him twice, and each time I got to take my blows at him.

The smarter move by the prosecution would have been to put him up once and get him out of there, but it just kept parading him up there. And I just kept going at him. Rather than going for a head shot in the first round to try to knock him out, instead what I did was I hit him with body shots throughout the entire six weeks of the trial. By the time the trial was over, he was done.

One of my favorite sayings is, "Persistence beats resistance every time."

By the time I was done with George, not only did the jurors believe he had something to do with the cover-up, but they even began to question whether he had intentionally murdered Caylee.

WHENEVER GEORGE TESTIFIED, and later when Cindy testified, Casey would get angry and would become more and more animated. She'd shake her head no. She'd make facial expressions, and I would constantly be on her about the faces she was making.

I was really angry with her. This was one of the three or four times during the trial when she and I would really go at it.

"I'm human," she'd say to me.

"I don't want you to be human," I'd reply. "I want you to sit there and not react to the evidence. Because at this point you're behaving no better than Ashton."

"People don't like it," I would tell her. "They're watching you."

One thing different about this case: we were facing the jury the entire time. Usually the defense table is off to one side, and you sit far away from the jury. This time we were face-to-face with the jury, and I think that worked in our favor.

"You need to stop that shit," I'd tell Casey.

And in fairness to her, I was asking her to do the impossible, which was to be emotionless during this incredibly emotional event she was going through.

At a certain point she realized she was disappointing me, and she'd keep her emotions in check. Overall, Casey did an excellent job keeping her emotions intact.

"I need you to keep focused on the task at hand," I kept telling her. "I can't be watching you. I can't spend my time thinking about what you're up to."

AFTER CALLING GEORGE, the prosecution for the next two weeks trotted out what they called The FOC-kers—Friends of Casey—to the stand. Their purpose was to talk about how she acted as though nothing was wrong—going to parties, smiling a lot, getting a tattoo—all of which was supposed to impress upon the jury that Casey wasn't at all sad over the disappearance and then death of her daughter.

The way the prosecution was figuring it, if the jurors saw that Casey had no remorse, then obviously she must have murdered her daughter. And why not do this? After all, the prosecution had spread these stories to the media, which had unanimously found Casey guilty of murder long before the trial began. In fact, after the media got through with unfairly and unconsciously besmirching her character, she was the most hated woman in America.

If it could convince the public, it figured, it could convince a jury.

The only difference, of course, is that for a jury to find Casey guilty of murder, the prosecutors had to come up with something called *evidence*. They would be hard-pressed to do so. Instead, the prosecution called her friends in an attempt to find her morally corrupt.

The first of the Fockers was Cameron Campana, one of Tony Lazzaro's two roommates. By calling Cameron, the prosecution was trying to show the jury that naughty Casey was living with three guys in a small apartment. I objected to his line of questioning, but Judge Perry overruled me.

I wanted to make a strong statement with the first witness, so that the jury could see how irrelevant these witnesses were, and in this case less was more.

"Where you in Casey's home on June 16, 2008, when Caylee drowned?" I asked Cameron.

"No," he said.

"Thank you," I said. "No further questions." The courtroom was stunned with a moment of silence—expecting much, much more. But the brevity of it made an impact.

The next witness was Nathan Lezniewicz, the third of the roommates. When Nathan took the stand, Ashton went to show him a photo of Casey at the Fusion nightclub as she was participating in a hot body contest.

I objected.

"This photo is clearly to show bad character," I said.

Judge Perry overruled me.

My co-counsel Cheney Mason then rose and moved for a mistrial under the *Mena v. State* case.

"This photo is not related to consciousness of guilt," said Cheney.

"Denied," said Judge Perry.

Frank George then asked Nathan whether he ever saw Casey distraught, depressed, scared, angry, or worried.

He said no.

"Did she ever go look for Caylee?" asked George.

"No."

On cross I got Nathan to admit that during the few times he saw Casey with Caylee the little girl was well fed, well taken care of, and that Casey never yelled at her.

A final question: "Were you present on June 16, 2008, at the Anthony home when Caylee drowned in the pool?"

"No."

George then questioned Clint House, who at one time lived with Tony and Cameron. Clint testified that Casey seemed like a "fun, party girl." George then wanted to ask him about a photo of Casey dancing.

I objected, but was overruled.

Maria Kish, who was Clint's girlfriend at the time, was next, and George got her to say that Casey really didn't have much to do with the shot girls, and then at the end of the testimony he gave me a special gift. He asked Maria a question that he didn't know the answer to.

George asked her, "Did you ever have occasion to ride in her car?"

Maria said yes.

"When was that?"

She said she couldn't remember, but it was *while* Casey was staying with Tony, which was the time period that the prosecution was arguing Caylee was decomposing in the trunk. She said she rode in the backseat of Casey's car with Tony and Clint.

Now it was my turn to cross-examine.

"When you sat in the backseat," I asked, "did you smell any foul odor?"

"No, sir."

"And Clint was with you in the backseat?"

"Yes."

"And did Clint say something stinks back here or anything like that?"

"No, sir."

"Okay, what about Tony. Did he say, 'Boy, does this car stink?'"

"No, sir."

And that really hurt them badly. It made the smell coming from the garbage a much more plausible explanation.

I had no idea Maria was going to testify to that. I never really thought, based on their sworn statements to law enforcement, that any of the Focker witnesses were very important to our defense. Until then.

It was a blunder on their part, a gift from the prosecution.

THEY CONTINUED TO CALL more Fockers, and I was able to get each one of them to testify to what a great mother Casey was. The Fockers were relatively insignificant witnesses up to the point where they put Tony on the stand. Tony talked a great deal about what Casey did during the thirty days Caylee was missing, and he testified to the issue of her not having any remorse, acting like nothing was wrong.

Then the prosecution asked Tony to discuss the "party photos." These were photos of Casey at the club Fusion having a good time. In one photo, for everyone including the jury to see, Casey was entered in a hot body contest. How those pictures were relevant to anything, I don't know, but I kept objecting, and Judge Perry kept overruling me. It didn't seem fair.

Under the law, the prosecution is not allowed to show evidence to show a defendant's lack of remorse because it's so subjective and unreliable. It is not only irrelevant; it is contrary to the law and is reversible error. A reversible error is an error serious enough to cause a reversal on appeal.

Not only did they show that hot body–contest photo, but they showed photos of Casey shopping at various stores like J. C. Penny, Winn-Dixie, and Blockbuster, in an attempt to show that after Caylee died, she carried on her life as though nothing had happened to her.

When I cross-examined Tony Lazzaro, I decided to make my point about how irrelevant those photos were to the case by taking my questions to the next level. I wanted the jurors to understand just how irrelevant those photos were and how ridiculous it was for the prosecution to ask him about them.

"I want to ask you about these photographs," I said to Tony. "You realize you're here to testify in a first-degree murder case, do you not?"

"Yes, sir."

George objected, arguing the question was beyond the scope.

"Sustained," said Judge Perry.

"It's irrelevant," said George.

I asked Tony, "In the first photograph that was taken, did Casey Anthony talk about murdering anyone?"

"No."

"Did she talk about murder she was planning on committing in the future?"

"No."

"Did she borrow duct tape from anyone there at the party?"

"No."

"Did she get any weapons, knives?"

"No."

"Guns?"

"No."

"Did you see a gun in her dress?"

"No."

"Did you have the opportunity to see her with any weapons on her?"

"No."

"Okay," I said, "as to the second photograph, did she talk about murdering anyone on that day?"

"No."

"Third photograph," I said. "Did you talk about murdering anybody on that day?"

"No."

"Did she wear a gun or did you have the opportunity to see if she had any weapons on her?"

"Nope."

"Did she borrow any duct tape from anyone?"

"No."

"Did she borrow any knives from anyone?"

"No."

"Guns?"

"No."

"Did she borrow anything that you think she could use to commit a murder on any of these three occasions from anyone?"

"No."

"That you could see?"

"No."

"What about when she went to JC Penny's with you. Did she buy any duct tape there at JC Penny's?"

"No."

"Did she buy any plastic bags?"

"No."

"Did she buy any chloroform there at the JC Penny's?"

"No."

"Did she go to the sporting goods department and look at the guns?"

"No."

"Did she buy any weapons there at Blockbuster?"

"No."

"Did she maybe snag a box cutter or something that you could see?"

"No."

"Did she talk about murdering anybody?"

"No."

"Did she talk about any murder she had previously committed?"

"No."

"She didn't buy any duct tape?"

"No."

I was making an important point. What I was doing was taking the silliness of the irrelevant evidence to the next level. I decided that the more irrelevant their evidence of bad behavior was going to be, the more atrocious my questions were going to be.

My point: the party photos had *nothing* to do with the murder of Caylee Anthony. Nothing.

Even though it's contrary to law, I can understand how people can talk about her lack of remorse. But as I saw it, the party photos were an obvious attempt by the prosecution to paint her negatively. So my goal was to do the polar opposite, to be extreme, just to show how ridiculous they were and to bring everyone back to the fact that this was a first-degree murder case.

Let's talk about the murder.

And I was making this point with Tony Lazzaro, because he was such an important witness.

After Tony told the jury what a good mother Casey had been, I asked him about an incident at the pool of his apartment complex. On direct George had asked Tony about the first time Casey brought Caylee to his apartment. He testified the three of them went to the pool. George quickly moved on, but it opened the door for me. This is a perfect example of why knowing the facts is so important. If George had known about the pool incident, he never would have gone in that direction and opened the door.

Tony testified that Caylee was going near the pool and Casey went after her and stopped her. He testified that Caylee really loved the pool.

During his deposition Tony had been very wishy-washy about what Casey had told him about her being sexually abused. He clearly remembered what she said about her brother, but he was unsure whether she said her father had physically abused her or sexually abused her.

During direct examination, Frank George had asked Tony whether the two of them shared secrets. In other words, was their relationship so close that she confided in him; he said yes. That was a perfect opening for me to start asking about the secret of the abuse of Casey by Lee and her father.

On cross-examination I asked Tony whether he and Casey had shared secrets, and he said they did. I asked him whether Casey had told him about the abuse by her father.

He said yes, and the prosecution rose and shouted their objection.

They wanted a proffer, meaning they wanted to know ahead of time what we were going to ask the witnesses. And the judge kept upholding the objections, and we had to go to sidebar and the jury had to leave.

In the end Tony testified that Casey told him her brother Lee had felt her up, but he wasn't sure what she had said about the father, whether it was physical or sexual abuse.

It didn't matter. The innuendo was very strong, so I left it alone. I let the jury ponder the extent.

FROM THE START OF THE TRIAL, during my opening and afterward, I noted the behavior of prosecutor Ashton, who everyone could clearly see was mocking me by laughing and making strange faces whenever I made my presentation. My feeling was that was just Ashton being Ashton, that he wasn't able to control himself. Among the members of the defense team, we had a nickname for him.

We called Ashton *Tourette's Boy*.

My wife, Lorena, had another opinion. She said she thought he was deliberately trying to distract and embarrass me. I'm not sure I buy that. I just don't think he was able to control himself.

If you remember, during a pretrial hearing, he had flipped out, and I knew that once the trial came, he would not be able to control himself.

Prior to the start of the trial, Judge Perry had sent us an order on court decorum, and in it was the warning, "No lawyer shall make any facial expressions," and what Ashton kept doing was a clear violation of his order. I was really hoping Judge Perry would lash out at him in front of the jury.

I had worked with the guy for two-and-a-half years, and so I knew his lack of decorum was going to play to our advantage, so I had an intern document every time he laughed or made a face, and I made a video of his disrespectful actions. The whole trial was on TV, so it was easy to do. I wanted to document his behavior for Judge Perry, hoping Judge Perry would stop attacking me and maybe start attacking him.

I was sure the jury would notice his behavior and realize how insensitive he was for smiling and laughing during the death penalty case of the death of a child. There was nothing funny about it, and it wasn't the time or place to be laughing or making jokes when you're talking about the death of a baby.

Later in the trial, my co-counsel, Lisabeth Fryer, would say to me every time we went to sidebar, "Do you notice that Ashton has these skinny, long fingers? They're like rat hands." Whenever I talked to Lisabeth about him, I would call him, "Rat Hands."

But generally within the team we preferred to call Ashton "Tourette's Boy."

CHAPTER 26

DAVID FINDS HIS ROCK

A T THE START OF DAY FOUR of the trial the prosecution filed a brief with the court in order to stop me from asking witnesses about Casey telling them if she was sexually abused. Their argument was that they noticed that Tony Lazzaro's testimony about abuse, while short, was powerful, and they wanted to know in advance when it was coming. I answered that the motion was untimely. Also it was a perfect move for the prosecution to try to stop me cold. I mean, the prosecution paraded witness after witness to the stand to talk about Casey's spending the night with men, her sexual partners, innuendos like a bruise one of them saw over Caylee's eye, all designed to bring in information totally irrelevant to this case. What does this have to do with how Caylee died? And now they wanted to preclude me from undoing their character assassination.

"To limit our cross-examination of a witness clearly obstructs the truth finding process," I argued.

"They're very capable prosecutors," I told the court. "They don't need advance notice of what the witness is going to testify to."

I told the court that the trial didn't have a script. I wanted to know, "How could I know in advance what questions I wanted to ask? Why should I have to hand the prosecutors the gift of telling them in advance what I want to ask?"

"We have a theory of defense, judge," I said. "We need to have the right to explore it, and we need to be able to have these witnesses on the spot and ask them specific questions. If there's an objection to the question, the prosecutors are more than capable of objecting—and this certainly does not require us to stop, proffer, and give them advance notice of what is going to be asked a particular witness."

I got nowhere with Judge Belvin Perry, who granted the state's motion.

I then renewed our motion for a mistrial based on the impermissible evidence of Casey's supposed lack of remorse that the state kept jamming down the throat of the jury.

"So far," I said, "the state has put on a case solely dealing with the bad character of my client, or the attempted character assassination of her past conducts, boyfriends, people she slept with, things that have absolutely nothing to do with the crimes charged, and has put us in a position where we are significantly prejudiced as to some of the impermissible character evidence that they have been successful in introducing."

Judge Perry stopped me. "Mr. Baez," he said, "How many times have you asked in cross-examination of witnesses whether or not Ms. Anthony was a quote, good mother, unquote?"

"Many times," I replied. "And I don't think one has anything to do with the other."

He said, "That can be construed as a question dealing with character evidence, which the state has objected to and I sustained the objection."

Judge Perry asked me if I was familiar with the case of *Greenfield v. State*.

"No, I am not," I said.

He explained while I looked on in disbelief that the question I asked about her being a good mother was not a pertinent character trait permissible as character evidence.

"You motion for a mistrial is denied," he said. We never expected him to grant it; however, in order to preserve the issue for appeal, the trial lawyer must make the motion for a mistrial. The theory being, why are you asking the appellate court now for a new trial when you never asked for one during trial.

THE NEXT WITNESS after Tony was the second appearance of George Anthony. I could see that the more time I spent cross-examining George, the more frustrated he was getting. This was why Jeff Ashton's decision to limit my cross the first time was an incredibly bad move. I had more time to develop my crosses, and I also was afforded more opportunities to see what angered George on the witness stand.

George kept wanting to fight me toe-to-toe, and I noticed that when I'd order him to come down from the witness stand and write things on my exhibits, he would become infuriated.

We were engaged in a psychological battle in which a man who couldn't have hated me any more was having to follow my instructions, even one as simple as writing something down on a calendar. I knew right then I getting under his skin, and because of that I also knew I was going to keep asking him to write things down on the board.

The purpose of his taking the stand this time was to talk about the fight he had with Casey over the gas cans. The idea was for the jury to believe that she had taken them and therefore she was responsible for putting the duct tape on them, and therefore she was the one who killed Caylee by putting duct tape across Caylee's mouth, supposedly because Caylee was keeping her from partying.

The key piece of the state's "evidence" was the duct tape on the gas cans, but I always felt the gas cans benefited the defense much more than the state. On cross-examination I wanted to introduce photos of the gas cans. They were entered as exhibits, but the prosecution was being slick by deliberately not introducing those photos.

My entire cross revolved around those gas cans, but the prosecution refused to stipulate I could show the pictures of them, and so I had to wait my turn—a month later as it was—and when I did, I would shove those photos down George Anthony's throat.

I really wanted to show the jury those photos. Ordinarily the defense is allowed to refer to an exhibit during cross—that doesn't mean it's admitted into evidence—however Judge Perry didn't even allow me to do that. In the end, because Ashton tried to get the tactical advantage at every twist and turn, he forgot about the jurors. They, too, wanted to see this photograph and in denying them that, they saw he was hiding the truth. A prosecutor should never look like he's hiding something from the jury, especially if you're the one arguing that it's the defense that's doing all of the hiding. This prosecution was hiding the ball on almost every play, and I do think the jury saw through that. In some instances it insulted the jurors' intelligence. When the state failed to call crucial witnesses and show them certain things, like the gas can photograph, it lost all credibility.

Judge Perry was shutting me down like crazy. He was on top of me to the extreme.

Some judges let you try your case; the theory behind that is if the defense does its best and the state does its best, true justice will come out in the end. It also lowers the risk of the case coming back on appeal because the judge hadn't restricted the defense in any way.

Every time a judge denies something from the defense, it increases the possibility of it coming back on reversal.

Judge Perry was no such judge. In his courtroom, I wasn't on a short leash; I was wearing a choke collar.

Not being able to show the photos of the gas cans was only one example. Later there came a point when Judge Perry was so angry with me that he stopped the trial, excused the jurors so they knew he was mad at me—because of something I had allegedly done wrong—and he kept them out for a long time, meaning the end result was the jurors would get pissed off at me for slowing down the trial because of my incompetence, thereby making me less persuasive.

Another time I asked George Anthony to step down and write something on an exhibit. Proper court decorum dictates that you ask permission from the judge. But sometimes you're on a roll when cross-examining someone, and he had just been down a second earlier when I did ask permission, and this time I told George to come down, and Judge Perry immediately said, "Stop." And he said, "Mr. Baez," and he began yelling at me for not asking permission. It was like, "You didn't say Simon Says, or pretty please."

This was in front of the jury.

What's important, the jury usually sees the judge as the wisest person in the room. It relies on the judge, who's in charge of taking them out for nice dinners, for arranging their accommodations, their comfort, so anything nice they received came from Judge Perry. It's always important that the judge appears to like or respect you as a lawyer before the jury. I was getting neither.

But what people don't realize is that a judge is a lawyer, and most people don't trust lawyers, but when a lawyer puts on a black robe, all of a sudden he is noble and all-knowing.

Another thing: a judge is an elected official, which means by definition he is a politician. So a judge is not only a lawyer but he's a lawyer who's a politician. Nevertheless, once he puts on that robe, he's cloaked with a certain amount of brilliance as it relates to a lay person, and I just find that fascinating.

The judge also gets to sit above everyone else. If you look at the rituals when it comes to the judiciary, it's interesting, to say the least.

AT THE END OF THAT DAY, because of the way Judge Perry was treating me, I really started to feel down. I was an emotional wreck. The adrenaline rush had subsided, and the fatigue started to build again. It was from a combination of the pressure, of getting my objections overruled time and time again by Judge Perry, who was shutting us down at every turn, of the pressure of being involved in a high-profile case, and the responsibility of it all. I was starting to come apart. Everything started to take its toll.

The toughest, most stressful times for me were the hours between leaving court in the evening and returning in the morning. It was bad leaving court, and the evenings were the worst. In fact, at times they were intolerable. But I was determined to never let it show. It's like they say, sharks smell fear. So do lawyers, and I never gave the first clue that something inside of me was wrong or hurting.

I called one of my very best friends, Michael Walsh, and I asked him to send me a Catholic prayer to help me get through this in my time of need.

He sent me a prayer and in addition he sent me a text that read:

"When the Philistines sent their most ferocious warrior out front to destroy the Israelites, God sent a small boy named David armed with a rock and a rag. David destroyed Goliath with a single shot. When God is with you it matters not who is against you, stand firm in the face of adversity and remain still knowing He is the lord."

It truly inspired me. It was as if it spoke to me. I was the underdog, feeling insulted and ridiculed every step of the way, and I was facing not only my very own Goliath, but several of them. I immediately changed the screen saver on my iPhone to a photo of Michelangelo's David.

The other thing I did was go to church every morning before court. I was born a Catholic, but I wasn't raised in a religious household. There's a Catholic church about a block from the courthouse, and most days before going to court, I would kneel and pray for fifteen minutes.

Some days I would just sit in church and stare at Jesus on the cross. I'd stare out and just think for a few minutes, and each day I would feel a message being given to me. It was more about my life than it was about the case.

Some days a voice would tell me, *You need to call your mother and tell her how much you love her.* Or, *You need to call your wife and daughter.* Or, *You need to be more grateful.*

And when I would sit and pray, I'd pray for wisdom. I'd pray for strength to handle those things I had no control over.

A calmness would usually come over me. I'd be in the zone, doing my thing, and I'd be fine.

One morning I was running late to court, so I skipped church that morning. We had a horrible day. I remember thinking, *Never again. Judge Perry is going to have to put me in jail for being late before I miss church again.*

I then made a decision as it related to Judge Perry: that was no matter how much he attacked me or berated me, I would be incredibly respectful. If he indeed had a bias against me, he would show that to the jury on his own. It would not be because any of my actions.

I knew this was going to be a long trial, and thanks to Cheney's constantly reminding me about just how long a marathon it would be, I was prepared to go the distance. People change opinions over time. I did not want the jury's opinion of me to change. I felt they liked and respected me, and I was going to be humble and straight while fighting for my client. After all this trial was about Casey, not Ashton, not Judge Perry, and certainly not about me.

THE NEXT WITNESS was Ricardo Morales, another former boyfriend of Casey's. I never liked Ricardo. I thought he was a creep. This was a guy who sold photos of Caylee to *Globe* magazine for $4,000. However, Ricardo's testimony was critical, because I was able to show the jury the "Win her over with Chloroform" photo he had posted on Myspace during the time they were dating. I was then able to explain to the jury that Casey had no idea what Ricardo was talking about, and that she looked up "chloroform" to understand the reference.

This contradicted the prosecution's ridiculous theory that Casey had used chloroform to sedate Caylee and then kill her.

After more Fockers, I cross-examined Mallory Parker, who was Lee Anthony's fiancée, and she concluded the good mother evidence for us. Mallory was a phenomenal witness because she came across as so sincere. She talked about what a great mother Casey was.

"Their relationship was amazing," she said.

She broke down in tears, and you could hear a pin drop in the courtroom. It was a powerful, powerful moment.

Yeah, the prosecution was able to spread the word that Casey partied, that she shopped, but I had set the framework for the jury to know *why* she was behaving this way. We constructed a backdoor mental health defense, and because of it, the jury understood that there was something off with this girl. So all the prosecution was doing was reinforcing our position.

Our strategy was always to take the negative things that the prosecutors threw at us and to adopt them as our own, rather than fight them, and I do think that helped us a great deal.

THE NEXT IMPORTANT WITNESS was Simon Birch, the manager of the tow yard company. We did very well with him. He helped the defense for several reasons. He had had the unique experience of having once worked for a sanitation company, and he said his first inclination on smelling the bad odor in Casey's car was that it was trash. Though he claimed to have smelled dead bodies before, and claimed he smelled a dead body in Casey's car, he testified he never called the police but rather allowed George to leave in the car. Furthermore, when he finally did speak to the police, he testified that he was influenced by what he had read in the media.

The exclamation point of his testimony was that George had told Birch that Casey's car had been at the Amscot parking lot for three days. He had known that, Birch said, because George Anthony had told him so.

Right after Birch, the prosecution called George to the stand again. What I found fascinating was that George, Cindy, and Lee were granted special permission during the trial to sit in the courtroom. Ordinarily, if you were testifying during the trial, you couldn't sit in court, but the rule of sequestration didn't apply to them, so they were able to listen to all the testimony.

George had just watched Birch testify that George had told him the car was at the Amscot lot for three days.

But when I asked George whether he had told Birch that, George said, "No, I didn't tell him that." And not only that, said George, but he had called Amscot right after he got to work that night.

So here we had an independent witness versus George, clearly showing that not only was George lying, but that he had access to that car for three days. You have to ask yourself: Why didn't George come and pick it up when Casey told him, and he said he'd come and get it? Did George leave it to get towed intentionally to start the ball rolling in an effort to pin Caylee's death on Casey? You have to wonder.

Casey, meanwhile, had told a number of her friends that she had told George and told him to pick up the car, so there was evidence that she wasn't making up the story.

As they say, the third time is a charm, and this is where the momentum really shifted to the defense as it related to George. He came across as unbelievable on so many points. For example, he was unable to tell the jury how long it takes a letter to get to his house from a mile and a half away. He went and picked up Casey's car knowing it "smelled of death," after not seeing Casey for three weeks, and he never even bothered to call Casey to inquire whether she or Caylee was okay?

The inconsistencies would also occur with Cindy.

At times George and Cindy would contradict each other. It was the weirdest thing.

While trying to explain why he didn't think Casey was pregnant in 2005, one time George said the reason Casey gained weight was because she would do athletics all the time, and when she'd run and exercise, she'd grow.

"She grew a potbelly from exercise?" I asked him.

And then I'd question Cindy, who was sitting right there listening to George's testimony, and Cindy would say, "No, she gained weight like that when she was sedentary." Meaning, Casey didn't do *any* exercise.

I couldn't believe how often they'd get up on the stand and contradict one another *while* they were listening to each other's testimony.

And people wonder how Casey was found not guilty?

I would later tell the jury, "They are *all* liars."

Cindy came on next to testify about her 9-1-1 call to the police. The rush I had gotten from being so successful with George was deflated because Cindy came across as a phenomenal witness for the prosecution. She was very sympathetic. She testified well, answering Linda Drane Burdick's questions in a calm and sympathetic way.

I never in a million years thought the hard-bitten, fast-talking Cindy could come off as sympathetic. Just knowing the way Cindy was, very powerful and aggressive, I thought that attitude was going to come through, but with Burdick on her side, she came off very well.

To watch her during that 9-1-1 call, you watched a woman being tortured. And when the jury looked at the photos of Caylee's playhouse, there wasn't a dry eye in the house.

I knew the one thing I couldn't do was get up there and attack a grieving grandmother, so my cross was very subdued and not very effective, because I knew that if I had gone after her, I would have done more harm than good.

What surprised me was that Cindy and Burdick, up until then, had been archenemies. Cindy had always defended Casey, and the two of them would battle. I used to joke with Burdick, calling it the Cindy Two-Step, meaning the two of them would go toe-to-toe with one another and dance. Cindy would sometimes get so aggressive with Burdick, that Burdick had to ask Judge Perry to step in and shut Cindy up. I used to laugh at Burdick all the time whenever she and Cindy would battle because Cindy was no pushover. I gather when Casey accused George of sexual abuse, Cindy went over to the prosecution's side.

Cindy had been extremely aggressive with Burdick, and I wanted the jury to see that, so right then and there, I started to think to myself, *I have to find a way to get the old Cindy back.*

Later on, we would, and it would be explosive.

AFTER CINDY TESTIFIED during court on June 13, there was a break in the case, and Judge Perry spoke to the jury. He said that depending on the length of the defense's presentation, deliberations should begin "hopefully the 25th or 27th, but that is subject to change."

Cheney objected and called for a sidebar.

"Listen," Cheney said, "We don't have any obligation to put on any evidence at all. And you just told the jurors you expect us to be putting on evidence, and we may or we may not."

"But you told me you were going to put on evidence," said Judge Perry.

Yes, we did tell him that, but nevertheless we felt that his discussion was signaling to the jury that somehow we had a burden, when we didn't.

Unfortunately, Judge Perry took it personally.

"Y'all lied to me," he said.

"No," Cheney said.

"Yes, the hell you did," said a very angry Judge Perry. "If you don't put on any evidence, then I will do that."

"Well, we are," Cheney said, "so don't worry about it."

"I will take it that I cannot trust one thing your side says anymore," said Judge Perry.

After that exchange we repaired to a room where our team sat down to discuss whether to try to recuse Judge Perry.

"This is getting out of hand," I said. "He's admitted that he can't trust a word we say, so how the hell can he give Casey a fair trial?"

We went back to sidebar with Judge Perry and told him what we were thinking, and he said, "Go ahead and file your motion, and I'll file my response."

Which in my estimation meant, *Do it and I'll retaliate.*

The proper response should have been, "I'm sorry you feel that way. It's not that way at all. But you're more than entitled to file your motion."

But the way he replied to me I took to be a threat.

We prepared the motion, and we went back and had another meeting, and every member of the team pretty much agreed that we shouldn't do it. We felt it was the right thing for the client, but the wrong thing for me.

"I fear he's going to retaliate against you, Jose," said Dorothy Clay Sims, and each member of the team agreed.

"I'll withdraw my vote because I'm biased and only thinking of myself," I said.

The vote remained the same.

I went to Casey and explained it to her, and told her the pros and cons; she too didn't want me to file it.

"Don't file it," she advised.

"I don't want anything to happen to you," said Casey.

And so we didn't.

CHAPTER 27

THE STATE'S CASE TURNS TO HUMAN DECOMPOSITION

OR A DAY AND A HALF, all the prosecution did was play videos of the jail visitations of George, Cindy, and Lee. That was a difficult time for everyone, because they were lengthy and repetitive. But the state did it because it was trying to prove several things. It wanted to show what a smart-ass Casey was to her parents, it was showing her lies about Zanaida, and it was showing her interaction with George, during which she told him what a great father he was.

What I realized and no one else did, was that this was right around the time Casey was trying to convince her parents to get her out on bail, and so she was trying an angle with Cindy in the context of, "Get me out so I can help you find Caylee," and her angle with George was, "You're the greatest father since sliced bread. Hey, I'm not going to roll over on you and tell everyone about the sexual abuse or about carrying away Caylee's body, so please bond me out."

Then there was the video that caused the public to think that the story about Caylee drowning in the pool was an invention. It occurred on August 14, when George and Cindy went to visit her. On the tape you can hear Cindy say, "The media is saying that Caylee drowned in the pool," and Casey says, "Oh well. Oh well," sounding like she's blowing her off.

We were going to counter that by putting either George or Cindy on the stand, and the testimony would have revealed that just before that moment, George and Cindy were walking to the jail when a reporter said to them, "So what do you guys think of this new theory that Caylee made have died *by accident*?"

It struck a chord with George, who turned around and blew up at the reporter.

"Shut up. Shut up," he started yelling.

Then they go into the jail, and you can hear Cindy saying to Casey, "George just blew up at the media."

"Oh really?" said Casey.

"They're saying that Caylee *drowned in the pool*," said Cindy.

And that's when Casey said, "Oh well. Oh well."

But here's the point. The media said, she died "by accident." But Cindy was the one who said "she drowned in the pool."

The inference had to be that at that point Cindy knew.

And I was going to ask her how she knew. But we never did that, because we didn't feel it was necessary.

The one thing everyone in the media forgets is that they knew they were being recorded. They knew their visits would be on all the news stations, because that's what happened after the first one. I even filed a motion to try to stop it. So her detractors who watched the video in which she told George what a great father he was—and to them that was proof she was lying about the sexual abuse—didn't know the backstory, how she was trying to get George and Cindy to bond her out.

I do believe the way the state presented it—playing all those videos for a day and a half straight—helped the defense. However, the prosecutors should have selected the best ones that made their points instead of using all of them.

The other interesting story relates to the state playing a recording of Casey's first phone call home after she was arrested. That's the call where her girlfriend says to her, "If anything happens to Caylee, I'll die," and all Casey can say to her is, "Oh my God. Calling you guys is a huge waste of time. All I wanted was my boyfriend's number."

From a defendant's standpoint, it was terrible. She sounded cold and heartless. All these people were trying to find out what happened to Caylee, and she's being bitchy with them. The prosecution used the tape to bash her at the trial.

I was sympathetic to Casey's trauma, but still, hearing her sound so heartless was infuriating. While it was being played I leaned over and said to her, "If this jury doesn't kill you, I will."

THE PROSECUTION called Amy Huizenga, who claimed to be Casey's best friend. The prosecution flew her in all the way from Spain, where she had been working on a cruise ship. Amy really wasn't able to contribute much, but the purpose of her testimony was for her to discuss one of the thousands of text messages that had gone back and forth between Amy and Casey, at least one of which had to do with Amy inviting Casey out to party, and Casey blowing her off, telling Amy she couldn't go out because she had to stay home with Caylee.

You see, this was another part of the prosecution's ridiculous accusations, Casey's supposed motive for murder. They were trying to argue that Casey had murdered Caylee because Caylee was preventing her from going out and partying. Again, when the charge was made in all the newspapers and on the all TV stations, the public took the state's word for it. Now, in court, the state would have to dig up evidence to support its absurd conclusion, and here was the "evidence," one of Amy's text messages where Casey complains she has to stay home and watch Caylee.

I have to say I never liked Amy. Yes, Casey stole some of her checks and cashed them, but that's no excuse for her stabbing her supposed best friend in the back. Everyone liked to portray Casey as the party girl, but I read every single one of her text messages between her and Amy, and it was usually Amy almost every night trying to get Casey to go out and Casey saying no.

Then came Lee Anthony, called to the stand to discuss July 16. I noticed during the direct examination that the prosecution was having a tough time getting anything out of him.

I sat up straight and took notice, because since the bond hearing, when he told the cops the nature of our private meetings and I found out about it, I hadn't trusted him again. Moreover, most of his public statements had been very pro-prosecution.

Then the prosecutors held a sidebar, during which Frank George admitted to Judge Belvin Perry that Lee had refused to meet with prosecutors before the trial to discuss his testimony, and he asked the judge if he could treat Lee as a hostile witness.

I knew right then and there we would have an opportunity, and that we needed to reach out to Lee's lawyer to see if he would meet with us.

Mark Lippman represented all the Anthonys, but it was clear that George and Cindy felt one way, and Lee another. I saw this a conflict of interest.

Due to the Rules of Professional Conduct, we couldn't approach Lee without his lawyer being present, but we got lucky. Out of the blue we got a call from Lee, informing me that Lippman no longer represented him. I explained to him my professional obligation to make certain of this. I asked him to send me a text message saying Lippman no longer represented him.

What he wanted was open access to the defense. In time Lee would prove to be a valuable ally.

THE NEXT WITNESSES were the first responders to Cindy's 9-1-1 calls, which started with Deputy Rendon Fletcher and ended with Detective Yuri Melich. They all testified to not smelling anything in Casey's car, and that while Cindy was a wreck, George was calm, and so was Casey.

At the end of my cross-examination of Melich, who spent an hour talking about how Casey had lied to him about working at Universal Studios, and how he had gone with her and trapped her into admitting to him that she no longer worked there, I asked him what I thought to be a logical and germane question.

"If you're about to sit down, what if Casey had told you, 'Don't sit there. Zanny the nanny is sitting there,' what would you have done?"

Linda Drane Burdick immediately objected, saying my question was speculative and irrelevant.

But it wasn't irrelevant at all. If Melich had seen a troubled, delusional young woman and had sought to find out why she acted the way she did, he would have discovered the reason behind her behavior. He would have discovered the abuse she had suffered at the hands of her father, and he would have found out how Caylee died.

But he didn't do that. Instead, he made the determination that Casey was guilty of something, threw her in jail, and made sure all the evidence pointed in her direction. As far as I was concerned, if there was any negligence on anyone's part, it was at the hand of Melich.

"I said it's a hypothetical, Judge," I told the judge.

"Sustained," said Judge Perry.

I asked Melich, "Are there psychologists or psychiatrists who you consulted with during this investigation?"

Again Linda objected, and her objection was sustained.

I asked to approach the bench, and I explained to Judge Perry that I was trying to establish that Melich's investigation should have taken the direction where he should have dealt with Casey's mental health issues.

"I think I should have the right to explore what this officer would have done under certain scenarios and whether he even considered that," I said.

"I'm trying to establish if instead of looking at this as a murder investigation or someone who is lying, as opposed to someone who doesn't have a grip on reality, this investigation would have taken a completely different direction. I think it's critical with this witness at this specific point of time."

"You haven't asked him one question in that direction," said Judge Perry.

"That's the question I'm getting at," I said.

Linda objected, arguing I had no good-faith basis to ask this question.

"She was evaluated right after her arrest, and they said she is normal," Linda said. "Is she insane?"

Judge Perry asked me whether there was a good-faith basis for my question.

I said there was.

"What is it?" he asked me.

"She has been evaluated," I began to say when Judge Perry cut me off.

"Just a second. Okay, what is the good-faith basis pursuant to the *Del Monte Banana Company* case? You cannot insinuate something out of thin air without a good-faith basis." He repeated, "You cannot dream up stuff out of thin air and bring it up, and that's precisely what this case says."

"I'm not dreaming this up," I said. "I do have a good-faith basis."

Judge Perry decided it was time for all of us to go to lunch.

And what "let's go to lunch" meant was that I was done. The issue was done. He ruled against me, and that was it. I couldn't go into that. Enough said.

This happened so often. I couldn't try this case the way I wanted to. He was forcing me to try it a certain way. It was absurd. It was like I was fighting the whole world.

When we returned the next day, I was determined to ask Melich why he didn't bother investigating the possibility that Caylee had drowned when Cindy told him the ladder to the pool had been up.

He said he didn't find the information to be important. Not only did he not ask Cindy about it, he said he never questioned Casey about it either. When asked about this by Burdick, Melich said he focused solely on Casey's statement that Caylee had been taken by Zenaida Fernandez-Gonzalez.

The state then called a couple of witnesses to show that Casey had lied about being employed at Universal Studios.

ON DAY ELEVEN of the trial, the state called Arpad Vass to the stand to testify as to his air evidence. I immediately objected because he had not adequately explained his database for his conclusions used in his research.

My motion was denied.

Dr. Vass got on the stand and talked of his expertise in anthropology, biology, chemistry, microbiology, clinical biology, and endocite biology. He said he had worked for the Oak Ridge National Laboratory for twenty years.

He discussed how he studied the decomposition of dead bodies, studied the chemical breakdown of soft tissue. He began to go through the process of decomposition in great detail, when I rose and objected, making the point that Dr. Vass was not a biologist.

I was overruled.

He continued, and I objected again, arguing he wasn't qualified to talk on the subject because he wasn't a chemist.

Again I was overruled. He blathered on, talking technically about the process of decomposition. I doubt if one person in the courthouse had any idea what he was talking about.

Through Dr. Vass's recitation I kept objecting, citing narrative improper predicate and nonresponsive.

Judge Perry overruled me every time, and finally he called a sidebar to explain why he was overruling me.

"I appreciate that, Your Honor," I began. "Part of the reason why we're objecting is this witness is going into areas that have no relevance to this case."

I continued, "The state alleges there may have been a body in the Pontiac Sunfire from June 16 to June 27, a period of nine days. And all this is doing is allowing this witness to give a lecture to the jury about his knowledge in various different areas that do not encompass the areas of which he's been asked to testify."

"I find that is improper bolstering."

Co-counsel Cheney Mason got up and told the judge that Jeff Ashton was getting dangerously close to testimony that he had already ruled was not admissible.

Ashton rose to say he didn't recall any restrictions in the court's order.

Cheney reminded him that the court order would not permit Dr. Vass to give an opinion as to whether the odor signature is that solely of a decomposing human body.

"He will not testify to that," said Ashton. "But he will testify that his own experience of smelling the odor, combined with all the other things, he will give his opinion as to whether he believes that there was a human body in the trunk of that car."

Say what?

"Hang on there just a second," said Cheney. "So what you're trying to do is say okay, the judge has made these findings or rulings, and you're still allowing him to give a backdoor quote *pure opinion* unquote?"

"He's going to give an opinion as many other witnesses already have about the nature of the odor having smelled it. He's going to combine that information with chemical information he's received, and he will answer a question about whether it's his opinion as whether there was a dead body in the trunk of that based on both—but no, he will not in any way vary from what he's said before about this scientific evidence."

Incredibly, Vass was allowed to do this.

He proceeded to explain his experiment with dead bodies to study how they decomposed. He talked of the tests he made to do that.

I stood and objected to his testimony. Vass hadn't made the chemical tests. Dr. Marcus Wise, Vass's partner, had, and he had sent the results to Dr. Vass.

I brought up the fact that there was no quantitative analysis of chloroform because the trunk is a free-flowing environment and it would be impossible to know how much chloroform was in the trunk of the car.

I also pointed out that Vass made corrections to his study.

I moved to strike the previous testimony, but my motion was denied.

Vass then testified that the amount of chloroform was "shockingly high." No it wasn't. I objected as it being outside his area of expertise, and I was overruled.

He then testified about tests to the carpet sample of Casey's car. He said he was able to identify fifty-one individual chemical components, and one of them was chloroform. And not only that, he testified there were "large peaks," that it was in much larger abundance than the other chemicals.

"Did that surprise you?" asked Ashton.

"We were shocked," said Vass.

He said he had never seen that level of chloroform in the twenty years doing his work. His conclusion: chloroform appeared in the trunk of the car at some point in time in the past.

I objected, of course. I told the court, "The witness has not testified as to where he obtained it, who conducted the tests, and anything related to its reliability."

Judge Perry asked Vass who conducted the tests.

"Dr. Wise and myself conducted the tests," he said.

"Is that the data that you reasonably rely upon in formulating your opinion in this case?" asked Judge Perry.

"Yes."

"Anything else, folks?" asked Judge Perry.

Dr. Vass then discussed the power of the odor coming from the sealed can that held the carpet sample. He said he jumped back a foot or two. He said he was shocked that "that little bitty can could have that much odor associated with it."

"What did you recognize that odor to be?" Ashton asked him.

"I would recognize it as human decomposition odor," said Vass.

"That you've smelled many, many times before?"

"Many times before," said Vass.

Vass then testified about paper towels and napkins sent to him by Dr. Neal Haskell for analysis. Vass said he did a chemical test and it revealed a number of fatty acids on the napkin.

His conclusion: those fatty acids are from decomposition.

"It is a product of the breakdown of the fat," he said.

"Is it associated with decomposition?" asked Ashton.

"Yes."

He then testified that the carpet was the source of the odor.

Said Dr. Vass with great finality, "Now, in the car sample, the car trunk sample, we identified fifty-one human decomposition [chemicals] based on the studies we've done over the last several years."

He said he started eliminating compounds found in the car trunk. He said he looked at decomposing pizza, squirrel remnants, the garage air, and that left approximately sixteen compounds.

"Of those sixteen compounds," said Vass, "seven of those are considered significant." He said there were six others, but they were eliminated because they had the same makeup as gasoline, which had been in the car.

He continued, "Those seven were found to be in the list of thirty compounds that we considered most relevant out of five hundred compounds in human decomposition."

"Can you come to any opinion about the source of the odor that you analyzed from the carpet?" asked Ashton.

"I consider it consistent with human decomposition," said Dr. Vass.

What I considered at that moment should not be set in type.

I KNEW WHEN VASS took the stand that Judge Perry was going to allow his testimony, even though according to my experts his methodology was faulty and his conclusions weren't based on reliable science.

Sometime in 2010 Judge Perry had conducted what is called a Frye hearing in which each side discusses the evidence they want to introduce, giving the other side the opportunity to object. I objected at every turn, but to no avail.

Judge Perry let everything come in. I know I sound like I'm whining, and I'm really sorry about that, but I can't help myself.

The Frye hearings were comprehensive, and so at the trial Vass knew exactly what it was that I was going to ask him. Often during the Frye hearing he was vague, or nonresponsive, or pretended he didn't get what I was saying.

It wasn't any different at trial. I did what I could to let the jury know that his science was junk, but I was stopped at every turn by Ashton's objections and Judge Perry's agreement. Vass had supposedly come up with a database which was supposed to identify the chemicals which indicated a dead body, but the way he collected his data was so totally unscientific, I couldn't believe it. Yet when I questioned him about it, I didn't get very far because of Ashton's objections and Judge Perry's upholding them.

I even had difficulty letting the jury know that Vass had a financial interest and stood to make a mint if he could sell his machine to police departments. His problem was that he needed his database study to be admitted in a court of law for him to sell these dead body detectors.

I fenced with him for an hour, getting him to admit he would get paid if his testimony stood up and his machine was sold to police departments around the country.

"These devices—the goal is to sell these to police departments all across the country?" I asked him on cross-examination.

"In my position at the national lab, we are required to file invention disclosures," was his answer. He then went on about how this involved a grant from the National Institute of Justice. He was totally unresponsive.

"Did you understand my question?" I asked him.

Ashton objected to my interrupting his witness.

"Sustained."

He said it was the laboratory's decision whether to file a patent or not. He said he had no say in the matter.

"Do you understand my question?" I asked again.

"I think I answered your question," Vass said.

"I don't think you did."

"The goal of this, sir, is to sell this to police departments all across the country?"

"No," he said. "My goal is not to sell these at all. My goal is to develop them."

"You have to have validation of that database in a court of law, do you not, sir?"

Ashton objected and asked to approach the bench.

The court sustained his objection.

"I do not know that," said Vass.

I pressed on.

"You get royalties as a result if this device is sold, and sold basically to the police, do you not, sir?" I said.

"I honestly don't know..." he said.

It went on like that for a while.

The owner of the patent and Vass stood to make a mint if he could show his data to prove decomposition was scientifically proven, and he was going to do all he could to make sure the jury didn't know. Unfortunately for Dr. Vass, they knew full well.

Fortunately for me, Vass loved giving interviews and writing articles. In researching his career, I found an article he wrote in which he said he could prove that divining rods work. A divining rod is like an unbent coat hanger, and he asserted that he believed in using divining rods to unearth hidden graves.

I started to question him about that, and Ashton objected, but I pushed the issue. In the end he admitted he used divining rods to teach, and that he believed in them. It was comical. In our research we also learned he had also tried to put electronic leashes on flies.

What was interesting, and germane to our case, was that a lot of the prosecution witnesses talked about how unique the smell of human decomposition was; however we were able to find an article where Vass said that a rotten potato sitting in a cupboard smelled very similar to human decomposition.

I was really bothered—it bothers me to this day—how many of Ashton's objections were sustained. Why shouldn't I have been allowed to show examples of outrageousness on the part of Vass? Why shouldn't I have been allowed to impeach his credibility? Vass was like any other witness, but whenever I went after him, I was shut down. Reliving this makes me as angry as when it was happening.

Vass had testified about how the chloroform levels were "shockingly high" and "unusually high," and as hard as I tried, I didn't get very far in my attempt to show there had not been a quantitative analysis, and that there was no way Vass could have known what the level of the chloroform had been.

Then the prosecutors handed us another gift. They did something so stupid I can't believe they did it. They brought on as a witness an FBI scientist by the name of Dr. Michael Rickenbach, who did very little if anything to bolster the prosecution's case. I can only think the reason they brought him in to testify was so they would have a second scientist to back up Dr. Vass.

But when I asked Rickenbach about the levels of chloroform found in the trunk of Casey's car, his answer was that the chloroform levels were very, very, very low.

"Were they shockingly high?" I asked him, mimicking Vass's high-pitched voice.

"No," he said.

"Were they unusually high?"

"No," he said.

And the fact they put him on the stand told me that Ashton did that because he totally lacked an understanding of the science. Not only did Rickenbach testify to the low levels of chloroform, he also testified that chloroform could be found in degreasers and other normal cleaning products, and that the levels found in the trunk were comparible to chloroform levels found in cleaning products. He was called for the prosecution, but it was as though he testified for the defense.

It wasn't one of Ashton's best days. During my cross-examination, Ashton went to make an objection, and he did it with a loud, aggressive shout. His screech was almost violent, and when he did it, I looked at the jury, and I could see juror number eight, the Caucasian woman who worked for Verizon, made a grimace as if to say, "You asshole." It was such a telegraph that she seemed to be signaling to anyone who noticed how much she didn't like Ashton.

As the trial dragged on, I never could be sure how well I was doing, how effective I was being. At times I felt good about how we were doing, but the pressure was intense every day, and the amount of preparation was great. Vass had been an important witness for us. If I had allowed him to get away with selling the cock and bull he was selling, I might have given the jury something to hang its hat on. If they had a suspicion or even a hint there might have been a dead body in the car instead of garbage, there was the chance they could have concluded that Casey had put it in the trunk of her car, because after all, it was her car. When it became clear that Vass could no more discriminate between decomposition and garbage, the prosecution's case became much weaker.

CHAPTER 28

HOPING IT STICKS

THE PROSECUTION next went to the dogs. In between our pretrial motions and actually going to trial, the Supreme Court of Florida handed down a ruling in the case of *Harris v. the State of Florida*. The ruling required law enforcement to provide records of their search and cadaver dogs to show that a dog was reliable. In the past, the training records had been acceptable, but the court ruled that because the one who did the training was the dog's handler, the results were biased. What would be needed were real-world results. Every time the dog went out what were the results?

In effect, the court wanted the results to come from blind testing.

In our case, neither Gerus nor Bones had any records to show their reliability as cadaver dogs, so under *Harris*, the testimony about what they may or may not have found should have been excluded.

I was baffled when Judge Belvin Perry allowed Officer Jason Forgey to play a video of Gerus finding another body in another case and tack that on to a couple of articles about other cases in order to allow in the testimony. These records were put together ghetto-style.

To me, hands down, this was reversible error.

I sat and watched the video, objecting all the way.

"You can't let the jury see this," I said.

"You've made your bed," Judge Perry said to me, "and now you're going to have to lie in it."

He took the *Harris* decision and turned it upside down.

It was so unfair.

After the dogs came the computer searches. Sandra Osborne Cawn was called to testify about her work with the home computer in Lee's old bedroom that everyone in the Anthony family had used.

One thing I noticed: though George was in his fifties he was an active user of that computer. He was always online. You can never categorically prove someone is behind a computer, but you can group searches to give you a very good idea who was using it. Casey, for example, spent hours on Facebook and Myspace. Based on the Internet history, it appeared George's favorite sites included job searches like Monster.com, but if he wasn't looking for a job, he was looking for prostitute and escort sites. Two of his favorites were Forty Plus and Single.com. He also looked up some gardening sites including Lowes.com. Again, you can never put someone behind a computer.

Cawn testified she found there were some deleted files, but she didn't know how to retrieve them, so she gave the computer over to Sergeant Kevin Stenger of the Orange County Sheriff's Department Computer Crimes Squad. Stenger used software called NetAnalysis to pull the reports of the deleted files and isolate them. He said he utilized a new type of software called CacheBack that was designed by the next witness, John Dennis Bradley, an ex-law enforcement officer from Canada. Bradley stayed up for three nights writing code and developing the Cache-Back program during the process after Stenger told him he couldn't get it to work.

So Linda Drane Burdick called Bradley to testify about Stenger's report because he was the developer of the software. While she was questioning him, she's going over each and every one of the searches. I saw one website for chloroform had been visited eighty-four times. I couldn't believe it.

I had already gone over these reports with a fine-tooth comb.

How could I have missed that? I wondered.

I even objected. We went to sidebar, and while we were standing before the judge, Burdick gave me this smirk, as if to say, "We got you. Finally, we've got you. She's going down."

Of course, I wasn't smiling.

Bradley's testimony came at the end of the day. I wanted more time to cross-examine him so I asked the court for a little more time, and Judge Perry agreed.

The prosecution liked to put a strong witness on at the end of the day so when the jury went home, the prosecution could leave on a very high note. It was a great strategy.

I went back to the back room, and I questioned Casey.

"What the fuck is this all about?" I said. "Eighty-four times looking for chloroform? Did you know anything about this?"

"I have no idea what this is," she said. "I'm telling you, I didn't visit any chloroform website eighty-four times. That's ridiculous, and it's not true."

I ended up believing her, because I looked at the page. It gave no information. This page had been clicked eighty-four times, but the page preceding it had only been clicked once. You needed to click the preceding page to get to the chloroform page. How could that page be clicked eighty-four times if the preceding page had only been clicked once?

It didn't make any sense.

I called Larry Daniels, my computer expert, and asked him if he would help me. He and I stayed up all night trying to find a way to cross-examine the issue. We needed to cross-examine Bradley the next day in court, but Bradley had not prepared the report. Stenger had. Larry was very frustrated over that.

The next day, the one strong point I could bring out on cross-examination was that Bradley hadn't prepared the report. The state called another witness to testify as to Stenger's report, which made me raise a serious question about Stenger. I would have to wait until I put on the defense case to talk about that NetAnalysis report, which would have shockingly different results, and that's when I would completely blow it out of the water.

We had to sit and wait on that for a while. It was unnerving.

Then they called Lee, who was there to testify that he wasn't the one who deleted files on the computer. My intention was to admit testimony about the searches for prostitutes and escort services, to argue that the conclusion was that George was the one who had deleted the files, because the logic was that he didn't want Cindy or anyone else to know about his philandering.

I wanted to say, "If you're a married man, and you're looking for whores on your computer, you better believe that from time to time you're going to make deletions of your Internet history."

But I couldn't. It was outside the scope of the direct examination.

NEXT, THE PROSECUTION delved into the crime scene. Deputy Edward Turso and Deputy Pamela Porter were the first two officers to arrive on the scene when Roy Kronk made his 9-1-1 call to report he had found a body on December 11, 2008. Given the fact that Kronk had said to Porter, "Do I still get the reward even though she's dead?" and the fact that Porter had been ordered by Internal Affairs not to say anything about Kronk, in effect keeping that little bit of information a secret, I didn't expect the state to call her, and they didn't. Instead they called Turso, who told the jury how he had arrived on the scene and found the body.

It was at this point we knew the prosecution wasn't going to call Kronk, which I just couldn't believe they were doing, but the reason they didn't call him, it turns out, wasn't just that they didn't trust Kronk's testimony. Worse than that, they flat out didn't believe him.

They thought he was "untruthful."

Here's what offends me deeply. They were asking the jury to believe the veracity of the crime scene that he delivered to them, while at the same time refusing to believe his story.

It was a case of, "Believe everything at the scene that I found, but don't believe me."

This was bad enough in a criminal case. In a capital case, which this was, it was so much worse and is really one of those things that makes you question capital punishment in this country. If this could happen in a high-profile case that everyone is watching, imagine a quiet case where no one is paying attention... It's scary.

AFTER CALLING A COUPLE MORE WITNESSES about the photographs of Caylee's remains, the state called medical examiner Dr. Gary Utz, who testified there was no evidence of trauma to Caylee.

After Utz, the state called Dr. John Schultz, their forensic anthropologist, whose job it was to show the jury the gory details of the scene.

They went so far as to show the jury photos of and testimony about animals chewing on Caylee's bones.

I objected strenuously. We went to a sidebar, and Judge Perry allowed it because of my opening statement that the remains had been moved. I didn't see how one thing had to do with the other, but that was his basis for allowing the jury to hear and see this prejudicial information that wasn't probative in any way. All it did was introduce an element of gore to the scene.

Casey, meanwhile, had to sit in court and watch these horrible photos of the bones of her beloved daughter, and I could see her get upset. Dorothy Clay Sims would put her arm around her shoulder to comfort her.

Jeff Ashton then took the time to complain about it.

"I do think that counsel's arm around the back, patting, needs to not be done in front of the jury," he said. "So we would ask that Ms. Sims and all counsel be instructed that the consoling really needs to stop, because it has the potential to influence the jury and getting sympathy. So we would ask that counsel stay out of it and leave the consolation for the breaks."

Judge Perry refused to do as Ashton asked, but he did warn me to watch myself, lest the court have to remove Casey from the courtroom.

Later in the day Casey became so upset watching those horrifying photos that she became ill, and Judge Perry called off court for the rest of the day. For all those bloggers who said that Casey didn't love her daughter, that she killed her so she could go dancing—well, you should have been in the courtroom on this day. Her pain was evident and terribly sad. This was a tragedy any way you looked at it, and I was sorry to be a part of it.

THE PROSECUTION THEN CALLED to the stand Dr. Jan Garavaglia, the medical examiner. The prosecution was touting her as being their star witness.

What I found her to be—and the jury found her to be—was over the top. Meaning she gave much more than what she was qualified to discuss. And it all had to do with the cause and manner of death—how this was a homicide case. As before, she repeated her justification for this to be ruled a homicide:

A. Caylee's disappearance was not reported to the authorities immediately,

B. her body was hidden in a wooded area, and

C. duct tape appeared to be applied to the lower face.

Again, these are not medical facts. These investigative facts say nothing about how Caylee died.

On cross-examination Dr. Garavaglia was very indignant, very abrasive, and yet I do really believe she felt she gave great testimony.

After the trial, she did something that really offended me. She made a documentary of the case, as we all knew she would. Instead of accepting the verdict, she commented that the jury had been made up of people who still believed Elvis was alive. She kept commenting about the defense's spin and how strong the prosecutor's case was. When I saw her say that, I wondered where she had heard all of this information.

She was a witness, which meant she wasn't allowed to sit in on the trial. The rule of sequestration dictated that she not listen to the testimony. Either she was in violation of the judge's order, or she was indicating her clear bias, when the medical examiner is supposed to be anything but.

THE NEXT WITNESS was Michael Warren and his absurd, offensive video superimposition of the duct tape around a photo of Caylee. On the stand Warren said this was a "possibility" and was "speculative." He failed to say it was entirely made up and sold to the public as reality.

I was offended on so many levels I don't know where to start.

I moved for a mistrial.

"I think the overwhelming prejudicial effect was outweighed by the probative value and we would hereby move for a mistrial based on the fact," I said.

Judge Perry asked me whether both sides had presented various theories about the location of the duct tape. And he asked me whether he had said there could be other possibilities, beyond the version of events implied by the video.

"The witness did," I said. "However, it's our position that it's not outweighed by the video, about two minutes long, seeing a photograph of this beautiful child with duct tape wrapped around her face and her skeleton, skull, in the background."

"Okay," he said.

"I think that served only one purpose, to inflame the jury, especially since this witness said he could describe and explain that opinion without the video."

Ashton argued that at one point Caylee did have duct tape over the area of her face, nose, mouth, or both, and that the exhibit was necessary to establish the state's theory that the duct tape was the murder weapon and was admissible for that purpose.

"Motion for a mistrial at this time will be denied," said Judge Perry.

NEXT WERE CRIME SCENE INVESTIGATORS Robin Maynard and Elizabeth Fontaine to talk about the phantom heart-shaped sticker. Dr. Neal Haskell testified about the flies coming from the trunk. Haskell's report may have overreached, but on the stand, he was fair. He was subdued and answered honestly. He talked about the single leg of the blowfly, and when I asked him on cross where all the bugs came from, he answered honestly—they came from the garbage in the bag.

The very last of the prosecution's long list of testifiers as to Casey's character—not to whether she killed anybody—was Bobby Williams, the tattoo artist who tattooed the words "La Bella Vita" on Casey.

The prosecutors wanted to end on an emotional bang; they wanted the jury to know that after Caylee had died, she had gone into town and had herself tattooed, which I suppose was to indicate to the jury that she was a person of bad morals.

During cross-examination I quickly pointed out that George and Cindy had also gotten tattoos to memorialize Caylee.

"If George and Cindy could do it," I said, "why couldn't Casey do it?"

And that was the end of their case, both literally and figuratively.

I MUST SAY THAT OVERALL the state did a very good job presenting the evidence that it had. The state didn't have much, but they made the most of it. All in all it was organized and well presented. Burdick was the reason for that. She was in charge of the case and its organization as far as the evidence was concerned.

Granted, there were a number of times when the prosecutors really let the case drag on, but what they wanted to do was err on the side of overkill, rather than under-try their case.

Aside from the fact they didn't have any evidence as to how, when, and where Caylee died, especially how she died, the prosecutors also engaged in the quintessential prosecutorial overkill—using the many Fockers, using that video superimposition, and really dragging out the case to the limit when they really had very little to back it up.

After the trial I heard from one of the alternate jurors, whom I will not name, that he and another juror told themselves the same thing: At the end of the prosecution's case, each said, "We were asking for more, expecting more. And we were shocked, at the end of their case, they didn't have more."

The alternate juror had this crazy phrase:

"It was like paying for a prostitute and not getting any," he said. But this case was far from over. Because of the circumstances, I feared the jury would find Casey guilty if it could find a reason to. I had to keep the pressure on.

CHAPTER 29

MY TURN

TO MAKE OUR CASE, we wanted to break it into themes. We thought it would be easier for the jury to follow. Also, the prosecution had argued its case in chronological order, and we figured the jury had already gotten an idea of what happened when.

Here are the five themes I intended to follow:

A: The forensics. This had to do with all the evidence concerning the chloroform, the carpet samples, the air in the trunk, the textile fibers, the lack of DNA evidence, the phantom heart-shaped sticker, bugs, and Dr. Arpad Vass's experimental air tests that there was decomposition in the trunk of Casey's car.

B: Caylee's accidental drowning. There was evidence to back this up.

C: The botched crime scene on Suburban Drive. I looked forward to questioning Roy Kronk.

D: Casey's sexual abuse at the hands of George Anthony. This would explain Casey's strange behavior during the thirty days before her arrest and in jail.

E: The final topic concerned the possible police misconduct and George's attempts to frame Casey in order to keep her from talking about the abuse. I couldn't wait to examine Krystal Holloway, George's mistress during this ordeal, to let the jury know what she had to say about the accident that snowballed "out of control."

FOR THE LONGEST TIME, I wanted to start with the forensics, and I wanted to start that way because the state had ended that way. It was a significant part of their case, and my intention was to put so many holes into their case that it would reek of reasonable doubt.

I wanted to accomplish two things with the forensics. One, I intended to show just how much the forensics actually exonerated Casey, and two, I wanted to show the jury just how much forensic evidence the state was hiding from them. And because of their poor strategy of hiding the ball, it made this really easy.

During the state's direct examination, whenever I tried to bring something up that Jeff Ashton would object to as being "outside the scope," Judge Belvin Perry would sustain the objection—these were points most judges would have allowed me to make—but what that did for me was really open up the door to show the jury just how much the prosecution was hiding from them.

Trying a case is a lot like playing a chess match. You always have to anticipate your opponent's next move. They began to preclude me from going into areas that exonerated Casey during my cross-examination which forced us to do it in our case. We were more than willing and happy to do this, because we could parade in front of the jury witnesses that the state should have called but didn't.

There's a case called *Haliburton*, which says that during closing arguments you cannot argue that the state has failed to call a witness unless you call that witness yourself. For example, if we had not called Roy Kronk, we could not then argue that the state didn't call him. And I knew come closing arguments, this was going to be especially important.

It would be fantastic to call as my first witnesses no one but FBI laboratory personnel to testify about all the evidence that *wasn't* brought forth by the prosecution, and all the evidence that exonerated Casey.

And that's precisely what we did.

This wasn't an easy task to pull off because all these experts were busy and had tight schedules, but this was where my associate Michelle Medina was at her best. Michelle is extremely organized and personable, and managed to arrange for all these witnesses to be in court in the order we needed to put them on.

We started with Gerardo Bloise, because he was the one who collected a lot of the evidence and sent it to the FBI so they could examine it. At this point I wish to note that I found the FBI lab employees to be extremely professional. Paula Wolf, the FBI lab's lawyer, was a straight shooter with the defense.

"Our personnel is going to testify to whatever the facts are," she told me, "whether it helps one side or the other."

I couldn't have asked for anything more.

The FBI asked if we would go over with each person the testimony before they testified in court, and so every evening after court I would meet with the FBI lab personnel and go over their testimony with them.

We began with Heather Seubert, who was a senior DNA analyst with the FBI lab.

DNA is always a very difficult topic to explain to jurors without losing them, and I have to say that some of my best lawyering in this case was making the science simple. I spent a lot of time preparing for it and to date it is the work I am most proud of.

I found Seubert to be a great witness. She was very personable and very good at explaining DNA, and she helped us out on several fronts. She testified that there was no blood on the car seat, in the trunk of Casey's car, or on the steering wheel; that there was no DNA on the duct tape; and that the duct tape was contaminated.

The state was arguing that there was human decomposition in the trunk of the car, but Heather testified that decompositional fluids should have DNA in them, yet there was none. She testified that she also tested for blood, semen, and saliva, and none of that was found.

The jury was able to reasonably conclude there was no body in the trunk.

She also testified about the foreign DNA found on the sticky side of the tape that excluded both Casey and Caylee.

That really hurt the prosecution's case.

~

THE NEXT THING I DID was attack the phantom heart-shaped sticker. The prosecution's theory was that Casey had taken one of Caylee's heart-shaped stickers and placed it on the duct tape to show her how much she loved her.

Taking this ridiculous theory apart was easy.

I called Ronald Murdock, who was in charge of processing the crime scene, and he testified that the sticker was thirty feet from Caylee's body.

After that we called Lorie Gottesman, and she testified that she inspected the duct tape and found no residue of any stickers.

Then we showed the jury that the stickers found in the house looked nothing like the one found at the scene thirty feet away.

The conclusion for the jury to make was that the state had in fact tried to trick it by giving it misleading information.

And what made it especially powerful was we were using the state's own people to do it. These were not our experts. These were the prosecution's witnesses, and the prosecution had to sit and watch us use their experts to put on our case.

Ashton, in particular, was getting all upset as his case disintegrated before his eyes. He was his usual self, making faces, carrying on, making objections, getting all angry as usual.

Slowly but surely we could see the agitated Ashton start to boil like a volcano ready to erupt at any moment.

The next day I called Dr. Tim Huntington, our entomologist, to the stand. Huntington did extremely well. He broke things down to their simplest forms for the jury to understand that based on the larval habits of flies, the ones in the trunk didn't come from human decomposition, which the prosecution tried to claim, but rather from the trash—and for no other reason.

When asked whether the leg of the blowfly was evidence of decomposition, he testified, "It doesn't mean anything." He said if there had been a body in the trunk, there should have been thousands of flies, not just one leg.

He also testified that, in his opinion, the body had been moved from another location to where it was found; it wasn't placed there originally.

Ashton spent several hours cross-examining him. He knew that Huntington was hurting his position badly, and he fought vigorously to attack him, cutting off his answers, bullying him, trying to control and manhandle him; in the end he failed because he didn't have the evidence on his side.

One of the most bizarre things Ashton did during the trial arose during his fencing with Dr. Huntington, who during his testimony was discussing pigs decomposing. Ashton thought it would be cute to talk about "wrapping pigs in a blanket." We were talking about the remains of a little girl, and he was cracking bad jokes.

Because Ashton was using an exhibit to question Huntington, I got to stand near the jury when Ashton made his "pigs in a blanket" quip. I looked over at the jurors. They didn't like it, and none of us thought it was funny.

I kept objecting to Ashton cutting off Dr. Huntington during his cross-examination. Ashton said, "Discovery issue. I'm just very concerned that we're going into other areas."

His real concern was that Huntington was turning his case into hamburger meat.

Judge Perry said to Ashton, "Don't do that again."

Ashton kept interrupting Dr. Huntington, until I couldn't stand it any longer.

"I'm going to object and ask that the witness be allowed to complete his answer," I said.

Ashton apologized. He saw how angry Judge Perry was.

"I thought he was done," said Ashton.

"I've lost my train of thought," said Dr. Huntington. "I don't remember where I was going with that."

Ashton asked if he would like the court reporter to read it back.

Judge Perry called a sidebar.

"You need to talk to your counsel," he said to Linda Drane Burdick about Ashton. "Because of what I'm about to do. If he continues to interrupt witnesses, and that goes the same for you, Mr. Baez, then I will prohibit counsel from participating. The only thing they can do is pass questions back and forth and so if you can't control your counsel, that counsel will be eliminated from actual participation."

"It's a simple rule. Ask a question. And when they finish answering the question, they'll stop talking. So if folks can't control their emotions, I'm going to control them. And that's one way I will do it."

In all of the bragging that I have seen Ashton do about his performance during the trial, I have never heard him tell anyone about the day Judge Perry nearly threw him off the case for not being able to control himself.

After that Ashton, his wrists slapped, calmed down considerably.

On June 18, I called Dr. William Rodriguez to the stand. I was calling him because he had a great deal of experience dealing with bodies and duct tape, and he was going to testify that unless the remains are buried, duct tape never stays near the remains. His conclusion was going to be that the crime scene had been staged, and any evidence surrounding it should not be considered.

He was also going to testify that the superimposition of the duct tape over the color photograph of Caylee's remains was "unheard of."

"There's no way scientifically that you can show where that duct tape was," he said.

Ergo, the state's cause of death—death by duct tape—was absurd.

But the jury would never hear his testimony. Ashton immediately objected because Rodriguez was an expert who hadn't been deposed, and under Judge Perry's order, if my witness had not included his opinions in his report or deposition, he couldn't testify.

But wait a minute: it was Ashton's responsibility to depose him. There was no way I could force Ashton to do that, and he purposely didn't depose this witness, just so he could object and try to keep him from testifying.

It was ridiculous on its face. And Judge Perry let him get away with it.

Judge Perry called for a recess at 1:00 P.M. so the prosecution could take Rodriguez's deposition.

But there was a hitch. Rodriguez worked for the United States Armed Forces, and somehow, some way, according to Ashton, Rodriguez's boss called Ashton's cell phone to tell him that Rodriguez hadn't gotten permission to testify. Ashton said if Rodriguez testified, he would be fired.

Ashton swore he hadn't called Rodriguez's boss, that his boss had called him. I have no evidence to say he was lying, but tell me, how did Rodriquez's boss get Ashton's cell number?

At first Rodriguez said he would testify anyway, but to make sure he didn't, Ashton made a motion to hold Rodriguez over for another day so he could review his deposition in order to be able to prepare for his testimony, knowing full well what Rodriguez's situation was.

For Ashton it was all about winning. Nothing else.

I told Rodriguez what Ashton had told me, that his boss said he was going to get fired if he testified, and under the pressure, we both agreed it wasn't worth his losing his job. At the end of the day I had to strike him from the witness list.

My next witness was Dr. Werner Spitz, who was nothing short of brilliant. You'd be hard-pressed to find a forensic pathologist with more experience.

He testified that the autopsy conducted by Dr. Garavaglia was "shoddy," and he talked about the fact that the skull had not been opened during the autopsy and that he had opened it. What he found was that there was important evidence that the body had decomposition on her left side, where she had been left. But when the body was discovered by Kronk, the skull was sitting upright. This was more scientific evidence that the crime scene had been staged.

Ashton cross-examined him. During his cross he tried to use an article written by lawyers to impeach his testimony. Ashton wanted Spitz to see it, and when he did, he exclaimed, "You know, this is written by lawyers for lawyers, and as I say, by lawyers. It's written in legalese. I don't understand it. I am not a lawyer. I have never been a lawyer. It's in lawyerese, and I don't know how to understand this."

Spitz was a riot on the stand, slapping Ashton around. He was also very persuasive. He was giving his direct testimony about decomposition in Caylee's skull to Cheney Mason, who was asking the questions. There was a moment when he said, "You see black flecks. These black flecks are material which represent the large and permanent result of decomposition. What that means is that the brain, which fills this entire space, is gone. The brain has dissolved but some parts, like iron, magnesium phosphate, sodium, chloride, all kinds of elements remain permanent. They don't disappear."

"This is ashes to ashes and dust to dust, what you read in the Bible. And this is the dust which is remaining. And this amount of dust would have been probably just less than an ounce, but of course there's not one ounce because some of the dust has been removed—has gone."

His "ashes to ashes, dust to dust" analogy was very interesting, and I looked over at the jurors, and each and every one of them was leaning forward listening to the professor, the dean of forensic pathology, teaching them about what he had found and how significant it was.

He was telling them that he had found the residue—the black flecks—on the top left-hand side of Caylee's skull to show she had initially been placed sideways.

The jurors saw that this was proof the crime scene had been disturbed and wasn't reliable. And when Spitz testified the duct tape had no DNA on it, they were convinced Caylee wasn't murdered by duct tape. During his cross-examination Ashton kept trying to nail Spitz with facts of the case that had nothing to do with the science. It was interesting, because when she was on the witness stand, all Garavaglia wanted to talk about were the facts of the investigation, that Caylee had been missing thirty days, investigative facts like that, while Spitz concentrated only on the work he did, not the investigative facts.

And because he couldn't recall any of the investigative facts, Ashton tried to paint him as a doddering old man who couldn't remember anything.

After court that day, it was one of the those days when I watched a bit of the news coverage afterward. The so-called experts out there who think they know what it's like to try a case were saying, "Ashton took him apart. Dr. Spitz is going to end his career on a low note because Ashton destroyed him. He looks like a senile old man."

Meanwhile, what these people didn't know because of their ignorance, what they didn't see from my seat in the courtroom, was that the jury hung on Spitz's every word. They liked him so much because of his personality that they were much more open to listening to what he had to say. And what he had to say was devastating to the prosecution's case.

After the trial one of the jurors confided in me, "After Dr. Spitz testified, the case was over for the prosecution."

Our next witness was Jane Bock, our forensic botanist specializing in plant ecology, plant anatomy, and forensic botany. Jane is an elderly woman, whom Ashton ridiculed left and right. She was discussing bones being buried and foraging by animals. When Ashton asked about a buried bone, she commented that a dog could have buried it.

He mocked her. "A dog buried? A dog buried?"

"They do," said Bock. "As do coyotes. I don't know if you have those here."

"We don't have coyotes..." Ashton said with contempt, when in fact there was a news article about coyotes being spotted in downtown Orlando.

You could argue whether her testimony hurt us or helped us, but the real impact of her testimony came from Ashton going overboard and treating this very kind, nice elderly woman badly.

"What a cocky asshole," one of the jurors said to me after the trial referring to the way Ashton treated Bock.

Then came Richard Eikelenboom, whom I flew in all the way from the Netherlands. He was another witness whom Ashton deliberately did not depose. And this time Ashton's tactics—with Judge Perry's wrath—almost pushed me to quit the case.

Ashton intentionally did not take the deposition of a lot of my experts that we gave him the reports for. I believe he did this so he could hold the judge to his order that said, "If it's not in the deposition and it's not in the report, they are not testifying to it." So throughout the trial, he kept bringing up the fact we were in violation of this order because *he* failed to take their deposition. You'd think there was something I could do about this, but there really wasn't. If I could have forced Ashton to depose my witnesses, I would have.

Ashton, meanwhile, was gaining a great deal of pleasure at my distress.

He kept saying, "Baez can't seem to follow that order, Your Honor." When in actuality, it was Ashton taking advantage of two things: one, the order, and two, the fact that Perry was playing along with the game.

I badly wanted to make a motion to recuse Judge Perry, accusing him of bias, but I feared making it, as I told Casey, because of what he could have done to me.

At any rate, after I put Richard Eikelenboom on the stand, and Ashton made a big show of his opinions being outside the scope of his report, Judge Perry read me the riot act.

Judge Perry ruled that my actions were not inadvertent, but willful. Eikelenboom should have been required to comply.

How was I supposed to force Ashton to depose him, Your Honor? I wanted to shout.

He refused to allow the witness to testify on the issue dealing with the possibility of DNA analysis on the decompositional fluid in the trunk of the car.

He also stated that he was going to consider holding me in contempt after the trial.

That shook me up, but good. What was he going to do to me? I didn't know. I had never been held in contempt before. He could have fined me. There could have been ramifications with the bar, something I certainly didn't want to go through. I could even go to jail.

And what of the public humiliation? I had worked hard to gain a good reputation as a lawyer, one who fights hard for his clients. I didn't care if the media bashed me because it was in the course of defending my client, but this was different. We had recessed for the day, and I went to see Casey.

"I have to confess something to you, Casey," I said to her. "I don't know if I can defend you anymore. The problem now is that I have to worry about myself more than about you. I'm worried for my family, for my son. It would be unfair for me to be your lawyer because you're no longer my main focus, and you deserve better than that."

Casey began to cry.

"Please don't give up on me," she begged.

"I'm not," I said. "But I just can't believe I'm telling you this."

I left her, went up to the bathroom, and I literally got on my knees and prayed for help and strength.

Cheney, meanwhile, went and spoke to Judge Perry. I walked in on them as Cheney was saying, "This kid is very concerned about his license and his career, and he's no longer focused on this case. We can't have this. This has got to stop."

Cheney suggested that we quit for the day and all go home to start anew tomorrow.

"Everyone go home," said Judge Perry. "I am not holding anyone in contempt."

I went back and spoke to Casey.

"We're breaking for the day," I told her, "Everything's going to be okay."

It was a very difficult time for me in the middle of this very difficult trial. The next day the *Orlando Sentinel* ran a cartoon of Judge Perry bending me over his knee spanking me. I am a lawyer, a father, and a husband. All I was doing was upholding my oath as an officer of the court. No lawyer should be spoken to or humiliated that way. I say this not for myself, because what's done is done, but for all of my brothers and sisters who fight for the poor, the underclass, and the underprivileged, as well as those who work for the private and endowed. But to those individuals responsible for this fiasco I offer them Plato's wisdom: *It is better to suffer injustice than to do injustice.*

CHAPTER 30

DESTROYING
THE FANTASY

W E PRESSED ON. As a lawyer, I learned to have a short-term memory, to put the past behind you and look forward. It's what we did on a daily basis. My whole approach was to fly straight. When we had a good moment, we didn't rejoice. When we had a bad moment, we didn't pout.

After a couple hours of extreme anxiety the previous day, I recovered. I vowed I wasn't going to let any of this affect my performance. I knew in the next few days the prosecution's fantasy—its made-up theory of how Caylee died—would be exposed.

We went after the prosecution's death-by-chloroform theory first by calling Detective Yuri Melich to testify that the police didn't find any chloroform anywhere in the Anthony home. He testified they didn't find any ingredients for making chloroform, didn't find receipts for buying chloroform, didn't find any chemistry kits, didn't find anything in any way, shape, or form in the Anthony home or anywhere else, for that matter, that indicated that Casey had been involved in making chloroform.

We then called Dr. Arpad Vass's partner, Dr. Marcus Wise. We didn't call Vass because he had already testified, and I had gotten what I wanted from him. And he wasn't a chemist; Wise was.

Dr. Wise was not happy to be there, and the jury clearly saw he was not being straightforward. When I attempted to get him to admit there

365

were no standard protocols for his test, he kept avoiding the answer. Jeff Ashton did his best to keep him from answering.

Dr. Wise explained that he had done a qualitative analysis of the chemicals in the trunk but decided not to do a quantitative one because of the nature of chloroform.

"Chloroform is what is called a volatile chemical," Wise said. "That means it evaporates easily. If you put a drop of chloroform on a surface, it's going to begin to evaporate, and over a period of minutes, hours, days, it's going to decrease."

He also said that because he didn't have a history of the carpet sample, didn't know the temperature of the trunk, how it varied every day, didn't know when the material was deposited, how much was there originally—in short, because there were so many unknowns—it was impossible to determine the amount of chloroform.

While it took pulling teeth from the guy he finally stated one crucial fact without equivocation: contradicting Vass, who had testified that there had been a "huge" amount of chloroform, Wise finally had to admit there was *no way* to determine how much chloroform was in the trunk of Casey's car.

So much for the state's theory that Casey used chloroform to drug Caylee.

We next called Maureen Bottrell, a soil expert from the FBI. She testified that she collected all of Casey's shoes—about thirty pairs—and tested them to determine whether any of her shoes had soil samples that matched the soil of the recovery site. None did.

There went state's theory that Casey dumped Caylee's body in the woods.

Madeline Montgomery of the FBI testified that there were no drugs found in Caylee's hair, and that included Xanax, chloroform, sedatives, or designer drugs. No drugs—period.

On cross-examination Ashton got her to say that such drugs are volatile and take a while to get into someone's system, and so the fact they were tested, and the tests came back negative was virtually meaningless.

I rose and said to her, "So what other meaningless work do you do over at the FBI?"

"My work is very important," she replied. "It's critical. We find evidence in cases."

As she did in this case.

WE CALLED DR. MICHAEL SIGMAN, who conducted the air sample tests. Sigman testified that the chloroform levels were low and that the main chemical in the trunk of Casey's car was gasoline.

Then we recalled Michael Rickenbach. If you remember, we tried to show he had conducted other tests during his initial appearance, only to be shut down by Ashton's objections. Here was my chance to throw it right into their faces—to show the jury what the state was hiding from them.

Rickenbach testified that he tested not only the trunk for chloroform but also the steering wheel cover, the door handle, and Caylee's doll, and none of those tests came back positive.

So much for the state's theory that Caylee was being knocked out by chloroform on a regular basis so Casey could go out and party.

We then returned to the issue of the hair—the one hair that supposedly had root banding, indicating there had been a dead body in the trunk.

We called Karen Lowe, and her testimony was especially impactful. On direct she had testified about the one hair, but this time I was able to ask her about the nine other tests she had conducted—the tests the prosecution wanted to keep from the jury. After making those nine inspections of more than a hundred other hairs, I was able to get her to tell the jury that not a single one of those other hairs had root banding—human decomposition—on them.

For example, they took Casey's clothes and took hairs from them, and not one hair had root banding.

They did vacuum sweepings from the house. None of them had decomposition on them.

They did vacuum sweepings from Casey's car. None of them had decomposition on them.

Everywhere they turned, they tested all these other hairs, and when the tests turned up negative, that increased the probability that the one hair that had root banding had changed not because it came from a dead body but because of environmental conditions in the trunk of Casey's car.

Her testimony wasn't conclusive, but it strongly suggested that the state's theory that Casey put Caylee in the trunk was weak at best.

WE THEN WENT AFTER the computer evidence. We called Cindy Anthony. Remember I said I wanted the old Cindy back? I found my opening. I realized how I could get her back.

I knew in her deposition she had claimed that she had been the one who had made the searches for the chloroform. However, her work records showed her to be at work that day. To get around that, she said she had worked from home that day, but her time records didn't reflect that.

I don't know if she was lying, because you can't be certain who is behind a computer, but we always felt our strongest argument that Casey had been on the computer was Ricardo Morales's Myspace posting of "Win her over with Chloroform."

This is a perfect opportunity for me to do two things: one, continue to cast reasonable doubt on these searches; and two, get Linda Drane Burdick to attack her best witness, Cindy, I thought to myself.

And that's exactly what I did.

We got Cindy up on the stand, and Cindy testified that she had made the searches for chloroform. She said she was doing research on chlorophyll, because she said she feared her dogs were eating bamboo and were acting lethargic, and by accident chloroform came up.

Looking back, I have mixed feelings about her testimony. You can certainly say what she was doing was lying to protect Casey, but there were plenty of other occasions when she could have stepped up and helped her a whole lot more.

I really don't know. Maybe she really believed she made those searches. Later, of course, it turned out she didn't. Maybe she was trying to save her daughter, but if she was, she wasn't doing a very good job of it.

And that was the big news of the day: Cindy falling on her sword for Casey.

When Burdick got up to cross-examine Cindy, boy, it was like the good old days, as Cindy and Burdick went back and forth at each other. An angry Cindy was pointing her finger at Burdick, and the two of them once again were doing the Cindy Two-Step.

I remember sitting back in my chair catching myself smiling at what was going on. I had to stop myself.

Oh shit, I thought, *I'm enjoying this way too much.*

Because up until then Cindy had been the perfect witness. But there came that moment, and it was on. She and Burdick would bump heads, and it was like the good old days.

And then Burdick did us a *big* favor. During her cross-examination, she asked her, "Did you run this search on how to make chloroform eighty-four times?

Cindy danced around the answer.

Burdick kept on the eighty-four searches. I could have objected as asked and answered, but I didn't. I wanted to give Linda enough rope to hang herself, and she was doing it over and over again.

Burdick repeated, "Eighty-four times," and all Burdick was doing was digging a bigger hole for the prosecution by repeatedly bringing up "eighty-four times."

Because with my next witness I was about to blow that theory out of the water.

We called Sergeant Kevin Stenger of the Orange County Sheriff's Department Computer Crimes Squad, and I got him to compare two different reports of the Internet histories of the Anthony family computer.

He testified that the report that he prepared using a program called NetAnalysis, had a problem with the times and dates, but otherwise was accurate. He said that according to his NetAnalysis program on March 21, Myspace was visited eighty-four times, and that there was one search for "How to Make Chloroform." This fit perfectly with Casey's explanation that one time she had gone to a chloroform site because her boyfriend at the time, Ricardo Morales, had posted that photo on Myspace that said, "Win her over with Chloroform."

To get rid of the notion that Cindy was the one doing the looking, I asked Stenger whether, if you type in chlorophyll, it could happen that chloroform might come up. He said no.

Stenger testified that the person who looked up the chloroform site during the two searches was on it for exactly three minutes.

On cross-examine Burdick tried to suggest that Casey might have stayed on the website a lot longer than three minutes, or might have printed out the results.

On redirect Stenger said that to say she might have stayed on longer was pure speculation.

"I do not know if that happened," he said.

I asked him whether anyone had recovered pages about chloroform that had been printed out and taken in as evidence.

"No one informed me of that," he said.

During Stenger's testimony, which pretty much blew to smithereens the notion that Casey had visited chloroform sites eighty-four times, Burdick, who had been pushing the theory, was turning red. That wasn't one of her finest moments, but it certainly was one of ours.

So much for the state's theory that Casey had looked up chloroform eighty-four times.

We left court that day, and it was one of the few days when I said to myself, *This evidence was so persuasive, these media folks are going to have no choice but to tell the public what a great session we had blowing a gaping hole in the state's case.*

But in the media the next day, all they were reporting was Cindy admitting to the searches for chloroform. Not one single reporter mentioned about how we had slammed a forensic issue in the state's case and made it look like a complete and total fraud.

My goodness, I said to myself, *how could they miss something huge like that?*

And what's funny is, after the trial I received an email from one of the jurors.

After asking why the state didn't check the phone records of anyone but Casey, including Roy Kronk, the juror wrote, "The computer evidence was just the final straw for me. What a joke!"

And I have to say, this is where having a quality expert makes a huge difference. Larry Daniel was the one who found the discrepancy, and he was nothing short of spectacular in his knowledge of what was on the Anthonys' computer. He knew it ten times better than the state.

When the trial was over, John Bradley, the designer of the software used by the state to determine that Casey had made eighty-four searches for chloroform, wrote an article saying that the searches were based on inaccurate data, and that there had only been one search, not the eighty-four searches as the state claimed.

Not only that, but according to *The New York Times*, "Mr. Bradley said he immediately alerted a prosecutor, Linda Drane Burdick, and Sgt. Kevin Stenger of the Sheriff's Office in late June through e-mail and by telephone to tell them of his new findings. Mr. Bradley said he conducted a second analysis after discovering discrepancies that were never brought to his attention by prosecutors or the police."

"Mr. Bradley's findings were not presented to the jury and the record was never corrected," said an article about it in *The New York Times*.

"I gave the police everything they needed to present a new report," wrote Bradley. "I did the work myself and copied out the entire database in a spreadsheet to make sure there was no issue of accessibility to the data."

Bradley, who lived in Canada, said he even volunteered to fly to Orlando at his own expense to set the record straight.

Bradley said that the first analysis report, conducted by Stenger, had been hidden from him.

And this was huge, because once again it showed the pattern of bad faith on the part of law enforcement and/or the prosecution when it came to this case.

The question arose: Did Linda Drane Burdick know that she was presenting false evidence? Where it gets fishy is that she called Bradley a civilian from Canada (we do not have subpoena powers in Canada) to testify about Sgt. Stenger's report. Then you have John Bradley's post trial comments. But I know Linda Drane Burdick, and John Bradley removed his statement off of his website after the *New York Times* wrote a big article on it and it began to get a lot of attention. Maybe Bradley got scared and back-pedaled because all of his business comes from law enforcement, or maybe he was mistaken. I will never know. If it had been any other prosecutor given these facts I would say absolutely they knew they put on false evidence, but Linda's character stands in the way of that, and I have the utmost respect for her character. So without first-hand knowledge, I would say no, she did not knowingly introduce false evidence. But nonetheless, the evidence was false.

AFTER THE COMPUTER TESTIMONY we wanted to delve more into the theme of shady police work. We called Detective Ryan Eberlin, who was the officer who first handcuffed Casey at her house, only to have her uncuffed a few minutes later.

We wanted to show the perfect example of law enforcement misleading the jury. Sergeant Reginald Hosey had testified that he had never told Eberlin to handcuff her, whereas on the stand, Eberlin testified Hosey had told him to do it.

That wasn't huge as it related to the case as much as it said to the jury, "Look, they are lying to you."

We then attempted to call to the stand Detective Eric Edwards and Linda Tinelli. We wanted to show that law enforcement wanted Tinelli, one of the women manning George's search-for-Caylee booth, to wear a wire and question George about Caylee's disappearance. Outside the presence of the jury, Judge Belvin Perry ruled that it wasn't relevant, so we never got them to testify.

We also got Melich to testify that the police had pulled Roy Kronk's phone records, when in truth they didn't. I got Melich to return the next day and admit to the jury that he "misspoke."

We then turned our attention to Suburban Drive. One of the issues we dealt with was the search in the woods conducted by Dominic Casey and Jim Hoover, who were working for the Anthonys. To bring the issue to the fore, on June 28, we called to the stand Cindy Anthony, Lee Anthony, and Yuri Melich.

In one of his reports, Melich had written that on December 20, when they went to the house to execute a search warrant, Cindy had said, "I had my people (Dominic and Hoover) search there a month ago, and they didn't find anything." Later Cindy would deny making that statement. She had denied it in her civil deposition, so I knew she'd deny it at trial. Sure enough, we called Cindy up, and she denied ever making it.

During my meetings with Lee, he had told me that in fact she did have Dominic and Hoover out in the woods searching for Caylee sometime in October. And as a result, said Lee, he and Cindy had had a fight, because Lee thought Caylee was still alive, and Cindy was sending Dominic into the woods to search for a dead Caylee.

How did Cindy know she was dead? While we will never know, you can insinuate in good faith that at some point Cindy learned the truth from George, and that's when she sent her guys into the woods.

At any rate, after Cindy testified, I called Lee to the stand. This was right after Cindy had testified, "No, I didn't make that statement, and no, I didn't send Dominic Casey into the woods."

Lee walked right up there after sitting next to his mother and said, "Yes, she did, and not only that, but we got into a big fight over it, and shortly after that fight I went back to work and stopped searching for Caylee."

It was huge, huge, and then I called back Melich, and he said, "Yeah, she made the statement."

For me the infighting among those three made such an impactful impression on the jury that it was one of the landmark reasons why Casey was acquitted.

And once again, not a word of it was mentioned in the media the next day.

ON SATURDAY, JUNE 24, in court Burdick came up to me, and she said, "You know, all I really want is the truth from Casey as to what happened."

When she said that, I thought, *This is a plea overture.*

"What do you have in mind?" I asked.

"Let's talk about it," she said.

Some other people have said I was the one who approached Burdick, but I will tell you, that wasn't the case. A plea bargain was the furthest thing from my mind, in large part because Casey had made it clear she was innocent and wouldn't entertain the possibility of a plea bargain.

"Listen," she said, "I'm willing to let her plead to count three."

Which was aggravated manslaughter of a child, with a thirty-year maximum. The problem was that there's no minimum, so Judge Perry would have discretion as to how many years he would sentence her to.

Judge Perry's involvement, for us, was the tricky part.

"If Casey will say that she would consider a plea," said Burdick, "Then we will go to Judge Perry, and he can tell us what he will sentence her to ahead of time, and then she can decide whether to accept it or not."

Hmmm. To me this was a no-lose situation, because once Judge Perry announced how many years he would sentence her to, say hypothetically twenty-five years, if afterwards she was convicted of murder and was sentenced to life, I could argue that it was vindictive sentencing in that he had already said, "Twenty-five years."

And if she was handed a death sentence, I could make an argument that might save her life.

All five of us on the defense team, Cheney, Lisabeth, Dorothy, Michelle, and I went to see Casey. I told her about the offer and that all she had to do was consider it.

"No," she said right away.

"Casey, you have got to at least think about it."

"Okay," she said. "I just thought about it. The answer is no."

We all went round and round talking to Casey, how this was a no-lose situation, but in the end, even listening to a plea deal was something she just couldn't do.

"No, I'm not guilty. I'm innocent," she said. "And I don't care what anyone has to say. I feel this jury is on our side. I'll plead guilty to lying to the cops, but I won't plead guilty to something I did not do."

Cheney and I left the room, and he said, "I don't know how to deal with this. I've never seen anything like this before."

Casey was taking a huge risk by not considering the deal, innocent or otherwise. Her life was at stake here, and she was trusting twelve strangers to decide whether she would live or die.

"I'm going to the judge," Cheney said. "I have issues about her competency."

We went to sidebar. Cheney was about to tell Judge Perry when I said, "Wait a minute, Cheney." And I asked the judge to give me a couple more minutes. I wanted another chance to talk to Casey.

I did, and I still didn't get anywhere with her. I went back, and Cheney and I told the judge.

"I have questions about her competency," said Cheney.

And whenever a lawyer does that, the trial has to stop, because any evidence that gets presented if the client isn't competent—it's a waste of time.

Judge Perry called a recess.

"I'll have some people go in and evaluate her today. We'll stop and say it's a legal issue. They'll evaluate her tonight, and tomorrow we'll see what the reports have to say."

We told Casey what they were doing, and she said, "Fine."

Doctors went in and talked to her, and they found her competent. The next day the trial continued.

When Judge Perry called off court for the day, saying it was a "legal issue," the media went crazy, inventing all the events it might be including Casey pleading guilty and one of the lawyers quitting the case. It was the usual garbage by reporters who needed a story for the news, whether there was truth to that story or not.

I can say a lot of things about Casey, but one thing I can never say is that she lacked courage. She looked death in the face and said, "A plea? Absolutely not." I know I wouldn't have had the same courage. To this day I'm amazed at how strong she was, and maybe that's what life taught her: how to be a survivor. But to this day I'm amazed for her actions on that day.

WHEN WE RESUMED, we called Kronk to the stand. Because of my fatigue, I turned over the questioning of Kronk to Cheney, who got Kronk to testify to all his calls in August. We outlined all the Kronk madness, went through the Kronk chronicles where he admitted to sticking his meter reading stick into the eye socket of Caylee's skull, lifting her up. We brought out his discussions of money. He denied that money was his motivation, denied calling his son, Brandon Sparks, around Thanksgiving and telling him he was about to become famous. He testified the cops never pulled his phone records, that the cops never spoke to him between August and December, the two times he called in to say he had found bones and remains.

He admitted his car needed $1,000 in repairs on December 10, and calling the police to report he had found Caylee's remains on December 11.

When Kronk finished testifying, I think it was clear to the jury that something was just not right about any of this.

We called Roy Kronk's son Brandon Sparks to the stand. Sparks, a very straightforward military kid, said that his father had called him a month before Caylee had been found in December and told him, "I'm going to be rich and famous."

We then called George to the stand to talk about his relationship with Krystal Holloway, whom he had met at the command center during the search for Caylee. It was a relationship that he denied. We showed that George sent her a text message in which he wrote, "I need you in my life," and he denied telling Krystal that Caylee's death was "an accident that snowballed out of control."

On the stand George began by saying Krystal was no different from any other volunteer. He denied ever being intimate with her and said he only went to her condominium on two or three occasions. And then he said something almost comical.

"She had relayed to me just a few days prior to me going there for the very first time that she has a brain tumor. She was dying," George said. "She needed someone to comfort her, and I felt as being a good guy or someone who had come to know a lot of people volunteered for us, I became very connected with a lot of people and her, and I felt because she was giving of herself to me and my family to help with my grand-daughter, that's the least I could do."

As he was giving his ridiculous recitation, I thought to myself, *In the closing argument I'm going to shove it right up this lying SOB by saying, "His wife was the one who needed comforting. They had a missing grand-daughter, not this woman who he barely knew. And not only that, she didn't have a tumor. She's still alive three years later. She didn't have any brain tumor."*

I pressed him.

"Is it your testimony to this jury that you weren't going there for any romantic interludes? It was just because you were going there to console her for her brain tumor?"

Ashton objected; his objection was overruled.

"Sir, yes, I did go there just to console her because she had confided in me that she had a brain tumor, or she was having medical issues, and she also explained that to my wife." He added, "I had nothing to hide, sir. Never have."

There isn't a man in American who has more *to hide*, I thought to myself.

Despite George's denials, I got everything I needed from him. I got that he had a relationship with her, though he denied it, and he also denied he ever made the statement to Holloway, "It was an accident that snowballed out of control."

I then called Krystal. I had met with her beforehand, and I found her to be a colorful character. She was who she was, and she wasn't going to apologize for it.

A scorned lover, she had a lot of anger toward George. Out of the kindness of her heart, during a period when George was telling Cindy he was working but really wasn't, she lent him more than $4,000 so he could keep his head above water financially.

Initially, she had wanted to protect George. When the relationship was made public, George not only kept denying its existence, he insulted and bad-mouthed her, claiming she was a criminal and a liar. As a result, she lost all sympathy for him. That and the fact he never paid her back.

Describing how their relationship ended, Krystal said, "Shortly after the memorial service for Caylee, I blew him, and he blew me off."

AFTER KRYSTAL WE CALLED Dominic Casey, who was the Kato Kaelin of our case. He was such a wacky character. A number of times during his testimony, the jury couldn't stop laughing at how crazy he was. I called him because he had emailed a psychic and included a Google map. Right where Dominic put the pin was where Caylee's remains were found, and this was in November, a month before she was found.

I showed the jury a blowup of an email with the spot where Caylee had been found. I had had Kronk's coworkers circle the area, had Melich do the same. And I got Dominic to say, "Yes, I sent this to a psychic because this was the area I had searched..." Right then and there, the jury and everyone in the courthouse knew there was something fishy going on.

I summarized it when I asked him, "This was the only time you searched for a dead Caylee?"

"Yes."

"Orlando is a hundred square miles?"

"Yes."

"The only place you searched was where she ultimately was found?"

"Yes."

The jury could have come up with but one explanation: either George or Cindy had told him, "Hey, you need to go to this spot and search."

Either they wanted Dominic to find her or wanted Dominic to be able to testify that he had searched the area and there was no body there.

Neither George nor Cindy have ever come forth and actually spoken about this. But, I have just about run out of excuses for all the coincidences.

I CALLED CINDY TO THE STAND to advance our theory that Caylee's death was an accident. She and I were talking about the layout of the house, the fact that there were no child-safety locks, and that Caylee was able to open the sliding-glass doors to the pool. It was at this point we introduced one of the most important exhibits in our entire case—the photo of Caylee opening the sliding-glass doors.

We didn't have this photo until the middle of the trial. Casey had been an inveterate photo-taker, taking thousands of photos of herself and Caylee, and she had had a lot of photos taken of herself, photos like the ones at her high school senior prom. Cindy had sold some of these photos to CBS, and we wanted to see them so we could use these photos to show to Cindy so she could talk about Casey being a good mother. At the same time I wanted to show Cindy had sold the photos.

There was a huge batch of photos that I put under the care of William Slabaugh, who was in charge of the Casey Anthony file.

"Here's what I want you to do," I said to him. "Go through these photos and pull out the ones that show Caylee by and in the pool so we have proof the ladder was always off."

"Sure, no problem," he said.

We worked weekends, and this was a Sunday. He was working on his assignment, and I was in my office preparing for upcoming witnesses, when William came over to me and said, "Jose, you've got to see this."

"What?" I said, walking over to his computer.

He clicked the button for the photo to come up, and just as it appeared, he slapped his hands together and yelled, "Pow, there it is."

And we couldn't believe it.

We sat around the conference room staring at a picture of Caylee opening the sliding-glass door to the pool. I have a three-year-old, and I have hundreds of pictures of him, but I don't have one of him opening a glass door.

No one had ever showed the picture because in and of itself it was so inconsequential. Caylee's face doesn't even show in the picture.

We all just stared.

It was the coup de grâce for the entire case.

We all sat in dead silence.

"It's as if she's trying to tell us something," said one of our interns.

CHAPTER 31

THE PET CEMETERY

A FTER WE FOUND THE PHOTO of Caylee opening the glass door on the way to the pool, we decided to look for more photos that would substantiate what George told Holloway, "It was an accident that snowballed out of control."

Casey had told me the same story, so I knew this to be the truth. But for the jury to believe it, we needed more, and we got it. We not only found the sliding door photo, but we also found a photo of Caylee walking up the ladder with Cindy, with Cindy barely touching her, we also found ones of Caylee jumping into the water and swimming in the pool.

We called Cindy to the stand to discuss these photos, which we blew up for all to see. Cindy talked about Caylee's ability to get out of the house on her own, that she had to be watched, that there were no locks to keep her from leaving. I showed her the photos and it was clear the jury was beginning to understand that this notion of ours that Caylee had drowned in the pool was not something we had pulled out of thin air.

It was huge.

We then talked about the shorts that had been found along with Caylee's remains. She had outgrown them. They were size twenty-four months, when Caylee wore a 3T. Whoever put them on her hadn't had much experience dressing her.

Cindy testified that she hadn't seen those shorts in six months.

When Dr. Henry Lee inspected the shorts, he had found rips in them. Whoever put them on her was so desperate to get them on, that he ripped them as he fought to get her body into them. It would have been nice to have had Lee's testimony. It was another piece of evidence we had that we never got to produce.

Who could have been the one to have dressed her like that? We believed we knew exactly who, but I don't know that the jurors made the connection.

We went to our grief expert, Dr. Sally Karioth. I had taken her class at Florida State University back in 1994. Her class was hard to get into, and she talked about grief and how people grieved in different ways.

The basic premise behind her testimony was that a person of sound mind and body grieved in the usual way, but those suffering from trauma, like sexual abuse or other mental health issues, grieve in a very different way—in a way that people just can't understand. She said that the way Casey pretended nothing was wrong was a common way that sexual abuse victims conduct themselves after suffering trauma or loss.

There aren't that many people who are qualified to testify about grief. Her specialty is unique, and she was criticized by many in the media who had no clue as to what they were talking about.

The day we were about to drop Sally off at the airport, she said to me, "Jose, when this trial is over, I want you to call me, because you're going through a traumatic event, and you're going to need me. In fact, not only you, but your whole defense team."

"Thank you," I said, "that's very kind of you."

And I thought to myself, *I don't think so. I'll be fine.*

And looking back, I can't tell you how right she was.

WE THEN CONCLUDED OUR CASE with the evidence that showed that in the past whenever one of the Anthony family pets died, George would wrap it in a blanket, put it in a trash bag, and wrap it with duct tape so it remained inside. And then he would bury the animal in the backyard.

Cindy had told that to Janine Barrett, our mitigation specialist. Oddly, Cindy hadn't told that to anyone else. She only told us. But I figured if Cindy knew, then Lee knew, and so I asked Lee about this—and again, this was the benefit of us having access to Lee—and Lee said, "Oh yeah, that was the way my dad did things. He would take the dead dog, wrap him in his favorite blanket, put him in a plastic bag, and put duct tape around the bag. That way the bag stayed tight to the body."

I thought, *Wow, as much as George has talked to the police, he never mentioned that to them?*

Our defense team held a meeting about how to use this little tidbit of information, and we all felt really strongly that this was the way we needed to end our case. I can't claim credit for it. Everyone in the room said, "The biggest impact and significance wasn't just that this was the way George buried his pets, but it was the fact he never said a word about it to the police. If he had buried his pets that way for so many years, and his granddaughter turns up the same way, the obvious conclusion had to be: If he hid this from the cops was it because he had something to hide?

His not telling anyone about the way he buried his pets pointed the finger right at him.

His silence was purely an act of self-preservation.

I put George on the stand and introduced the video of George talking at the command center. On the table, in full sight, was the Henkel duct tape, sitting next to the donation jar. Both sides stipulated facts about the command center, including its location.

When I asked George about where the command center was, he said it wasn't that location. He fought me on the point.

I thought to myself, *George is lying about facts stipulated to by the prosecution!*

After he dodged my questions about his access to the Henkel duct tape found at the command center, I asked him, "When you lived in Ohio, sir, did you have a dog named Mandy?"

Jeff Ashton objected, asking for relevance.

I told him it would come soon enough.

"Twenty years ago?" said Ashton.

"I will be tying it in," I said.

Ashton called for a sidebar.

"The witness will testify that, yes, he went to a vet, that they began burying their pets in a manner of putting them in a blanket, a black plastic bag, and wrapping them in duct tape," I said to Judge Belvin Perry.

"What he did..." said Ashton.

"He won't say duct tape," said Linda Drane Burdick.

"What he did with a dog twenty years ago," said Ashton.

They didn't like where this was going. This piece of information was was not going to turn out well for them.

"And that tradition continued when they buried numerous pets in their backyard," I continued.

Ashton continued to state his objections.

"It is relevant because it shows that my client was two or three years old and couldn't have been the one who learned how to do this and bury their pets in this manner," I said.

"I stand on my objection," said Ashton.

"He knows there's more testimony that would suggest his client did know," said Burdick.

"Well, yeah, she did know, but this began long before..."

"Who began the tradition isn't relevant if counsel wants to ask about what they did in this millennium. But twenty years ago in Ohio is not," said Ashton. His argument was ridiculous.

"Because it shows that this began before—while she was at the age of three..." I said.

"Go ahead," said Judge Perry.

"Is counsel planning on bringing out more recent..." said Ashton.

He was hoping beyond hope that I wasn't.

"I am," I said. "I will."

"I stand on my objection, Judge," said Ashton.

"Overruled," said Judge Perry. It was one of the rare times when Judge Perry overruled one of Ashton's objections, and it came at a crucial time.

I asked George whether he had a dog named Mandy in Ohio.

"Yes."

"Did there come a time where the dog had to be either put down or was deceased?"

"Yes."

"And how was that dog buried?"

"In our yard where we used to live."

"Did you pick the dog up at the veterinarian?"

"Yes."

"Okay, and was the dog wrapped in a blanket?"

"To the best of my recollection, probably, yes."

"Was the dog then placed in a plastic bag?"

"I don't remember that exactly, but the dog was deceased and the dog was taken to our home and placed there, yes."

"Was it also wrapped in duct tape?"

"Sir, I have no idea," said George. "You're going back almost thirty years."

"And was that before Casey was born?"

"Yes."

"Okay, when you moved here, did you have a dog named Bo?"

"Yes."

"When did Bo pass away?"

"I can't remember the exact year, sir."

"Okay, was it fifteen years ago? Ten years ago?"

"Could have been more than fifteen or more years ago."

"Okay. How old was Casey at the time?"

"Probably about four or five years old. I'm just rough guessing here."

"Okay. And was Bo buried in a blanket, in a plastic bag, wrapped with duct tape?"

"I do not remember exactly what he was buried in."

I asked him about another dog by the name of Ginger. I asked him if Ginger was wrapped in a bag with duct tape wrapped around it.

Again he said he didn't remember exactly how the animals were finally put to rest.

"What about Cinnamon?"

"Again, that would be the same answer."

"Okay, when you found out that your granddaughter was found with a blanket and with a plastic bag and with duct tape, did you tell law enforcement at any time over the last three years that that is the way you used to bury your pets?"

Ashton jumped up, objected, and asked for a sidebar.

I fully understand why he was objecting. His case of innuendos and phony evidence was unraveling so fast, his head was spinning. At this point, if I could have, I would have put Ashton on the stand, and I would have asked him why law enforcement never bothered to investigate George for the things Casey was accused of doing.

AND AGAIN, this was the amazing drama unfolding, three family members sitting together in the courtroom, watching each other testify, with George getting on the stand and making his denials, and Cindy and Lee getting on the stand and impeaching his credibility.

Cindy went so far as to describe exactly how George used the duct tape to secure the bags holding the deceased pets.

"The tape was used to secure the top of the bag so it wouldn't open?" I asked Cindy.

She replied, "The tape was placed around the bags in two locations, the top and the bottom so that when we rolled it to keep the air out—we were trying to keep things from getting into the bag. So we placed tape like at thirds, one-third and two-thirds."

Added Lee, "She was placed in a plastic bag, and I do recall there being duct tape used to secure the bag."

We couldn't have asked for anything better.

Lying takes its toll, and during this trial the one who constantly was lying was George. That's the primary reason these jurors couldn't stand him.

During the state's rebuttal case it called to the stand Dr. Michael Warren to impeach Dr. Werner Spitz. Warren is a forensic anthropologist and Spitz is a forensic pathologist, so that was like calling a podiatrist to impeach an optometrist. It was ridiculous and so off the mark.

The state's desperation was starting to show.

CHAPTER 32

THE LAUGHING GUY

AFTER WE RESTED, we were feeling really good about how the case was going. One of our most important decisions was whether or not to let Casey testify, and there were times throughout the case that I thought she might have to. However, it all changed when we started to make some progress with George, which was the result of Jeff Ashton parading him up on the stand time after time, giving me more and more shots at him.

We made up a lot of ground with George, especially when you consider the last time he testified, he lied about the pet cemetery, about the duct tape when he wrapped the plastic bags to bury his pets. As I said, the man couldn't tell the truth to save his life, and I was sure that was the way the jury was seeing him.

My office staff met, and we tossed back and forth the question of Casey's testifying.

"What do we have to gain?" I asked.

What could she talk about? What happened the day Caylee died?

I thought we had made our case with Cindy and the pool photos, and at the end of our discussions, I said, "You know what? She doesn't need to."

If we had been in a more desperate position, maybe. By why should we give the prosecution a strong day when it hadn't had one in a while?

We had everything to lose and very little to gain.

I talked it over with Casey, and Casey agreed; it turned out to be the right decision.

In the courtroom Judge Belvin Perry asked if I intended to present more live witnesses.

"No, sir. We do not."

"Will the defendant be testifying?" he asked.

"No, sir."

He asked Casey, "Is it your decision not to testify?"

"Yes, sir," she said.

"Has anyone used any force or pressure in making you arrive at that decision?"

"No, sir."

"Okay, and that decision is your decision freely and voluntarily?"

"Yes, sir."

"Thank you, ma'am."

The jury returned.

"Okay, Mr. Baez," said Judge Perry. "You may call your next witness."

"The defense rests," I said.

The prosecution's rebuttal mostly had to do with proving that Cindy Anthony wasn't the one who looked up chlorophyll and accidentally came up with chloroform on her computer. They obviously had to do this, because if Cindy made the search for chloroform, then Casey didn't, but I had to laugh at the lengths they went to prove Cindy a liar in order to convict Casey.

They called the chief compliance officer of Gentiva Health Services, Inc. where she worked to testify she was at work, not at home when she said she was looking for chlorophyll because, according to her story, her dog had eaten bamboo and had become lethargic, and she wanted to check out the connection.

They called on Sergeant Kevin Stenger to testify that there had been no search for chlorophyll.

Another computer expert testified that she couldn't find any reference on the Internet that showed bamboo leaves were poisonous substances.

I must say, they did a fine job making Cindy out to be a liar. Our strategy paid off big-time. They could have gone through our case and called rebuttal witnesses in any number of areas, but instead they were consumed with impeaching Cindy's testimony.

We accomplished our two goals:

1) occupy their rebuttal case with things that benefit the defense and
2) get the old Cindy back.

They also called on Dr. Michael Warren to testify that opening up Caylee's skull was a bad idea. He had been the one who had super-imposed the duct tape on the color photo of Caylee, and I asked him, "That was done in Photoshop?"

Ashton objected of course, but not as much as I objected to the despicable montage created by Dr. Warren.

JUDGE PERRY ONLY GAVE US one day to prepare for closing arguments, and I knew my closing arguments were going to be around four hours long. It was mostly a matter of organizing the exhibits and the order I wanted to present my arguments.

If you remember, I wrote my closing arguments first—before anything else, so I would know where we were and where we wanted to end up.

On the day of closing arguments, Judge Perry ruled that we had submitted enough evidence to show that Caylee had died by accidentally drowning in the pool, but that I couldn't argue anything about Casey being sexually molested by her father or her brother because we hadn't proved it or shown any evidence of it. As far as I was concerned, there was as much evidence of sexual abuse in this trial as there was about murder, and I could reasonably make the argument that there was significantly more.

There was no direct evidence. It was all circumstantial. I get that. But I argued that we showed that there was plenty of evidence: the paternity test done by the FBI to see if Lee was the father; that Casey hadn't been to a gynecologist until she was nineteen years old; and that she had had her menstrual cycle since she was ten and that she had had an irregular menstrual cycle and other female problems. I mean, wasn't that a pretty good indication that her parents were keeping her from a doctor so her sexual activity wouldn't be found out?

Judge Perry sarcastically commented that he had never had one of those exams in his life.

"It is common sense," I said. "Both sides will ask the jurors to use their common sense."

I continued, "The court can make a reasonable inference from the hidden pregnancy, and there is evidence about Ms. Anthony's sexual background and behavior that stems from sexual abuse. I spoke of her other behavior, the compartmentalization, the lying which is consistent with someone who has been sexually abused.

"There's no more evidence that this child was killed by chloroform than there is of sexual abuse. I think they're equal. Both of these theories ask the jurors to draw from inferences, and the jury is going to hear arguments of chloroform and of duct tape, of which there is also no evidence.

"While there are no witnesses, there is the testimony of Tony Lazzaro, that they had shared secrets. As the court knows, and as everyone knows, the testimony and the good faith basis is that the secret has to do with molestation, improper sexual behavior and incest. To ignore it or to pretend none of it exists just because someone didn't get up on the stand and actually say it doesn't make it less real. It's the equal to what the state says about chloroform."

After my argument, Judge Perry issued his findings.

He said, "The court hereby finds that there's no facts in evidence or reasonable inference that can be drawn therefrom that there is evidence that either Mr. George Anthony or Mr. Lee Anthony molested or attempted to molest Ms. Anthony."

Here's the crazy part. Judge Perry decided this on his own. The state didn't make a motion to exclude this. He brought it up, and he ruled on it. In all my years of trying cases, I had never seen a judge do this before. Maybe some do, and I hadn't seen it until then.

Maybe the prosecutors wanted the issue to go before the jury so they could argue against it, ridicule it, criticize it.

I don't believe a judge should be making motions and objections.

Just before I got up to do my closing arguments, I was very calm and ready. I was actually anxious, looking forward to it, ready to do it. My co-counsel Dorothy Clay Sims, one who was never shy about holding back what she was thinking, was worried; just before I was about to get up, she handed me a list of things to say during the closing.

"How am I going to look at this now?" I asked, and I handed it back to her.

"Don't worry, Dorothy," I said to her. "I got this."

With that I arose and did my thing.

I began by telling the jurors that I was sure they had more questions than they had answers. I'm also sure that you, my reader, do too.

"One question that will never be answered," I said, "can never be proven, and that is, *how did Caylee die? What happened to her?* That evidence was never presented to you. In fact there were a great deal of things that you were probably looking for and never received."

I told the jury that the state has to prove its case beyond a reasonable doubt and to the exclusion of every reasonable doubt, that the prosecution gets to go last because it's the state's burden.

"It's not a two-sided affair," I said. "The state has the only burden here."

I told the jury we had put on evidence and testimony, but that we weren't required to do so.

"We could have sat back, not questioned one single witness, and done absolutely nothing throughout the course of this trial, and the prosecution still had the burden to prove every element and every charge."

I then told the jury, after talking about my biggest fear, I would outline the state's case piece by piece, and then talk about the defense's case, "even though we weren't required to do anything."

"Let me start with my biggest fear," I said. "This case deals with so much emotion. I know there were times where every single person here felt something deep inside." I talked about the guidance the law gives them when it comes to their emotions.

I then showed them a huge exhibit of the Florida Rules for Deliberation, which read in part, "This case must not be decided for or against anyone because you feel sorry for anyone, or are angry at anyone." And then I added, "and that's because we want you to base your verdict on the evidence, not on emotion. And it's my biggest fear because it's such a difficult thing for you to push aside. Caylee Anthony was a beautiful, sweet, innocent child who died too soon. But to parade her up here to invoke your emotions would be improper."

"It's improper under the law, and it's improper to the rules of your deliberation. And I submit to you, that is the way the state presented its case."

"They started with—let me start with Mr. Ashton's remarks to you today.

"Mr. Ashton started out showing you a video of little Caylee, started talking to you about parenting, about what a mother should or should not do. He went on for a great length of time talking about this beautiful child. They gave you two weeks of testimony that was completely irrelevant and served only one purpose, and that was to paint Casey Anthony as a slut, as a party girl, as a girl who lies, and that has absolutely nothing to do with how Caylee died. And you would dishonor the law, and even Caylee's memory, if you were to base your decision on anything but the evidence—to use emotion to get you angry is improper."

There's a backstory behind Ashton using that video of Casey and Caylee to begin their case. I also had possession of that video, and before I gave my closing arguments, Dorothy told me I should play it.

"You have to show the jury how much these two loved each other," she said. "It's important."

"That's come out already in the testimony," I said. "What that's doing is playing on the jury's emotions, and I've been arguing from the very beginning that the prosecutor is the one playing on their emotions, so I can't do that."

"But this is too good a video not to play it," she said.

"Sorry, Dorothy," I said, "I just don't think it's the right thing to do. And I won't do it."

Lo and behold, Ashton got up to give his closing argument, and starts it by playing that same video!

I leaned over to Dorothy and said, "I told you he was on our side."

"Though the state called a string of witnesses to testify to Casey's bad behavior, what's interesting is that everyone the state called kept coming back with the same thing: Casey was a good mother. Caylee loved Casey. I asked many questions as to how Caylee reacted to Casey because I thought it important that you understand that a child cannot fake this. A child cannot fake love. A child knows when someone is loved. It behaves a certain way. And I did this not to appeal to your emotion. It was especially directed at the child abuse charges."

"You didn't hear one single instance having anything to do with child abuse. Not one. Ask yourself, when did someone get on this stand and tell me or demonstrate to me in any way that Caylee was abused?" I could literally see jurors number three and ten nodding their heads.

"Child abuse cases are sad. They're one of the most horrible crimes imaginable. One thing is for certain. If there's an abused child, people know about it. People see bruises. People see different things about the child. There will be broken bones. But there was nothing other than the fact that this child was loved and well taken care of."

The implication was clear. In discussing what happened to Caylee, the jurors would have to rely on the evidence.

"What was put before you? I agree with one statement that Mr. Ashton said, and that is you can't speculate. Don't speculate. Don't guess. If you don't know what happened, it wasn't proven. There are no mysteries to solve here."

This statement was directed to juror number one based on a conversation that she and I had during jury selection. I was reinforcing it, and when you do that you'll have no greater ally in the deliberation room than someone who has been educated on the law.

I concluded, "If you have questions, then it was not proven. And that's as simple as it goes."

When I began my closing arguments, Ashton sat in his chair laughing, and grimacing, and making faces. It was something he did during my opening statement to the jury. Three or four times during the trial I brought it to Judge Perry's attention at sidebar, and each time he dismissed my concerns about it.

We had a break, and I could see he was still doing it, so when we came back into court the very first thing I said to Judge Perry was, "Your Honor, I want to point out that Mr. Ashton continues to make faces and he is laughing during my closing arguments."

"I haven't seen him making any faces," was Judge Perry's response.

He was apparently blocked from seeing Ashton by the exhibits I had brought for my closing.

He's going to let him get away with it, I told myself.

I resumed my closing arguments and was on a roll, talking about George's connection to the duct tape and the gas cans, and out of the corner of my eye I could see the laughter coming from Ashton. He was acting so inappropriately that I didn't miss a beat when instinctively, reflexively, I pointed to him and said, "It doesn't matter who's asking the questions, whether it's this laughing guy right here..."

Ashton jumped up and objected, and we went sidebar.

I was done with him.

This is not the way a trial should be run, I felt. I was disgusted with the whole process and ready to accept responsibility for my actions.

This is not justice, I told myself.

At sidebar Judge Perry could not have been more upset with me, and after sending out the jury for fifteen minutes, he laid into me.

"Tell me why I shouldn't hold you in contempt of court for violation of this court's order about not making disparaging personal remarks against counsel," he said.

"I don't believe that was a disparaging remark about counsel. I was just merely pointing out his behavior."

He said I should approach the bench, and when I did, he said he could not see Ashton because of the exhibits.

"If you would move those signs where I can see Mr. Ashton, then I would be able to see him."

"Sir, would you like me to move a seat over?" Ashton asked in his most unctuous way.

"Yeah," said the judge.

I hadn't gotten a lot of words out, when one of the court administrators told him, "It's on TV, and you can see Ashton laughing."

Judge Perry went into his back room and watched the video of Ashton carrying on. When he came back his anger was directed at Ashton.

He told everyone, "Go look at it, and I'm going to do what I need to do."

"Your honor," said Ashton, sucking up as only he could, "I trust your judgment about whatever it is you saw, and I don't need to see it." He went anyway.

He told us to go back and look at the video if we wanted to. We did, and there he was, laughing like he was at a comedy club, rather than a murder trial of a baby.

When we came back, Ashton told the judge, "Your honor, as I viewed the video, I appear to be smiling behind my hand. I wasn't laughing. I wasn't nodding. I was doing what I could to make sure that my expression was not seen by the jury. If I exceeded the court's order, I apologize."

I could see Judge Perry was about to do something—I didn't know whether he was going to hold Ashton in contempt or not—or hold me in contempt for that matter—but I knew he was about to crack the whip and do something extremely harsh. I stepped up and said to him, "I would not request that Mr. Ashton be held in contempt because of his facial expressions. This case has been highly emotional for both sides, and all I really request is that it stop."

When I did that, Judge Perry calmed down, and he let us off with a warning.

That day Kerry Sanders, a correspondent for NBC, called me and said, "What you did was a very gentlemanly thing to do. It was a class act."

I thanked him, but at the end of the day when I look back, I did that as much to save my own hide as Ashton's. I knew once he was done holding Ashton in contempt, he was going to do the same to me. I didn't think for a second he would have disciplined just Ashton alone.

Some people say I won the case right then and there, or at least it was one reason the jury voted the way it did, but that's nonsense. At the same time Ashton didn't do himself any favors by acting that way.

As I said, he was always on our side.

I NOTED THAT THE PROSECUTION spared no expense hiring the finest crime labs in the country, but with all its resources, it had to create new areas of forensic science. I said that for the first time ever, a jury heard about air evidence. For the first time, they heard about hair banding, and they were the first to hear about a dog trainer testifying about his dog.

"You're the first ones to ever hear any of these types of evidence," I said. "That's what I told you from the very beginning, that this prosecution would raise the level of desperation to make up for their lack of evidence."

"I told you at the very beginning this was an accident that snowballed out of control, and while it was a very common accident, what made it unique is not what happened but who it happened to."

I said the jurors sat and watched some bizarre things during the trial, "bizarre things that have been going on long before Caylee was ever born and throughout her early life. You saw all of these things."

"There's something wrong here. There's something not right," and I told the jury that was what made Casey's behavior after Caylee's death irrelevant. I reiterated: "It's irrelevant to the number one question that you all came to answer: How did *Caylee* die?"

THE NEXT TOPIC of my closing was to let the jury know that there was not one single strand of real evidence to the state's case.

Since it was Casey's car, one thing the prosecution did was try to show Casey had put Caylee's body in her car, drove to the woods, and dumped her there. There's only one problem with that theory: even though the prosecution rounded up a posse of scientists, and even though it made up theories in a desperate attempt to show there was a body decomposing in the car, there was no evidence of that.

The prosecutors brought up a stain of decomposition in the trunk, when no stains existed. They kept bringing up how the smell in the trunk reeked of decomposition, when at the end of the day all their scientists turned out to be full of it. The trunk smelled of garbage, not decomposition, it turned out.

They needed to tie the duct tape found near Caylee's body to Casey, and so when a gas can was found with some of the same duct tape on it, they trumpeted that Casey had used the gas can, and therefore she had been the one to put the duct tape on Caylee. But it turned out there was no DNA on the duct tape found near Caylee and no fingerprints. The theory also turned out to be made up by the cops and the prosecution.

I asked the jury, "Why were there so many lies surrounding the gas cans and the duct tape? It's not a coincidence."

Then there was the sense that the police did everything they could to make sure the finger was never pointed at George.

When George went to pick up Casey's car at the lot, he not only brought his keys, but he also brought a full can of gas, because Casey had told him the car had run out of gas. He told the tow lot manager that the car had been at the Amscot lot for three days. How did George know that? Because Casey told him when it ran out of gas, and he knew.

And he smelled the smell you never forget, and he did what every responsible parent would do when his daughter and granddaughter were missing.

Nothing.

He went home and went to work.

I talked about the great lengths the police went to to make sure Casey was convicted. A dog who was inconsistent at identifying the smell of dead bodies alerted to Casey's car. The next day the dog came back and smelled—nothing. And not only that, when a dog did a test like that, he was supposed to choose among three different cars, but he only smelled one car. When asked about it, the dog handler testified that the dog had chosen between two cars, yet everyone else's testimony impeached him. Why? Because even though there turned out to be no evidence that a body had ever been in that car, the cops wanted you to think there was.

Was there the smell of death in the car? George certainly pointed it out that first night, but then Catherine Sanchez, the manager of the Amscot, said she smelled garbage. Casey's boyfriend, Tony, who rode in the car, didn't smell anything. Charity Beasley, who picked up the car and took it to the tow yard, didn't smell anything. Maria Kish also rode in the car and didn't smell anything. Sergeant Reginald Hosey smelled something. Did he call the crime scene investigators? No. There was trash in the car for three weeks.

Deputy Ryan Eberlin didn't smell anything. Detective Yuri Melich? Didn't smell anything. Corporal Rendon Fletcher? He walked right by the car while the trunk was open.

But once Casey was arrested, everyone smelled death in that car.

Is there reasonable doubt about the smell in the car?

I told the jurors to decide that for themselves.

Then there was the day Casey borrowed a shovel from her neighbor for forty minutes, and therefore the state's conclusion was that she was burying Caylee in the backyard in broad daylight. What she was doing was trying to break the lock on the garage to find some gas for her car. But to the state, her borrowing that shovel was cause for it to trumpet she was digging a hole. But when she brought the shovel back, the neighbor testified, she wasn't sweaty. When the shovel was inspected by the FBI, no DNA or any other evidence was found on it.

Is that reasonable?

What was the state doing here? They were speculating. That's not the law, but that's what they wanted the jury to do.

To win, I speculated that the police may have consciously altered and destroyed evidence. Take the trash. It was our alternate theory to their contention that the smell came from a dead body. How did they try to get rid of our contention? They dried the garbage so that it didn't smell any more.

"How can this create a smell?" the prosecution asked.

Well, it sure smelled when it was garbage—before the police altered it so it wouldn't smell.

I then talked about what I liked to call the state's fantasy of forensics. If I have made a mark in trying this case, that expression will live forever in legal history. I didn't use it to make a name for myself. I used it because it was true. The state's case was a mixture of invented evidence and science fiction.

Early on, the cops leaked that there was blood in the trunk of Casey's car. There was a stain from human decomposition. They said there were maggots in the car, and that was proof of human decomposition.

None of it was true, but all this "evidence" was spread through the media to trial fans throughout the country. The anger against Casey grew because she was a woman who killed her daughter in order to go out and party, a series of charges of which NONE WERE TRUE.

But here's what the state hoped: if the jury was angry enough at Casey, if its emotions were riled up, if it stared hard enough and long enough, it just might see a stain in the back of that car.

That's not evidence. Evidence would be a DNA report. It was a phantom stain. It's there—you just can't see it.

The state's case was nothing but desperation.

Dr. Neal Haskell and Dr. Tim Huntington talked about the bugs in the trunk of the car. Or should I say bugs in the trash bag? The insect the state found is commonly found in garbage. Since the state had no DNA evidence or any blood, it instead gave us speculation: if the police found maggots, there must have been a dead body.

Anger and emotion: that's what the state wanted to fill in the gaps with.

Why were there allegations that there was a body in the trunk?

It's to make up for a lack of evidence. To keep the jury guessing. To have it take that leap of faith into a place where it should not and could not go under the law.

Next the prosecutors talked about the hair. Or rather *one* hair. And they said it had post-mortem root banding, proof that the one hair came from a dead Caylee, hence Caylee's body was in the trunk of the car.

But it turned out that the science was unable to determine whether the hair came from a dead body or from a hair that was discolored from spending a long time in the trunk while it was being subjected to chemicals and heat.

One thing we did know: they were talking about *one hair*. They had taken hair from the trunk, hair from the trash bag, hair from her home—they went crazy trying to find more hairs so they could say the hair came from a dead body. And they found hundreds more hairs, but not one more with post-mortem root banding.

What are they doing here? Let's throw it all against the wall and see what sticks, right down to the cause of death. One week it was chloroform. Later it's duct tape. Let's make up our minds.

Then we get to the chloroform. When I first heard chloroform mentioned in this case, I thought it was a joke. This issue came up because of Dr. Arpad Vass. He testified that the levels of chloroform were "shockingly high." But all he performed was a qualitative analysis, not a quantitative one. He had no idea what the levels were. But what did he say? He said the levels were "unusually high." And it was spread to the world by the media like a radioactive cloud from an atomic bomb. Casey had killed her daughter using chloroform.

And it turned out this guy was selling a machine which was supposed to be able to identify whether chemicals came from a dead body. Someone stood to make millions if only he could make it known how great his data was in this trial. The trouble was that the data was faulty, and as it turns out, there is no reliable chemical signature of human decomposition yet. It's in its infancy stage, and some of his work is groundbreaking, but it doesn't make it sound science. That doesn't make it true.

The prosecution was pushing the boundaries of science. That's what Vass was doing here. When I questioned Dr. Marcus Wise, his colleague, Wise said it was impossible to tell how much chloroform there had been in the trunk because a quantitative test was scientifically impossible. Meanwhile, another chemist said the main component found in the trunk of the car was gasoline.

Was the state giving jurors the truth when someone's life hangs in the balance?

The jury had to look at the lack of evidence and wonder why some of these questions weren't answered. I suggest that this lack of straightforwardness is unacceptable.

This is the level of absurdity, the desperation that the prosecutors will take it to. They asked the jurors to see things that weren't there. They asked the jurors to imagine fictional science. It was a fantasy of forensics. That's what it was. And nothing more.

We have the most advanced crime-fighting tools available to us anywhere in the world, and they couldn't find a single link from Casey to Caylee's death. Not a single link. But yet they wanted to create things? For what? The cameras? Because it was a high-profile case? No. Because it was all about winning. Winning at all costs. No matter how much it cost. No matter what it cost. No matter how much justice was perverted.

Then I took the jury to where I thought the evidence showed where this case reached its most outrageous level, and that is the computer searches. A report came in that someone—the state said it was Casey—had visited a chloroform site one time. But at trial the man who made the report, Sergeant Kevin Stenger, didn't testify. Instead, John Bradley testified that he developed a new program that indicated that someone had visited a chloroform site eighty-four times.

"There were eighty-four searches for chloroform" was what was spread to the world via another atomic blast from the media via the police.

It was a jaw-dropping moment for me, and it turned out the second program was faulty. The reality was Casey had looked up chloroform once after Ricardo Morales had sent her a Myspace photo entitled "Win her over with Chloroform." And it turned out she had spent exactly three minutes finding out what her boyfriend was referring to.

The evidence he testified to, when challenged, failed and in the faulty report, the Myspace searches weren't even there.

We called the man who wrote the report to the stand to expose the truth. You see why even though we had no burden to do so, we called witnesses, police officers to the stand, to bring the truth to light so the jury could render a just verdict.

This was their murder case? How could they come forward with this evidence? How was that the truth? That's why there were more questions than answers. Fantasy searches, phantom stains, all of this nonsense and no real hard evidence. No DNA. No fingerprints. Nothing but Casey was a liar and a slut. Convict her on that. And she lied. And she didn't act the way she needs to. She made some stupid decisions, but let's make her pay with her life.

That's what the case was all about.

I continued in that vein for another couple of hours. As I was standing there in the courtroom reciting act after act of duplicity by the cops and the prosecution, I became angrier and angrier. Was I the only sane one in this courtroom? If you read the papers and watched the TV, you never would have guessed it. Here I was, the rookie lawyer from Kissimmee, spending twenty hours a day in a battle with trained scientists and veteran police officers to free a client who the world wanted to see jailed and even put to death.

I felt I was someone out of *Alice in Wonderland*, where some crazy queen was going around hollering "off with her head." The only way the lunacy was going to stop, I knew, was with a not-guilty verdict.

After the prosecution closed with its usual rant about Casey's bad character and how badly she behaved during the thirty days after Caylee's death, it rested.

The case would soon be in the hands of the jury.

CHAPTER 33

JUSTICE

I FINISHED MY CLOSING ARGUMENTS, and I sat down. Cheney followed with a very good closing argument explaining reasonable doubt to the jurors in a very eloquent and patriotic way.

My work was done. There was nothing more I could say or do in this trial before the jury would deliberate. We then took a break, and I did with Casey what I do with all my clients in all my trials. I walked over to her, knelt down, and I said to her, "That's it, Casey. There's nothing more I can do. I hope you know I fought like hell for you, want you to know I tried my best, left no stone unturned, and I hope you're satisfied with the work I did. I really do."

"I know you did," she said, "and I will never be able to thank you enough for it."

It was an intimate moment, and a reporter from *In Session*, Jean Casares, reported on it, saying that Casey and I had a "tender moment," and she speculated on what she was seeing—she couldn't hear what we were saying—and it was a rarity—the very first time in three-and-a-half years that any of those speculative reports got it right.

After Cheney spoke, we took a break for the day. The morning Jeff Ashton made his closing arguments, and while I was listening to him, I kept wishing I could have had another shot at him, because some of the things he was saying amazed me.

One thing made my jaw drop. He admitted that the prosecution didn't believe that Roy Kronk was credible, that he wasn't being truthful. Once again it was, don't trust the messenger but trust the message. After saying that there was no way that George Anthony could have been involved in any way, shape, or form, he began to give crazy arguments of alternative ways in which Caylee might have died, either with duct tape or chloroform. He was saying, "If she died this way, you can find the defendant guilty. If she died that way, you can find the defendant guilty," and it was right about then that I looked over toward the jury and I could see juror eleven, who would soon be the jury foreman, look at Ashton with his eyebrows clenched together as if to say, *Are you kidding me? What is this that you're throwing at us?*

I just shook my head. From start to finish, instead of giving the jury evidence, he fed the jury emotion and anger.

Linda Drane Burdick closed out the prosecution's case. Before, Burdick was always monotone, but when she got up this time I witnessed a totally different Linda Drane Burdick. Her arguments were perfectly delivered. She was articulate, and she was brilliant. I was watching a lawyer in the zone.

She finished on an incredibly high note, asking whose life benefitted from Caylee's death, and she put up on the screen a photo of Casey partying side by side with a photo of her tattoo La Bella Vita, and she said, "There's your answer," and she sat down, walking away leaving the images there for the jury to ponder.

The jury broke to deliberate, and I walked over to Burdick and said to her, "That was incredible. I'm not sure I've seen a prosecutor give a better closing argument than that."

"Well," she said, "I watched yours, and you had me really scared."

We agreed at a future date to sit down and talk about the case, one professional to another and hopefully learn from each other's presentation as well as mistakes.

We broke for the day. The case was over for the lawyers. The members of our defense team, including our interns, went across the street from the courthouse to a restaurant called Terrace 390, where we had beers and a couple of drinks.

We were relaxing at the bar, unwinding, when the prosecution team, Frank George, Burdick, and Ashton walked in.

"Hey, let me buy you a drink," I said to George. I did that, and I bought Burdick a drink, and I said to them all, "Hey, let's all sit down together and have a well-deserved drink."

George and Burdick started to come over, when Ashton said to them, "No, I don't want to sit with them. Let's go sit over here," and they went and sat at the other end of the bar.

"If he tried, I don't think he could be a bigger asshole," said one of our interns.

The next day was the fourth of July, and we stayed in court as the jury continued to deliberate. I wasn't nervous during deliberations. A lot of lawyers are, and I used to be when I first tried cases, but it's futile. I can't go bang on the door of the jury room and try to say one or two more things to them to change their minds. It is what it is, and there's nothing I can do to change it.

I was relaxed, and during that day I went to church a couple of times. As I sat there in a pew, I was thinking about wanting to save Casey's life, and praying for my family. Right then and there, I realized how much I had sacrificed for Casey, how much this case took me away from my family, and how it took something away that I may never be able to get back, including my life savings, my home, and nearly my practice.

I gave everything I had in this case, I said to myself. *Maybe I gave too much of me.* I prayed about that, asking God to make me a better person, a better father, a better husband, because I knew I hadn't been any of those.

In my search for serenity that day, I drove to the Ritz-Carlton hotel in Orlando. It's a beautiful property, and there's a spot I find very peaceful, and I went back there to relax and take my mind off things. I sat down, admiring the palm trees and the flowers, and not twenty minutes went by when my phone rang. Karen Levy, the court administrator said, "I've been instructed to call you to say that the jury has reached a verdict."

She said it with such a happy tone, and I was trying to figure out, *Does she know? Does she have the verdict forms? Does she know what the verdict is? If so, why is she so happy?*

The jury had been out a day and a half for approximately ten-and-a-half hours. I drove to the courthouse and brought my car around to the sheriff's bay so I could escape the mob, and I walked upstairs.

I was led through the side entrance, but the prosecutors walked through the normal entrance past a legion of spectators. Ashton was so sure Casey was going to be found guilty that he was seen by numerous people high-fiving the spectators on his way in for the verdict.

When I arrived in the courthouse everybody was already there. I was the last to arrive. Judge Belvin Perry had set a time limit for us to get there, and I made it with ten minutes to spare.

I could see Burdick over at the defense table talking to Cheney.

"Hey, how are you?" I said to Burdick.

"I want you to know that I wish you the best of luck in your career and in your future," she said.

"I wish you the same," I replied, "but only after the next fifteen minutes."

We both had a chuckle, and she walked back over to her side of the room.

Judge Perry took his place, and he called everyone to order.

"I understand the jury has reached a verdict," he said.

The jury walked in. A lot of lawyers say they can tell what the jury has decided by looking at their faces. If the jurors do not look at the defendant or at the defense table, a lot of times it's because they have found the defendant guilty.

A couple of the jurors had looked over at me frequently during the trial, but this time they weren't doing it. They all were stone-faced, but I could not get a sense whether their vibe was negative or positive. I just couldn't read them.

The foreman, it turned out, was the physical education teacher, the juror who had taken the most notes. This wasn't a surprise. He seemed the most likely candidate for the job.

He handed over the verdict forms. Judge Perry also was stone-faced, and I could see him look down at the verdict forms and see his face turn angry.

He checked each form, and then he checked them again.

Why's he doing that? I asked myself. *Why is he checking them again?*

My antennae went up.

"Madame clerk," he said, "you may read the verdict." He handed her the forms.

Then Judge Perry took a quick glance over at us, and I thought, *This is going to be interesting.* It told me he was not happy with the verdict.

The clerk started to read and stumbled as she spoke, but she regained her composure and said, "As to the count of murder in the first degree . . . not guilty."

When she said that, I said to myself, *I did it. I saved her life.* And at that moment, I reached over and squeezed Casey's hand.

Then the verdict came in as to aggravated child abuse.

"Not guilty." I squeezed her hand even tighter.

Then the verdict as to aggravated manslaughter of a child.

"Not guilty." And I squeezed her hand so hard I feared that I had broken a bone.

I was looking at the clerk, and as to the next charges of lying to law enforcement, the clerk announced: "Guilty." But I thought to myself, *Wait a minute. The serious charges are gone. It's over. It's over. Oh my God. This is incredible. We did it.*

The jury was polled, and then I hugged Casey and put my hand on the side of her head, and I said, "We did it, kiddo."

"Thank you," was all she said, and she hugged me.

The judge put a stop to that by calling us over. He said he was adjudicating her not guilty on the first three charges but guilty on the fourth and that he would set sentencing two days hence, on Friday.

What a phenomenal, incredible rush for all of us. We were all crying and hugging. When I hugged Jeanine Barrett, our mitigation specialist, she completely lost it. At one point William and Michelle and Cheney and I all hugged together. We were so happy for Casey. This poor girl had suffered through her childhood, suffered through the loss of her daughter, was thrown to the wolves by her father, and was ripped to shreds by the media. We were hoping that after being found innocent, she would be able to resume a normal life. George and Burdick walked over and shook our hands. Ashton did not.

We remained in the courtroom after the judge, the jury, the prosecution, and all the spectators left. All that remained were members of the media who wanted to watch us and report on how we were reacting.

I won't lie. Numerous times I had allowed myself to dream about what I would say to the legion of all my media detractors when Casey was actually found not guilty, and I thought to myself, *Wow. You're finally going to have the opportunity to rub their noses in it and really tell them where they can stick it.*

But as I looked over at them, I then decided, *You know what? It's not worth it. They're not worth it,* and when we held our after-trial press conference, I was very subdued. I thought of Caylee, and I thought of the prosecutors, and I said, "There are no winners here. We're happy for Casey, but at the same time Caylee passed far too soon." I took the high road and complimented the prosecutors, saying they had worked hard and had served the state of Florida very well.

"They didn't deserve anyone's criticism," I said, calling them out individually. And by that I mean I included Ashton.

For me this was like a boxing match. During the match you try to rip the other guy's head off, but when it's over you shake hands and have a mutual amount of respect for each other.

I thought it would be that way, but unfortunately, this case proved otherwise.

We were taken out of the courthouse by a SWAT team, who didn't want us going out the front door because it was too crazy out there. We got into white vans under SWAT team cover. We were literally dropped off across the street in front of the Terrace 390 restaurant. It was a *very* short ride.

Once in the restaurant we were alone. The owners had closed it down for us, and we had a very badly needed drink. We figured, *Okay, let's watch the media coverage*, and for the first time we really did that. We ordered champagne, and we had a toast, and Cheney said, "To the Constitution of the United States." And we toasted the U.S. Constitution.

A crowd began to form outside the restaurant. There are few secrets anymore, as fifty media representatives, many with cameras, pressed their noses to the windows.

Geraldo Rivera was the only media representative I allowed in. He came in and gave me a hug and said he was proud of me. Cheney let in Jean Casares, but before I knew it, she was on her phone reporting what she was seeing inside, and I made her stop. This was for us, not for the media.

Other media people wanted to come in, but I said no. I wanted to be with the team, and this was our time to spend together in celebration. We loosened our ties and relaxed, and while we were chatting, members of the national media called me on my cell phone and each network said the same thing, "Jose, your first media interview is a big one. You can have any correspondent out there to conduct it. Name the person, and we'll make it happen."

I knew exactly who I wanted: the incomparable Barbara Walters. A few years earlier, I had watched her interview Tom Mesereau after he had won the Michael Jackson case, the biggest trial of the time, and I said to myself, *One day I'd like to be in that position. If I were to work hard, I would hope my talents would be recognized.*

And here it was, a dream come true.

I didn't hesitate to say I wanted the interviewer to be Barbara Walters, and not twenty minutes later I got the call, "Barbara wants to talk with you."

Barbara and I spoke briefly on the phone, and she said, "We'll fly you up tonight, and we'd love to have you here."

I couldn't believe it. I had been talking on the phone to Barbara Walters.

I didn't have to be back in court for two more days for the sentencing, so that night I was picked up and I flew to New York, and I did my first—and only—post-trial interview with Barbara Walters.

Everyone came calling, everyone, but at the end of the day I thought, *The verdict speaks for itself. I'm not going to make the rounds and gloat. It's not the right thing to do.*

I wanted to be gracious in victory. I didn't want to come across as a blowhard.

IF YOU WERE TO ASK ME whether Casey received a fair trial, my personal opinion would be no. A lot of Judge Belvin Perry's rulings would have come back on appeal. But having said that, what the judge did extremely well was make sure Casey had a fair jury.

During jury selection he gave us ample time to interview the jurors, to speak to them. He also was very strict when it came to protecting the jurors from outside influences. He sequestered them, and he also kept up their mood and their stamina. He went out of his way to make sure this jury wasn't influenced, and that was no easy task. It was a massive undertaking, and he did it with flying colors.

WE RETURNED TO THE COURTROOM for sentencing. Ashton wasn't in attendance. As soon as the trial was over, he immediately announced his retirement. He retired literally within hours of the verdict. And then he flew to New York to do media appearances.

When we were celebrating at Terrace 390 after the verdict, one of the media people calling me informed me that Ashton was going to be on the *Today* show. I texted Linda Drane Burdick asking her if she knew.

"I know now," she texted back.

What I ended up finding out was that even before the trial began, Ashton had hired Annie Scranton, a publicist, who three weeks before the verdict had booked him for the *Today* show. This appearance was supposed to be his victory dance. The idea was for him to fly the next morning after the verdict, and the only reason he wouldn't be on the show was if there was a first-degree murder conviction, and then he would do the show after the penalty phase. There were rumors that early on in the trial she was going around looking for a ghostwriter for him.

Now I don't have a problem with Ashton writing a book. I'd be a hypocrite if I did, but when I was trying this case, a book was the furthest thing from my mind, and it appears it was the *only* thing on his mind while trying this case. His book came out in November—the verdict was in July—so you can imagine how quickly they had to put it together.

What bothers me the most is that he had filed a motion accusing me of having a conflict of interest, when in fact there could be no more of a conflict of interest for a prosecutor—a minister of justice on a death penalty case—when your intention is to profit. I am appalled that someone had that much authority and was able to do what he did. And I'll take it a step further. Hands down the thing that bothered me the most about Jeff Ashton was that he didn't bother to show up for the sentencing.

If I had lost this trial, and Casey would have been convicted of first-degree murder, I would have had to turn over the case to Ann Finnel, our death penalty lawyer, and I wouldn't have had a role in the penalty phase. It would have been the most difficult thing for me to do, passing all the "I told you so" guys in the media, the public, everyone, who were saying for months, "I told you she was going to fry." But I would have done it. I would have gone to court, and I would have been there every single day. This guy didn't even have the decency to show up and sit next to his team at sentencing. I felt horrible for Burdick and George, having to sit there without Ashton, who was in part responsible for the not-guilty verdict. He was off to New York making media appearances and book deals, instead of being at the sentencing with his team.

It's what cowards do—run away when they lose. They refuse to face the music. I can think of nothing worse to do to your team, and all I have to say about that is that Jeff Ashton, you're a coward.

AFTER THE VERDICT WAS ANNOUNCED, the only person who called to thank me for saving Casey's life was Lee Anthony. He called with a very touching message.

Afterward I said to Cindy, "You never even thanked me for saving your daughter's life."

"Yes, I did," she said.

But in actuality, she hadn't.

WE WERE HOPING JUDGE PERRY would give Casey credit for time served rather than make her stay in jail for ten more days, but we had no illusions about that happening.

Sure enough, he gave her the maximum time, and she was released ten days later on July 17, 2011.

Now the hard part: where does she go from here?

CHAPTER 34

A PRISONER IN
HER OWN FREEDOM

A FTER SENTENCING, I had ten days to formulate a plan for getting Casey out of jail. I asked my California lawyer friend Todd Macaluso if he would fly his plane to Orlando so we could fly Casey out of the Orlando Executive Airport to someplace safe. There were too many crazies who were convinced she had killed Caylee while she danced the night away, and I feared for her safety.

I met a couple times with jail officials. We talked to the tactical-support team members, and they suggested that Casey and I wear bulletproof vests when leaving the jail.

"If you remember Timothy McVeigh," said one of them, "every time he came and went, he wore a bulletproof vest."

"She's not Timothy McVeigh." I replied sternly. Timothy McVeigh had bombed a federal building in Oklahoma City and killed more than a hundred people. Casey stood trial and had been found not guilty.

"No," I said, "we're walking out the front door, and you're going to protect us."

I had a meeting in our office with our entire staff to discuss how we were going to get Casey from the jail to the airport. In addition to avoiding an army of media, we knew we were going to also duck the surveillance of a half dozen helicopters.

To help us get away, the police agreed to shut down the John Young Parkway for three minutes once we left the jail to give us enough time to get on the highway, but I knew the media would stake out both sides of the highway, and getting to the airport wouldn't be so easy.

William Slabaugh came up with the idea of our driving to a multilevel garage, where the helicopters couldn't see us, driving a bunch of cars in the garage, and making them guess which car Casey was in as all the cars left the building.

Cheney's building had such a garage and it was across the street from the courthouse. It was perfect.

We brainstormed and came up with different ideas. We talked of driving into the garage, walking out, and taking a different car to the airport. Or taking the elevator to a different floor and leaving in a different car. Or switching to a second car, sitting there for an hour, waiting until the media left, and then leaving.

At the airport, Todd put his plane in a hangar so no one would see it. According to Todd, the media helicopters were based at the executive airport. We'd be driving into the lion's den.

Even worse, someone learned of our plan and alerted the media that we intended to fly out of the Orlando Executive Airport. So not only were we going to be followed from the jail, but the media would be staking out the airport.

Part of the plan was to drive to a shopping center near the executive airport, and from there an executive of the airport would drive up through a back gate to the plane. But we first had to get to the mall to meet him.

Casey wasn't going to be released until midnight, so we spent the entire day working on our getaway plans. An hour before our departure time, we made a quick drive-by of the jail, and outside in the dark, two hundred protesters and gawkers were setting up tents, carrying the usual hateful signs like "The Bitch Should Be Fried," and "Boycott Casey." She did have two supporters. One carried a sign saying, "Casey, will you marry me?" and the other's said, "She's not guilty. Get over it."

I thought to myself, *One sane person out of two hundred. Not bad.*

I looked up in the sky, and there was a small plane pulling a big *She's Guilty and She Should Die* banner. Someone had gone to a lot of expense to express his or her anger.

We returned to the office. My law school interns met us there. All of them were going to drive into Cheney's garage. Robert Haney was our security guard. Casey and I would start in his car and then switch to William's car inside the garage where no one could see us. It would be midnight, and no one else would be there. After all our cars entered the garage, our plan was for Pat McKenna to stop his car at the garage entrance and prevent anyone else's car from entering.

Then all the cars would leave. One would have Casey and me. One car would go east, one west, one north, one south, and the fifth car would go to the airport.

With our plan set, we went through the back way of the jail, as film crews shot us going in. After they patted me down, I went to a back room where Casey was sitting. She was wearing a dark pink polo shirt with jeans and some funky tennis shoes that had two-colored laces.

"Hey," I said

"Hey," Casey said.

Looking at her sneakers, I said, "What the hell is that all about?"

"They don't exactly have a shopping mall here at the jail," she said. "It's what your office gave me, remember?"

As we sat there for the ten minutes until the clock struck midnight, I explained our plan to her, how Haney would pull up in his SUV, and I told her about the three options once we arrived inside the parking garage. As I looked at my watch, waiting for midnight, I said, "I can't believe this day has finally come."

"I can't either," she said, shaking her head. "I'm still trying to figure out, what am I going to do next?"

"The good thing is that you have the option of what to do next," I said.

A small tear fell down her cheek. She smiled, and at that moment the chief of the jail came over and said, "Okay, we're ready to go."

We had made sure Casey had packed all her stuff so she could leave unencumbered, and as she walked out the jail door to freedom, she was escorted by a SWAT team in full riot gear. As she passed one of the guards, she turned to him and whispered, "Thank you." He was one of the guards who had escorted her from the jail to the courthouse every day, and she told me he had been really decent with her.

When we walked out, some photographers from the Associated Press were allowed to be in attendance, and I could hear the clicking of cameras. I was focused on making sure we had an unobstructed walk to

Haney's SUV, and as soon as we walked out that door, I heard screams, the way teenagers screamed for Justin Bieber at one of his concerts. I'm certain they were yelling "Baby Killer" and the like, but after going from total silence to the sound of insanity, neither one of us could make out a single word they were saying.

We got in the car, and Haney drove away. We sat in the back of the SUV trying to stay out of sight. The streets were completely empty because of the two-minute head start they gave us, and Haney drove at a good rate of speed, six helicopters flying above us—when we drove into the parking garage across the street from the courthouse. The media freaked out.

"They're going into the courthouse. I don't understand."

It was midnight, and at night Cheney's parking garage only has one entrance. After we entered, McKenna parked his car at the entrance as we had planned. No one would be able to follow us in the garage.

Haney started speeding up the ramp to the next floor and then the next, and when we got to the third floor I saw our intern Shakema Wallace's car sitting there, and I yelled, "Stop." On the spot, I discarded our plans one, two, and three, and decided what we should do was get in Shakema's car.

I previously told Casey, "When we stop, hold my hand and stay close, because we're going to do this fast."

"Got it," said Casey.

I opened the door, grabbed Casey's hand, pulled her out, and I was so hopped up with adrenalin, I forgot she was there and slammed the car door on her leg before she could even get out of the car.

"Owwwwww," she yelped.

"Oh, I'm so sorry," I said. "I'm really sorry."

Shakema couldn't have been more surprised. This bright-eyed law student was in a civil procedure class one day and the next acting as the getaway driver for the most hated woman in America.

"Let's go," I said, and she headed down the ramps to the exit. Shakema and all the other interns had taped paper to their windows, so when the five intern cars left the garage, there was no way of knowing which car Casey was in. I had someone stand at the ticket booth paying for each car as it left.

One car went east, one north, one west, one south. Shakema headed east, and as we drove we didn't see anyone following us. We did, however, have a helicopter above us. A different helicopter followed each one of us.

We drove until we were about ten miles from the airport, but that damn helicopter kept us in sight. We got on the phone to William who suggested we drive to Lake Mary where there was a heavily wooded area. We could part under the big oak trees and sit there quietly until the helicopter went away.

We switched into William's car, and finally, the helicopter lost patience and went away.

I called Todd.

"Dude," he said, "there are another five or six helicopters flying over this airport."

"How can that be? There were six helicopters following us."

"They must have all come here after you lost them. They apparently know we're flying out of here."

Great.

Okay, I thought, *we've got to kill some time, and maybe they'll think we've already left, and they'll go away.*

We drove around, and I had no idea where we were, but Casey did.

"You know about three blocks up on the left, do you know who lives there?" she asked.

"Zanny?" I blurted out.

We cracked up laughing.

"Don't make me punch you," she said.

William and I kept laughing.

"Are you hungry?" I asked her.

Jail food is miserable, and the first thing someone who's spent a long time in jail wants is a decent meal, and Casey said, "Yeah, I could eat something."

William pulled into an all-night Steak 'n Shake, and he got us cheeseburgers, fries, and milkshakes.

Her first meal of freedom was a cheeseburger, fries, and a chocolate shake.

I called Todd.

"We'll head over in a little while," I said. We drove to the shopping mall where we met with the airport executive. He drove us into a back area of the airport.

"It's still dangerous to drive to the hangar," he said, "because they'll be able to see you. The helicopters are still flying above the airport."

We literally waited three hours for them to get tired and go away. We sat in the car with our lights off, and two did. Then came a moment when the remaining choppers had to come in and refuel, and boom, we hit the gas and sped into the hangar.

"So what's our destination?" the pilot wanted to know.

"St. George Island," I said. It's on the Florida panhandle near Panama City and not far from Apalachicola, the oyster capital of the world. I had been there once for a weekend when I was a student at Florida State University. You can rent a house on the beach and have complete privacy. Our entire team was going to spend the weekend relaxing and talking about where Casey was going to go.

Dorothy Clay Sims drove in her car from Orlando with Michelle and my wife Lorena, and Pat McKenna also drove down after his duties in the parking garage were over. It's about a six-hour drive from Orlando.

We took off, and even though one of the helicopters saw us, they had no way of knowing whether Casey was inside. It didn't take an hour before we were flying high above St. George's Island.

I called Dorothy and told her to meet us at the airport, which was less than a mile from the house we rented.

As we were arriving the pilot called Todd into the cockpit. Todd said to me, "Can you call Dorothy?"

"Sure, why?"

"Tell her to flash her lights so we can find the airport."

"What do you mean, flash her lights?" I wanted to know.

"The airport is closed," Todd said, "and it doesn't have any of its runway lights on."

"What good is that going to do?"

"If she flashes her lights, we can land the plane," Todd said.

"You're going to land the plane with Dorothy on the ground flashing her headlights?"

"Yeah."

I looked down, and I could see Dorothy down below, flashing her lights.

"Okay, I know where the airport is," said the pilot. "Tell her to drive to the runway."

And that's what she did.

Meanwhile I said to myself, *Oh my God. After all this, I'm going to die in a fucking plane crash with Casey Anthony. This is a blogger's dream come true.*

With Dorothy's lights leading the way, the pilot made a perfect landing. As we got off the plane, Dorothy was mimicking Hervé Villechaize in *Fantasy Island,* shouting, "Da plane. Da plane." On the deserted runway she hugged Casey, and as soon as we left the plane, the pilot headed for the West Coast. Along the way he stopped for gas in Arizona and California, and every place he landed, the media sent their reporters in a fruitless search to find Casey.

AFTER DRIVING TO THE HOUSE, I was too wound up to sleep. The beach house had a ladder that allowed you to climb on the roof and watch the water, and I did that. It was five in the morning, and the sun was just about to peek out from the horizon. I heard Pat McKenna arrive and then I could hear someone else climbing to the roof. It was Casey.

"Jose, what am I going to do," she said.

"I don't know, Casey, but we will figure it out together."

"Thank you. I will never forget all that you did for me."

She looked at the ocean, which was turning from black to blue, and she said, "It's the most beautiful thing I've ever seen, and I'm going to sit here and watch the sun come up."

And she did. She took photos of her first sunrise of freedom.

I went to bed.

The next day we were all walking around the house cooking, talking, when the phone rang.

"Is Jose Baez there?" The person claimed to be from the media. But the house had been rented in someone else's name. Who knew I was there?

Apparently earlier that day I had stood on the veranda to make a phone call, and someone had recognized me and called someone.

I knew I had to get Casey out of there immediately.

There were Casey sightings across the country, as if she were Elvis. An ABC News report had placed her in a rehab place in Arizona. The *Today* show was stalking an airport in California. The *National Enquirer* had her living with some rich guy in Mexico. One tabloid had her moving in with Octomom as a part-time nanny. It was beyond ridiculous.

I had one of my investigators drive Casey to New York. While the entire national media was searching for her in Arizona and California, she was within walking distance of all of their offices.

She ended up having to come back to Florida to serve her probation.

I no longer represent Casey Anthony, and I'll tell you why. After the Casey Anthony case I landed another big case, representing Gary Giordano, who was accused of murdering his travel companion, Robyn Gardner. We got him out of prison after demonstrating that law enforcement didn't have sufficient evidence to hold him. After working closely with an Aruban attorney, I moved on and in January of 2012 I had an incredible opportunity when Harvard Law School asked me to come and be a faculty member in its trial advocacy program. It was a tremendous honor, and I was very excited to be there. I flew to Cambridge, and I was in the middle of the program when videos of Casey talking on her computer were made public.

No one had seen a photo of her since she got out of jail, so when these videos were released to the media, I was bombarded with phone calls and requests for camera crews to come to Harvard to speak with me. Basically, I was bringing the circus to town, and I didn't like it. Here I was trying to move forward. Lorena was with me, and it bothered me to no end when seven months after the Casey Anthony case the media was all over me wanting to know about her.

"What did the videos mean?" everyone wanted to know.

I'm never going to shake this, I told myself.

Before the trial I attended a Hispanic media event, and I was asked, "Do you think the Casey Anthony case will define you as a lawyer?"

My answer was no, and that's because I'm going to do other cases, and some of them are going to be high-profile cases like the Gary Giordano case. And here I was in academia, moving into the next chapter of my life, and because Casey sneezed, everyone wanted to talk to me about it. And it really ruined what was supposed to be a special moment for me. I was supposed to be looking forward, not back.

This is not the way I want to pursue my career, I said to myself.

My job representing Casey, after all, ended with the verdict. Lisabeth Fryer was handling Casey's appeal on the lying to law enforcement charges, and I had nothing to do with her civil case. I knew Casey would have no other criminal matters for me to handle.

My work was done. The only thing that really troubles me is that she is a prisoner of her own freedom.

When she was in jail, we'd talk about her getting out, where she'd go. I used to say to her, "You'd be best off leaving this country." I'd tell her about one of the *Bourne Identity* movies I had seen where in the end the girl who's in hiding is in some resort town in Greece renting mopeds.

"Go to Greece and rent mopeds," I would tell Casey.

I don't think she'll do it, but it sure would be a fitting end to the story.

I just hope if Casey does stay in this country that one day she will be allowed to live in peace. She was found not guilty by a jury of her peers, by a jury that made so many sacrifices, and to attack her and to criticize her after she had the finality of a trial is not justice. It goes against everything that we as Americans believe in.

I am reminded of a quote from Martin Luther King, Jr., when he said, "Injustice anywhere is a threat to justice everywhere."

Meanwhile Casey Marie Anthony is hiding in an undisclosed location in the state of Florida. She is due to get off probation on August 21, 2012.

AFTERWORD

PRESUMED GUILTY was published on July 3, 2012—just two days before the anniversary of Casey's acquittal. In the days before publication,
one-star reviews of the book began appearing on Amazon.com. Haters
writing under fake names warned potential readers not to buy the book.
They called it "garbage," "disgusting," "rubbish," "absolute trash," and
"made-up lies." I couldn't believe that Amazon refused to delete or block
these comments. (For a company whose job it is to sell books, I couldn't
help thinking that this was a ridiculous way to run a business.) People
who openly admitted that they were not going to read the book wrote
comments such as, "This has to be one of the worst things anyone can
do... make money from the horrible murder of an innocent child." I
could hear the raspy voice of Nancy Grace in my head as I read comments like this.

On the day the book was published, there were almost a hundred
one-star reviews on Amazon. Then people began to read it. I was relieved and gratified to see that many readers wanted to know the true
inside story. The five-star reviews began pouring in; as of this writing,
there are 264 one-star reviews, 47 four-star reviews, and 200 five-star
reviews. For all of you who took the time to set the record straight, I
thank you.

When Peter Golenbock called me to tell me that I was now a *New
York Times* bestselling author, I cried. While I was really happy after the
verdict, I don't think it compared to my satisfaction with the success of
the book, because I always felt that this book was about *my* experience,
not Casey's. I cannot express enough gratitude to all of those who made
it possible. I then had an amazing two weeks in New York City as a guest
on a number of national radio and television shows. It was exciting to be

a guest on *The View* and *Good Morning America*. The whole experience—the book and radio tour—I found to be fascinating, overwhelming, and truly rewarding. I am blessed to be able to say I'm an author. To be a best-selling author is something very special to me.

Part of the public's skepticism about Casey's innocence had to do with the fact that the defense team didn't put Casey on the stand during her trial and didn't present enough evidence to satisfy the public that she was factually innocent. But that's not how criminal cases work. When you are trying a criminal case, someone's life is on the line. Everyone who hates Casey gets to go back to their lives and judge her. A citizen accused—Casey in particular—has no such luxury. People who are accused of crimes do not—and should not—try their cases to curry the public's favor. If a person is truly self-evaluating, when asked whether he or she cares about public opinion the answer would be, "Sure." But if told that by accepting public opinion he or she might spend the rest of his or her life in prison or, worse, be executed, anyone would certainly answer, "Hell no." Many wouldn't care to spend even a single night in jail.

I presented the defense's complete case in the book. When people who read the book with an open mind came to its end, they were able to see how the police, prosecutors, and media had deceived them into pressing for the death penalty for Casey Anthony—despite the fact that the medical examiner and the prosecution could not conclude how Caylee died.

It still amazes me that so many people remain so outraged at her acquittal. It tells me something very disturbing: some people would much rather see an innocent person go to jail than see a guilty person go free. Our laws are based on the premise that says, "May ten guilty people go free before one innocent person is convicted." That's the ideal, but unfortunately our media-driven society apparently doesn't feel that way. All you have to do is look at all the anger directed at Casey. They expressed deep outrage.

But when the Innocence Project, for example, found that a man serving thirty years on death row for a crime he didn't commit had been wrongly convicted on evidence found to be factually incorrect, where was the outrage over that? You didn't see it anywhere, and it's shameful. This small nonprofit organization has been able to accomplish this about 305 times in the last fifteen years. Why are we not crying out for major reform for those people? This is an astounding number if you consider that a majority of these are DNA exonerations and do not include the number of people wrongfully convicted where there was no DNA evidence, either because the police didn't collect it or because the accusations do not allow for DNA to clear them.

The one legal institution that came out looking good in this case was the jury system. Those twelve jurors sat in the courtroom day after day, listened to the evidence, and quickly concluded what they should have concluded: Casey was not guilty.

And yet after the verdict, the way they were treated in the press and by the public may cause the next jury to think twice about doing the right thing. The jurors' privacy was compromised when Judge Belvin Perry decided to release their names to the public. The media immediately went knocking on their doors, violating their privacy. It was nothing short of outrageous. These men and women hadn't volunteered for the job—they were drafted. And after the verdict, they had to go into hiding to escape the vicious comments and death threats that came their way. It's just another example of how broken our legal system is.

For me, the case has one loose end that really haunts me. According to Casey, George held Caylee's lifeless body in his arms and, after accusing Casey of being responsible for her death, told Casey he'd "take care of it." Caylee's body was found dumped in the woods. That was all I was ever able to uncover about how Caylee ended up where she did.

Several months after the verdict, I invited lead prosecutor Linda Drane Burdick to lunch. It was something we had wanted to do for a long time. She's my colleague, and I respect her as a lawyer and a person. I will not disclose the contents of our conversations, but I will tell you we talked about the case extensively. We asked each other about the strategies used during the trial since we wanted to learn from each other. Linda listened to some of my arguments about the case and understood my points. By the end of the lunch, we both agreed on one point.

"Regardless of what happened," Linda said, "whoever threw Caylee into those woods like that deserves to rot in hell. You don't do that to a baby."

I agreed. This fact disturbs me greatly. It's the one fact that will never change. *You don't do that to a baby.* Whoever put Caylee there, I curse you.

People have commented that they don't understand why I went to the lengths that I did in order to represent Casey and gain an acquittal. There are a couple of reasons. Clients can grow on you, especially when you see an injustice firsthand. As an officer of the court, I felt a deep responsibility to make sure Casey wasn't railroaded into a guilty verdict or, worse, a death sentence. Casey Anthony didn't get a fair shake from anyone. I was all she had to defend herself from the police, the prosecution, and even her own family.

I vowed that I would do what I could to put the state's evidence to the test, and I did. When it turned out the prosecution had no real evidence, the jury did the only thing it could do. It found Casey not guilty. In the aftermath, the greatest response came from those who were looking for excuses and for someone to blame for what they felt was an unjust verdict.

Even after the publication of *Presumed Guilty*, law enforcement and the press continued to tell stories about "evidence" they claimed pointed to Casey's guilt. Funny how these stories are never news stories unless they paint her in a negative light.

For example, on November 25, 2012, four months after the release of *Presumed Guilty,* after reading about it in the book, Orlando news reporter Tony Pipitone "revealed" that the Florida Sheriff's Office had overlooked a computer search for "foolproof suffocation" made from the Anthony home on the day Caylee was last seen alive. (This is extensively covered in Chapter 14, "What Happened on June 16, 2008 [The Evidence No One Ever Told You About].")

The conclusion made by Pipitone and spread by media across the country was if this information had been discovered and presented at trial, it would have been further proof that Casey was searching for a way to kill Caylee. Pipitone made it sound like it was a confession on Casey's part.

Nothing could be further from the truth.

It was a Google search, not a confession, and the search could have been made by anyone. Furthermore, the logical conclusion is that whoever made the search was thinking about suicide, not murder, because after the person made a Google search for "foolproof suffocation," the link that was clicked next was "Venturing into the pro-suicide pit," a blog post about suicide. That removed any question about whether the person making the search was looking to kill another person. The searcher was looking for a way to commit suicide, not murder.

I can't get past the crazy idea that one needs a Google search to kill a two-year-old. It's pretty simple. Grab the kid, throw her in the pool, walk away, and come back in an hour. Then you say, "Oh my God, she's drowned." Or throw a bag over her head or poison her with rat poison. If Casey had wanted to murder her daughter, she didn't need to do any research. She could have done any number of things to kill a baby. You don't need a Google search to do it.

However, it's much more reasonable to do a Google search if you're thinking about killing yourself in such a way that you don't end up a vegetable.

Let's say for argument's sake it was Casey who did the search for a way to kill herself. Her daughter was dead. Many people in the process of grief think of suicide. It's an overwhelming emotion, especially if one is so consumed. If Caylee had wandered into the pool and drowned while Casey was sleeping or on the computer, she certainly would have felt responsible. Wouldn't most mothers have felt that way?

And if George had been doing the searches, which I believe to be the case, the same thing could be said for him. According to Casey, and partly George's own testimony, George was supposed to be watching Caylee on the day she wandered into the pool and died. (He testified they had breakfast together and he watched her that morning.) George did in fact later try to commit suicide.

Pipitone's report said that the information had been "overlooked" by the sheriff's department. I don't believe that for a second. I am convinced the sheriff's department deliberately kept it hidden and for good reason: the department kept it under wraps for fear the information would have unraveled its case.

Why is this? Because the information about the searches would have thrown a black cloud over George Anthony. The computer records indicated activity throughout the day, and that includes the time frame during which George said that Casey had already left the house. If she left the house, she couldn't be on the computer. In the same way the prosecution showed that Cindy was lying throughout the trial by showing her work's computer records, we would have been able to show George was lying using similar computer records.

It would have proved that George was lying when he said that Casey and Caylee had walked out of the house at 12:50 P.M. It would have cast doubt on his entire testimony about her leaving the house and wearing a certain outfit and about his opening the door for her, giving her a kiss goodbye, and waving as she left. All of that would have been called into question, and all of that would have been disproved by these computer searches.

The news report made a big deal claiming that the defense's timeline was off by an hour—the searches were run at 2:50 P.M., not 1:50 P.M., thereby exonerating George and implicating Casey. (George was supposed to be at work at 3:00 P.M., and if he left at 2:30, so goes the argument, he couldn't have done the searches.) But the cops never pulled George's cell tower records, George didn't have to punch a clock at work, and there is nothing in the entire case file other than his work schedule to prove that he in fact showed up to work on time that day, or even at all. No one seemed to care that I had two independent computer experts review the actual computer. The media used a computer-savvy blogger to do it for them. They also claimed that the computer had a password-protected account. This is not true. Everyone accessed both user accounts on that computer, and it was always left on. Unless it was rebooted, it would not be password protected. Additionally, Pipitone failed to mention one crucial fact because it did not help his "blame Casey" story line—there was computer activity all day until Casey's cell tower records indicated that she left the house shortly after 4:00 P.M.

Thus the time of the searches is completely irrelevant for two reasons: 1) As far as we know, the police never pulled George's phone records, so there's no way to verify where he was. 2) More importantly, if Casey did do these searches, on cross-examination of George, it wouldn't have mattered whether I used my timeline or the timeline created by the media's blogging computer expert. The natural question for George would have been, "Why are you lying about the last time you saw your granddaughter alive?" In any murder case, if someone is lying about the last time he saw the decedent alive, he automatically becomes a suspect.

The great irony is that was exactly why they prosecuted Casey: for lying about the last time she saw Caylee and saying that she had dropped Caylee off with her nanny. It was the strongest evidence they had against her.

You can't have Casey both on the computer and driving away at the same time. The information throws a real monkey wrench into the state's case. With this information, the issue of George lying to the police would have come to the forefront. The suspicion would have fallen on him.

To date there still has been no investigation into George Anthony's role in any of this.

The questions I am often asked are, "If Casey has accused George of doing all those things she accused him of doing, why doesn't anyone believe her?" and, "Why hasn't George been investigated by the police?" Simple. When the police first investigated Casey, she told a number of lies consistent with her imaginary world that protected her emotionally from her painful life as a victim. She told me she made up a nanny so her parents wouldn't find out she was taking Caylee out of the house to protect her from George's incestuous behavior. She told police she worked at Universal Studios to further her ruse. She told the police a series of lies that the police then revealed to the media, causing everyone to declare Casey a pathological liar. Had the police investigated her charges of incest, they might have understood *why* she lied to them as she did. They never did that. They were convinced she had murdered her child, in part because of those lies, and they refused to investigate anyone else, even when the evidence against George slapped them upside the head. Moreover, once the police's allegations against Casey became known, the public had no interest in hearing Casey's side of this sordid story. Casey's reputation as a liar was so entrenched in the public's mind that nothing Casey could say could change the way they felt about her.

Public perception could have sent Casey Anthony to the death chamber. What saved her, of course, was the jury system: twelve citizens who listened to the evidence and weren't swayed by the relentless drumbeat of false and phony media reports.

And so justice was served. Even so, Casey Anthony will be hunted down and reported on by the media for the rest of her life. And all of the reporting will be negative. To them she is still a baby killer, and no amount of evidence or argument will change that. There have been reports she has a sugar daddy in Mexico. There have been reports she was getting married. There have been reports she's pregnant. There are Casey Anthony sightings, stories about her being "driven from cover." There are reports she's going to write her own book, stories that she has been offered money *not* to publish her own book, and already third parties are taking steps to make sure she doesn't earn any money from it if she does publish her own book. It's all despicable and an abridgment of her right to privacy, but in this age of social media, all's fair in love and ratings.

For myself, life goes on. I have opened a dream office in Coral Gables, Florida, while still maintaining my office in Orlando. My practice has grown; we have excellent lawyers who represent crime victims and criminal defense cases. My practice and I are going to continue to grow. We may open up other offices, depending on my stamina. Most importantly, I am slowly putting together the pieces of my life that had fallen apart during the case and afterward.

I am moving forward and continuing to do what I love, which is practice law, so if ever you need a robust defense, you know where to find me. As I did with Casey, I promise you I will give you everything I've got. She, and you, deserve no less.

— JOSE BAEZ
April 6, 2013

ABOUT THE AUTHORS

JOSE BAEZ is one of the most sought-after attorneys in the country. After successfully defending Casey Anthony in what became one of the nation's most high-profile trials, he took on the case of Gary Giordano, which caught international headlines. Baez fought hard to successfully obtain Giordano's release from a prison in Aruba where he had been held for several months. Baez continues to practice criminal defense law, handling cases throughout the country, especially those involving complex forensic issues for which he has shown strong interest and expertise.

Baez is fluent in Spanish and Portuguese, extremely active in various charitable endeavors in the Hispanic community, and enjoys traveling and spending time with his family. He currently has offices in Orlando and Miami, Florida.

PETER GOLENBOCK, one of the nation's best-known sports authors, graduated Dartmouth College in 1967 and the NYU School of Law in 1970. He has written seven *New York Times* bestsellers, including *The Bronx Zoo* (with Sparky Lyle) and *American Prince* (with Tony Curtis).